Religion and the American Constitutional Experiment

Religion and the American
Constitutional Experiment

THIRD EDITION

JOHN WITTE, JR.
Emory University

AND

JOEL A. NICHOLS
University of St. Thomas School of Law

**WESTVIEW
PRESS**
A Member of the Perseus Books Group

Westview Press books are available at special discounts for bulk purchases in the United
States by corporations, institutions, and other organizations. For more information,
please contact the Special Markets Department at the Perseus Books Group, 2300
Chestnut Street, Suite 200, Philadelphia, PA 19103, or call (800) 810-4145, ext. 5000,
or e-mail special.markets@perseusbooks.com.

Cover image, "Freedom of Worship" (SEP 1943) by Norman Rockwell, printed by
permission of the Norman Rockwell Family Agency
Copyright © 1943 The Norman Rockwell Family Entities

Set in 10 point Adobe Garamond by the Perseus Books Group

Library of Congress Cataloging-in-Publication Data
Witte, John, 1959–
    Religion and the American constitutional experiment / John Witte, Jr. and Joel A.
Nichols. — 3rd ed.
        p.   cm.
    Includes bibliographical references and index.
    ISBN 978-0-8133-4475-1 (alk. paper)
    1. Freedom of religion—United States—History. 2. Church and state—United
States—History. 3. Freedom of religion—United States. 4. Church and state—
United States. 5. United States. Constitution. 1st Amendment. I. Nichols, Joel A.
II. Title.
KF4783.Z9W58 2011
342.7308'52—dc22   2010003209

ISBN: 978-0-8133-4475-1

10 9 8 7 6 5 4 3 2 1

For Our Students in Law and Religion
Past, Present, and Future

Contents

Tables, Figures, and Appendices

Preface

This volume is at once an introduction for students, a provocation for specialists, and an invitation for the public to view afresh the American experiment in religious rights and liberties. We combine historical, doctrinal, and comparative methods to tell the unique American story of religious freedom—from the formation of the First Amendment in 1789 to the Supreme Court's most recent interpretations of its guarantees of no establishment and free exercise of religion.

This volume is calibrated to press uninitiated readers beyond simple incantation of Jefferson's wall of separation as the source and summary of the First Amendment. It is also calculated to lift seasoned readers above common lamentation over the Supreme Court's recent First Amendment cases. We have sought to provide just enough historical, case law, and comparative analysis for readers to appreciate the ingenuity of the American founders and the intricacies of the experiment they unleashed. We have also sought to provide just enough of an argument for the principled integration of religious liberty for readers to see the robust promise that the American experiment still holds.

The first edition of this volume, published in 2000, was designed as an accessible introduction to the American story of religious liberty viewed in interdisciplinary and international perspective. Few books of the sort were then on the market, and no book sought to reach students and scholars of law, theology, history, ethics, political science, human rights, and American studies alike. It was gratifying to see the generous reception of the book by scholars of many specialties, and the ready adoption of the book in a number of college, law school, divinity school, and graduate school classrooms. Given its success, the second edition of the book, published in 2005, was largely an update on recent Supreme Court cases and congressional acts affecting religious liberty. The second edition has continued to do well in the classroom.

In this new edition, we have retained the main organization and main themes of the first two editions. But this edition features more substantial revisions, better division of chapters, and clearer presentation of trends in modern Supreme Court case law. We have updated the historical chapters, taking into account the latest scholarship and weaving into our analysis additional relevant primary sources from the founding era. We have broken up the overly long chapters on free exercise and establishment law into shorter chapters dealing, respectively, with free exercise and statutory protections of religious liberty, the establishment clause, religion and public education, government and religious education, and religion in public life. We have also added a chapter on religious organizations and the law. We have expanded the final chapter, which compares the American experiment on religious liberty with international norms of religious freedom, drawing on recent comparative constitutional scholarship and the use of international law materials in Supreme Court cases. We have continued to call for an integrative theory of religious liberty grounded in principles of liberty of conscience, free exercise of religion, religious equality of a plurality of faiths, separation of church and state, and no establishment of religion. We have done more to show the utility of our integrative theory of religious liberty and to compare it to other recent theories. The updated appendixes present a chronological list of the drafts of the religion clauses considered in 1788 and 1789, a table showing common patterns in earlier state constitutional laws on religious liberty, and a tabular summary of all relevant Supreme Court cases on religious liberty from 1815 until 2010.

The new edition takes into account the latest Supreme Court cases. Since the second edition went to press in 2004, the Court has issued seven cases on religious liberty—*Cutter v. Wilkinson* (2005), *McCreary County v. ACLU* (2005), *Van Orden v. Perry* (2005), *Gonzales v. O Centro Espirita Beneficiente Uniao Do Vegetal* (2006), *Hein v. Freedom from Religion Foundation* (2007), *Pleasant Grove City v. Summum* (2009), and *Salazar v. Buono* (2010). *Christian Legal Society v. Martinez* (2010) is pending as this book goes to press. These cases have continued to weaken the First Amendment protections of religious liberty. The *Cutter* and *O Centro* cases, upholding the application of two federal statutes on religious freedom, have further encouraged a trend, begun in 1990, of leaving the protection of free exercise of religion more to Congress than to the federal courts. The *Hein* case has further narrowed the standing rights of private parties to challenge government actions under the establishment clause. The four other cases, dealing with the constitutionality of religious symbols in public life, have featured such convoluted and conflicting approaches to the establishment clause that lower federal courts have increasingly been left to sort out their own preferred approaches, even if those differ sharply from those of other federal courts.

Both the shifting jurisprudence and the substantial weakening of the First Amendment religion clauses have triggered a small explosion of new federal and state legislation on religion, yielding an intricate mosaic of special religious preferences and exemptions that are now being further tested in the lower courts. It has also sparked a new industry of *state* constitutional litigation, which is further diversifying the law of religious liberty governing the nation. This rise of state constitutional laws has encouraged a number of jurists, not least Justice Thomas of the Supreme Court, to propose new federalist understandings of religious liberty. In particular, these writers are pressing for a "selective deincorporation" of the First

Amendment establishment clause from the Fourteenth Amendment due process clause, leaving states much freer to operate in accordance with their own state constitutional provisions in their treatment of religion.

We are troubled by this emerging shift from the judiciary to the legislature, and from the federal to the state governments in the protection of religious liberty in America. Such a shift leaves what should be common national rights of religious liberty vulnerable to fleeting political fashions and contingent on a claimant's geographical location. In our view, the federal courts, sometimes aided by Congress, should provide common and firm religious liberty protections for all American parties, no matter where they reside or where they file their lawsuit. This need for firm common laws on religious liberty, in the face of bigotry at home and abroad, was among the compelling reasons that led the Supreme Court in the 1940s to "incorporate" the First Amendment religion clauses into the Fourteenth Amendment due process clause and make them binding on state and local governments. It was also the reason that America and the world embraced religious freedom in the 1940s as a universal and nonderogable human right of all persons—one of the famous "four freedoms" that Franklin Roosevelt championed (and our book cover depicts) to rebuke the horrific abuses inflicted on Jews and other religious minorities during World War II. We think this vision of a national theory of religious liberty remains an important aspiration for America, and we think the federal courts are in the best position to achieve it.

We are also troubled by a growing tendency among some scholars to deny that religion is special and deserving of special constitutional protection. Various writers now say that such a constitutional vision of religion, if it even existed in the eighteenth century, has become obsolete in this postmodern and postreligious age. Religion is too dangerous, divisive, and diverse in its demands, the argument goes, to be accorded special protection. Religion is better viewed as just another category of liberty and expression and given no more preference than its secular counterparts. Indeed, to accord religion special treatment is an unconstitutional establishment of religion and discriminates against the nonreligious. We reject this argument and some of the revisionist historiography that inspires it. The founders' vision was that religion is more than simply a peculiar form of speech and assembly, privacy and autonomy and deserving of separate and special treatment. They thus placed freedom of religion alongside freedom of speech, press, and assembly, giving religion special protection and restricting government interaction with religion. Although our religious demographics have changed dramatically, today, as much as in the founding era, religion remains for many a unique source of individual and personal identity, involving "duties that we owe to our Creator, and the manner of discharging them," in Madison's words. Religion is also a unique form of public and social identity, involving a vast plurality of sanctuaries, schools, charities, missions, and other forms and forums of faith. All peaceable exercises of religion, whether individual or corporate, private or public, properly deserve the protection of the First Amendment. And such protection sometimes requires special immunities, exemptions, protections, and privileges not afforded by neutral and general laws.

Finally, we are troubled by a growing tendency among some jurists and scholars to dismiss the principle of separation of church and state as an obsolete if not odious teaching. A small cottage industry of important writings has emerged in recent years arguing that the principle of separation of church and state was an invention of nineteenth-century anticlerical and antireligious elites, starting with Thomas Jefferson, and was hijacked by nineteenth-century anti-Catholic and antireligious nativists who introduced all manner of prejudicial changes in later American law in the name of separation of church and state but to the detriment of religious liberty. Because of its recent paternity and because of its odious pedigree, it is now argued, we should jettison the principle of separation of church and state and some of the harsher laws that it occasioned, including old laws against state funding and support of religious institutions. We respectfully disagree. Our reading of the sources leads us to conclude that separation of church and state has a much longer history, and much more complex and wholesome pedigree than some recent historiography allows. Long before Jefferson drafted his famous 1802 letter to the Danbury Baptists that used the "wall of separation" phrase, the American founders had at least five understandings of separation of church and state, several with deep Western roots. Each of these understandings made important contributions to the protection of religious liberty in the eighteenth and nineteenth centuries, and each holds enduring lessons for us today.

It is a special privilege for me to have Professor Joel A. Nichols join as a coauthor of this third edition of the volume. Professor Nichols was one of the very best of the six thousand–plus students I have had the privilege to teach over the past quarter century, and he was my prize research assistant when I prepared the first edition of this volume in 1998. He has already established himself as a distinguished authority on law and religion, religious liberty and human rights, and religion and family law. He has written several definitive law review articles on religious liberty in the founding era, and has a major new title on *Multi-Tiered Marriage* in press with Cambridge University Press that maps the frontier of issues on law, religion, and family life. He has done invaluable work on this third edition, and he took the lead on drafting the chapter on religious organizations and the law. This latter topic is becoming a hot area of litigation as churches and other religious bodies today divide over issues of same-sex rights and then find themselves unable to divide religious property without judicial intervention.

I wish to thank Amy Wheeler for her dedicated work on the production of this third edition, and Will Haines, Chris Hudson, and Kelly Parker of the Emory Law Library for their valuable library services. A large number of student assistants have helped in the production of each edition of this volume. But this edition was greatly improved by the insights and criticisms of the sixteen bright Emory law students in my Advanced Religious Liberty course in the spring semester of 2009. They worked systematically through the text and made numerous edifying suggestions, which are reflected on these pages. I am also grateful for the excellent research assistance of Amos Davis, Justin Latterall, Trevor Pinkerton, and Judd Treeman on this new edition.

Finally, I wish to thank Dr. Craig Dykstra and his colleagues at the Lilly Endowment for their generous grant in support of my project on law, religion, and the Protestant tradition, which has provided research support for this and several other book projects. I also wish to thank Dr. Alonzo L. McDonald and his colleagues in the Alonzo L. McDonald Family Foundation for their generous grant in support of my related project on Christian foundations of religious liberty and rule of law, which has supplied further research support for this new edition.

JOHN WITTE, JR.
Emory Law School

Introduction

Thomas Jefferson once described America's new religious liberty guarantees as a "fair" and "novel experiment."[1] These guarantees, set out in the new state and federal constitutions of the later eighteenth century, defied millennium-old assumptions inherited from Western Europe—that one form of Christianity must be established in a community and that the state must protect and support it against all other forms of faith. America would no longer suffer such governmental prescriptions and proscriptions of religion, Jefferson declared. All forms of Christianity had to stand on their own feet and on an equal footing with all other religions. Their survival and growth had to turn on the cogency of their word, not the coercion of the sword; on the faith of their members, not the force of the law.

This bold constitutional experiment of granting religious liberty to all remains in place, and in progress, in the United States. From 1776 to 1940, principal governance of the experiment lay with the states, operating under their own state constitutions. The First Amendment applied, by its terms, only to the federal government: "*Congress* shall make no law respecting an establishment of religion, or prohibiting the free exercise thereof." And these First Amendment guarantees of no establishment and free exercise of religion were only superficially enforced in the federal courts. Most questions of religious liberty were left to individual state legislatures and courts to resolve, with little involvement from Congress or the federal courts.

After 1940, principal control of the experiment shifted to the federal courts. In *Cantwell v. Connecticut* (1940) and *Everson v. Board of Education* (1947), the United States Supreme Court applied the First Amendment religion clauses for the first time to state and local governments.[2] Beginning in 1925, the Court had already applied the First Amendment free speech clause ("Congress shall make no law . . . abridging the freedom of speech") to the states, and in the next decade it added the freedom of press and freedom of assembly clauses as well. The *Cantwell* and *Everson* Courts used the same methodology the Court had employed in those earlier cases. It read the First Amendment guarantees of religious liberty into the general liberty guarantee of the Fourteenth Amendment: "No state shall deprive any person of . . .

liberty . . . without due process of law." "Religious liberty" as defined by the First Amendment was considered part of the body of "liberties" protected by the Fourteenth Amendment, and thus it could be applied against states as well. This interpretive move, which the Court would repeat several more times for other Bill of Rights provisions, made possible a national law of religious liberty enforceable by and in the federal courts. The First Amendment establishment and free exercise clauses had always bound the federal government and had long served as a source and inspiration for states as well. But after 1940, these constitutional clauses also bound state and local governments through their "incorporation" into the Fourteenth Amendment due process clause. Thousands of cases poured into the federal courts after 1940, with more than 160 reaching the Supreme Court.

The American experiment in religious liberty initially inspired exuberant rhetoric throughout the young American republic and well beyond. "Our act for freedom of religion is extremely applauded," Thomas Jefferson wrote enthusiastically from Paris. "The ambassadors & ministers of the several nations in Europe resident at this court have asked of me copies of it to send to their sovereigns. . . . I think it will produce considerable good even in those countries where ignorance, superstition, poverty, & oppression of the body and mind in every form, are so firmly settled on the mass of the people."[3] "[W]e know of no country in the world, at any period since the first establishment of Christianity, where there has been such perfect liberty of conscience, and such entire freedom in the exercise of religion," a Philadelphia Baptist pamphleteer wrote in 1787.[4] Preacher Elhanan Winchester declared proudly to a London audience in 1788:

> There is but one country in the world where liberty, and especially religious liberty, is so much enjoyed as in these kingdoms, and that is the United States of America: there religious liberty is in the highest perfection. All stand there on equal ground. There are no religious establishments, no preference of one denomination of Christians above another. The constitution knows no difference between one good man, and another. A man may be chosen there to the highest civil offices, without being obliged to give any account of his faith, subscribe [to] any religious test, or go to the communion-table of any church.[5]

Yale president Ezra Stiles robustly predicted in 1783:

> The United States will embosom all the religious sects or denominations in christendom. Here they may all enjoy their whole respective systems of worship and church government, complete. . . . All religious denominations will be independent of one another . . . and having, on account of religion, no superiority as to secular powers and civil immunities, they will cohabit together in harmony, and I hope, with a most generous catholicism and benevolence.[6]

Dozens of such enthusiastic endorsements of the American experiment in religious liberty can be found in the writings of America's founders.

Today, though, the American experiment often inspires more criticism than praise. The United States does "embosom" all religious sects and denominations, not only from Christendom but from around the world: America is home to more than one thousand religious traditions, with more than two-thirds of the American population claiming religious membership. And American citizens and groups do enjoy remarkable religious freedom. But the laboratory of the American experiment since 1940—the United States Supreme Court—no longer inspires confidence. The Court's record on religious rights and liberties has become vilified for its lack of consistent and coherent principles, its uncritical use of mechanical tests and misleading metaphors, and its massive jumble of divided and discordant opinions. Leading scholars are now writing with open dismay and disdain that the First Amendment experiment was a "foreordained failure" and that its promise of religious freedom is "impossible" to achieve.[7]

The United States Supreme Court is not the only body grappling with the experiment. In the past two decades, the testing ground has partly shifted away from the federal government to the states and away from the courts to the legislatures—a trend encouraged by the Supreme Court's generous nods toward federalism and separation of powers as well as by the Court's firmer standing requirements and weakened First Amendment tests. Accordingly, state legislatures and courts have become bolder in conducting their own experiments in religious liberty, which seem calculated to revisit, if not rechallenge, prevailing Supreme Court interpretations of the establishment and free exercise clauses. At the same time, Congress has issued a number of laws to defend the religious rights of a number of individuals and groups. The Supreme Court has responded with a host of divided and conflicting opinions. Among them is Justice Thomas's repeated proposal that the establishment clause should be applied only to Congress, not to the states, and Justice O'Connor's holding that the free exercise clause should apply only if government explicitly "prohibits" religion. Some interpreters regard such dicta as indications that the Court may try to "unincorporate" the religion clauses from the Fourteenth Amendment due process clause and explicitly return the nation to the two-track constitutional system of religious freedom that existed before the 1940s.

When an experiment becomes a "kind of wandering inquiry, without any regular system of operations, . . . prudence commends three correctives."[8] So wrote Francis Bacon, the great seventeenth-century English jurist and scientist and the "father" of the experimental method in science. First, said Bacon, we must "return to first principles and axioms," reassess them in light of our experience, and "if necessary refine them." Second, we must assess "our experience with the experiment" in light of these first principles, to determine where "the experiment should be adjusted." Third, we must "compare our experiments" and experiences with those of fellow scientists—and where we see in that comparison "superior techniques," we must "amend our experiments" and even our first principles accordingly.[9] Although Bacon offered these prudential instructions principally to correct scientific experiments that had gone awry, his instructions commend themselves to legal and political experiments as well—as he himself, as Lord Chancellor of England, sought to demonstrate in the seventeenth century.[10]

This volume applies Bacon's prudential instructions to the American constitutional experiment in religious rights and liberties—an experiment that today is indeed, as Bacon put it, "wandering, without any regular system of operations." Applying Bacon's first instruction, Chapters 1–4 return to the "first principles" that inspired and informed the original American experiment. Looking backward from 1789, the year the First Amendment was drafted, these chapters survey the theological and political movements that were most critical to the formation of the new constitutional laws on religious liberty—the Puritan, Evangelical, Enlightenment, and Republican movements, each viewed in broader European context. These four groups of founders, we argue, despite their vast differences, helped to forge the "first principles" of the American experiment in religious liberty.

Six principles stand out in these founders' writings: (1) liberty of conscience, (2) free exercise of religion, (3) religious pluralism, (4) religious equality, (5) separation of church and state, and (6) no establishment of a national religion. These six principles were part of the First Amendment religion clauses as well as a number of state constitutional bills of rights. They remain the guiding principles of the American experiment today—in their original form as well as in provocative new constructions and combinations such as "religious accommodationism," "no religious coercion," "equal access," "equal treatment," and "substantive neutrality."

Applying Bacon's second instruction, Chapters 5–11 analyze the American constitutional experience in light of these first principles. We begin by reviewing the use of these principles in the state constitutions before 1940 and as they were carried into the seminal Supreme Court cases (*Cantwell v. Connecticut*, 1940; and *Everson v. Board of Education*, 1947) that rendered the free exercise and establishment clauses applicable to the states. We then analyze the 160-plus First Amendment cases on religious liberty issued since 1940. These modern cases have served both to enhance and to frustrate the American experiment, we argue, in part because these two lines of cases have not been effectively merged, and in part because the Court has often dealt inconsistently with the first principles of the experiment in religious liberty.

Applying Bacon's third instruction, Chapter 12 compares the principles and practices of the American experiment with prevailing international norms of religious rights and liberties. Somewhat ironically, the first principles of religious liberty seen in the American experiment have been exported, reified, and reformulated in international legal instruments where they now enjoy greater coherence than they do in First Amendment law. While international human rights norms, we argue, are no panacea to the current constitutional confusion, they do open promising new pathways toward a more integrated approach to the First Amendment religion clauses and offer a fresh look at how to interpret America's own first principles. The priority given to liberty of conscience, free exercise, and religious equality principles at international law might well serve as a prototype for the integration of the guarantees of free exercise and no establishment of religion. The firm insistence of international human rights instruments that state abridgments of religious rights be both "necessary" and "proportionate" encourages a stricter free exercise test than is currently in vogue. The growing emphasis in international law on the rights of religious groups and the need for affirmative state action toward them encourages greater protection of religious minorities in America and greater cooperation of religious and political officials on vital social tasks.

The concluding chapter returns to the first principles of religious liberty of the American experiment and offers an assessment of the current law of religious liberty in America.

The methodology at work in this volume is more expansionist than revisionist in intention. The argument that the First Amendment religion clauses reflect both the theology and the politics of the eighteenth century is not new. But we do give voice to some religious groups and theological sources that have not been conventionally included among the founders. Moreover, we argue that a more candid acknowledgment of the theological pedigree of the First Amendment is an instance of constitutional correction, not "religious correctness."[11] It is irresponsible to hold up as normative only those eighteenth-century texts that happen to anticipate contemporary secular fashions and deprecate others that do not have modern equivalents. And it is irresponsible to pretend that the First Amendment is a purely secular trope, or just another category of liberty and autonomy that can be collapsed into generic guarantees of free speech, free press, and free assembly. It is better, in our view, to acknowledge the explicitly religious sources that helped to form the First Amendment and then seek to include more religious and nonreligious voices and values in the modern constitutional dialogue. It is better to recognize that the founders regarded freedom of religion as a special category of liberty that is vital to the constitutional rule of law and then seek to be sure that all peaceable forms and forums of faith are adequately protected. A more candid acknowledgment of these religious sources and dimensions of the First Amendment enriches more than endangers our understanding.

The six principles of religious liberty analyzed and advocated herein are not new creations. But we have grounded these principles in several European legal traditions, eighteenth-century American texts, and modern human rights instruments that have not been part of the conventional literature. We have labeled and grouped them in a way that does not always follow current linguistic and conceptual fashions. And we have stripped them of some of the thick accretions of casuistry, which have tended to obscure their essential value and vigor in informing and integrating the twin religious liberty guarantees of the First Amendment.

In our view, these six principles of religious liberty allow for an integrated understanding of the First Amendment religion clauses. The free exercise clause outlaws government *proscriptions* of religion—actions that unduly burden the conscience, unduly restrict religious action and expression, intentionally discriminate against religion, or invade the autonomy of churches and other religious bodies. The establishment clause, in turn, outlaws government *prescriptions* of religion—actions that coerce the conscience, unduly mandate forms of religious action and expression, intentionally discriminate in favor of religion, or improperly ally the state with churches or other religious bodies. Both the free exercise and the establishment clauses thereby provide complementary protections to the first principles of the American experiment— liberty of conscience, freedom of religious expression, equality of plural faiths before the law, and separation of church and state.

The call for a more integrated framework of religious liberty in America built on these first principles is also not new. But we warn against efforts to reduce the religion clause guarantees to one or two principles alone—even to such vaunted principles as coercion, neutrality, or equal treatment that are currently in vogue. Religion is simply too vital and valuable a source of individual flourishing and social cohesion to be left to one or two legal defenses. As both the eighteenth-century American founders and twentieth-century international jurists have repeatedly argued, a variety of principles must be integrated into an interlocking and interdependent shield of religious liberties and rights for all. The principles of liberty of conscience, free exercise, pluralism, equality, separation, and no establishment form the essential amalgam of the American shield.

Notes

1. Saul K. Padover, ed., *The Complete Jefferson, Containing His Major Writings* (1943), 538, 673–676, 1147; P. L. Ford, ed., *The Works of Thomas Jefferson*, 12 vols. (1904–1905), 11:7; Julian Boyd, ed., *The Papers of Thomas Jefferson*, 9 vols. (1950), 1:537–539. See analysis in Sidney E. Mead, *The Lively Experiment: The Shaping of Christianity in America* (1963), 55–71. The concept of an "experiment" in religious liberty goes back at least to John Locke. See Locke, "A Second Letter Concerning Toleration (c. 1690)," in *The Works of John Locke*, 12th ed. (1824), 5:59–138, at 63ff. It was also used by American colonists Roger Williams and William Penn in the seventeenth century (pp. 15–16).

2. 310 U.S. 296 (1940); 330 U.S. 1 (1947).

3. Letter to George Wythe (August 13, 1786), in *The Works of Thomas Jefferson*, vol. 5, http://oll.libertyfund.org/title/802/86631/1991245.

4. "To the Baptist Churches Belonging to the Philadelphia Association," *The Documentary History of the Ratification of the Constitution*, ed. John P. Kaminski et al. (2003), 19:334.

5. Elhanan Winchester, "A Century Sermon on the Glorious Revolution (London, 1788)," in *Political Sermons of the American Founding Era, 1730–1805*, ed. Ellis Sandoz (1991), 969, 988–989.

6. Ezra Stiles, *The United States Elevated to Glory and Honor* (1783), 54–55 (spelling modernized and original italics removed).

7. Steven D. Smith, *Foreordained Failure: The Quest for a Constitutional Principle of Religious Freedom* (1995); Winnifred Sullivan, *The Impossibility of Religious Freedom* (2005).

8. Francis Bacon, "The Great Instauration (1620)," preface, reprinted in Bacon, *The New Organon and Related Writings*, ed. Fulton H. Anderson (1960), 3, 11.

9. Francis Bacon, "The New Organon (1620)," Aphorisms Book 1, 70, 82, 103, 104, reprinted in *The New Organon and Related Writings*, 31, 67–69, 78–80, 97–98.

10. Barbara Shapiro, "Sir Francis Bacon and the Mid-Seventeenth Century Movement for Law Reform," *American Journal of Legal History* 24 (1980): 331.

11. Cf. Isaac Kramnick and R. Laurence Moore, *The Godless Constitution: The Case Against Religious Correctness* (1996).

1

The American Experiment in Historical Context

The American founders did not create their experiment in religious liberty out of nothing. They had more than a century and a half of colonial experience and more than a millennium and a half of European experience from which they drew both examples and counterexamples.

A host of historical examples and exemplars of religious liberty were readily at hand. Foremost among the sources was the Christian Bible, by far the most widely used and commonly cited text in the American founding era. American politicians, preachers, and pamphleteers alike quoted the Bible's many bracing aphorisms on freedom: "For freedom, Christ has set us free." "You were called to freedom." "Where the Spirit of the Lord is, there is freedom." "You will know the truth, and the truth will make you free." "You will be free indeed." You have been given "the glorious liberty of the children of God."[1] Equally important were the Bible's calls to believers to "render to Caesar the things that are Caesar's and to God the things that are God's," and to remain "separate" from worldly temptations.[2] Christians are, at heart, "strangers and foreigners on the earth"; their true "citizenship is in heaven."[3] St. Paul even used the phrase "wall of separation" (*paries maceriae*), albeit very differently from the way it came to be used in law and politics.[4] Such biblical passages inspired hundreds of impassioned sermons in defense of religious liberty for Christian individuals and groups. Indeed, political sermons, issued in both churches and statehouses, constituted some 80 percent of all the American political literature published in the 1770s and 1780s.[5]

Beyond the Bible, the American founders also turned for inspiration to the martyred prophets of religious liberty in the West. These included the early English heroes of the faith—Thomas Becket, John Wycliffe, and Thomas More—and the sundry English Levellers, Quaker dissenters, and Catholic missionaries who followed them. They turned for instruction to a host of European theologians and philosophers, from the sixteenth-century Protestant reformers Martin Luther and John Calvin to early modern Catholic champions of rights, Francisco de Vitoria and Francisco Suarez, to later European voices of liberty such as Montesquieu, Voltaire, and Condorcet of

France; Frances Hutcheson, David Hume, and Adam Smith of Scotland; and John Locke, William Blackstone, and Edmund Burke of England.[6]

Historical counterexamples also came to mind, particularly to those founders who denounced traditional religious establishments and defended religious freedom for all peaceable believers. In defending the novelty of the American experiment, these founders often dismissed the Western inheritance as a veritable "career of intolerance," in the words of Virginia statesman James Madison.[7] "In most of the Gov[ernment]s of the old world," Madison declared, "the legal establishment of a particular religion and without or with very little toleration of others makes a part of the Political and Civil organization. . . . [I]t was taken for granted, that an exclusive & intolerant establishment was essential, and notwithstanding the light thrown on the subject by that experiment, the prevailing opinion in Europe, England not excepted, has been that Religion could not be preserved without the support of Gov[ernmen]t, nor Gov[ernmen]t without the support of Religion."[8]

Many founders laid the blame for this traditional arrangement squarely on the first Christian emperor, Constantine, in the fourth century. A New Hampshire conventioneer put it thus in 1781:

> Who, sir, since that ever to be lamented era, when Constantine the great connected the church and the state together, has ever been able to fix an exact equipoise between the prerogatives of princes and claims of dignified priests. Visionaries have written about it, politicians have labored, but it is all in vain. The prince or priest must govern the whole. Priests when connected with the prince will sound the dread alarm, cry out infidel, infidel—the church, the church is in danger: and then lead armies under the banner of the cross, to exterminate heretics and massacre whole nations.[9]

Another Massachusetts preacher put it thus:

> No doubt, Constantine the Great, who first established christianity, had a good intention in the same; but all the darkness that has since overspread the Christian church, the exorbitant power of the popes and church of Rome, all the oceans of blood that have been shed in the contests about religion, between different sects of Christians, the almost total cessation of the progress of christianity, the rise of mahometanism, the rise and spread of deism, the general contempt in which christianity is fallen; all may fairly be laid at the door of that establishment.[10]

Jefferson concurred that the "age of Constantine" has been disastrous for the Western church and state alike: "Millions of innocent men, women, and children, since the introduction of Christianity, have been burnt, tortured, fined, imprisoned; yet we have not advanced one inch towards uniformity."[11] Madison wrote similarly:

> During almost fifteen centuries has the legal establishment of Christianity been on trial. What has been its fruits? More or less in all places, pride and indolence in the Clergy, ignorance or servility in the laity, in both, superstition, bigotry and persecu-

tion. . . . Torrents of blood have been spilt in the old world, by vain attempts of the secular arm, to extinguish Religious discord, by proscribing all differences in Religious opinion. Time has at length revealed the True Remedy. . . . The American Theatre has exhibited proofs that equal and compleat liberty, if it does not wholly eradicate it, sufficiently destroys its malignant influence on the health and prosperity of the state.[12]

James Iredell of North Carolina reflected commonplaces of the day when he declared:

Every person in the least conversant in the history of mankind, knows what dreadful mischiefs have been committed by religious persecutions. Under the color of religious tests the utmost cruelties have been exercised. Those in power have generally considered all wisdom centered in themselves, that they alone had a right to dictate to the rest of mankind, and that all opposition to their tenets was profane and impious. The consequence of this intolerant spirit had been that each church has in turn set itself up against every other, and persecutions and wars of the most implacable and bloody nature have taken place in every part of the world. America has [now] set an example to mankind to think more modestly and reasonably; that a man may be of different religious sentiments from our own, without being a bad member of society.[13]

Anyone who remained unconvinced could turn to Massachusetts jurist John Adams's massive three-volume *A Defense of the Constitutions of Government in the United States of America* (1788) for an exhaustive account of the "gory ecclesiastical or civil tyranny" of the Western tradition and the "glorious new experiment" of the American republic.[14]

In this chapter, we stand with the eighteenth-century American founders and look back with them on the development of Western understandings of church-state relations and religious liberty. We focus first on the Roman Empire, then on medieval and early modern Western Europe, and finally on colonial America. We also focus on the shifting Christian understandings of church-state relations and religious liberty, and the emerging challenges to them during the eighteenth-century Enlightenment. We analyze the novelty of the eighteenth-century American experiment in disestablishing a national religion and granting religious freedom to all peaceable believers. But we will also consider important prototypes for these developments from earlier eras, and a number of ancient legal and theoretical ideas on which the American founders depended. The American founders revolutionized the Western understanding of church-state relations and religious liberty. But they ultimately remained firmly within the Western tradition, drawing on its enduring and evolving postulates about God and humanity, authority and liberty, church and state.

The First Millennium

During the first three centuries of its existence, the Christian church was largely isolated from official Roman society. It received virtually no support from the Roman political authorities and virtually no protection against oppression by them. Christians refused to acknowledge the divinity of the emperor, as required by Roman law, or to swear the oaths or to join the pagan rituals necessary for participation in Roman civic, political, or military life. Early Christians taught obedience to the authorities but only to the limits of Christian conscience, following Christ's call to "render to Caesar the things that are Caesar's, and to God the things that are God's."[15] But they also sought to expand their faith and reform society, following Christ's call for them to "make disciples of all nations, teaching them to observe all that Christ had taught them."[16] This combination of nonconformity and agitation for reform brought government reprisals. Even before the infamous reign of Emperor Nero (r. 54–68), the Roman authorities began to repress Christians, departing from Rome's usual policy of indifferently tolerating all faiths that remained politically subservient and religiously sequestered. By the end of the first century, Rome had declared Christianity an illicit religion and pronounced Christians guilty of treason unless they recanted their faith. Imperial edicts outlawed Christian worship, charity, and education, and instituted intermittent waves of brutal persecution against Christians.[17]

After the conversion of Emperor Constantine in 312, the Roman authorities began to tolerate Christian beliefs and practices. The imperial Edict of Milan (313) for the first time guaranteed to Christians, alongside all other faiths, "freedom to follow whatever religion each one wished," "a public and free liberty to practice their religion or cult," and a "free permission to follow their own religion and worship as befits the peacefulness of our times." The edict also recognized the rights of Christian groups to property and places of worship, "which belonged by right to their body—that is, to the churches not to individuals," and the right to restitution of properties confiscated in earlier persecutions. Such guarantees of individual and group religious rights were granted, the edict provided, "so that the supreme Divinity, whose religion we obey with free minds, may be able to show in all matters His accustomed favour and benevolence towards us."[18]

Had this law on the books remained the law in action, Rome would have instituted a regime of religious toleration that the West would not see again for more than a millennium. Even in Constantine's reign, however, and increasingly thereafter, the Roman emperors moved from a policy of open religious toleration of most peaceable faiths to a policy of increasing preference for Trinitarian Christianity. They also began to persecute "Jews, pagans, apostates, and heretics" who opposed orthodox church teachings, subjecting them to the same repressive and bloody measures that Christians had faced before the fourth century. An imperial edict of 380 sealed this shift in policy. This edict for the first time legally established Trinitarian Christianity as the official state religion and declared all other forms of faith to be heretical and deserving of retribution:

> [T]here is one Godhead, Father, Son, and Holy Spirit, in an equal Majesty and Holy Trinity. We order that those who follow this doctrine to receive the title of Catholic Christians, but others we judge to be mad and raving and worthy of incurring the dis-

grace of heretical teaching, nor are their assemblies to receive the name of churches. They are to be punished not only by Divine retribution but also by our own measures.[19]

This formal legal establishment of Trinitarian Christianity as the official religion of the Roman Empire brought the church under both the support and the control of Roman political authorities. On the one hand, orthodox Christian clergy were given special military protection, legal privileges, and financial support to spread the faith, to educate the young, to care for the poor, and to build new churches, monasteries, schools, and charities. Heretics, pagans, and Jews, in turn, were subject to severe repression and legal disability, which Christian bishops sometimes led at the behest of the emperor.[20] On the other hand, the Roman emperors declared themselves to be the supreme rulers of both civil and religious affairs in the empire. The Roman emperors and their delegates convoked and presided over the major church councils, appointed and removed bishops and other clergy, and chartered and administered churches and monasteries. Numerous imperial laws regulated the internal activities of the church, the lives of its clerics and monks, the acquisition and disposition of church property, and the definition of church doctrine and liturgy. The great compilations of Roman law—the *Theodosian Code* (438) and Justinian's *Corpus Iuris Civilis* (529–534) and *Novel Constitutions* (c. 565)—were filled with hundreds of new laws that governed the doctrine, liturgy, polity, and property of the established Christian church.

This new form of church-state relations in Christian Rome gave rise to a variety of new Christian political theories. The most famous theory was developed by Augustine, the bishop of Hippo in North Africa (354–430). Augustine saw in this new church-state arrangement not a betrayal of apostolic ideals of separatism but a better way of understanding the spiritual and temporal dimensions and powers of this earthly life. In *City of God* (ca. 413–427),[21] Augustine contrasted the city of God that coexists on this earth with the city of man. The city of God consists of all those who are saved from sin, bound by the love of God, and devoted to a life of Christian piety, morality, and worship led by the Christian clergy. The city of man consists of all the things of this sinful world, and the political and social institutions that God had created to maintain a modicum of order and peace on the earth. Augustine sometimes depicted this dualism as two walled cities separated from each other—particularly when he was describing the sequestered life and discipline of monasticism, or the earlier plight of the Christian churches under pagan Roman persecution. But Augustine's more dominant teaching was that, in the Christianized Roman Empire, these two cities overlapped in responsibility and membership. Christians would remain dual citizens until these two cities were fully and finally separated on the return of Christ and at the Last Judgment of God. A Christian remained bound by the sinful habits of the world, even if he aspired to greater purity of the Gospel. A Christian remained subject to the power of both cities, even if she aspired to be a citizen of the city of God alone. If the rulers of the city of man favored Christians, rather than persecuting them, so much the better.

It was crucial, however, that the spiritual and temporal powers in these two cities remain separate in their core functions. Even though Christianity became the one established religion of the Roman Empire, patronized and protected by the Roman authorities, Augustine and other church fathers insisted that political authorities not intrude upon core spiritual functions. All magistrates, even the Roman emperors, were not ordained clergy but laity. They had no power to administer the sacraments or mete out religious discipline. They were bound by the teachings of the Bible, the decrees of the ecumenical councils, and the traditions of their predecessors. They also had to accept the church's instruction, judgment, and spiritual discipline. Thus, for example, Ambrose, bishop of Milan (ca. 337–397), excommunicated Emperor Theodosius the Great for massacring the people of Thessalonica and readmitted him to Communion only after he had done public penance for his immoral act. Pope Gelasius I (r. 492–496) put the matter famously in 494 in a letter rebuking Emperor Anastasius:

> There are, indeed, most august Emperor, two powers by which the world is chiefly ruled: the sacred authority of the Popes and the royal power. Of these the priestly power is the more important, because it has to render account for kings of men themselves at [the Last Judgment]. For you know, our clement son, that although you have the chief place in dignity over the human race, yet you must submit yourself faithfully to those who have charge of Divine things, and look to them for the means of your salvation.[22]

This "two powers" passage became a *locus classicus* for many later theories of a basic separation between pope and emperor, clergy and laity, *regnum* and *sacerdotium*.[23]

This system of tempered imperial or royal rule within the church largely continued in the West after the Roman Empire fell in the fifth century. Before their conversion, many of the pagan Germanic kings and tribal rulers were considered to be divine and were the cult leaders as well as the military leaders of their people. When they converted to Christianity, they lost their divinity yet continued as sacral rulers of the church within their territories. Christianity legitimated their efforts to extend their rule over the diverse peoples who made up their regimes. In addition to supporting these efforts to suppress tribal religions, the clergy looked upon such figures as the Frankish emperor Charlemagne (r. 768–814) and the Anglo-Saxon king Alfred (r. 871–899) as spiritual leaders. In turn, Christian rulers supported the clergy in its struggle against heresy and extended military protection, political patronage, and material support. Feudal lords within these Germanic domains further patronized the church, by donating lands and other properties to the church in return for the power to appoint and control the priests, abbots, and abbesses who occupied them.

The Papal Revolution

This model of church-state relations was turned upside down after 1050. In the name of "freedom of the church" (*libertas ecclesiae*), Pope Gregory VII (r. 1073–

1085) and his successors threw off their political and feudal patrons and declared the Catholic Church to be an independent and superior legal and political authority of Western Christendom.[24] In his revolutionary manifesto, *The Dictates of the Pope* (1075), Gregory proclaimed that emperors and kings had no authority over the church, its clergy, or its polity. Only the pope, Gregory declared, had authority to ordain, discipline, depose, and reinstate bishops, to convoke and control church councils, and to establish and administer abbeys and bishoprics. Only the pope had authority "to enact new laws according to the needs of the time" that were binding on all persons and parts of Christendom. Only the papal court was "the court of the whole of Christendom" open and available to all Christians. The pope "may depose emperors," and "the pope is the only one whose feet are to be kissed by all princes."[25] Gregory's bold proclamation did not go unchallenged. For more than three generations thereafter, a good deal of Europe was locked in bitter religious and civil war, with the papacy and its supporters ultimately prevailing.

In the course of the twelfth and thirteenth centuries the Roman Catholic Church began to make good on Gregory's grand claims. The pope and the clergy now claimed more than a spiritual and sacramental power over the church's affairs. They claimed a vast new jurisdiction, an authority to proclaim and enforce law—literally the power "to speak the law" *(jus dicere)* for Christendom. They claimed exclusive personal jurisdiction over clerics, pilgrims, students, heretics, Jews, and Muslims. They claimed subject matter jurisdiction over doctrine, liturgy, patronage, education, charity, inheritance, marriage, oaths, oral promises, and moral crimes. And they claimed concurrent jurisdiction with state authorities over secular subjects that required the church's special forms of Christian equity. A torrent of new church laws, called canon laws, issued by popes, bishops, and church councils came to govern Western Christendom. A vast network of church courts, headquartered in the papal court, enforced these laws throughout the West.[26] Between 1150 and 1350, the Roman Catholic Church, ironically, became "the first modern state" in the West.[27] Church law became the first modern international law, presumptively trumping local secular laws in the event of conflict.

This late medieval system of church government and law was grounded in part in a new theory of "two swords" that supplanted the traditional Gelasian formula of "two powers." The two swords theory taught that the pope is the vicar of Christ on earth, in whom Christ vested his whole authority.[28] This authority was symbolized in the "two swords" mentioned in passing in Luke 22:38, which medieval writers identified as a spiritual sword and a temporal sword. According to conventional medieval formulations of the two swords theory, Christ had metaphorically handed both swords to the pope, the vicar of Christ on earth. The pope and the Christian clergy wielded the spiritual sword, in part by establishing canon law rules for the governance of all Christendom. The clergy, however, were too holy to wield the temporal sword. They thus delegated this temporal sword to those authorities below the spiritual realm—emperors, kings, princes, dukes, and their civil retinues—who held their swords "of" and "for" the sake of protecting and supporting the church. These civil magistrates were to promulgate and enforce civil laws in a manner consistent with canon law. Under this two swords theory, civil law was by its nature inferior to canon law. Civil jurisdiction was subordinate to ecclesiastical jurisdiction. The state answered to the church.[29] Pope Boniface VIII distilled this two swords theory forcefully in 1302:

> We are taught by the words of the Gospel that in this Church and in its power there are two swords, a spiritual, to wit, and a temporal. . . . [B]oth are in the power of the Church, namely the spiritual and [temporal] swords; the one, indeed, to be wielded for the Church, the other by the Church; the former by the priest, the latter by the hand of kings and knights, but at the will and sufferance of the priest. For it is necessary that one sword shall be under another and that the temporal authority should be subjected to the spiritual. . . . If, therefore, the earthly power err, it shall be judged by the spiritual power; if the lesser spiritual power err, it shall be judged by the higher, competent spiritual power; but if the supreme spiritual power [i.e., the pope] should err, it could be judged solely by God, not by man.[30]

The church further predicated these jurisdictional claims on Christ's famous delegation of "the keys of the kingdom of heaven" (Matt. 16:18) to St. Peter, who was regarded as the first pope. According to the "two keys theory," Christ delegated a key of knowledge to discern God's word and will and a key of power to implement and enforce that word and will by law. The church further predicated its specific subject matter jurisdiction on its traditional authority over the form and function of the Christian sacraments. By the fifteenth century, the church had gathered whole systems of canon law around the seven sacraments—baptism, Eucharist, penance, orders, extreme unction, confirmation, and marriage—whose rules and procedures were enforced in church courts.

The church's canon law made regular use of the concept of individual and corporate rights (*iura,* the plural of *ius* in Latin). It defined the rights of the clergy to their liturgical offices and ecclesiastical benefices, their exemptions from civil taxes and duties, and their immunities from civil prosecution and compulsory testimony. It defined the rights of ecclesiastical organizations like parishes, monasteries, charities, and guilds to form and dissolve; to accept and reject members; to establish order and discipline; and to acquire, use, and alienate property. It defined the rights of church councils and synods to participate in the election and discipline of bishops, abbots, and other clergy. It defined the rights of the laity to worship, evangelize, maintain religious symbols, participate in the sacraments, travel on religious pilgrimages, and educate their children. It defined the rights of the poor, widows, and needy to seek solace, succor, and sanctuary within the church. A good deal of the rich latticework of medieval canon law was cast, substantively and procedurally, in the form and language of rights.[31]

To be sure, such rights were not unguided by duties. Nor were they available to all parties. Only the Catholic faithful—and, notoriously, not Jews, Muslims, or heretics—had full rights, which were to be exercised with appropriate ecclesiastical and sacramental constraints administered by the church. But the basic medieval rights formulation of exemptions, immunities, privileges, and benefits, as well as the rights of religious worship, travel, speech, and education, have persisted, with ever greater inclusion and application, to this day. The core religious rights and liberties that came to prevail in the eighteenth-century American experiment were first forged as legal concepts not by James Madison or Thomas Jefferson in the eighteenth century but by obscure Catholic theologians and canon lawyers half a millennium before them.

In the course of the fourteenth century and thereafter, this intricate system of religious rights, and of church-state relations, began to break down. Strong monarchs began to increase their control over the church, and clerical authority began to wane—in part because of widespread corruption and compromise even at the highest levels of church government. In 1309, the papal seat was moved from Rome to Avignon, France, and there came under increasing constraint and control by the kings of France. In 1377, the pope returned to Rome, only to have a rival pope appointed the next year in Avignon, claiming the same prerogatives as his Roman rival. In 1415 yet a third pope was appointed in Pavia, Italy, compounding the already widespread confusion and dissent within the church hierarchy.

In response, the German emperor Sigismund convoked at Constance the first of a series of great church councils that declared authority over church polity and canon law, despite papal disapproval. In the Pragmatic Sanction of Bourges (1438) and again in the Concordat of Bologna (1516) French kings banned various papal taxes, limited appeals to Rome, required French bishops to be elected by French church councils called by the king, subjected French clergy to royal discipline, and increased royal control over church property.[32] In fifteenth-century Germany, strong princes and city councils passed numerous "legal reformations" that placed limits on church property and taxation, disciplined wayward clergy, and curtailed the jurisdiction of church courts over crime, family, inheritance, and contracts. Fifteenth-century Spanish monarchs subordinated the ecclesiastical courts to the civil courts and assumed political and legal control over the prosecution and execution of heretics, Jews, and Muslims, eventually unleashing the terrifying Spanish Inquisition.

The Protestant Reformation

In retrospect, such developments can be seen as storm signals that heralded the coming of the Protestant Reformation. The Reformation—inaugurated by Martin Luther's famous posting of the Ninety-Five Theses in 1517 and burning of the Catholic canon law books in 1520—began as a call for religious freedom. Martin Luther (1483–1546), John Calvin (1509–1564), Thomas Cranmer (1489–1556), Menno Simons (1496–1561), and other sixteenth-century reformers all began their movements with a call for freedom: freedom of the individual conscience from intrusive canon laws and clerical controls, freedom of political officials from ecclesiastical power and privileges, and freedom of the local clergy from both central papal rule and oppressive princely controls. "Freedom of the Christian" became the rallying cry of the early Reformation.[33] It drove theologians and jurists, clergy and laity, princes and peasants alike to denounce canon laws and ecclesiastical authorities with unprecedented alacrity and to urge radical constitutional reforms. The reforms that these Protestants eventually instituted, however, often simply reestablished new forms of Christian faith, again under political control and with various Protestant denominational accents.

The Protestant Reformation broke the unity of Western Christendom and eventually laid the foundation for the modern Western system of religious pluralism. Four different patterns of church-state relations emerged in Protestant lands. The Lutheran Reformation *territorialized* the faith. Luther replaced the two swords theory of the papal revolution with a new two kingdoms theory. The "invisible" church of the heavenly kingdom, Luther argued, is a perfect community of saints, where all stand equal in dignity before God, enjoy perfect Christian liberty, and govern their affairs in accordance with the Gospel. The "visible" church of this earthly kingdom, however, embraces saints and sinners alike. Its members still stand directly before God and still enjoy liberty of conscience, including the liberty to leave the visible church and the territory where the church is located. Unlike the invisible church, however, the visible church needs both the Gospel and human laws to govern its members' relationships with God and with fellow believers. The clergy must administer the Gospel. But the magistrate must administer the law, for the magistrate is God's vice regent, called to appropriate and apply God's law in all aspects of earthly life, including within the visible church on earth.

This Lutheran understanding of the role of the magistrate in religious affairs, predicated in part on Roman law precedents, was cast into enduring constitutional form. The Peace of Augsburg (1555) established the principle of *cuius regio eius religio* ("whose region, his religion") for much of Germany and surrounding polities.[34] Under this principle, princes, dukes, or city councils were authorized to establish by civil law the appropriate forms of religious doctrine, liturgy, charity, and education for their polities—with religious dissenters granted the right to worship privately in their homes or emigrate peaceably from the territory. This new constitutional policy rendered Germany, with its 350 distinct polities, intensely pluralistic (though decidedly Christian), eventually setting off endless political, theological, and economic rivalries.

The Anglican Reformation *nationalized* the faith. When the papacy refused to annul his marriage to Catherine of Aragon, King Henry VIII (r. 1509–1547) ultimately severed all ties between the church in England and the pope. The Act of Succession (1534) denied papal authority over marriage and divorce, and granted Henry his annulment. Succeeding acts effectively divested the Catholic Church of its remaining jurisdiction and banned tithes, annates, and appeals to Rome. These acts also dissolved the church's numerous monasteries and guilds and confiscated massive holdings of church property in England. The Supremacy Act (1534) declared the monarch to be "the only Supreme Head in Earth of the Church of England called *Anglicana Ecclesia*."[35] The church *in* England had become the Church *of* England.

As spiritual and temporal heads of the Church of England, Henry VIII and his successors, through their councils and parliaments, established a uniform liturgy, doctrine, and administration of the sacraments. They issued *The Book of Common Prayer* (1559) and *The Thirty-Nine Articles of Religion* (1571), and ordered the preparation of the Authorized Version of the Bible (1611) in English translation, which came to be known as the King James Version. The Crown and Parliament also claimed jurisdiction over poor relief, education, marriage, and other activities that had previously been carried on under Catholic auspices, subject to Catholic canon law. Communicant status in the Church of England was rendered a condition for citizenship status in the Commonwealth of England. Contraventions of royal religious policy were punishable both as heresy and as treason. Catholics and dissenting Protestants were subjected to severe repression, and hundreds were executed for their religious nonconformity.

The Anabaptist Reformation *communalized* the faith by introducing a "wall of separation" between the redeemed realm of religion and the fallen realm of the world.[36] Anabaptist religious communities withdrew from the world into small, self-sufficient, intensely democratic communities. These ascetic religious communities were governed internally by biblical principles of simplicity, charity, hospitality, and discipleship. When such communities grew too large or experienced divisions, they colonized themselves, eventually spreading the Anabaptist communities from Russia to Ireland to the North American frontier—under such variant denominational labels as Amish, Hutterites, Mennonites, and Baptists.[37]

The Calvinist Reformation *congregationalized* the faith by introducing rule by a democratically elected consistory of pastors, elders, and deacons. During John Calvin's tenure from 1541 to 1564, the Geneva consistory was still an appointed body and exercised wide legal authority within Geneva and surrounding rural areas. By the later sixteenth century, however, Calvinist consistories in many communities had become elected, representative bodies whose jurisdiction was limited to their congregations. These consistories separated the offices of preaching, discipline, and charity, and established a fluid, dialogical form of religious polity and policing centered upon collective worship, the congregational meeting, and the regular election of church officers. This flexible form of ecclesiastical polity rendered the Calvinist churches and communities mobile and adaptable. They eventually spread throughout Europe under such labels as Scottish Presbyterians, English Puritans, Dutch Pietists, French Huguenots, and various Reformed groups.

The Protestant Reformation broke not only the unity of Western Christendom but also the primacy of corporate Christianity. Protestants gave new emphasis to the role of the individual believer in the economy of salvation and the individual rights that should attach thereto. The Protestant Reformation did not invent or discover the individual or the concept of individual rights; there were ample precedents for this in Greek, Roman, Patristic, and medieval Catholic sources. But the sixteenth-century Protestant reformers, more than most of their Catholic contemporaries, gave new emphasis to the (religious) rights and liberties of the individual in both religious law and civil law.

The Anabaptist doctrine of adult baptism gave new emphasis to a voluntarist understanding of religion. The adult individual was called to make a conscious choice to accept the faith through adult baptism—metaphorically, to scale the wall of separation between the fallen world and the realm of religion to come "within the perfection of Christ."[38] Later Free Church followers converted this cardinal image into a powerful platform of liberty of conscience and free exercise of religion—not only for Christians but eventually for all peaceable believers.

The Calvinist and Lutheran branches of the Reformation laid the basis for an even more expansive theory and law of (religious) rights. Classic Protestant theology teaches that a person is both saint and sinner. On the one hand, a person is created in the image of God and justified by faith in God. The person is called to a distinct vocation, which stands equal in dignity and sanctity to all others. The person is prophet, priest, and king and is responsible to exhort, minister, and rule in the community. Every person, therefore, stands equal before God and before his or her neighbor. Every person is vested with a natural liberty to live, to believe, to serve God and neighbor. Every person is entitled to the vernacular Scripture, to education, to work in a vocation. On the other hand, the person is sinful and prone to evil and egoism. He needs the restraint of the law to deter him from evil and drive him to repentance. She needs the association of others to exhort, minister, and rule her with law and with love. Every person, therefore, is inherently a communal creature, a member of a family, a church, a political community.

Protestant groups in Europe and America cast these theological doctrines into democratic forms designed to protect religious and civil rights. Protestant doctrines of the person and society were cast into democratic social forms. Since all persons stand equal before God, they must stand equal before God's political agents in the state. Since God has vested all persons with natural liberties of life and belief, the state must ensure them of similar civil liberties. Since God has called all persons to be prophets, priests, and kings, the state must protect their freedom to speak, to preach, and to rule in the community. Since God has created persons as social creatures, the state must promote and protect a plurality of social institutions, particularly the church and the family.

Protestant doctrines of sin were also cast into democratic political forms. The political office must be protected against the sinfulness of the political official. Political power, like ecclesiastical power, must be distributed among self-checking executive, legislative, and judicial branches. Officials must be elected to limited terms of office. Laws must be clearly codified and discretion closely guarded. If officials abuse their office, they must be disobeyed; if they persist in their abuse, they must be removed, even if by force. Such views would eventually have a monumental influence on the theories of inalienable rights and political revolution in early modern Europe and eighteenth-century America.[39]

Religious Establishment Versus Religious Freedom

When the Reformation splintered Western Christendom into competing religious polities—each with its own preferred forms and norms of religious governance—it

catalyzed both religious warfare and persecution and corresponding movements toward religious freedom. For example, in the 1570s the Spanish monarch Philip II
(1527–1598), who was also lord of the Netherlands, ordered a bloody inquisition
and eventually declared war against the growing population of Dutch Protestants,
killing thousands of them and confiscating huge portions of private and church
property. This sparked the revolt of the seven northern provinces on the strength of
Calvinist principles of revolution. Presaging American developments two centuries
later, the Dutch revolutionaries established a confederate government by the Union
of Utrecht of 1579, which included a provision that "each person must enjoy freedom of religion, and no one may be persecuted or questioned about his religion."
The confederacy led the revolutionary war against the Spanish monarch. In 1581
the confederacy issued a declaration of independence—the Act of Abjuration—
invoking "the law of nature" and the "ancient rights, privileges, and liberties" of the
people in justification of its revolutionary actions. When the war was settled, each
of the seven Dutch provinces instituted its own constitution. These provincial constitutions were among the most religiously tolerant of the day and helped make the
Netherlands a haven for religious dissenters from throughout Europe—and a common point of departure for American colonists, from the Mayflower Pilgrims of
1620 onward.[40] When later comparing this sixteenth-century Dutch experience
with the eighteenth-century American experience, American founder John Adams
wrote: "The Originals of the two Republicks are so much alike, that the History of
one seems but a Transcript from that of the other."[41]

In the opening decades of the seventeenth century, much of northern Europe
was locked in bitter warfare between and among Catholic and Protestant forces—
sometimes based on religious differences but often triggered by economic, territorial, and cultural disputes. The Thirty Years' War, as it came to be called, finally
ended with the Peace of Westphalia (1648).[42] Confirming and extending the principles of the 1555 Peace of Augsburg, this new treaty authorized each ruler to establish by civil law either Catholicism, Lutheranism, or Calvinism in his or her
territory. Dissenting religious groups, though denied the right to worship publicly,
were granted special privileges to assemble and worship privately and to educate
their children in their own faith (and eventually in their own private religious
schools). The spiritual jurisdiction of the canon law and papal authority over clergy
and church property were guaranteed for Catholic territories. But canon law was
barred from use in the Protestant territories, and Catholic clerics and groups therein
were divested of any remaining privileges of forum, tax exemptions, and other civil
immunities.

While this policy of balancing religious establishment with religious toleration
proved effective to securing peace for a good deal of Europe for the remainder of
the seventeenth century, it did not ultimately constrain France and England, two
of the main national powers of the day.

In France, the monarchy gradually abandoned its earlier policies of religious
toleration—particularly as they had been set out in the Edict of Nantes (1598),

which had granted modest toleration to Calvinist and other Protestant noncon-formists.[43] Supported by the antipapalism of the revived Gallican party and by the new theories of absolute monarchy expounded by Jean Bodin (1530–1596) and others on the strength of Roman law precedents, the French monarchs consolidated their control over a national Catholic Church. The French monarchy sharply cur-tailed remaining papal power over church property, ecclesiastical courts, and clerical nomination. King Louis XIV (1638–1715) passed more than one hundred acts against religious dissenters, constraining their freedom and imposing crushing taxes on them. Finally, in the Edict of Fontainebleau (1685), Louis ordered all Protestant churches and schools destroyed, proscribed all liturgies and theologies that deviated from officially sanctioned Gallicanism, and banished all dissenting clerics from France.[44] Protestants fled from France by the tens of thousands, with many making their way to Belgium, the Netherlands, Switzerland, and Germany—and eventually to distant colonies in North America and southern Africa.

Similarly, in early seventeenth-century England, the Stuart kings James I (1566–1625) and Charles I (1600–1649) issued through their parliaments a series of in-creasingly repressive laws against the few remaining Catholics and the growing number of Protestant dissenters in England. As official and unofficial persecution mounted in the 1620s and 1630s, tens of thousands of Puritans, Anabaptists, Lu-therans, and other "sectaries," as English law called them, "flew out of England, as if out of Babylon" to make their way to the Continent, and often from there to North America.[45] When the English monarchy persisted in its abuse, the remaining Puritans led a revolutionary struggle against the English Crown. The revolutionaries ultimately deposed and beheaded King Charles I. In 1649 they passed a law "declar-ing and constituting the People of England to be a commonwealth and free state."[46] They further outlawed the establishment of the Church of England and granted tol-eration to all Protestants—although not to Catholics or Jews. This experiment was short-lived. In 1660 royal rule was restored, Anglicanism was reestablished, and dis-senters were again repressed. But when the dissenters threatened a new civil war, Par-liament ultimately passed the Toleration Act of 1689 which guaranteed freedom of association and worship to all Protestants dissenting from the Church of England.[47] Many of the remaining legal restrictions on the civil and political liberties of Protes-tants fell into desuetude in the following century. Catholicism and Judaism, however, continued to be outlawed until the Jewish and Catholic Emancipation Acts of 1829 and 1833.[48]

Colonization and Experimentation

This checkerboard of rival religious and political groups in early modern Europe was projected in part onto the New World. European powers, eager to extend their po-litical and religious regimes, issued charters and privileges to colonial companies that would establish themselves in the New World under the rule of the distant mother country and mother church. Thus Spanish and Portuguese Catholic rulers from the early sixteenth century onward extended their regimes through much of Latin America, the Caribbean, Mexico, and modern-day Florida. From the later sixteenth century onward, Jesuits and other missionaries made frequent forays into the American frontier, reaching north to the Carolinas and Virginia, and more successfully west to modern-day Alabama, Louisiana, Texas, New Mexico, and California. French Catholics sent colonists to Quebec and the Canadian Maritimes, many of whom migrated south into New England. By the eighteenth century, numerous Catholic families from Quebec had also settled in New York and Pennsylvania, and hundreds more had moved down the Midwest corridor and the Mississippi River to Louisiana and from there westward. Dutch Protestant authorities chartered companies of Dutch Calvinists to New York (called New Amsterdam) and parts of New Jersey and Pennsylvania. These companies, though only modestly successful, were amply bolstered in the eighteenth century by new waves of Calvinist colonists from the German Palatinate. Scandinavian Lutheran monarchs sponsored scattered colonial companies in Delaware and eventually in Maryland, Pennsylvania, and New York.[49]

The most prominent colonizers of all, however, were the British, who established colonial companies all along the Atlantic seaboard—from Ontario and the Maritimes in the north to the southern colonies of Virginia, the Carolinas, and Georgia. Among the earliest and most influential colonies was Virginia, which was founded in 1607 as an Anglican "Christian colonie," to be populated by a "peculiar people, marked and chosen by the finger of God."[50] The British eventually assumed formal control of the Middle and New England colonies as well. The royal charters of all these colonies confirmed the rule of English laws and liberties, including ecclesiastical laws. By the time of the American Revolution in 1776, there were Anglican churches in every American colony, and every American colony was formally under the jurisdiction (albeit not the active rule) of the Bishop of London and the Archbishop of Canterbury.

Colonial America was not only a frontier for European establishments but also a haven for European dissenters, many of whom introduced their own experiments in religious liberty. Both the Plymouth Colony of 1620 and the Massachusetts Bay Colony of 1629 were founded by Puritan dissenters from the Church of England and eventually became havens for Calvinist refugees from throughout Europe, though for few others, until well into the eighteenth century. Providence Plantation was established in 1636 as "a lively experiment [for] full liberty in religious concernments," in the words of its founder, Roger Williams, who had been banished from the Massachusetts Bay Colony because of his heretical views. Providence Colony's remarkably progressive policies of protecting "liberty of conscience" and "the free exercise and enjoyment of all their civil and religious rights" eventually attracted Anabaptists and other Christian dissenters from Europe and other North American colonies, and became a model for various religious liberty advocates of the eighteenth century.[51]

In 1633 Maryland was founded by the Catholic leader Lord Baltimore as an experiment in Catholic and Protestant coexistence. Its famous Act of 1649 provided that "noe person . . . professing to believe in Jesus Christ, shall from henceforth bee any waies troubled . . . for his or her religion nor in the free exercise thereof . . . nor any way compelled to the beliefe or exercise of any other Religion against his or her consent."[52] Though ultimately frustrated by persistent Catholic-Protestant rivalries and slowly eclipsed by new Anglican establishment policies from the 1660s onward, the Maryland experiment provided ample inspiration during the constitutional debates of the next century.

Equally inspirational—and controversial—was the "holy experiment" in religious liberty instituted by Quaker leader William Penn in Pennsylvania in 1681. The Great Law of 1682 captured Penn's cardinal convictions about Christian liberty:

> [N]o person now or at any time hereafter living in this province, who shall confess and acknowledge one almighty God to be the creator, upholder, and ruler of the world, and who profess[es] himself or herself to be obliged in conscience to live peaceably and quietly under the civil government, shall in any case be molested or prejudiced for his or her conscientious persuasion or practice. Nor shall he or she at any time be compelled to frequent or maintain any religious worship, place, or ministry whatever contrary to his or her mind, but shall freely and fully enjoy his, or her, christian liberty in that respect, without any interruption or reflection.[53]

This early Quaker experiment in religious liberty, though often denounced by mainline Protestants and Catholics, provided a talisman of religious liberty that later American writers would make real. William Penn's brilliant defense of religious liberty, on the strength of liberty of conscience for all peaceable religions and disestablishment of all state religions, would prove to be axiomatic for the American logic of religious liberty.

Some fifty years after the founding of Pennsylvania, England set up its thirteenth colony in America. Georgia was not, as common lore would have it, primarily a debtors' colony, but instead a home for European religious misfits. A host of European dissenters settled in the new colony alongside Anglicans, including Scottish Presbyterians, Austrian Lutherans, German Moravians, Jews, Baptists, Methodists, and others. Georgia's Royal Charter (1732) both created and reflected this reality, as it proclaimed:

> [F]orever hereafter, there shall be a liberty of conscience allowed in the worship of God, to all persons inhabiting, or which shall inhabit or be resident within our said province, and that all such persons, except papists, shall have a free exercise of their religion, so they be contented with the quiet and peaceable enjoyment of the same, not giving offence or scandal to the government.

Although the Church of England was later established in 1758, there remained ample space for dissenters' beliefs and practices both before and after the Revolution.[54]

The eighteenth-century American experiment in religious freedom was thus, at once, very old and very new. For a nation to contemplate not establishing religion at all and granting religious liberty to all peaceable faiths without obstruction was, indeed, a novel exercise in the history of the West. But legal precedents for such an experiment lay closely at hand in the constitutional example of sixteenth-century Holland and, more distantly, in the Edict of Milan in 313. And firm legal principles to implement this experiment—liberty of conscience, freedom of religious exercise, separation of religious and political authorities, guarantees of religious group rights, and the like—were readily at hand in Catholic canon law, Protestant civil law, European peace treaties, and the protests of religious dissenters throughout the ages. Even so, as James Madison observed, "it remained for North America to bring the great & interesting subject to a fair, & finally, to a decisive test."[55]

This Western pedigree of the American experiment in religious liberty might be a source of comfort to modern skeptics, who see the experiment as a betrayal of the classic ideals of Western Christendom. This Western pedigree might also be a source of warning to modern enthusiasts, who see it as a universal formula of the good life and good society to be enforced throughout the world. We shall return to this question in our final chapters when we ask whether religious freedom is a natural right that Americans were merely the first to discover fully and implement constitutionally or a distinctly American invention that might not work in other cultures (pp. 263–271). We shall argue that the American experiment in religious liberty was more a discovery of a natural right than the invention of an American product, and thus it deserves universal application. But we also argue that the American formulation of the natural rights of religion was distinctive, particularly its prohibition on a national establishment of religion.[56]

Notes

1. Galatians 5:1,13; 2 Corinthians 3:17; John 8:32, 36; Romans 8:21. All biblical quotes in this volume are taken from the Revised Standard Version.

2. Matthew 22:21; Mark 12:17; Luke 20:25; Romans 12:2; Ephesians 2:14; 2 Corinthians 6:14–18.

3. Hebrews 11:13, Philippians 3:20.

4. Ephesians 2:14.

5. Donald S. Lutz, *The Origins of American Constitutionalism* (1988), 140–141. See Ellis Sandoz, ed., *Political Sermons of the American Founding Era, 1730–1805* (1991); J. W. Thornton, *The Pulpit of the American Revolution* (1860).

6. See Lutz, *Origins,* 139–149. Of all citations in the founders' writings, those to the Bible constituted 34 percent, Montesquieu 8.3 percent, Blackstone 7.9 percent, and Locke 2.9 percent.

7. James Madison, "Memorial and Remonstrance Against Religious Assessments," in *The Papers of James Madison,* ed. W. T. Hutchinson et al. (1962), 8:298.

8. James Madison, Letter to Rev. Adams (1833), in Daniel L. Dreisbach, *Religion and Politics in the Early Republic: Jasper Adams and the Church-State Debate* (1996), 117–121, at 118.

9. *New Hampshire Patriot,* July 23, 1781, 4.

10. Elhanan Winchester, "A Century Sermon on the Glorious Revolution (1788)," in Sandoz, *Political Sermons,* 969, 989–990.

11. Thomas Jefferson, "Notes on the State of Virginia (1781–1785)," Query XVII, in *The Complete Jefferson,* ed. Saul K. Padover (1969), 673–676.

12. Madison, "Memorial and Remonstrance," sec. 8, 11.

13. North Carolina Ratification Debates, July 30, 1788, in Jonathan Elliot, ed., *The Debates in the Several State Conventions, on the Adoption of the Federal Constitution* (1854), 4:196–197 [hereafter Elliot, ed., *Debates*]. Baptist leader Isaac Backus opined similarly to fellow members of the Massachusetts ratification convention: "Nothing is more evident both in reason and the Holy Scriptures, than that religion is ever a matter solely between God and individuals; and therefore, no man or men can impose any religious test, without invading the essential prerogatives of our Lord Jesus Christ. Ministers first assumed this power under the Christian name; and then Constantine approved the practice, when he adopted the profession of Christianity, as an engine of state policy. And let the history of all nations be searched from that day to this, and it will appear that the imposing of religious tests hath been the greatest engine of tyranny in the world." Intervention February 4, 1788, in Elliot, *Debates,* 2:148, with slightly different wording in *The United States Chronicle: Political, Commercial, and Historical,* August 21, 1788, 1.

14. Reprinted in *The Works of John Adams,* ed. C. F. Adams (Boston, 1850–1856), vols. 4–6; see further John Adams, "A Dissertation on the Canon and Feudal Law (1774)," in *The Works of John Adams,* 3:447, 451ff.

15. Matthew 22:21; see also Romans 13:1–7.

16. Matthew 28:19–20; see also Acts 1:8.

17. Robert L. Wilken, *Christians as the Romans Saw Them* (1984); Charles Cochrane, *Christianity and Classical Culture,* repr. ed. (2003).

18. Lactantius, *De Mortibus Persecutorum [c. 315],* 48.2–12, ed. and trans. J. L. Creed (1984), 71–73.

19. In Sidney Z. Ehler and John B. Morrall, eds., *Church and State Through the Centuries: A Collection of Historic Documents with Commentaries* (1954), 7.

20. Harold A. Drake, *Constantine and the Bishops* (2000).

21. St. Augustine, *City of God,* trans. G. G. Walsh et al., ed. Vernon J. Bourke (1958), bk. 4.1–4; 19.15–22; 20.1–2, 30; 21; see also *The Political Writings of St. Augustine,* ed. Henry Paolucci (1962).

22. In Ehler and Morrall, *Church and State,* 10–11.

23. Karl F. Morrison, *The Two Kingdoms: Ecclesiology in Carolingian Political Thought* (1964); Ernst Kantorowicz, *The King's Two Bodies: A Study in Medieval Political Theology* (1957).

24. Harold J. Berman, *Law and Revolution: The Formation of the Western Legal Tradition* (1983).

25. In Ehler and Morrall, *Church and State,* 43–44.

26. Berman, *Law and Revolution,* 199–254; R. H. Helmholz, *The Spirit of the Classical Canon Law* (1996).

27. F.W. Maitland, in Berman, *Law and Revolution,* 113–115.

28. Brian Tierney, *The Origins of Papal Infallibility, 1150–1350* (1972), 39–45, 82–121.

29. Otto von Gierke, *Political Theories of the Middle Age,* trans. F. W. Maitland (1958), 7–21; Ewart Lewis, *Medieval Political Ideas* (1954), 2:506–538; Lester L. Field, *Liberty, Dominion, and the Two Swords: On the Origins of Western Political Theology* (1998).

30. In Ehler and Morrall, *Church and State,* 89–92; Brian Tierney, *The Crisis of Church and State, 1050–1300* (1964), 180ff.

31. Brian Tierney, *The Idea of Natural Rights: Studies on Natural Rights, Natural Law, and Church Law, 1150–1625* (1997).

32. In Ehler and Morrall, *Church and State,* 96–144.

33. Martin Luther, "Freedom of a Christian (1520)," in Jaroslav Pelikan, ed., *Luther's Works* (1955–1968), 31:327.

34. In Ehler and Morrall, *Church and State,* 164–173.

35. In Carl Stephenson and Frederick G. Marcham, eds., *Sources of English Constitutional History,* rev. ed. (1972), 311–312.

36. See, e.g., *The Complete Writings of Menno Simons, c. 1496–1561,* trans. L. Verduin, ed. J. C. Wenger (1984), 29, 117–120, 158–159, 190–206.

37. Walter Klaassen, ed., *Anabaptism in Outline: Selected Primary Sources* (1981); George H. Williams, *The Radical Reformation,* 3d ed. (1992).

38. The phrase is from the foundational text of Anabaptists, the Schleitheim Confession (1527), in Howard J. Loewen, *One Lord, One Church, One Hope, and One God: Mennonite Confessions of Faith in North America* (1985), 79–84.

39. John Witte, Jr., *The Reformation of Rights: Law, Religion, and Human Rights in Early Modern Calvinism* (2007); Witte, *Law and Protestantism: The Legal Teachings of the Lutheran Reformation* (2002).

40. E. H. Kossmann and A. Mellink, eds., *Texts Concerning the Revolt of the Netherlands* (1974).

41. John Adams, "Memorial to the States General" (April 19, 1781), in *The Papers of John Adams,* ed. Gregg Lint et al. (2006), 11:277.

42. In Ehler and Morrall, *Church and State,* 193–198.

43. Ibid., 204–207.

44. Ibid., 208–213.

45. Harold J. Berman, *Faith and Order: The Reconciliation of Law and Religion* (1993), 104.

46. C. H. Firth and R. S. Rait, eds., *Acts and Ordinances of the Interregnum,* 1642–1660 (1911), 2:18, 24, 120, 122.

47. In Stephenson and Marcham, *Sources,* 607–608.

48. Ibid., 678–679.

49. See details in Edwin S. Gaustad and Philip L. Barlow, *New Historical Atlas of Religion in America* (2001), chap. 1.

50. William Strachey and John Rolfe, quoted and discussed in Frank Lambert, *The Founding Fathers and the Place of Religion in America* (2003), 46.

51. "Plantation Agreement of Providence (1640)"; and "Charter of Rhode Island and Providence Plantations (1663)," in *The Federal and State Constitutions, Colonial Charters, and Other Organic Laws,* ed. F. Thorpe (Washington, DC, 1909), 6:3205–3206, 3211–3213.

52. In W. Browne, ed., *Archives of Maryland* (1883), 1:244, 246.

53. In J. T. Mitchell and J. Flanders, eds., *Statutes at Large of Pennsylvania* (1911), 1:107–109; see further *The Political Writings of William Penn,* ed. Andrew R. Murphy (2002); J. William Frost, *A Perfect Freedom: Religious Liberty in Pennsylvania* (1990).

54. See Joel A. Nichols, "Religious Liberty in the Thirteenth Colony: Church-State Relations in Colonial and Early National Georgia," *NYU Law Review* 80 (2005): 1693.

55. James Madison, Letter to Rev. Adams (1833), in Dreisbach, *Religion and Politics,* 118.

56. See T. Jeremy Gunn and John Witte, Jr., eds., *No Establishment of Religion: America's Contribution to the World of Religious Liberty* (2011).

2

The Theology and Politics
of the Religion Clauses

In Chapter 1, we stood with the American founders and looked backward with them at the history of church-state relations and religious liberty in the West. The founders understood that they were creating something new in the religion clauses of the state constitutions and the First Amendment—especially in their efforts to remove traditional national establishments of religion and extend religious liberty to all peaceable believers. But the founders also understood that the Western tradition offered many prophets and prototypes and that drawing on these sources was vital to creating a law of religious liberty that was constitutionally cogent and politically acceptable in the new nation.

If Chapter 1 had us peeking over the shoulders of the founders as they surveyed the long history of the West, this chapter has us listening in on their informal and formal conversations about the origin, nature, and purpose of their new constitutional guarantees of religious liberty. Drawing on everything from private diaries and letters to formal constitutional provisions and drafting and ratification debates from the later eighteenth century, we shall let the American founders tell us what they were trying to achieve with this new constitutional experiment.

The American experiment in religious liberty cannot be reduced to the First Amendment religion clauses alone, nor can the framers' understanding be determined simply by studying the debates on these clauses in the First Session of Congress in 1789. The record of these debates is very slender—a mere three pages in modern edition, as we shall see in Chapter 4. And the First Amendment religion clauses, by design, reflect only a small part of the early constitutional experiment and experience. The First Amendment religion clauses formally define only the outer boundaries of appropriate national governmental action respecting religion: government may neither prescribe ("establish") religion nor proscribe ("prohibit") the freedom to exercise or practice religion. Precisely what governmental conduct, short of outright prescription or proscription of religion, is constitutionally permissible is left open for debate and development. Moreover, the religion clauses on their face bind only the federal government ("Congress"), rendering prevailing state constitutional provisions and the sentiments of their drafters equally vital sources of the original understanding. Finally, the drafters of the religion clauses urged interpreters to look not only to the drafters' intentions but, in James Madison's words, "to the text itself [and] the sense attached to it by the people in their respective State Conventions, where it received all the authority which it possesses."[1] The state convention delegates derived their understandings from their own state constitutional experiments and experiences, which are reflected in contemporaneous pamphlets, sermons, letters, and speeches. Thus we must consult a wide range of eighteenth-century textual and contextual materials in order to come to terms with the prevailing sentiments on religious rights and liberties in the young American republic.

Within the ample eighteenth-century sources at hand, four views on religious liberty were critical to constitutional formation. These we label *Puritan, Evangelical, Enlightenment*, and *Civic Republican*. Exponents of these four views often found common cause and used common language, particularly during the constitutional convention and ratification debates. Yet each group offered its own distinct teachings on religious liberty and had its own preferences for their implementation as law. Together, these groups held up the four corners of a wide canopy of opinion about religious liberty in the eighteenth century.

The image of a "canopy" of opinions—which swayed and stretched even while covering the same basic ground—underscores the notion that the founders' views on religious liberty defy easy description and classification. Many other views on religious liberty besides these four circulated, and many other labels besides Puritan, Evangelical, Enlightenment, and Civic Republican can be used to describe even these four views. Moreover, the founders often moved freely between two or more perspectives, shifted their allegiances and alliances over time, or changed their tone and tune as they moved from formal writing to the pulpit, letter desk, or political platform. The four perspectives are presented here as heuristic models—typical clusters of argument and adherence in eighteenth-century American discussions and debates about religious rights and liberties.

The founders' original understanding regarding government and religion cannot be reduced to any one of these views. It must be sought in the tensions among them and in the general principles that emerged from their interaction. What follows in this chapter is a snapshot of these four views on religious liberty. The next chapter provides a distillation of the first principles of religious liberty that they held in common, even though each group defined and prioritized these principles differently.

Puritan Views

The Puritans of the New England states of Massachusetts, Connecticut, New Hampshire, Vermont, and Maine were heirs of the theology of religious liberty taught by the Reformed or Calvinist tradition. This was the Protestant tradition inspired by the sixteenth-century Genevan reformer John Calvin that had spread through early modern Switzerland, France, the Netherlands, Scotland, the Rhineland, and England.[2] The New England Puritans had refined this European Calvinist legacy through the efforts of John Winthrop, John Cotton, Cotton Mather, and others in the seventeenth century. They had liberalized some of this legacy through the writings of John Wise, Charles Chauncy, Jonathan Mayhew, and others in the eighteenth century. They had propagated their views throughout colonial America through their relentless publications, and through the further writings of such Calvinist coreligionists as the Presbyterians, Huguenots, and Dutch and German Reformed who had settled in other colonies all down the Atlantic seaboard. But it was in the New England states that the Puritans had the occasion to cast their Calvinist theological principles into constitutional practice.

The Puritans who wrote on religious liberty were concerned especially with the nature of the church, the state, and the relationship between them. They conceived of the church and the state as two separate covenantal associations, two seats of godly authority within a broader covenant community formed by a founding covenant. The founding communal covenant or compact, beginning with the Mayflower Compact of 1620, set the basic moral and religious ideals of each local community. The separate institutions of church and state served to implement these local communal ideas. Each institution, they believed, was vested with a distinct power, polity, and calling. The church held the power of the Word, and was governed by pastoral, pedagogical, and diaconal authorities who collaborated to preach the word, administer the sacraments, teach the young, and care for the poor and the needy. The state held the power of the sword, and governed by executive, legislative, and judicial authorities who were called to enforce law, punish crime, cultivate virtue, and protect peace and order.

In the New England communities where their views prevailed, the Puritans adopted a variety of rules designed to foster this basic separation of the institutions and operations of church and state. Church officials were formally prohibited from holding political office, serving on juries, interfering in governmental affairs, endorsing political candidates, or censuring the official conduct of a statesman. Political officials, in turn, were prohibited from holding ministerial office, interfering in internal ecclesiastical government, performing the sacerdotal functions of clergy, or censuring the official conduct of a cleric. To permit any such officiousness on the part of church or state officials, Governor John Winthrop averred, "would confound those Jurisdictions, which Christ hath made distinct."[3]

Although church and state were not to be confounded, they were still to be "close and compact."[4] To the Puritans, these two institutions were inextricably linked in nature and function. Each was an instrument of godly authority. Each did its part to establish and maintain the community and its founding moral and religious ideals. As Puritan preacher and Harvard President Urian Oakes put it, "I look upon this as a little model of the gloriou[s] kingdom of Christ on earth. Christ reigns among us in the commonwealth as well as in the church, and hath his glorious interest involved and wrapped up in the good of both societies respectively."[5]

The Puritans, therefore, countenanced both the coordination and the cooperation of church and state.

State officials provided various forms of material and moral aid to churches and their officials. Public properties were donated to church groups for meetinghouses, parsonages, day schools, hospices, and orphanages. Tax collectors took tithes and special assessments to support the ministers and ministry of the congregational church. Tax exemptions and immunities were accorded to the religious, educational, and charitable organizations that they operated. Special subsidies and military protections were provided for missionaries and religious outposts. Special criminal laws prohibited interference with religious properties and services. Sabbath day laws prohibited all forms of unnecessary labor and uncouth leisure on Sundays and holy days and required faithful attendance at worship services.

Church officials, in turn, provided various forms of material and moral aid to the state. Church meetinghouses and chapels were used not only to conduct religious services but also to host town assemblies, political rallies, and public auctions; to house the community school and library; and to maintain census rolls and birth, marriage, and death certificates. Parsonages were used not only to house the minister and his family but also to harbor orphans, widows, the sick, the aged, and victims of abuse and disaster. Church officials preached obedience to the authorities and imposed spiritual discipline on parishioners found guilty of crimes. They encouraged their parishioners to be active in political affairs and each year offered "election day sermons" on Christian political principles. They offered learned expositions on the requirements of godly law and occasionally offered advice to legislatures and courts, particularly on heated questions of public morality and law, such as the execution of criminals.

Initially the New England leadership left little room for individual religious experimentation. Despite their adherence to a basic separation of the offices of church and state, the New England authorities established a common Calvinist congregationalism for each local community. Separatism for them did not connote disestablishment of one religion or the toleration of other religions. Already in the 1630s, dissidents from the established faith, such as Anne Hutchinson and Roger Williams, were summarily dismissed from the Massachusetts Bay Colony.[6] Immigration restrictions in Massachusetts Bay and other New England colonies throughout the seventeenth century left little room for Catholics, Jews, "Familists, Antinomians, and other Enthusiasts"—notably Quakers.[7] In the late 1650s special laws banned the Quakers and their teachings from the colony. Those Quakers who had newly arrived or newly converted were banished. Those who failed to leave were subject to flogging and confiscation of their property. Four Quakers who returned after banishment were hung in the Boston Common in 1659 and 1660.

Although Quakers remained unwelcome, Baptists, Episcopalians, and other Protestant groups came to be tolerated in the New England colonies—partly on account of the Toleration Act (1689) passed by the Parliament, which required all the colonies to be open to Protestant nonconformists. Although tolerated, these non-Puritan groups had limited political rights and social benefits and were subjected to various tithe rates as well as restrictions on property and profession. Massachusetts and Connecticut introduced a complex system of religious taxation or tithing. The state collected tithes but allowed each tithe payer to select which church should receive the tithe revenue. Only properly registered and incorporated churches were eligible to receive these tithes, however. Various Baptists and other Evangelical groups could not or would not incorporate and thus proved ineligible. Moreover, only persons who could prove regular church attendance enjoyed the right to direct their tithes to nonestablished churches; persons who would not or could not satisfy the authorities that they regularly attended church also proved ineligible. This system persisted until the constitutional reforms of Connecticut in 1819 and Massachusetts in 1833.[8]

Over time, the growing presence of religious nonconformists in New England shifted the Puritan understanding of liberty of conscience. Classic Calvinism taught that each person has the liberty to enter into a personal covenant relationship with God. Seventeenth-century Puritans had treated this covenant in narrow and nonnegotiable terms. God set the covenantal terms for salvation in the Bible; a person had the freedom only to accept or reject them. Such sentiments can be seen in a 1682 tract on "covenant liberty" by Samuel Willard, a leading Puritan systematizer and political theorist of his day. Willard argued that every person has the "equal right," "title," "claim," "liberty," and "prerogative" "to enter and to enjoy every blessing of the covenant." But by the time Willard finished spelling out all the standard terms and conditions of the covenant, there seemed to be few at liberty to enter the covenant and little liberty left for those few who could.[9]

Confronted by the realities of religious pluralism, eighteenth-century Puritan writers began to view the covenantal relationship between God and persons in more open and voluntarist terms. The covenant was made more accessible to parties of various Christian faiths, and its terms were made more open to personal deliberation and innovation. Elisha Williams, the distinguished Puritan preacher, jurist, and rector of Yale University, put the matter thus in 1744:

> Every man has an equal right to follow the dictates of his own conscience in the affairs of religion. Every one is under an indispensable obligation to search the Scriptures for himself . . . and to make the best use of it he can for his own information in the will of God, the nature and duties of Christianity. And as every Christian is so bound; so he has the unalienable right to judge of the sense and meaning of it, and to follow his judgment wherever it leads him; even an equal right with any rulers be they civil or ecclesiastical.[10]

"Religious liberty is a divine right," wrote the New Hampshire Congregationalist preacher Israel Evans, "immediately derived from the Supreme Being, without the intervention of any created authority. . . . [T]he all-wise Creator invested [no] order of men with the right of judging for their fellow-creatures in the great concerns of religion."[11]

It was only a short step from this formulation to the more generic and generous religious liberty guarantee of the 1780 Massachusetts constitution, drafted principally by John Adams, a cradle Puritan who had decided to forgo the pulpit in favor of a legal and political career:

> It is the right as well as the duty of all in society, publicly, and at stated seasons, to worship the Supreme Being, the great Creator and Preserver of the universe. And no subject shall be hurt, molested, or restrained, in his person, liberty, or estate, for worshipping God in the manner and season most agreeable to the dictates of his own conscience, or for his religious profession of sentiments; provided he doth not disturb the public peace or obstruct others in their religious worship.[12]

It was also a natural next step to find political, if not theological, virtue in the religious pluralism of the community. Zabdiel Adams put the prevailing opinion well in a sermon of 1782:

> Modes and forms of religion; sentiments concerning doctrines, etc., people should be indulged in, without molestation. If coer[c]ion would bring mankind to a uniformity of sentiment, no advantage would result therefrom. It is on the contrary best to have different [sects] and denominations live in the same societies. They are a mutual check and spy upon each other, and become more attentive to their principles and practice. . . . [W]here Papists and Protestants live intermingled together, it serves to meliorate them both. . . . With madmen and enthusiasts there can be no agreement, except among people as distracted as themselves. But even such, where they put on a religious guise, and do not interrupt the peace of society, are not to be disturbed by the civil arm. . . . [Only] that part of religion which has an immediate aspect on the good of the community falls under the cognizance of the ruler.[13]

Evangelical Views

The eighteenth-century American Evangelical[14] tradition of religious liberty had its roots in sixteenth-century European Anabaptism. This branch of the Protestant Reformation originally included groups like Amish, Hutterites, Mennonites, Baptists, Brethren, and others. They emphasized that religion was a voluntary choice signaled by adult baptism, and that the church was an independent institution protected from the state by a "wall of separation." The American Evangelical tradition also had roots in the seventeenth-century "lively experiment" of Rhode Island that granted "full liberty in religious concernm[en]ts" and allowed for "no establishment of a religion."[15] The Evangelicals found strong political allies in the Quakers, who had created their own "holy experiment" in religious liberty in Pennsylvania in 1681, centered on liberty of conscience, freedom of exercise, and separation of church and state. By the mid-eighteenth century, the Quakers had spread their distinctive teachings and practices into a number of other colonies. They were ardent and eloquent champions of conscientious objection to military service, oath swearing, mandatory tithes, and compulsory worship.[16]

Evangelicals did not emerge as a strong political force in America until after the Great Awakening of 1720–1780, which dramatically expanded their membership and message. Numerous spokesmen for the Evangelical cause rose up in the course of the later eighteenth century all along the Atlantic seaboard—Isaac Backus, John Leland, John Wesley, George Whitefield, and a host of other preachers and pamphleteers. Their numbers grew exponentially, and by 1820 their adherents outnumbered mainline Anglicans and Puritans. Numerous denominational labels became attached to their followers—sundry types of Baptists and Methodists most prominently, but also Moravians, Enthusiasts, and hybrid polities such as the African Methodist Episcopal Church. These denominational labels sometimes signaled real differences in theological emphasis among these early groups, which later hardened into bitter denominational divisions. Despite these theological differences, however, early American Evangelicals were largely united in their insistence on liberty of conscience, no establishment of religion, and separation of church and state. While Evangelicals had fewer opportunities (outside of Rhode Island and Pennsylvania) than Puritans to institutionalize their views in the colonial era, their relentless preaching and pamphleteering had a formidable political influence on the early American experiment.

Like the Puritans, the Evangelicals advanced a theological theory of religious liberty. They likewise advocated the institutional separation of church and state—the construction of "a wall of separation between the garden of the Church and the wilderness of the world," as Roger Williams put it famously in 1643.[17] Most Evangelicals, however, went beyond the Puritans—and battled with them in the New England states—both in their definition of the rights of religious individuals and groups and also in their insistence on a fuller separation of the institutions of church and state. Evangelicals sought to protect the liberty of conscience of every individual and the freedom of association of every religious group. Their preferred method for achieving these ends was to prohibit all legal establishments of religion and, indeed, all admixtures of religion and politics.

"The notion of a Christian commonwealth should be exploded forever," wrote John Leland, a fiery Baptist preacher.[18] Summarizing the Evangelical view, he decried all religious establishments as "evil"—whether Constantine's establishment of Trinitarian Christianity, the Ottoman Empire's establishment of Islam, Spain's establishment of Catholicism, England's establishment of Anglicanism, or New England's establishment of Puritanism. Establishments are evil, Leland argued, first, because when "uninspired, fallible men make their own opinions tests of orthodoxy," then religion is stunted and stilted, and "ignorance and superstition prevail, or persecution rages." Second, establishments are evil because "the minds of men are biased to embrace that religion which is favored and pampered by law, and thereby hypocrisy is nourished." Third, "establishments not only wean and alienate the affections of one from another," but they drive nonconformists away from the state, taking their loyalty, work, and taxes with them and leaving dull, anemic religions to propagate themselves or convert others by force. Fourth, "establishments metamorphose the church into a creature, and religion into a principle of state, which has a natural tendency to make men conclude that religion is nothing but a trick of state." Fifth, even in so-called Christian lands, "there are no two kingdoms and states that establish the same creed and formalities of faith." This brings neighbors and families into inevitable conflict and war, as European history has too often shown. Sixth, establishments merely cover for the insecurity and doubt of church leaders. Instead of having faith in the cogency of their views, they "dictate for others" and betray an "overfondness for a particular system" that becomes its own theological idol. And seventh, establishments also cover the insecurity of politicians. "Rulers often fear that if they leave every man to think, speak, and worship as he pleases, that the whole cause [of statecraft] will be wrecked in diversity."[19]

In place of religious establishment, religious voluntarism lay at the heart of the Evangelical view. "[N]othing can be true religion but a voluntary obedience unto [God's] revealed will," declared Isaac Backus, the leading Baptist light of the eighteenth century.[20] God called the adult individual to make a conscientious choice to accept the faith and to signal that acceptance through adult baptism. State coercion or control of this choice—either directly through persecution and repression or indirectly through withholding civil rights and benefits from those who made this choice—was an offense to the individual and to God. A plurality of religions should coexist in the community. It was for God, not the state, to decide which religions would flourish and which would fade.

Autonomy of religious governance also lay at the heart of this Evangelical view. All religious bodies, Evangelicals argued, should be free from state control of their assembly and worship, state regulation of their property and polity, state incorporation of their society and clergy, state interference in their discipline and government, and state collection of religious tithes and taxes. "I am as sensible of the importance of religion and of the utility of it to human society" as the Puritans are, Backus wrote. "And I concur with [them] that the fear and reverence of God and the terrors of eternity are the most powerful restraints upon the minds of men. But I am so far from thinking with [them] that these restraints would be broken down if equal religious liberty was established." Consider the long history of Christian establishment, where such forms of state intrusion on religious groups had long been countenanced. Such establishment never led to pure religion, Backus pronounced, but instead, "tyranny, simony, and robbery came to be introduced and to be practiced under the Christian name." Consider communities with no religious establishments: religion, state, and society all flourish without fail. And consider the parallel to this in the principles of the American Revolution: "[A]ll America [was] up in arms" against taxation without representation. But just as certainly as Americans were not represented in the British Parliament, so religious dissenters are not represented among the civil authorities in an establishment state. Yet dissenters are still subject to religious taxes and regulations. Finally, Backus urged consideration of biblical principles:

> God has expressly armed the magistrate with the sword to punish such as work ill to
> their neighbors, and his faithfulness in that work and our obedience to such authority,

is enforced [by the Bible]. But it is evident that the sword is excluded from the kingdom of the Redeemer. . . . [I]t is impossible to blend church and state without violating our Lord's commands to both together. His command to the church is, Put away
from among yourselves that wicked person. His command to the state is, Let both
grow together until the harvest. But it has appeared for these thousand years that pure
Gospel discipline in the church is very little if at all known in state establishments of
religion.[21]

Some Evangelicals extended the principle of church autonomy and no establishment to argue against state support of religion too, in the form of tax exemptions,
civil immunities, or property donations. Such Evangelicals feared state benevolence
toward religious bodies almost as much as they feared state repression. Religious
bodies that received state benefits would invariably become beholden to the state
and distracted from their divine mandates. "[I]f civil Rulers go so far out of their
Sphere as to take the Care and Management of religious affairs upon them," reads
a 1776 Baptist declaration, "Yea . . . Farwel to 'the free exercise of Religion.'"[22]

The chief concern of the Evangelicals was theological, not political. Having suffered as religious minorities for more than a century in colonial America and more
than two centuries in Europe, Evangelicals sought a constitutional means to free all
religion from the fetters of the law, and to relieve all churches from the restrictions
of the state. In so doing, most Evangelicals of the founding era—save Isaac Backus,
building on his seventeenth-century hero Roger Williams—developed only the
rudiments of a political theory.[23] Most Evangelicals were content with a state that
created a climate conducive to the cultivation of a plurality of religions and accommodated all religious believers and religious bodies without conditions or controls.

Enlightenment Views

The Enlightenment movement in America provided a political theory that complemented the Evangelical theology of religious liberty. The Enlightenment was not a
single, unified movement but a series of diverse ideological movements, in various
academic disciplines and social circles throughout Europe and North America.
Among its chief exponents were Montesquieu, Condorcet, and Voltaire in France,
along with John Locke, Adam Smith, and David Hume in England and Scotland.
Among its leading lights in America were Thomas Jefferson and Thomas Paine,
flanked on some causes by Benjamin Franklin and James Madison.[24] It was the
American Revolution, especially, that catalyzed these American figures to convert
Enlightenment ideals into constitutional imperatives.

The writings of English philosopher and theologian John Locke provided ample
inspiration for this movement. In his famous *Letter Concerning Toleration* (1689),
Locke had distilled the liberal English and Dutch learning of the seventeenth century into an elegant plea for church and state to end their corrosive alliances and
destructive abridgments of the liberty of conscience. "[A]bove all things," Locke
pleaded, it is "necessary to distinguish exactly the business of civil government from

that of religion, and to settle the just bounds that lie between the one and the other." The church, Locke wrote, must be "absolutely separate and distinct from the commonwealth," for the church is simply "a voluntary society of men, joining themselves together of their own accord in order to [exercise] the public worshipping of God in such manner as they judge acceptable to Him, and effectual for the salvation of their souls." Church members are free to enter and free to exit this society. They are free to determine its order and organization and arrange its discipline and worship in a manner they consider most conducive to eternal life. "Nothing ought nor can be transacted in this society relating to the possession of civil and worldly power. No force is to be made use of upon any occasion whatsoever. For force belongs wholly to the civil magistrate."[25]

State force, in turn, cannot touch religion, Locke argued. The state exists merely to protect persons in their outward lives, in their enjoyment of life, liberty, and property. "True and saving religion consists in the inward persuasion of the mind," which only God can touch and tend. A person cannot be compelled to true belief of anything by outward force—whether through "confiscation of estate, imprisonments, [or] torments" or through mandatory compliance with "articles of faith or forms of worship" established by law. "For laws are of no force without penalties, and penalties in this case are absolutely impertinent, because they are not proper to convince the mind." "It is only light and evidence that can work a change in men's [religious] opinions: which light can in no manner proceed from corporal sufferings, or any other outward penalties" inflicted by the state. Every person "has the supreme and absolute authority of judging for himself" in matters of faith.[26]

Locke did not press this thesis to radical secular conclusions. His *Letter Concerning Toleration* presupposed a magistracy and community committed to a common Christianity. State laws directed to the common good, he believed, would only "seldom" "appear unlawful to the conscience of a private person" and would only seldom run afoul of conventional Christian beliefs and practices. Catholics, Muslims, and other believers "who deliver themselves up to the service and protection of another prince" have no place in this civil community. Moreover, "those are not at all tolerated who deny the being of a God"—for "promises, covenants, and oaths which are the bonds of human society, can have no hold upon an atheist."[27] Locke strengthened these qualifications even more in his theological writings, arguing for the cogency of a simple biblical natural law in his volumes *The Reasonableness of Christianity, Essays on the Law of Nature*, and *Thoughts on Education* and endorsing the utility of a moderate Christian republicanism in his glosses on several books of the New Testament.[28]

A century later and an ocean away, American Enlightenment writers pressed Locke's theory of religious toleration further, and into more concrete legal and political forms.[29] American writers pressed beyond mere toleration to a more robust freedom of conscience and exercise for all peaceable parties. As Thomas Paine put it: "Toleration is not the opposite of intoleration, but is the counterfeit of it. Both are despotisms. The one assumes to itself the right of withholding liberty of conscience, and the other of granting it."[30] What was needed instead was a legal and political system that gave full freedom to every peaceable religion and no political privilege to any one religion.

The state, Enlightenment writers taught, should not give special aid, support, privilege, or protection to religious doctrines or groups through special tax appropriations or collections of tithes, special donations of goods and realty, special laws of religious incorporation, or special criminal laws against blasphemy, sacrilege, and Sabbath breaking. The state should neither predicate its laws on explicitly religious premises nor direct them to exclusively religious purposes. The state should neither draw on the services of religious officials to discharge its political tasks nor interfere in the order, organization, or orthodoxy of religious bodies. As Madison put it in 1822: "[A] perfect separation between ecclesiastical and civil matters" is the best course, for "religion and Government will both exist in greater purity, the less they are mixed together."[31]

Like Locke, Madison did not press this logic to absolutist conclusions, particularly when it came to the "unessentials" of church-state relations. In an 1833 letter to Reverend Jaspar Adams, he wrote:

> [I]t may not be easy, in every possible case, to trace the line of separation between the rights of Religion and the Civil authority, with such distinctness, as to avoid collisions & doubts on unessential points. The tendency to a usurpation on one side, or the other, or to a corrupting coalition or alliance between them, will be best guarded against by an entire abstinence of the Government from interference in any way whatever, beyond the necessity of preserving public order, & protecting each sect against trespasses on its legal rights by others.[32]

Such views were based on both skepticism toward organized religion and fear of an autocratic state. To allow church and state to be unrestricted, it was thought, would be to invite arbitrariness and abuse. To allow them to combine would be to their mutual disadvantage—to produce, in Paine's words, "a sort of mule-animal, capable only of destroying, and not of breeding up."[33] Jefferson was particularly strident in his opposition to organized religion, especially Trinitarian Christianity. As he wrote in a private letter to John Adams:

> It is too late in the day for men of sincerity to pretend they believe in the Platonic mysticisms that three are one, and one is three; and yet that the one is not three, and the three are not one. . . . [T]his constitutes the craft, the power, the profit of the priests. Sweep away their gossamer fabrics of factious religion, and they would catch no more flies. We should all then, like the Quakers, live without an order of priests, moralize for ourselves, follow the oracle of conscience, and say nothing about what no man can understand, nor therefore believe; for I suppose belief to be the assent of the mind to an intelligible proposition.[34]

Such views were also based on the assumption that a person is fundamentally an individual being and religion is primarily a matter of private reason and conscience, and only secondarily a matter of communal association and corporate confession. "My own mind is my own church," wrote Paine.[35] Every person, Madison wrote, has the right to form "a rational opinion" about "the duty he owes the Creator and the manner in which that duty is to be discharged."[36] Whether that religious duty is to be discharged individually or corporately is of secondary importance.[37]

Such views were based on a contractarian view of society. Religion was one of the natural and unalienable rights that God had given to each person upon birth. Neither the state nor the church could take away this natural right of religion, nor could a person transfer this right to anyone else. Instead, the state and church, through their founding contracts, could simply set appropriate conditions for the exercise of this natural right in their respective societies. As state citizens, all persons have full freedom to exercise their religion up to the point of violating their neighbor's rights or the public order. The state may intervene only if a person's religious exercise violates these conditions, and then only because that person has violated the basic terms of the social contract. As church parishioners, all persons have the right and duty to exercise religion in accordance with the rules and rituals of the church they voluntarily joined. The church may insist on compliance with its rules and rituals, and the state cannot interfere in those internal church decisions. But the church has no power to bind the conscience, obstruct the exit, or violate the life, limb, or property of its parishioners; when it does, the state must intervene to protect them. For the church enjoys only those powers and rights that its parishioners alienated to it through the founding church contract. No parishioner can alienate to the church rights over conscience (which belong to God) or over life, limb, and property (which only the state can touch through due process of law).

Postrevolutionary Virginia proved to be fertile ground for political exponents of the Enlightenment tradition to cultivate these views.[38] The 1776 Virginia Bill of Rights opened with a famous declaration: "That all men are by nature equally free and independent, and have certain inherent rights, of which, when they enter into a state of society, they cannot, by any compact, deprive or divest their posterity; namely, the enjoyment of life and liberty, with the means of acquiring and possessing property, and pursuing and obtaining happiness and safety." Religious liberty was one of these "inherent rights" whose full and free exercise was considered essential to "obtaining happiness." Article 16 of the bill of rights, shaped by Madison, provided:

> That religion, or the duty which we owe to our Creator, and the manner of discharging it, can be directed only by reason and conviction, not by force or violence; and therefore, all men are equally entitled to the free exercise of religion, according to the dictates of conscience; and that it is the mutual duty of all to practise Christian forbearance, love, and charity, towards each other.

Article 15 of the bill of rights elaborated this understanding of mutual duties: "That no free government, or the blessings of liberty, can be preserved to any people, but by a firm adherence to justice, moderation, temperance, frugality, and virtue, and by frequent recurrence to fundamental principles."[39]

This early Virginia constitutional text was one of the most influential formulations of religious liberty in the young republic, and was echoed in many other early state constitutions, texts, and ratification debates. Its appeal lay in part in its clever combination of Enlightenment and Evangelical accents (on liberty of conscience, freedom of exercise, and equality of faiths) with Civic Republican and traditional Christian emphases (on the "Creator" God and the mutual duties of all to practice "Christian forbearance, love, and charity" and other virtues toward others). This commingling of various inspirational sources was key to the text's early acceptance in a state whose traditional Anglican establishment was giving way to growing ranks of Evangelicals, Presbyterians, and others. And it also explains its eventual widespread appeal among the other states.

The famous and cleverly titled Virginia Statute for the Establishment of Religious Freedom, drafted by Thomas Jefferson in 1779 and enacted in 1786, provided less qualified Enlightenment language. The statute began by celebrating that "Almighty God hath created the mind free; that all attempts to influence it by temporal punishment, or burthens, or by civil incapacitations, tend only to beget habits of hypocrisy and meanness, and are a departure from the plan of the Holy Author of our religion." The statute recounted the ravages of religious establishment and repression, and their resulting injuries to God, religion, churches, states, and individuals. It then guaranteed:

> That no man shall be compelled to frequent or support any religious worship, place, or ministry whatsoever, nor shall be enforced, restrained, molested, or burthened, in his body or goods, nor shall otherwise suffer on account of his religious opinions or belief; but that all men shall be free to profess, and by argument to maintain, their opinions in matters of religion, and that the same shall in no wise diminish, enlarge or affect their civil capacities.[40]

These lofty protections of individual religious rights went hand in hand with the close restrictions on corporate religious rights that were also advocated by Enlightenment exponents. Before the turn of the nineteenth century, the Virginia legislature outlawed religious corporations, a prohibition still in place in West Virginia today—although Virginia recently amended its state constitution after a federal court struck down the ban on religious incorporation as a violation of the free exercise clause.[41]

Republican Views

Just as the Enlightenment movement provided a political theory to complement the Evangelical theology of religious liberty, so the Civic Republican movement provided a sturdy political philosophy to complement the Puritan theology of religious liberty. The Civic Republicans themselves were an eclectic group of politicians, preachers, and pamphleteers who strove to cultivate a set of common values and beliefs for the new nation.[42] Their principal spokesmen included George Washington, John Adams, Benjamin Rush, John Jay, Oliver Ellsworth, Samuel Adams, and other civic leaders—though the movement attracted considerable support among the spiritual and intellectual laity of the young republic as well. While many of the core ideas of this movement were grounded in earlier Anglican and Puritan ideals of a Christian commonwealth designed to give glory to God, Civic Republicans cast these ideas in more generic and utilitarian form as an argument about the basic place and utility of all peaceable religions in a well governed society.

Although Republican leaders had, by the later eighteenth century, found their most natural theological allies among the Puritans, they still shared much common ground with Evangelical and Enlightenment exponents. They too advocated liberty of conscience for all and state support for a plurality of religions in the community. They too opposed religious intrusions on politics that rose to the level of political theocracy and political intrusions on religion that rose to the level of religious establishment. Particularly at the national level, full religious liberty for all was essential. George Washington put this powerfully in a 1790 letter to the Hebrew Congregation in Newport: "The Citizens of the United States of America have a right to applaud themselves for having given to mankind examples of an enlarged and liberal policy; a policy worthy of imitation. All possess alike liberty of conscience and immunities of citizenship. It is now no more that toleration is spoken of, as it was by the indulgences of one class of people, that another enjoyed the exercise of their inherent natural rights. For happily the Government of the United States, which gives to bigotry no sanction, to persecution no assistance requires only that they who live under its protection should demean themselves as good citizens, in giving it on all occasions their effectual support."[43]

But contrary to Evangelical and Enlightenment writers and consistent with Puritan writers, Republican writers sought to imbue the public square with a common religious ethic and ethos—albeit one less denominationally specific and theologically rigorous than that countenanced by the Puritans. Key to the Republicans' understanding was that religion, and particularly Christianity, was foundational for the prosperity and happiness of citizens, and the efficacy and efficiency of good government.[44]

"Religion and Morality are the essential pillars of Civil society," Washington declared. "Of all the dispositions and habits which lead to political prosperity, religion and morality are indispensable supports."[45] "[W]e have no government," John Adams echoed, "armed with power capable of contending with human passions unbridled by morality and religion."[46] "Religion and liberty are the meat and the drink of the body politic," wrote Yale president Timothy Dwight.[47] According to Republican lore, society needs a fund of religious values and beliefs, a body of civic ideas and ideals that are enforceable both through common law and communal suasion. This was what Benjamin Franklin in 1749 had called the "Publick Religion" (and what Robert

Bellah has called the "civil religion") of America, which undergirded the plurality of sectarian religions.[48] This Publick Religion taught a creed of honesty, diligence, devotion, public spiritedness, patriotism, obedience, love of God, neighbor, and self, and other ethical commonplaces taught by various religious traditions at the time of the founding. Its icons were the Bible, the Declaration of Independence, the bells of liberty, and the Constitution. Its clergy were public-spirited ministers and religiously devout politicians. Its liturgy was the proclamation of prayers, songs, sermons, and Thanksgiving Day offerings by statesmen and churchmen. Its policy was government appointment of legislative and military chaplains, government sponsorship of general religious education and organization, and government enforcement of a religiously based morality through positive law.

These Republican views found favor in the Continental Congress, which authorized the appointment of tax-supported chaplains to the legislature and military, tax appropriations for religious schools and missionaries, diplomatic ties to the Vatican, recitations of prayer to open legislative sessions, and various proclamations of Thanksgiving.[49] The Continental Congress also passed the Northwest Ordinance in 1787, which provided in part: "Religion, morality and knowledge, being necessary to good government and the happiness of mankind, schools and the means of education shall forever be encouraged."[50]

These Republican views also found strong support among some of the states. Republicans countenanced state support and accommodation for religious institutions, for they were regarded as essential allies of good government and critical agents of the common good. Preacher Nathan Strong declared that "religion and its institutions are the best aid of government, by strengthening the ruler's hand, and making the subject faithful in his place, and obedient to the general laws."[51] Similarly, Connecticut senator Oliver Ellsworth declared: "Institutions for the promotion of good morals, are objects of legislative provision and support: and among these . . . religious institutions are eminently useful and important."[52] Pennsylvania preacher Thomas Reese was "fully convinced of the utility, and even necessity of religion, to the well being" and even "the very existence of civil society": religion provides citizens with the understanding of "reward and punishment," "restraint and respect," and loyalty and duty—all essential to "a society dedicated to life, liberty, and the pursuit of happiness."[53] Civic Republicans, therefore, endorsed tax exemptions for church properties and tax support for religious schools, charities, and missionaries; donations of public lands to religious organizations; and criminal protections against blasphemy, sacrilege, and interruption of religious services.[54]

John Adams was an important and influential proponent of these Civic Republican views, as he sought to balance the freedom of all private religions with what he called the "mild and equitable establishment" of one public religion that was essential to civic prosperity. We must begin "by setting the conscience free," Adams wrote. For "[w]hen all men of all religions consistent with morals and property, shall enjoy equal liberty, . . . [and] security of property, and an equal chance for honors and power . . . we may expect that improvements will be made in the human character and the state of society." Moreover, a plurality of private religions in the community provides the best safeguard against religious persecution.[55] But just as certainly as we must guarantee the freedom of all private religions, Adams insisted, we must set a public "religion at the fore and floor of society and government." "Statesmen may plan and speculate for liberty, but it is religion and morality alone which can establish the principles upon which freedom can securely stand." "[R]eligion and virtue are the only foundations, not only of republicanism and of all free government, but of social felicity under all governments and in all the combinations of human society."[56]

Adams wrote these principles into the 1780 Massachusetts constitution. This state constitution, which remains in place as the oldest constitution of America, sought to balance the freedom of all private religions with "a mild and equitable establishment" of a public religion, as Adams described it. Article II provided: "It is the right as well as the duty of all men in society, publickly, and at stated seasons to worship the SUPREME BEING, the great Creator and preserver of the Universe." Article III stated the reason for this: "[T]he public worship of GOD and instructions in piety, religion, and morality . . . promote their happiness, and secure . . . the good order and preservation of their government."[57] The same constitution also insisted that all persons, particularly political leaders, maintain rigorous moral and religious standards, which they must confirm publicly when taking their oaths of office. It also rendered these same moral qualities essential ingredients of education within the state, since "the encouragement of arts and sciences, and all good literature, tends to the honor of GOD, the advantage of the Christian religion, and the great benefit of this and the other United States of America."[58]

Summary and Conclusions

These four views—Puritan, Evangelical, Enlightenment, and Civic Republican—helped inform the early American experiment in religious rights and liberties. Each view was liberally espoused by federal and state leaders in the early American republic—informally in their letters and pamphlets and formally in the constitutional convention and ratification debates. Each view left indelible marks on the documents and developments of early American constitutionalism.

The common point of departure for all four views was their rejection of the traditional Anglican establishment that had been the formal law of the American colonies until the American Revolution. The Anglican establishment combined church and commonwealth in a uniform society. The king was its supreme head. Bishops sat in Parliament. The Anglican clergy were political appointees. They held numerous special exemptions and privileges, tax and tithe supports, state-funded parsonages and benefices. Parliament passed ecclesiastical laws, and church courts enforced them. Parliament mandated the nation's doctrine, liturgy, and canonical texts. Criminal law enforced religious morality, mandated religious worship and loyalty oaths, and protected the established church's property and personnel. Communicant status was tied to citizenship status; heresy was a form of treason. Protestant religious dissenters were legally tolerated, but subject to special taxes and restrictions. Jews and Catholics had no legal status. No important American founder wanted this full blown form of religious establishment.[59]

The Puritans and Civic Republicans wanted only a "mild and equitable establishment" of religion. The Puritans wanted each local community to establish its own distinctive religious and moral ideals, protected by the local church and state authorities, against dissenting religions. The Civic Republicans pressed for a more generic form of religion, which the state embraced for reasons of utility and expediency. Evangelicals and Enlightenment exponents opposed any kind of establishment and called for a stronger separation of church and state. The Evangelicals' main concern was to protect the church and religion from the state and politics. The Enlightenment exponents' main concern was to protect politics and the state from religion and the church.

Despite their differences, exponents of all four of these rival views eventually countenanced liberty of conscience, freedom of religious exercise, and the equality of a plurality of rival religions before the law. The Puritans and Civic Republicans cast these principles of religious liberty more narrowly; Evangelical and Enlightenment exponents cast them more broadly. What these principles entailed, how they were prioritized, and how they squared with the principle of no establishment of religion and separation of church and state are the topics of the next chapter.

Notes

1. James Madison, "Letter from James Madison to Thomas Richie (September 15, 1821)," in *Letters and Other Writings of James Madison*, 4 vols. (1884), 3:228. See also the quote from Madison in *The Debates and Proceedings in the Congress of the United States, March 3, 1789–May 27, 1824*, 42 vols. (1834–1856), vol. 5, column 776: "As the instrument came from [the drafter] it was nothing more than the draft of a plan, nothing but a dead letter, until life and validity were breathed into it by the voice of the people, speaking through their several State conventions" [hereafter Gales and Seaton, *Annals*].

2. For sample primary texts, see Edmund S. Morgan, *Puritan Political Ideas, 1558–1794* (2003 [1965]); Perry Miller and Thomas H. Johnson, *The Puritans*, rev. ed., 2 vols. (1963).

3. Quoted by Timothy Breen, *The Character of the Good Ruler* (1970), 42 n. 24. See samples in Max Farrand, ed., *The Book of the General Laws and Liberties Concerning the Inhabitants of Massachusetts (1648)* (1929), 18–20; "The Cambridge Synod and Platform (1648)," in *The Creeds and Platforms of Congregationalism*, ed. Williston Walker (1960), 234–237.

4. John Cotton, Letter from The Rev. John Cotton to Lord Say and Seal (1636), in Morgan, *Puritan Political Ideas*, 209–212.

5. Urian Oakes, *New England Pleaded with, and Pressed to Consider the Things Which Concern Her* (1673), 49.

6. David D. Hall, *The Antinomian Controversy, 1636–1638*, 2d ed. (1968).

7. Nathaniel Ward, *The Simple Cobler of Aggawam in America*, 5th ed. (1713), 43.

8. William G. McLoughlin, *New England Dissent, 1630–1833*, 2 vols. (Cambridge, 1971).

9. Samuel Willard, *Covenant-Keeping the Way to Blessedness* (Boston, 1682); Willard, *Morality Not to Be Relied on for Life* (1700); Willard, *Walking with God* (1701).

10. Elisha Williams, *The Essential Rights and Liberties of Protestants* (1744), 7–8.

11. Israel Evans, "A Sermon Delivered at Concord, Before the Hon. General Court of the State of New Hampshire at the Annual Election (1791)," in *Political Sermons of the Founding Era, 1730–1805*, ed. Ellis Sandoz (1991), 1057, 1062–1063.

12. Massachusetts Constitution (1780), Pt. I, Art. II; see also Vermont Constitution (1793), Ch. I, Art. III.

13. Zabdiel Adams, "An Election Sermon (1782)," in Charles S. Hynemann and Donald S. Lutz, eds., *American Political Writing During the Founding Era, 1760–1805*, 2 vols. (1983), 1:539, 556. Original capitalization and italics removed.

14. For the changing meaning of this label in American history, see Mark A. Noll, "Evangelicals in the American Founding and Evangelical Political Mobilization Today," in James H. Hutson, ed., *Religion and the New Republic: Faith in the Founding of America* (2000), 137.

15. The phrase is from Baptist leader Dr. John Clarke in c. 1662, quoted in Charles M. Andrews, *The Colonial Period in American History*, 2 vols. (1936), 2:42. The phrase recurs in the 1663 Charter of Rhode Island, which remained the state's constitutional text until 1843. See Francis N. Thorpe, ed., *The Federal and State Constitutions*, 7 vols. (1909), 6:3211.

16. J. Willard Frost, *A Perfect Freedom: Religious Liberty in Pennsylvania* (1990); *The Political Writings of William Penn*, ed. Andrew R. Murphy (2002).

17. Roger Williams, *Complete Writings*, 7 vols. (1963), 1:392.

18. *The Writings of the Late Elder John Leland* (1845), 118.

19. John Leland, "The Rights of Conscience Inalienable," in *The Writings of John Leland*, ed. L. F. Greene (1969), 179–192.

20. Isaac Backus, "A Declaration of the Rights, of the Inhabitants of the State of Massachusetts-Bay in New England (1779)," in *Isaac Backus on Church, State, and Calvinism*, 487.

21. *Isaac Backus on Church, State, and Calvinism*, 351, 357–358, 373–375 (emphasis omitted).

22. "Declaration of the Virginia Association of Baptists (December 25, 1776)," in *The Papers of Thomas Jefferson*, ed. Julian P. Boyd (1950), 1:660–661.

23. Backus and a few other Evangelicals who propounded political views tended to agree with Puritans and Republicans that the political office should be restricted to Christians and that the state had a role to play in the cultivation of public morality through laws against blasphemy, theatergoing, card playing, and violations of the Sabbath day of rest. See William G. McLoughlin, *Soul Liberty: The Baptists' Struggle in New England, 1630–1833* (1991), 194–195, 267–268.

24. Henry May, *The Enlightenment in America* (1976).

25. John Locke, *Letter Concerning Toleration* (1689), in *The Works of John Locke*, 12th ed., 9 vols. (1824), 5:1–58, at 9, 13, 16, 21. Locke wrote two subsequent such letters and had a fragment of a fourth letter under way on his death in 1704. It was the first letter of 1689 that was best known in America.

26. Ibid., 11, 41.

27. Ibid., 47.

28. John Locke, *The Reasonableness of Christianity*, in *Works*, 6:1–158, at 140–143; Locke, *Essays on the Law of Nature*, ed. W. von Leyden (2002 [c. 1662]); *The Educational Writings of John Locke*, ed. James Axtell (1968).

29. For example, Jefferson incorporated a number of ideas from Locke's *Letter Concerning Toleration* in his "Bill for the Establishment of Religious Freedom" (1779). See Jefferson, "Notes on Locke and Shaftesbury," in *The Papers of Thomas Jefferson*, 1:544–551. See Sanford Kessler, "Locke's Influence on Jefferson's 'Bill for Establishing Religious Freedom,'" *Journal of Church and State* 25 (1983): 231.

30. Thomas Paine, *The Rights of Man*, pt. 1, in Philip Kurland and Ralph Lerner, eds., *The Founders' Constitution*, 5 vols. (1987), 5:95–96.

31. Letter to Edward Livingston (July 10, 1822), in *The Writings of James Madison*, ed. G. Hunt (1900–1910), 9:98, 102.

32. James Madison, Letter to Rev. Adams (1833), in Daniel L. Dreisbach, *Religion and Politics in the Early Republic: Jasper Adams and the Church-State Debate* (1996), 120.

33. Thomas Paine, *The Rights of Man* (1791), in *The Complete Writings of Thomas Paine*, ed. P. S. Foner, 2 vols. (1945), 1:243–462, at 292.

34. Letter to John Adams (August 22, 1813), in *The Works of Thomas Jefferson*, ed. P.L. Ford, 12 vols. (1904–1905), 11:328–329.

35. Thomas Paine, *Age of Reason*, 1, in *Collected Writings*, ed. Eric Foner (1995), 666.

36. James Madison, "Memorial and Remonstrance Against Religious Assessments," in *The Papers of James Madison*, ed. W. T. Hutchinson et al., 17 vols. (1962), 8:298, sec. 1.

37. In his "Detached Memoranda" of c. 1817, Madison highlights his distaste for corporate organized religions by criticizing laws that allowed ecclesiastical bodies to incorporate, to be exempt from taxation, to accumulate property, and to gain political access through legislative chaplains and other means. See Elizabeth Fleet, "Madison's 'Detached Memoranda,'" *William and Mary Quarterly*, 3d ser., 3 (1946): 534, 554.

38. Thomas E. Buckley, *Church and State in Revolutionary Virginia, 1776–1787* (1977).

39. Madison, *Papers*, 1:175.

40. William Waller Hening, ed., *The Statutes at Large . . . of Virginia* (1768–1828), 12:84–86.

41. Virginia Constitution, Art. IV, Sec. 14 (as amended effective January 1, 2007); *Falwell v. Miller*, 203 F.Supp. 2d 624 (W.D. Va. 2002).

42. Nathan O. Hatch, *The Sacred Cause of Liberty* (1977); Gordon S. Wood, *The Creation of the American Republic, 1776–1787* (1969); Paul Rahe, *Republics Ancient and Modern* (1992); Catherine L. Albanese, *Sons of the Fathers: The Civil Religion of the American Revolution* (1976).

43. Letter to the Hebrew Congregation in Newport, Rhode Island (August 18, 1790), in *The Papers of George Washington*, ed. W. W. Abbot et al. (1987), 6:285.

44. See samples in James H. Hutson, *Forgotten Features of the Founding: The Recovery of Religious Themes in the Early American Republic* (2003), 1–44; Michael W. McConnell, "Establishment and Disestablishment at the Founding: Part I: Establishment of Religion," *William and Mary Law Review* 44 (2003): 2105, 2181ff.

45. Letter to the Clergy of Philadelphia (March 3, 1797), in *The Writings of George Washington from the Original Manuscript Sources, 1745–1799*, ed. J. C. Fitzpatrick, 39 vols. (1931), 35:416; Washington, Farewell Address (September 17, 1796), in ibid., 35:214, 229.

46. "Letter of John Adams to a Unit of the Massachusetts Militia (1798)," in *The Works of John Adams*, ed. C.F. Adams (Boston, 1850–1856), 9:229.

47. Timothy Dwight, "The Duty of Americans at the Present Crisis, Illustrated in a Discourse Preached on the Fourth of July, 1798," in Sandoz, ed., *Political Sermons*, 1380.

48. Benjamin Franklin, "Proposals Relating to the Education of Youth in Pensilvania (1749)," quoted and discussed in Martin E. Marty, "On a Medial Moraine: Religious Dimensions of American Constitutionalism," *Emory Law Journal* 39 (1990): 9–20, at 16–17; Robert N. Bellah, "Civil Religion in America," *Daedalus: The Journal of the American Academy of Arts and Sciences* 96 (1967): 1–21.

49. Derek H. Davis, *Religion and the Continental Congress, 1774–1789: Contributions to Original Intent* (2000). See numerous resolutions excerpted in Daniel L. Dreisbach and Mark David Hall, eds., *The Sacred Rights of Conscience: Selected Readings on Religious Liberty and Church-State Relations in the American Founding* (2009), 215–239.

50. Article III, 1 Stat. 50, 51–53, ch. 8. See also discussion in pages 76, 93, and 114. On various earlier drafts of the Northwest Ordinance, with more expansive language, see Edwin S. Gaustad, *Faith of the Founders: Religion and the New Nation, 1776–1826*, 2d ed. (2004), 115–117, 151–156.

51. Nathan Strong, *Election Sermon* (1790), 15.

52. *The Public Records of the State of Connecticut*, ed. Christopher Collier (1967), 11:371, 373.

53. Thomas Reese, *An Essay on the Influence of Religion in Civil Society* (1788), in Dreisbach and Hall, eds., *The Sacred Rights of Conscience*, 316–335.

54. See below, pp. 115–120, 175–177, 257–258.

55. Letter to Thomas Jefferson (June 25, 1813), in *The Adams-Jefferson Letters*, 2 vols., ed. Lester J. Cappon (1959), 333, 334.

56. Adams, *Works*, 8:232; 9:401, 635, 636.

57. Massachusetts Constitution (1780), Pt. I, Arts. II and III; this language is retained in Amendment, Art. XI (1833), which replaced Pt. I, Art. III. See below, pp. 116–118.

58. Ibid., Pt. II, Ch. V.

59. See, e.g., "Dr. Price's Observations on the American Revolution, of Liberty of Conscience, and Civil Establishments of Religion," in *Massachusetts Spy: Or, Worcester Gazette*, April 21, 1785, 2.

3

The Essential Rights and Liberties of Religion

Puritans, Evangelicals, Republicans, and Enlightenment exponents—these four groups of founders held up the four corners of a wide and swaying canopy of opinion on religious liberty in eighteenth-century America. Beneath this canopy were gathered what they called the "essential rights and liberties" of religion: (1) liberty of conscience, (2) free exercise of religion, (3) religious pluralism, (4) religious equality, (5) separation of church and state, and (6) disestablishment, at least of a national religion.[1] While these four groups of founders gave different accents and interpretations to these six principles, they held the core notions of these principles in common.

These six principles appear regularly in the debates over religious liberty in the eighteenth century, though with varying definitions and priorities. They were commonly incorporated into the original state constitutions, though with different emphases and applications. And they remain at the heart of the American experiment today—as central commandments of the American constitutional order and as cardinal axioms of a new American logic of religious liberty. The goal of this chapter is to work systematically through each principle as it was commonly understood in the founding generation. We shall highlight what the founders held in common and how they differed with respect to each of them. We shall also, in the conclusion, highlight the interdependence of these essential principles of religious liberty.

Liberty of Conscience

The principle of liberty of conscience was almost universally embraced in the young republic—even by ardent proponents of continued religious establishments.[2] The phrase "liberty of conscience" is of ancient vintage, rooted in early Roman and Christian sources and laden with multiple meanings in canon law, common law, and civil law.[3] The plasticity of the phrase was not lost on the American founders. Like their predecessors, they often conflated or equated the phrase with other favorites, such as "free exercise of religion," "religious freedom," "religious liberty," "religious privileges," and "religious rights." James Madison, for example, simply rolled into one linguistic heap "religious freedom" or "the free exercise of religion according to the dictates of conscience."[4] In another passage, he spoke of "liberty of conscience" as the "religious rights and privileges . . . of a multiplicity of sects."[5] Such patterns of interwoven language appear regularly in writings of the day. One term often implicated and connoted several others.[6] To read the guarantee of liberty of conscience too dogmatically is to ignore its inherent elasticity.

That said, the founders did ascribe distinct content to the phrase "liberty of conscience," which won wide assent in the early republic. First, liberty of conscience protected *voluntarism*—"the unalienable right of private judgment in matters of religion," the unencumbered ability to choose and to change one's religious beliefs and adherences, the unfettered freedom to believe the dictates of one's own heart and mind.[7] The Westminster Confession (1644), an anchor text for Presbyterians and other Calvinists, emphasized the God-given qualities of this freedom: "God alone is Lord of the Conscience, and hath left it free from the Doctrines and Commandments of men."[8] The English scientist and philosopher Joseph Priestly, whom John Adams befriended for a time, thought granting "universal liberty of conscience" was the best way to live out the Golden Rule: "[D]o unto others as we would that they should do to us."[9] Every person must be "left alone" to worship God "in the manner and season most agreeable to the Dictates of his own conscience," John Adams echoed. For the rights of conscience are "indisputable, unalienable, indefeasible, [and] divine."[10] "I am an enemy to every appearance of restraint in a matter so delicate and sacred as the Liberty of Conscience."[11] James Madison wrote: "The Religion then of every man must be left to the conviction and conscience of every man; and it is the right of every man to exercise it as these may dictate."[12] Evangelical preacher Samuel Stillman concurred: "[S]ome of the natural rights of mankind are unalienable and subject to no control but that of the Deity. Such are the sacred rights of conscience."[13] Baptist leader John Leland echoed these sentiments in 1791:

> Every man must give an account of himself to God, and therefore every man ought to be at liberty to serve God in that way that he can reconcile it to his conscience. . . . It would be sinful for a man to surrender to man [that] which is to be kept sacred for God. A man's mind should be always open to conviction, and an honest man will receive that doctrine which appears the best demonstrated; and what is more common for the best of men to change their minds?[14]

Puritans, Republicans, Evangelicals, and Enlightenment exponents alike could agree on this core meaning of liberty of conscience.

Second, and closely related, liberty of conscience *prohibited* religiously based *discrimination* against individuals. Persons could neither be penalized for the religious choices they made nor swayed to make certain choices because of the civil advantages attached to them. Liberty of conscience, Puritan preacher and Yale president

Ezra Stiles opined, permits "no bloody tribunals, no cardinal inquisitors-general, to bend the human mind forcibly to control the understanding, and put out the light of reason, the candle of the Lord in man."[15] Liberty of conscience also prohibited more subtle forms of discrimination, prejudice, and cajolery by state, church, or even other citizens. "[N]o part of the community shall be permitted to perplex or harass the other for any supposed heresy," wrote a Massachusetts pamphleteer. "[E]ach individual shall be allowed to have and enjoy, profess and maintain his own system of religion."[16]

Third, in the view of some founders, liberty of conscience guaranteed "freedom and *exemption* from human impositions, and legal restraints, in matters of religion and conscience."[17] Persons of faith were to be "exempt from all those penal, sanguinary laws, that generate vice instead of virtue."[18] Such laws not only included the onerous criminal rules that traditionally encumbered and discriminated against religious nonconformists and led to fines, whippings, banishments, and occasional executions of dissenting colonists. They also included more facially benign laws that worked injustice upon certain religious believers—conscription laws that required religious pacifists to participate in the military; oath-swearing laws that ran afoul of the religious scruples of certain believers; and tithing and taxing laws that forced believers to support churches, religious schools, and other causes that they found religiously odious.[19] Liberty of conscience, Thomas Jefferson wrote, required that the conscientiously opposed be "totally free and exempt from all Levies, Taxes and Impositions whatever towards supporting and maintaining the [established Anglican] church" as a means of ensuring "equal Liberty as well religious as civil" to all "good People."[20] Pamphleteer Henry Cumings put it similarly: "Liberty of conscience requires not [only] that persons are . . . exempt from hierarchical tyranny and domination, from the usurped authority of pope and prelates, and from every species of persecution on account of religion." It also requires that they "stand on equal ground, and behaving as good members of society, may equally enjoy their religious opinions, and without molestation, or being exposed to fines or forfeitures, or any other temporal disadvantages."[21]

In the eighteenth century, it was commonly assumed that the laws and policies of benevolent legislators would rarely tread on the religious scruples of their subjects.[22] George Washington put it thus in a letter to a group of Quakers: "In my opinion the conscientious scruples of all men should be treated with great delicacy and tenderness: and it is my wish and desire, that the laws may always be as extensively accommodated to them, as a due regard for the protection and essential interests of the nation may justify and permit."[23] Even so, it was also commonly understood that the growing religious pluralism in America might make such legislative accommodation of all religions increasingly difficult. Where general laws and policies did intrude on the religious scruples of an individual or group, liberty of conscience demanded protection of religious minorities through exemptions from such laws and policies. James Madison understood clearly how majoritarian legislation can "narrow" and "invade" "the rights of Conscience in particular." "Wherever the real power in a Government lies, there is the danger of oppression. In our Governments the real power lies in the majority of the Community, and the invasion of private rights is chiefly to be apprehended, not from acts of Government contrary to the sense of its constituents, but from acts in which the Government is the mere instrument of the major number of the constituents."[24] Hence the need for religious exemptions to protect the private rights of conscience for religious minorities. Whether such exemptions should be accorded by the legislature or by the judiciary, and whether they were a constitutional right or an equitable exception—the sources of much scholarly contention today—the eighteenth-century sources at our disposal do not dispositively say.[25]

These three aspects of liberty of conscience—voluntarism, nondiscrimination, and exemption—were embodied in early state constitutional laws. All the early state constitutions included some guarantee of liberty of conscience, and many expanded on the particular goods and goals it promoted for religious believers. The 1776 Delaware constitution had typical language:

> That all men have a natural and inalienable right to worship Almighty God according to the dictates of their own consciences and understandings; and that no man ought or of right can be compelled to attend any religious worship or maintain any religious ministry contrary to or against his own free will and consent, and that no authority can or ought to be vested in, or assumed by any power whatever that shall in any case interfere with, or in any manner controul the right of conscience and free exercise of religious worship.[26]

The 1776 Pennsylvania constitution added a protection against religious discrimination: "Nor can any man, who acknowledges the being of a God, be justly deprived or abridged of any civil right as a citizen, on account of his religious sentiments or peculiar mode of religious worship." It also provided a state constitutional exemption for conscientious objectors: "Nor can any man who is conscientiously scrupulous of bearing arms, be justly compelled thereto, if he will pay such equivalent."[27] The 1776 constitution of New Jersey provided exemptions from religious taxes, using typical language: "nor shall any person . . . ever be obliged to pay tithes, taxes, or any other rates, for the purpose of building or repairing any other church, . . . or ministry, contrary to what he believes to be right."[28] The 1777 constitution of New York addressed both state and church intrusions on conscience, endeavoring "not only to expel civil tyranny, but also to guard against that spiritual oppression and intolerance . . . wherewith the bigotry and ambition of weak and wicked priests have scourged mankind." It thus declared "that the free exercise and enjoyment of religious profession and worship, without discrimination or preference, shall forever hereafter be allowed, within this State, to all mankind."[29] Conscientious objection, nondiscrimination, noncompulsion in matters of religion, freedom of belief and worship—these provisions and more were all subsumed in state guarantees of "liberty of conscience."

The principle of liberty of conscience also informed some of the federal constitutional debates on religion. Article VI of the Constitution explicitly provided:

"[N]o religious Test [oath] shall ever be required as a qualification" for public office, thereby protecting those religiously opposed to oath swearing.[30] Early versions of the First Amendment religion clauses, debated in the First Congress of 1789, included such phrases as the following: "That any person religiously scrupulous of bearing arms ought to be exempted, upon payment of an equivalent to employ another to bear arms in his stead"; "persons conscientiously scrupulous of taking an oath" are protected; "[t]he civil rights of none shall be abridged on account of religious belief or worship . . . nor shall the full and equal rights of conscience be in any manner, or on any pretext, infringed"; "no State shall violate the equal rights of conscience"; and "Congress shall make no law . . . to infringe the rights of conscience." Such phrases were ultimately abandoned (although not argued against in the surviving records) in favor of blunter language: "Congress shall make no law . . . prohibiting the free exercise" of religion.[31] In Chapter 4, we shall review whether the principle of liberty of conscience is missing from the First Amendment or left implicit in the free exercise clause.

Free Exercise of Religion

For many founders, freedom of conscience was closely tied to free exercise of religion. Liberty of conscience was the right to be left alone to choose, to entertain, and to change one's religious beliefs—without state coercion or control and without benefits or burdens imposed by the state. Free exercise of religion was the right to act publicly on the choices of conscience once made—up to the limits of encroaching on the rights of others, disturbing the public peace, or otherwise violating criminal laws.[32] This organic tie between religious conscience and religious exercise was well known in the Western tradition and was not lost on English and American writers.[33] Already in 1670, the Quaker leader William Penn had linked these two guarantees, insisting that in "plain English" religious liberty entails "not only a mere Liberty of the Mind, in believing or disbelieving" but equally "the free and uninterrupted exercise of our consciences, in that way of worship, we are most clearly persuaded, God requires us to serve Him."[34] The American founders followed this view. Religion, Madison wrote, "must be left to the convictions and conscience of every man; and it is the right of man to exercise it as these may dictate."[35] Religious practices must be protected because they are inseparable from religious beliefs, Madison wrote; religion consists of both "the duties that we owe to our Creator, and the manner of discharging them."[36] This sentiment was common to most eighteenth-century writers. In its early free exercise cases concerning polygamy, we shall see, the Supreme Court held that the free exercise clause protects beliefs only, not actions. No eighteenth-century founder to our knowledge supported this view, and the Supreme Court later abandoned this belief/act distinction as well.

In the view of most founders, "free exercise" rights—or "the right freely and peaceably to exercise one's religion," as the New York ratification convention termed it[37]—generally connoted freedom to engage in a variety of public religious actions informed by the dictates of conscience: religious worship, religious speech, religious assembly, religious publication, religious education, and more. It was assumed, however, that such actions would not only be civilly peaceable but also morally exemplary. As George Washington put it: "While all men within our territories are protected in worshipping the Deity according to the dictates of their consciences; it is rationally to be expected from them in return, that they will be emulous of evincing the sincerity of their profession by the innocence of their lives, and the beneficence of their actions: For no man, who is profligate in morals, or a bad member of the civil community, can possibly be a true Christian, or a credit to his own religious society."[38] Particularly for Evangelicals, aglow with the missionary zeal of the Great Awakening, free exercise also included the right to evangelize for converts. But this too had to be done peaceably, as New York lawyer Henry Livingston reminded his readers: "I Believe, that to defend the Christian religion is one Thing, and to knock a Man in the Head for being of a different [faith], is another Thing."[39]

Free exercise of religion also embraced the right of the individual to join with like-minded believers in religious societies, which were free to devise their own modes of worship, articles of faith, standards of discipline, and forms of liturgy.[40] The founders did not use our current terminology of "religious group rights" or "corporate free exercise rights." But they did speak of "ecclesiastical liberty," "the equal liberty of one sect . . . with another," and the right "to have the full enjoyment and free exercise of those purely spiritual powers . . . as may be consistent with the civil rights of society."[41] By these phrases they intended to capture certain rights of religious societies themselves.

Every early state constitution guaranteed "free exercise" rights of some sort—often adding the familiar caveat that such exercise not violate the public peace or the private rights of others. Most early states limited their guarantee to "the free exercise of religious worship" or the "free exercise of religious profession," thereby leaving the protection of other forms of religious expression and action beyond worship to other constitutional protections, if any. A few states provided more generic, and thus more robust, free exercise guarantees. The 1776 Bill of Rights of Virginia, for example, guaranteed "the free exercise of religion, according to the dictates of conscience."[42] It thereby expanded free exercise protection to cultic and noncultic religious expression and action, provided these were mandated by conscience. The 1777 Georgia Constitution provided even more flatly: "All persons whatever shall have the free exercise of their religion; provided it be not repugnant to the peace and safety of the State."[43] The First Amendment drafters too chose the more expansive language of "free exercise [of religion]"—without defining or delimiting the kinds of religious exercises that might be protected—and at the same time they explicitly guaranteed the freedom of speech, press, and assembly for religious and nonreligious parties alike.

Religious Pluralism

The founders regarded "multiplicity," "diversity," or "pluralism" as an important and independent principle of religious liberty. In one sense, of course, religious pluralism was not a principle but rather a cause, condition, and consequence of giving freedom of conscience and free exercise rights to all, with the assurance of equality before the law. In another sense, religious pluralism was just a sociological fact. The young American republic had dozens of different religious groups to consider, most of them Christian, but some fiercely covetous of their particular denominational identity. That said, several eighteenth-century founders regarded religious pluralism as an essential principle of religious liberty that rebuked the traditional establishment ideal of only one faith allowed per territory.

The founders distinguished two kinds of pluralism pertinent to religion: confessional pluralism and structural pluralism. Evangelical and Enlightenment writers stressed the protection of *confessional pluralism*—the maintenance and accommodation of a plurality of forms of religious expression and organization in the community. Evangelical writers advanced a theological argument for this principle, emphasizing that it was for God, not the state, to decide which forms of religion should flourish and which should fade. "God always claimed it as his sole prerogative to determine by his own laws what his worship shall be, who shall minister in it, and how they shall be supported," Isaac Backus wrote.[44] "God's truth is great, and in the end He will allow it to prevail."[45] Confessional pluralism served to respect and reflect this divine prerogative.

Enlightenment writers advanced a rational argument for this principle of confessional pluralism. Madison wrote that "freedom arises from the multiplicity of sects, which pervades America, and which is the best and only security for religious liberty in any society; for where there is such a variety of sects, there cannot be a majority of any one sect to oppress and persecute the rest."[46] "Difference of opinion is advantageous in religion," Jefferson wrote similarly. "The several sects perform the office of a *Censor morum* over each other. Is uniformity attainable? Millions of innocent men, women, and children, since the introduction of Christianity, have been burnt, tortured, fined, imprisoned; yet we have not advanced one inch towards uniformity. . . . Reason and persuasion are the only practicable instruments."[47] When Jefferson seemed to be wandering from these early sentiments, John Adams wrote to him: "Checks and balances, Jefferson," in the political as well as the religious sphere, "are our only Security, for the progress of Mind, as well as the Security of Body. Every Species of these Christians would persecute Deists, as [much] as either Sect would persecute another, if it had unchecked and unbalanced Power. Nay, the Deists would persecute Christians, and Atheists would persecute Deists, with as unrelenting Cruelty, as any Christians would persecute them or one another. Know thyself, human Nature!"[48] It is much better for the liberty of all, Adams elaborated elsewhere, to recognize that religious and moral liberty are God-given qualities that "reside in Hindoos and Mahometans, as well as in Christians; in Cappadocian monarchists, as well as in Athenian democrats; in Shaking Quakers, as well as in the General Assembly of the Presbyterian clergy; in Tartars and Arabs, Negroes and Indians, as well as in the people of the United States."[49]

As this last quote from Adams illustrates, Puritan and Republican writers endorsed confessional pluralism as well. Governor Randolph of Virginia, for example, declared to the Virginia ratification convention: "I am a friend to a variety of sects, because they keep one another in order. . . . There are now so many in the United States, that they will prevent the establishment of any one sect, in prejudice to the rest, and will forever oppose all attempts to infringe religious liberty."[50] But Puritan and Republican writers added an argument for structural or *social pluralism* as well. They encouraged each community to maintain and accommodate a variety of social units to foster religion. Churches and synagogues were not the only "religious societies" that deserved religious liberty protection. Families, schools, charities, and other learned and civic societies were equally vital bastions of religion, and they were equally deserving of the special protections of religious liberty. These diverse social institutions had several redeeming qualities. They provided multiple forums for religious expression and action; important bulwarks against state encroachment on natural liberties (and particularly religious liberties); and vital sources of theology, morality, charity, and discipline in the state and broader community. John Adams put it thus:

> My opinion of the duties of religion and morality comprehends a very extensive connection with society at large. . . . The benevolence, charity, capacity and industry which, exerted in private life, would make a family, a parish or a town happy, employed upon a larger scale, in support of the great principles of virtue and freedom of political regulations might secure whole nations and generations from misery, want and contempt.[51]

Benjamin Rush concurred: "Religion is best supported under the patronage of particular societies. The differentiation of religion into multiple forums and forms "is as necessary to the perfection and government of the whole as regiments and brigades are in an army."[52] Another pamphleteer argued that not only "magistrates [but] ministers of the gospel and heads of families, all of who have a regard for the future happiness of their country . . . [ought] to use all possible means to destroy vice and immorality of every kind and to cultivate and promote the fear of God and a love of religion in the minds of our young people."[53]

Pluralism was thus not just a sociological fact for the founders. It was also a constitutional condition for the guarantee of religious liberty. This was a species and application of Madison's famous argument about the virtues of republican pluralism in *The Federalist Papers,* numbers 10 and 51. In a federalist republic, Madison had argued in *Federalist* 10,

> The influence of factious leaders may kindle a flame within their particular States but will be unable to spread a general conflagration through the other States. A religious sect may degenerate into a political faction in a part of the Confederacy; but the variety of sects dispersed over the entire face of it must secure the national councils against any danger from that source.[54]

He summarized this general point crisply in *Federalist* 51: "In a free government, the security for civil rights must be the same as that for religious rights; it consists in the one case in the multiplicity of interests, and in the other in the multiplicity of sects."[55]

Religious Equality

The efficacy of the principles of liberty of conscience, free exercise of religion, and religious pluralism depended on a guarantee of equality of all peaceable religions before the law. For the state to single out one pious person or one form of faith for either preferential benefits or discriminatory burdens would skew the choice of conscience, encumber the exercise of religion, and upset the natural plurality of forms and forums of faith. Many of the founders therefore called for equality of all religions before the law. Madison captured the prevailing sentiment: "A just Government . . . will be best supported by protecting every Citizen in the enjoyment of his religion, with the same equal hand which protects his person and property; by neither invading the equal rights of any sect, nor suffering any sect to invade those of another."[56] John Adams concurred: "[A]ll men of all religions consistent with morals and property [must] enjoy equal liberty, . . . security of property . . . and an equal chance for honors and power."[57] Baptist leader Isaac Backus wrote similarly that religious liberty requires that "each person and each [religious] society are equally protected from being injured from others, all enjoying equal liberty to attend the worship which they believe is right."[58]

The founders' arguments for religious equality became particularly pointed in their debates over religious test oaths as a condition for holding federal political office and other positions of public trust. Oaths were commonly accepted in the day as "one of the principal instruments of government." They induce "the fear and reverence of God, and the terrors of eternity," one Puritan preacher put it, and thus impose "the most powerful restraints upon the minds of men" as they exercise their political office.[59] Eleven of the original thirteen states prescribed such oaths. These ranged in specificity from a general affirmation of belief in God or in (Protestant) Christianity to the Trinitarian confession required by Delaware: "I, A. B., do profess faith in God the Father, and in Jesus Christ His only Son, and in the Holy Ghost, one God, blessed for evermore; and I do acknowledge the holy scriptures of the Old and New Testament to be given by divine inspiration."[60] Both before and after the American Revolution, a number of Quakers, Moravians, Baptists, and other groups had condemned such oaths as a violation of liberty of conscience and as an "invading of the essential prerogatives of our Lord Jesus Christ."[61] The few Jewish voices of the day likewise protested oaths as a violation of their liberty of conscience and civil rights.[62] In response, most colonies and states legislatively exempted Quakers (and sometimes others with conscientious objections) from oaths in deference to the principle of liberty of conscience.

The addition of an argument from religious equality proved particularly persuasive in outlawing religious test oaths entirely—first at the federal level and eventually in many states as well. This equality argument first came to prominence in the state ratification debates in 1787 and 1788 on the draft United States Constitution.

Article VI of the Constitution provided that "no religious Test shall ever be required as a Qualification to any office or public Trust under the United States." Some state ratification conventioneers feared that this provision was "dangerous and impolitic." "[I]f there be no religious test required," Henry Abbot of North Carolina declared to his fellow conventioneers, "pagans, deists, and Mahometans might obtain office amongst us." "We ought to be suspicious of our liberties. We have felt the effect of oppressive measures, and know the happy consequences of being jealous of our rights."[63] Fellow Carolinian James Iredell countered, defending the prohibition on federal test oaths by resort to an argument from equality: "This article is calculated to secure universal religious liberty, by putting all sects on a level."[64] Richard Spaight elaborated: "No sect is preferred to another. Every man has the right to worship the Supreme Being in the manner that he thinks proper. No test is required. All men of equal capacity and integrity are equally eligible to offices."[65] A Massachusetts ratification conventioneer argued similarly: "That as all have an equal claim to the blessings of the government under which they live, and which they support, so none should be excluded from them for being of any particular denomination in religion."[66] "A test in favor of any one denomination of Christians would be to the last degree absurd in the United States," a Connecticut ratification conventioneer added. "If it were in favor of either Congregationalists, Presbyterians, Episcopalians, Baptists, or Quakers, it would incapacitate more than three-fourths of American citizens for any public office."[67]

Such equality arguments proved persuasive enough to convince the states to accept the no religious test oath provision in Article VI and to ratify the Constitution. This argument also led several states to remove their religious test oath requirements for state political officeholders. Georgia (1789), Delaware (1792), and Vermont (1793) dropped their religious test oaths. Pennsylvania (1790) adjusted its constitution to allow Jews to swear a political oath. And the new state constitutions of Kentucky (1792) and Tennessee (1796) included no religious test oaths, although they still required that political officials be theists, if not Christians.[68]

Most founders extended the principle of equality before the law to all peaceable theistic religions, including Jews, Muslims, and Hindus. A few founders pressed the principle even further, arguing for the equality of religions and nonreligions before the law—particularly on issues of test oaths and religious taxes. Anti-federalist Luther Martin of Maryland grumbled about the solicitude for nonreligious individuals shown by some of his fellow politicians: "[I]n a Christian country, it would be at least decent to hold out some distinction between the professors of Christianity and downright infidelity or paganism," he wrote.[69] James Madison was one object of Martin's criticism. Madison had obliquely suggested that even nontheists should enjoy religious freedom: "While we assert for ourselves a freedom to embrace, to profess and to observe the religion which we believe to be of divine origin, we cannot deny an equal freedom to those whose minds have not yet yielded to the evidence which has convinced us. If this freedom be abused, it is an offence against God, not against man."[70] Thomas Jefferson similarly wrote: "The legitimate powers of government extend to such acts only as are injurious to others. But it does me no injury for my neighbor to say there are twenty gods, or no god. It neither picks my pocket or breaks my leg. . . . Constraint may make him worse by making him a hypocrite, but it will never make him a truer man. It may fix him obstinately in his errors, but not cure them. Reason and free enquiry are the only effectual agents against error."[71] These rare passages from the eighteenth century that flirt with the idea of extending equal religious rights to atheists, polytheists, and nontheists alike should not be overread, though. The principal concern of most founders, unlike that of the modern Supreme Court, was directed to equality among theistic religions before the law, not equality between religion and nonreligion.

A number of early state constitutions embodied this principle of equality of all religions before the law. The New Jersey constitution, for example, insisted that "there shall be no establishment of any one religious sect in . . . preference to another."[72] The Delaware constitution guaranteed Christians "equal rights and privileges"—a guarantee soon extended by judicial interpretation and later amendment to include all religions.[73] The Maryland constitution insisted that Christians "are equally entitled to protection in their religious liberty."[74] The Virginia bill of rights guaranteed that "all men are equally entitled to the free exercise of religion."[75] The New York constitution guaranteed all persons "free exercise and enjoyment of religious profession and worship, without discrimination or preference."[76] Even Massachusetts, which maintained a Puritan establishment, nonetheless guaranteed in its constitution that "all religious sects and denominations, demeaning themselves peaceably, and as good citizens of the commonwealth, shall be equally under the protection of the law; and no subordination of one sect or denomination to another shall ever be established by law."[77]

The principle of equality also found its place in early drafts of the First Amendment religion clauses, yielding such phrases as: "nor shall the full and equal rights of conscience be in any manner, or on any pretext, infringed"; "Congress shall make no law establishing One Religious Sect or Society in preference to others"; and "Congress shall make no law establishing any particular denomination of religion in preference to another." Madison regarded protection of the "equal rights of conscience" as the "most valuable" guarantee for religious liberty, and he argued that it should be guaranteed to apply to both federal and state governments.[78] At the federal level, however, these explicit provisions and their supporting arguments were eventually abandoned for the more generic guarantees of no establishment and free exercise of religion. In Chapter 4, we shall consider whether the principles of religious equality for a plurality of faiths find their way into the final text of the First Amendment.

Separation of Church and State

While the principle of separation of church and state is often regarded as a distinctly modern American invention, it is in reality an ancient Western teaching. It has its

roots in biblical passages that speak of "separation" and "walls of separation" between believers and nonbelievers, and between priests and commoners, and the
need to maintain "two swords" to govern earthly life. Such biblical passages inspired a long Western tradition of reflection upon the (wall of) separation between
the faithful and the fallen, the religious and the political, the clergy and the laity,
the spiritual and the temporal, the sacerdotal and the secular, the church and the
state.

American Puritan adherents were drawn to early modern Protestant formulations. Martin Luther, for example, spoke of "a paper wall" "between the spiritual
estate [and] the temporal estate" and elaborated these views in his complex two
kingdoms theory.[79] John Calvin argued that the "political kingdom" and "spiritual
kingdom" must always be "considered separately," for there is "a great difference
between the ecclesiastical and civil power" and it would be "unwise to mingle these
two which have a completely different nature."[80] The seventeenth-century English
philosopher John Milton protested the Anglican and Presbyterian establishments
of his day: We must not "suffer the two powers, the ecclesiastical and the civil,
which are so totally distinct, to commit whoredom together, and, by their inter-
mingled and false riches, to strengthen indeed in appearance, but in reality to undermine, and at last to subvert one another." We should learn "to distinguish rightly
between civil power and ecclesiastical." The Bible makes clear, Milton went on, that
"Christ's kingdom is not of this world," and his church "does not stand by force or
constraint, the constituents of worldly authority." Nor is Christ's church like some
"vine" that "cannot subsist without clasping about the elm of worldly strength," or
some building that cannot support itself "without the props and buttresses of secular authority." The opposite is true, Milton argued: "[I]t is because the magistracy
and church have confuse[d] their jurisdictions" that "all Christendom" has reaped
a "bitter harvest" of crusades and wars, inquisitions and pogroms, bloodshed and
persecution. It is because church and state have "conflated" their powers and offices
that the church has become "a pontifical despotism decked, under pretense of religion, with the spoils of civil power, which it has seized unto itself contrary to
Christ's own precept."[81] Such early Protestant views were echoed in a number of
New England Puritan writings and laws that called for a basic separation of the offices and officers of church and state.

American Evangelical writers also had a trove of historical Anabaptist confessional
statements, sermons, and pamphlets calling for a "wall of separation" between the
redeemed church of Christ and the fallen world that lay "beyond the perfection of
Christ."[82] These early Free Church views recurred in a number of Baptist pamphlets
that called for the church, as the "pure bride of Christ," to be free from "adulterous
unions" with the state.[83] They recurred in other American Evangelical writings that
called for a "wall," "hedge," "line," or "fence" between church and state and an "absolute divorce" between the church and the state.[84]

The principle of separation of church and state also had solid grounding in political sources that appealed to American Enlightenment and Republican writers.

John Locke, for example, argued that the authority of the clergy, "since it is ecclesiastical, ought to be confined with the bounds of the church, nor can it in any manner be extended to civil affairs, because the church itself is a thing absolutely separate and distinct from the commonwealth. The boundaries on both sides are fixed and immovable."[85] James Burgh, a Scottish Whig who was popular among several American founders, pressed for the principle in his influential writings of the 1760s and 1770s, which echoed some of Milton's views.[86] Burgh lamented the "ill consequences" of the traditional "mixed-mungrel-spiritual-secular-ecclesiastical establishment." Such conflations of church and state, he said, lead to "follies and knaveries," and make "the dispensers of religion despicable and odious to all men of sense, and will destroy the spirituality, in which consists the whole value, of religion." "Build an impenetrable wall of separation between sacred and civil," Burgh enjoined. "Do not send the graceless officer, reeking from the arms of his trull [i.e., prostitute], to the performance of a holy rite of religion, as a test for his holding the command of a regiment. To profane, in such a manner, a religion, which you pretend to reverence, is an impiety sufficient to bring down upon your heads, the roof of the sacred building you thus defile."[87]

The French revolutionary Marquis de Condorcet, who influenced Thomas Paine, put his case "to separate religion from the State" in the shriller, anti-Catholic terms that would dominate the 1789 French Revolution. While it was important "to leave to the priests the freedom of sacraments, censures, [and] ecclesiastical functions," Condorcet conceded, the state must take steps to remove the traditional influence and privileges of the Catholic Church and clergy in society and the state. The state was "not to give any civil effect to any of their decisions, not to give any influence over marriages or over birth or death certificates; not to allow them to intervene in any civil or political act; and to judge the lawsuits which would arise, between them and their citizens, for the temporal rights relating to their functions, as one would decide the similar lawsuits that would arise between the members of a free association, or between this association and private individuals."[88] Such anti-clerical and anti-Catholic separationist sentiments were quite typical of French revolutionaries. In the following decades, such sentiments stirred up a devastating political and populist attack on the clergy and property of the Catholic Church that left the French Catholic Church in tatters for more than half a century.

This range of theological and political sources formed the background for the American founders, and these quotations evidence the variety and scope of sentiments that informed the principle of separation of church and state. The American founders sifted through this European and colonial legacy of church-state separation to distill five major themes.

First, the founders invoked the principle of separation of church and state as a means to protect the church from the state. This had long been a dominant motif in European Catholic and Protestant writings—captured in the Christian clergy's perennial call for "freedom of the church." The concern was to protect church affairs from state intrusion, the clergy from the magistracy, church properties from state encroachment, and ecclesiastical rules and rites from political coercion and control. This understanding of separation of church and state continued and grew in eighteenth-century America. Puritan theologian and jurist Elisha Williams spoke for many churchmen when he wrote in 1744: "[E]very church has [the] right to judge in what manner God is to be worshipped by them, and what form of discipline ought to be observed by them, and the right also of electing their own officers" without interference from political officials.[89] A Baptist pamphleteer saw "separation of church and state" as the political equivalent of the "fundamental principle" of the Bible that "the kingdom of Christ is not of this world." The church is "to observe the law of Christ in all things" and "not be governed by worldly maxims, influenced by worldly hopes or fears, ambitious of worldly power or honours."[90] At the turn of the nineteenth century, Enlightenment libertarian Tunis Wortman wrote:

> It is your duty, as Christians, to maintain the purity and independence of the church, to keep religion separate from politics, to prevent an union between the church and the state, and to preserve the clergy from temptation, corruption and reproach. . . . Unless you maintain the pure and primitive spirit of Christianity, and prevent the cunning and intrigue of statesmen from mingling with its institutions, you will become exposed to a renewal of the same dreadful and enormous scenes which have not only disgraced the annals of the church, but destroyed the peace, and sacrificed the lives of millions.[91]

This understanding of separation of church and state was captured in the many state and federal constitutional guarantees of freedom for religious groups, sects, and societies (pp. 47–48, 55).

Second, the founders sometimes adduced the principle of separation of church and state as a means to protect the state from the church. Just as Wortman had argued for independence of the church, so too he argued for the independence of the state: "Religion and government are equally necessary, but their interests should be kept separate and distinct."[92] "Upon no plan, no system can they become united, without endangering the purity and usefulness of both—the church will corrupt the state, and the state pollute the church."[93] Cato's *Letters* reviewed much "ecclesiastical history, and the history of the Turks and Saracens," to drive home the point that the state needs protection from the church: "Nor have churchmen, when they ruled states, had ever any other view; but having double authority, had generally double insolence and remarkably less mercy and regard to conscience or property, than others who had fewer ties to be merciful and just. And therefore the sorest tyrants have been they, who united in one person the royalty and priesthood."[94] John Adams similarly devoted much of his *Dissertation on the Canon and the Feudal Law* (1774) to a lengthy history of the "tyrannous outrages" that the Catholic Church and the papacy had inflicted through its control of the state; this was "a wicked confederacy between two systems of tyranny."[95] Drawing on these same historical lessons, John Jay urged his fellow constitutional conveners in New York "not only to expel civil tyranny, but also to guard against that spiritual oppression and intolerance wherewith the bigotry and ambition of weak and wicked priests and princes have scourged mankind."[96]

This understanding of separation of church and state helped to inform the movement in some states to exclude clergy and other church officials from holding political office. While such clerical exclusions were commonplace among seventeenth-century Puritans, they later became attractive to Evangelicals and Enlightenment exponents as well. Some argued that clerics in political office could use the threat of spiritual reprisal to force their congregants, including fellow politicians who sat in their pews, to acquiesce in their political positions. Others argued that clerics would inevitably be conflicted over whose interests to represent and serve: the interests of their religious congregants or their political constituents. Still others claimed that clerics who tried to serve both God and the state would be distracted from their fundamental callings of preaching and teaching, and tempted to bend their religious messages toward political causes. Finally several critics insisted that clerics could not enjoy both the benefit of exemption of taxation for themselves and the power to impose taxation on all others; this was even more odious than the great offense of taxation without representation.[97]

But not all founders opposed political office-holding by religious ministers. For example, Thomas Jefferson initially favored such clerical exclusions for "the clergy, by getting themselves established by law, & ingrafted into the machine of government, have been a very formidable engine against the civil and religious rights of man." But he thought such measures were only temporarily necessary in the aftermath of the American Revolution. "It now appears," he wrote in 1800, "that our means were effectual. The clergy seem to have relinquished all pretensions to privilege and to stand on an equal footing with lawyers, & physicians, etc. They ought therefore to possess the same rights."[98]

The arguments for clerical exclusions led seven of the original thirteen states to ban ministers from serving in political office. The 1778 South Carolina constitution had typical language: "And whereas, ministers of the Gospel are by their profession dedicated to the service of God and the cure of souls, and ought not to be diverted from their great duties of their function, therefore no minister of the Gospel or public preacher of any religious persuasion, while he continues in the exercise of his pastoral function, and for two years after, shall be eligible either as governor, lieutenant-governor, a member of the senate, house representative, or privy council in this State."[99] A few states retained these clerical exclusions until the twentieth century; the Supreme Court finally banned these provisions in 1978 as a violation of the free exercise rights of the clergy.

Third, the principle of separation of church and state was invoked as a means to protect the individual's liberty of conscience from the intrusions of both church and state. This understanding of separationism was strongly held by Anabaptists in Europe and some Evangelicals and Quakers in early colonial America.[100] It became more prominent in eighteenth-century America. "Every man has an equal right to follow the dictates of his own conscience in the affairs of religion," Elisha Williams wrote in 1744. This is "an equal right with any rulers be they civil or ecclesiastical."[101] "Religion is altogether personal and the right of exercising it inalienable," wrote a Presbyterian pamphleteer in 1776; "it is not, cannot, and ought not to be, resigned to the will of the society at large" let alone "to the authorities of church and state."[102] Madison called for a "great barrier" between church and state to protect the rights of individuals:

> Their jurisdiction is both derivative and limited. It is limited with regard to the co-ordinate departments; more necessarily is it limited with regard to the constituents. The preservation of a free government requires not merely, that the metes and bounds which separate each department of power be invariably maintained; but more especially that neither of them be suffered to overleap the great barrier which defends the rights of the people.[103]

Jefferson's famous 1802 letter to the Danbury Baptist Association—often invoked as the source of the phrase "separation of church and state"—also tied that principle directly to the principle of liberty of conscience:

> Believing with you that *religion is a matter which lies solely between a man and his God,* that he owes account to none other for his faith or his worship, that the [legitimate] powers of government reach actions only, and not opinions, I contemplate with sovereign reverence that the act of the whole American people which declared that their legislature should "make no law respecting an establishment of religion, or prohibiting the free exercise thereof," *thus building a wall of separation between church and State.* Adhering to this expression of the supreme will of the nation *in behalf of the rights of conscience,* I shall see with sincere satisfaction the progress of those sentiments which tend to *restore to man all his natural rights,* convinced he has no natural right in opposition to his social duties.[104]

In Jefferson's formulation, separation of church and state assured individuals of their natural, inalienable right of conscience, which could be exercised freely and fully to the point of breaching the peace or shirking social duties. But Jefferson was not speaking of separating politics and religion altogether. Indeed, in the very next paragraph of his letter, President Jefferson performed an avowedly religious act of offering prayers on behalf of his Baptist correspondents: "I reciprocate your kind prayers for the protection and blessing of the common Father and Creator of man."[105]

Fourth, the principle of separation of church and state was occasionally used to argue for the protection of individual states from interference by the federal government in governing local religious affairs. As Daniel Dreisbach has shown, Jefferson sometimes used the principle of separation of church and state in this federalist jurisdictional sense as well.[106] Jefferson said many times that the federal government had no jurisdiction over religion; religion was entirely a state and local matter. As he put it in his second inaugural address: "In matters of religion, I have considered that its free exercise is placed by the constitution independent of the general [federal] government. I have therefore undertaken, on no occasion, to prescribe the religious exercises suited to it; but have left them, as the constitution found them, under the direction and discipline of State or Church authorities."[107] The separation that Jefferson had in mind was between local church-state relations and the federal government. The federal government could not interfere in the affairs of local churches, *and* the federal government could not interfere in the affairs of local states vis-à-vis these local churches. Under this federalist jurisdictional reading of separation, state governments were free to patronize and protect religion, or to establish or abridge religion, as their own state constitutions dictated—but the federal government was entirely foreclosed from the same. Thus Jefferson as governor of Virginia supported religion in a variety of ways, including making religious proclamations on behalf of the state. But Jefferson as president of the United States insisted firmly on separation and refused to give Thanksgiving Day proclamations on behalf of the country.[108]

Fifth, the principle of separation of church and state was occasionally adduced as a rationale to protect society and its members from unwelcome participation in and support for religion and its morals in positive law. In the eighteenth-century colonies, some religious dissenters used the language of separation to argue against established church policies of mandatory payments of tithes, required participation in swearing oaths, forced attendance at religious services, and compulsory registration of church properties. This formulation tied the principle of separation of church and state closely to the principle of liberty of conscience.[109] At the turn of the nineteenth century, however, the language of separation of church and state also began to fuel broader campaigns to remove traditional forms and forums of religion in law, politics, and society altogether. This was the most novel, and controversial, understanding of separation of church and state in the young American republic, but it began to gain rhetorical currency. As Philip Hamburger has shown, in the course of the nineteenth century, separation of church and state became an increasingly useful rhetorical weapon in the battles over dueling, freemasonry, lotteries, drunkenness, Sunday laws, slavery and abolition, marriage and divorce, women's suffrage, religious education, blasphemy prosecutions, enforcement of Christian morals, and more.[110]

Disestablishment of Religion

For some eighteenth-century founders, the roll of "essential rights and liberties" of religion ended here. They saw no inconsistency between having one established religion in a state yet guaranteeing liberty of conscience, free exercise, religious equality of a plurality of faiths, and separation of church and state to all others. Seven of the original thirteen states still had religious establishments when the First Amendment was being drafted in 1789. The New England states of Massachusetts, Connecticut, and New Hampshire (along with the independent territories of Vermont and Maine) all retained their "mild and equitable" establishments of Puritan congregationalism, although individual townships occasionally went their own way. Georgia, South Carolina, North Carolina, and Maryland replaced the exclusive Anglican establishments of the prerevolutionary era with "multiple establishments" of "all denominations of Christian Protestants."[111] The four counties that comprised much of New York City retained an establishment as well.

Though local practices varied in these establishment states, their governments still exercised some control over religious doctrine, governance, clergy, and other personnel. They still required church attendance of all citizens, albeit at a church of their choice. They still collected tithes for support of the church that the tithe payer attended, and often gave state money, tax exemptions, and other privileges preferentially to one religion. They still imposed annoying restrictions on education, voting, and political involvement of religious dissenters. They still obstructed the organization, education, and worship activities of dissenting churches, particularly Catholics and Quakers. They still conscripted established church institutions and their clergy for weddings, education, poor relief, political rallies, and distribution of state literature. They still administered religious test oaths for political officials, and sometimes even for petty state bureaucrats. To be sure, these formal state establishments of religion, particularly the controversial practice of state funding for religion, were losing support by 1789 when the First Amendment was being forged. Such state establishments of religion ended formally in 1833, when Massachusetts became the last state to abandon its state tithing system. Yet many states retained vestiges of traditional establishments throughout the nineteenth century, as we shall see in Chapter 5.

Despite the remaining state establishments, disestablishment movements were gaining support, especially as Evangelical forces grew stronger and as Enlightenment arguments for disestablishment cut deeper into traditional practices. By 1789, six of the original thirteen states had formally disestablished religion. Rhode Island and Pennsylvania never had establishments from the time of their founding. New Jersey, Delaware, and New York (except for the four counties that comprised New York City) had constitutionally abandoned establishment after the American Revolution. Virginia had just passed its 1786 Act for the Establishment of Religious Freedom. And even in establishment states—perhaps especially in these states—virtually all founders feared a national establishment of religion. Newspapers of the day were filled with hyperbolic projections of Anglican bishops or Presbyterian divines presiding tyrannically over the vulnerable young nation. Such a national establishment of religion simply could not be allowed, even in places where local state establishments persisted.[112]

The term "establishment of religion" was an ambiguous phrase in the eighteenth century, as much as it is today. In the dictionaries and common parlance of the founders' day, "to establish" meant "to settle firmly," "to fix unalterably," "to settle in any privilege or possession," "to make firm," "to ratify," "to ordain," "to enact," "to set up," and "to build firmly."[113] Such was the basic meaning of the term, for example, when used in the text of the 1787 Constitution: "We the people of the United

States, in order to form a perfect union, to *establish* justice . . . do ordain and *establish* this Constitution" (preamble); Congress shall have power "[t]o *establish* an uniform rule of naturalization" and "[t]o *establish* post offices" (Art. I.8); governmental offices "shall be *established* by law" (Art. II.2); Congress may "ordain and *establish* . . . inferior courts" (Art. III.1); the ratification of nine states "shall be sufficient for the *establishment* of this Constitution" (Art. VI).[114]

Following this basic sense of the term, most founders understood the establishment of religion to mean governmental actions to "settle," "fix," "define," "ordain," "enact," or "set up" the religion of the community—whether its religious doctrines and liturgies, its religious texts and traditions, or its clergy and property. To the founders, the most notorious example of religious establishment in this sense was the Anglican establishment, as already noted. The king, as supreme head, together with the Parliament, mandated the Thirty-Nine Articles of Religion as the established doctrine, prescribed the Book of Common Prayer as the established liturgy, and instituted the King James Version of the Bible as the established Authorized Version. They vested, disciplined, and removed the clergy as political appointees, collecting tithes and taxes for their support and granting them privileges and immunities from civic duties. They instituted special criminal laws to protect the church's doctrine and liturgy, clergy and property. They consigned all nonconformists to second-class status, officially tolerating only Protestants, not Catholics, Jews, Muslims, or others. For many eighteenth-century American founders, such an establishment of religion could not coexist with a guarantee of liberty of conscience, religious equality of a plurality of religions, or the separation of church and state. The establishment of any one religion, they argued, necessarily abridged the other principles of religious liberty. These founders thus called for the disestablishment of all religion, whether by federal or state government.

Disestablishment of religion, under this understanding, protected the principle of liberty of conscience by foreclosing government from coercively prescribing mandatory forms of religious belief, doctrine, and practice. As both the Delaware and Pennsylvania constitutions put it: "[N]o authority can or ought to be vested in, or assumed by any power whatever, that shall in any case interfere with, or in any manner controul, the right of conscience in the free exercise of religious worship."[115] Every major religion in America, Benjamin Franklin wrote, had a history of violating freedom of conscience and exercise of other faiths when given the chance to establish its own faith. Consequently it was better not to give any religion that chance:

> If we look back into history for the character of the present sects in Christianity, we shall find few that have not in their turns been persecutors, and complainers of persecution. The primitive Christians thought persecution extremely wrong in the Pagans, but practiced it on one another. The first Protestants of the Church of England blamed persecution in the Roman church, but practiced it against the Puritans; these found it wrong in the Bishops, but fell to it themselves both here and in New England. To account for this we should remember, that the doctrine of toleration was

not then known. . . . By degrees more moderate and more modest sentiments have taken place in the Christian world; and among the Protestants particularly all disclaim persecution, none vindicate it, and few practice it. We should then cease to reproach each other with what has been done by our ancestors, but judge of the present character of sects or churches by their present conduct only.[116]

Thomas Paine, who is usually branded as a religious skeptic, put this same argument:

All religions are in their nature mild and benign, and united with principles of morality. They could not have made proselytes at first, by professing anything that was vicious, cruel, persecuting or immoral. . . . Persecution is not an original feature in any religion; but it is always the strongly marked feature of all law-religions, or religions established by law. Take away the law-establishment, and every religion reassumes its original benignity.[117]

Disestablishment of religion further protected the principles of equality and pluralism by preventing government from singling out certain religious beliefs and bodies for preferential treatment. Read this way, the problem was not establishment per se but the preference given to the established church versus the others. This concept of disestablishment came through repeatedly in both state and federal debates. In the Virginia ratification convention, for example, Madison and several other conventioneers stressed that religious pluralism would "prevent the establishment of any one sect in prejudice, to the rest, and will forever oppose all attempts to infringe religious liberty."[118] South Carolina conventioneer Francis Cummins likewise stated that it was "his duty and honor to oppose the ideas of religious establishments; or of states giving preference to any religious denomination." "It would be impolite for a state to give preference to one religious order over any others in matters of state, and to dictate and prescribe in points of religion, in which men have from different modes of education and circumstances of one kind or other, will and must split in opinion."[119] The New Jersey constitution provided "there shall be no establishment of any one religious sect . . . in preference to another."[120] Both the New York and the Rhode Island ratifying conventions suggested amendments to the Constitution that "no religious sect or society ought to be favored or established by law in preference to others."[121] Two drafts of the religion clauses debated in the First Congress included a similar guarantee: "Congress shall make no law establishing one religious sect or society in preference to others"; "Congress shall make no law establishing any particular denomination of religion in preference to another."[122]

Disestablishment of religion also served to protect the basic principle of separation of church and state. Disestablishment, in Jefferson's words, prohibited government "from intermeddling with religious institutions, their doctrines, discipline, or exercises" and from "the power of effecting any uniformity of time or matter among them. Fasting & prayer are religious exercises. The enjoining them is an act of disci-

pline. Every religious society has a right to determine for itself the times for these exercises, & the objects proper for them, according to their own peculiar tenets."[123] To
allow such governmental meddling in the internal affairs of religious bodies would
inflate the competence of government. As Madison wrote, it "implies either that the
Civil Magistrate is a competent judge of religious truth; or that he may employ religion as an engine of civil policy. The first is an arrogant pretension falsified by the
contradictory opinions of rulers in all ages, and throughout the world, the second
an unhallowed perversion of the means of salvation."[124]

According to Madison, the wisdom and utility of disestablishment of religion
can be seen by contrasting the erosion of religion in establishment states with the
flourishing of religion in nonestablishment states. In establishment states of the
New England and the South, he wrote, "[t]he old churches, built under the establishment at the public expense, have in many instances gone to ruin, or are in a very
dilapidated state, owing chiefly to a transition desertion of the flocks to other wor-
ships." It had been "the universal opinion" in such states "that civil government
could not stand without the prop of a religious establishment, and that the Christian religion itself, would perish if not supported by a legal provision for its clergy.
The experience of Virginia [together with that of Rhode Island, Pennsylvania, New
Jersey, and Delaware] conspicuously corroborates the disproof of both opinions.
The civil government, though bereft of everything like an associated hierarchy, possesses the requisite stability and performs its functions with complete success; whilst
the number, the industry, and the morality of the priesthood, & the devotion of the
people have been manifestly increased by the total separation of the church from
the state" and the complete disestablishment of religion.[125]

The question that remained controversial—in the eighteenth century as much as
in our own—was whether more gentle and generic forms of state support for religion
could be countenanced. Did disestablishment of religion prohibit governmental support for religion altogether, or did it simply require that such governmental support
be distributed nonpreferentially among all religions? It takes a bit of historical imagination to appreciate this question in eighteenth-century terms. State governments
still patronized religion in a variety of ways, although less lavishly than in prerevolutionary times. Many new American states still donated land and personnel for the
building of churches, religious schools, and charities. They collected religious taxes
and tithes to support ministers and missionaries. They exempted church property
and ministers from taxation. They had special forms of religious incorporation for
churches, religious schools, charities, mission groups, and other religious bodies.
They supported Christian education in schools and colleges. They outlawed blasphemy, sacrilege, and unnecessary labor on the Sabbath and religious holidays. They
administered religious test oaths and foreclosed dissenters from political office.[126]

Historically, such forms of state patronage and protection of religion were reserved to one established church alone. All other faiths, if tolerated at all, were left
to depend on their own resources. During the later seventeenth and eighteenth centuries, the growth of religious pluralism in the colonies often entailed the gradual

extension of these forms of state privilege and patronage to other churches besides the established churches—often in piecemeal and painful fashion: benefit by benefit, congregation by congregation, county by county. By the later eighteenth century, states faced a hard constitutional question: Should state patronage for religion be ended altogether? Or should state patronage be extended to all religions indiscriminately or nonpreferentially, rather than granted in piecemeal fashion? Given the overwhelmingly Christian, indeed Protestant, character of the new nation,[127] a policy of nonpreferential governmental support for all religions could be quite realistically envisioned—particularly if accommodation were made for Jewish Sabbatarian beliefs or Quaker aversions to religious oaths. (No founder seriously thought of having to accommodate the African religions of the slaves or the traditional religions of the Native Americans.)

The historical sources do not resolve whether a guarantee of no establishment of religion outlaws all governmental financial and other support for religion or instead outlaws only preferential governmental support for some religions to the exclusion of others. The eighteenth-century founders were divided on the question. A number of Evangelical and Enlightenment writers viewed the principle of no establishment as a firm ban on all state support, particularly financial support, of religious beliefs, believers, and bodies. Any such support, direct or indirect, would erode the freedom of religion and religious bodies. A number of Puritan and Republican writers understood no establishment only as a prohibition against direct financial support for the religious worship or exercise of one particular religious group. For these founders, general governmental support for religion—tax exemptions to religious properties, land grants and tax subsidies to religious schools and charities, tax appropriations for missionaries and military chaplains—were not only licit but necessary for good governance.

The state constitutions were likewise divided on the question. A number of states explicitly authorized such support for religion in their original constitutions, although they sometimes defined "religion" as Christianity (or even Protestantism).[128] The constitution of Maryland (1776) was typical. It included strong guarantees of religious liberty that touched each of the principles of religious liberty. "[A]ll persons, professing the Christian religion, are equally entitled to protection in their religious liberty." This includes freedom from "molestation" "on account of his religious persuasion or profession, or for his religious practice"; "nor ought any person to be compelled to frequent or maintain, or contribute, unless on contract [i.e., by agreement] to maintain any particular place of worship, or any particular ministry." But the 1776 Maryland constitution continued without pause: "[T]he Legislature may, in their discretion, lay a general and equal tax, for the support of the Christian religion; leaving to each individual the power of appointing the payment over of the money, collected from him, to the support of any particular place of worship or minister, or for the benefit of the poor of his own denomination, or the poor in general of any particular county."[129] A similar juxtaposition of provisions was included in the original constitutions of Massachusetts, New Hampshire, Connecticut, and Georgia. The other original state constitutions simply repeated the general principles of religious liberty, without touching the issue of whether government could support religion(s).

Interdependence of Principles

For all the diversity of opinion that pervades the constitutional convention debates, pamphlets, sermons, editorials, and broadsides of the eighteenth century, most influential writers embraced this role of "essential rights and liberties of religion"—liberty of conscience, free exercise of religion, religious pluralism, religious equality, separation of church and state, and disestablishment at least of a national religion. While many of these terms carried multiple meanings in the later eighteenth century and several other terms were under discussion, these six principles are foundational in the eighteenth-century sources. James Madison reflected this nicely in 1823, when he summarized what he considered the main features of religious liberty in the founding era:

> The settled opinion here is that religion is essentially distinct from civil government and exempt from its cognizance; that a connexion between them is injurious to both; that there are causes in the human breast, which ensure the perpetuity of religions without the aid of the law; that rival sects, with equal rights, exercise mutual censorships in favor of good morals; that if new sects arise with absurd opinions or overheated [i]maginations, the proper remedy lies in time, forbearance, and example; that a legal establishment of religion without a toleration could not be thought of, and without a toleration, is no security for public quiet and harmony, but rather a source of itself of discord and animosity: and finally that these opinions are supported by experience, which has shown that every relaxation of alliance between law and religion, from the partial example of Holland, to its consummation in Pennsylvania, Delaware, N[ew] J[ersey, Rhode Island], etc., has been found as safe in practice as sound in theory.[130]

Eighteenth-century writers designed these principles to work together to prevent repressive religious establishments. Liberty of conscience protected the individual from coercion and discriminatory treatment by church or state officials and guaranteed unencumbered, voluntary choices and changes of faith. Free exercise of religion protected the individual's ability to discharge the duties of conscience through self-selected religious worship, speech, publication, assembly, and other actions. Pluralism protected multiple forms and forums of religious belief and action, in place of a uniformly mandated religious doctrine, liturgy, and polity. Equality protected religious individuals and bodies from special benefits and from special burdens administered by the state or by other religious bodies. Separationism protected individual believers, as well as religious and political officials, from undue interference or intrusion on each other's processes and practices. Disestablishment precluded governmental prescriptions of the doctrine, liturgy, or morality of one faith.

At the same time, eighteenth-century writers designed these principles to be mutually supportive and mutually subservient to the highest goal of guaranteeing "the essential rights and liberties of religion" for all. No single principle could by itself guarantee such religious liberty. Simple protection of liberty of conscience provided insufficient protection of religious actions or organizations. Free exercise alone could be mere toleration at best, without adequate support in the community or by the government. Pure pluralism could decay into religious relativism and render the government blind to the special place of religion in the community and in the constitution. Simple guarantees of the equality of religion could render governments indifferent to the widely divergent needs of different forms of religion. Pure separationism could deprive the church of all meaningful forms and functions and deprive states of an essential ally in government and social service. Pure disestablishment could rob society of all common values and beliefs and prevent religion from playing a salutary role in civic and political life. Eighteenth-century writers, therefore, arranged these multiple principles into an interlocking and interdependent shield of religious liberties and rights for all. Religion was simply too vital and too valuable a source of individual flourishing and social cohesion to be left unguarded on any side. Religious liberty was simply too essential a foundation of other civil rights and liberties to be in any way deprecated; it is, as Thomas Jefferson said, "the most inalienable and sacred of all human rights."[131]

Notes

1. The term "essential rights and liberties" was common among the founders. This was the title of Elisha Williams's tract, *The Essential Rights and Liberties of Protestants* (1744). The Virginia ratifying convention provided "that, among other essential rights, the liberty of conscience, and of the press, cannot be cancelled, abridged, restrained, or modified, by any authority of the United States." Elliot, ed., *Debates,* 1:327. James Madison spoke of the "essential rights" of religious freedom and rights of conscience in his speech of August 17, 1789, in the House debates. See Gales and Seaton, *Annals,* 1:784; and W. T. Hutchinson et al., eds., *The Papers of James Madison,* 17 vols. (1962), 11:404–405. John Adams included religious rights among "our most essential rights and liberties." C. F. Adams, ed., *The Works of John Adams* (Boston, 1850–1856), 3:465. The Federal Framer also saw "the free exercise of religion" as one of the "essential rights." Letter IV (October 12, 1787), in *The Anti-Federalist,* ed. Herbert J. Storing (1985), 58.

2. See prevailing sentiments collected in *The Palladium of Conscience, or, The Foundation of Religious Liberty Displayed, Asserted and Established, Agreeable to its True and Genuine Principles* (1773). The strongest early formulations in America came from Roger Williams. See "Religious Liberty in America and Beyond: Celebrating the Legacy of Roger Williams on the 400th Anniversary of His Birth," *Roger Williams University Law Review* 10 (2005): 279–536.

3. See sources and discussion in Brian Tierney, "Religious Rights: An Historical Perspective," in *Religious Human Rights in Global Perspective: Religious Perspectives,* ed. John Witte, Jr. and Johan D. van der Vyver (1996), 17–45; Karl Schwarz, "Der Begriff Exercitium Religionis Privatum," *Zeitschrift der Savigny-Stiftung (Kan. Ab.)* 105 (1988): 495–518.

4. Virginia Bill of Rights (1776), Art. 16.

5. Virginia Ratifying Convention (June 12, 1788), in Elliot, ed., *Debates*, 3:113–114, 330; Madison, *Papers,* 11:130–131; Anson P. Stokes and Leo Pfeffer, *Church and State in the United States*, rev. ed. (1975), 61.

6. John Mellen, *The Great and Happy Doctrine of Liberty* (1795), 17–18; Amos Adams, *Religious Liberty an Invaluable Blessing* (1768), 39–40, 45–46.

7. Williams, *Essential Rights and Liberties*, 42; John Lathrop, *A Discourse on the Peace* (1784), 29; Hugh Fisher, *The Divine Right of Private Judgment, Set in a True Light*, repr. ed. (1790).

8. Westminster Confession, chap. 20, sec. 2, in *The Confession of Faith, Together with the Larger and Smaller Catechisms* (1658), 63.

9. Quoted in *Joseph Priestly, Scientist, Philosopher, and Theologian,* ed. Isabel Rivers and David L. Wykes (2008), 131.

10. Adams, *Works*, 3:452–456; Massachusetts Constitution (1780), Pt. I, Art. II.

11. John Adams, Letter to Robert R. Livingston (October 8, 1782), in *The Papers of John Adams,* ed. Gregg C. Lint et al. (2006), 13:392.

12. James Madison, "Memorial and Remonstrance Against Religious Assessment," in Madison, *Papers,* 8:298, para. 1.

13. Quoted in Daniel L. Dreisbach and Mark David Hall, eds., *The Sacred Rights of Conscience: Selected Readings on Religious Liberty and Church-State Relations in the American Founding* (2009), vii.

14. John Leland, "The Rights of Conscience Inalienable" (1791), in *Political Sermons of the American Founding Era, 1730–1805*, ed. Ellis Sandoz (1991), 1079, 1085; Israel Evans, "A Sermon Delivered at Concord, Before the Hon. General Court of the State of New Hampshire at the Annual Election (1791)," in Sandoz, ed., *Political Sermons,* 1063.

15. Ezra Stiles, *The United States Elevated to Glory and Honor* (1783), 56.

16. Worcestriensis, IV (1776), in *American Political Writing During the Founding Era*, ed. Charles S. Hyneman and Donald S. Lutz (1983), 1:449–450.

17. Mellen, *The Great and Happy Doctrine of Liberty*, 17 (emphasis added).

18. Ibid., 20.

19. Jonathan Parsons, *Freedom from Civil and Ecclesiastical Slavery* (1774); Isaac Backus, *Appeal to the Public for Religious Liberty Against the Oppressions of the Present Day* (1773).

20. Thomas Jefferson, "Draft of Bill Exempting Dissenters from Contributing to the Support of the Church, 30 Nov. 1776," in Philip Kurland and Ralph Lerner, eds., *The Founders' Constitution*, 5 vols. (1987), 5:74. These arguments were sometimes extended to claiming "exemptions" and "immunities" from the jurisdiction, discipline, and confessional statements of a local church. See, e.g., Isaac Foster, *A Defense of Religious Liberty* (1780) (a 192-page tract arguing for exemptions from compliance with the imposition of a new confession, the Saybrook Platform, in a local church).

21. Henry Cumings, *A Sermon Preached at Billerica* (1797), 12–13.

22. John Locke had made this point in his *Letter on Toleration* (1689): "But some may ask: 'What if the magistrate should enjoin anything by his authority that appears unlawful to the conscience of a private person?' I answer that, if government be faithfully administered and the counsels of the government be indeed directed to the public good, this will seldom happen." Locke, *The Works of John Locke*, 12th ed., 9 vols. (1824), 5:43–46.

23. Letter to the Religious Society Called Quakers, October, 1789, in Washington, *Writings,* 30:416; see also *George Washington on Religious Liberty and Mutual Understanding: Selections from Washington's Letters,* ed. Edward F. Humphrey (1932).

24. Letter to Thomas Jefferson (October 17, 1788), in Madison, *Writings,* 5:272; and in *Letters of Delegates to Congress, 1774–1789,* ed. Paul H. Smith, 26 vols. (1976), 25:428.

25. See a careful critical sifting of recent arguments in Douglas Laycock, "Regulatory Exemptions of Religious Behavior and the Original Understanding of the Establishment Clause," *Notre Dame Law Review* 81 (2006): 1793–1842.

26. Delaware Declaration of Rights (1776), sec. 2.

27. Pennsylvania Declaration of Rights (1776), II, VIII.

28. Constitution of New Jersey (1776), Art. XVIII.

29. Constitution of New York (1777), Art. XXXVIII.

30. Joseph Story, *Commentaries on the Constitution* (Boston, 1833), 3:703.

31. See Appendix 1 for each of these draft versions.

32. Luther Martin put it crisply: "The declaration, that religious faith shall be unpunished, does not give impunity to criminal acts, dictated by religious error." *Federal Gazette & Baltimore Daily Advertiser,* March 19, 1799, 2.

33. Schwarz, "Der Begriff Exercitium Religionis Privatum," 502ff.

34. William Penn, *The Great Case of Liberty of Conscience* (1670), in *The Political Writings of William Penn,* ed. Andrew R. Murphy (2002), 79, 81–82.

35. Madison, "Memorial and Remonstrance," para. 1; Levi Hart, *Liberty Described and Recommended* (1775), 14–15.

36. Virginia Bill of Rights, Art. 16.

37. Elliot, ed., *Debates,* 1:328.

38. Letter to the General Assembly of the Presbyterian Church (May 1789), in *The Papers of George Washington,* ed. W. W. Abbot et al. (1987), 2:420

39. Quoted by Thomas A. Lambert, *The Founding Fathers and the Place of Religion in America* (2003), 189.

40. Williams, *Essential Rights and Liberties,* 46ff.; *Isaac Backus on Church, State, and Calvinism,* 348ff.; Parsons, *Freedom from Civil and Ecclesiastical Slavery,* 14–15; Stiles, *The United States Elevated,* 55ff.; Amos Adams, *Religious Liberty,* 38–46.

41. Hart, *Liberty Described and Recommended,* 14; *Backus on Church, State, and Calvinism,* 348–349; "A Declaration of Certain Fundamental Rights and Liberties of the Protestant Episcopal Church in Maryland," quoted by Anson P. Stokes, *Church and States in the United States,* 3 vols. (New York, 1950), 1:741.

42. Virginia Declaration of Rights (1776), Sec. 16.

43. Constitution of Georgia (1777), Art. LVI.

44. *Backus on Church, State, and Calvinism,* 317; *The Freeman's Remonstrance Against an Ecclesiastical Establishment* (1777), 13.

45. Isaac Backus, *Truth Is Great and Will Prevail* (1781); John R. Bolles, *A Brief Account of Persecutions, in Boston and Connecticut Governments* (1758), 47, 59. See also *George Washington on Religious Liberty,* 12.

46. Debates of June 12, 1788, in Elliot, ed., *Debates,* 3:330.

47. Thomas Jefferson, "Notes on the State of Virginia, Query 17," in *The Complete Jefferson*, ed. Saul K. Padover (1969), 673–676; Stiles, *The United States Elevated*, 55–56; Thomas Paine, *Common Sense and the Crisis* (1960 [1776]), 50.

48. Letter to Thomas Jefferson, June 25, 1813, in *The Adams-Jefferson Letters*, ed. Lester J. Cappon, 2 vols. (1959), 333, 334.

49. Adams, *Works*, 6:474.

50. Intervention on June 10, 1788, in Elliot, ed., *Debates*, 3:204.

51. Letter to Abigail Adams (October 29, 1775), quoted by John R. Howe Jr., *The Changing Political Thought of John Adams* (1966), 156–157 (capitalization modernized).

52. Letter to John Armstrong (March 19, 1793), in *The Founders' Constitution*, 5:78.

53. Hyneman and Lutz, eds., *American Political Writing*, 1:38–39.

54. *The Federalist Papers: Alexander Hamilton, James Madison, John Jay*, ed. Clinton Rossiter (New York, 1961), 84.

55. Ibid., 324.

56. Madison, "Memorial and Remonstrance," paras. 4, 8.

57. Letter to Dr. Price, April 8, 1785, in Adams, *Works*, 8:232; Frank Donovan, ed., *The John Adams Papers* (New York, 1965), 181.

58. *Backus on Church, State, and Calvinism*, 333.

59. Phillips Payson, "Election Sermon of 1778," in Hynemann and Lutz, eds., *American Political Writing*, 1:523, 529. See also Jaspar Adams, *Elements of Moral Philosophy* (1837), 190ff. on the importance of oaths to institute political integrity and trustworthiness.

60. Delaware Constitution (1776), Art. XXII (outlawed by a 1792 amendment).

61. Speech of Isaac Backus (February 4, 1788), in Elliot, ed., *Debates*, 2:148; see also *The Founders' Constitution*, 4:633ff.

62. Petition of the Philadelphia Synagogue to the Council of Censors of Philadelphia (December 23, 1783), in Kurland and Lerner, eds., *The Founders' Constitution*, 4:635; "Jonas Phillips to the President and Members of the Convention (September 7, 1789)," in *The Records of the Federal Convention of 1787*, ed. Max Farrand, 3 vols. (1911), 3:78–79.

63. Speech of July 30, 1788, in Elliot, ed., *Debates*, 4:191–192.

64. Speech of July 30, 1788, in Elliot, ed., *Debates*, 3:204. See also Speech of Governor Randolph, 3:207.

65. Speech of July 30, 1788 in Elliot, ed., *Debates*, 4:208.

66. Intervention by Mr. Dawes (January 30, 1788), in *The Massachusetts Sentinel*, February 20, 1788, 179.

67. "A Landholder VII," *Connecticut Courant*, December 17, 1787, in *The Documentary History of the Ratification of the Constitution*, ed. Merrill Jensen, 27 vols. (1978–), 3:497–498. See also Zachariah Johnston of Virginia (June 25, 1788): "the exclusion of tests willl strongly tend to establish religious freedom." Bernard Bailyn, ed., *The Debate on the Constitution: Federalist and Anti-Federalist Speeches, Articles, and Letters During the Struggle over Ratification* (1993), 2:752.

68. Chester J. Antieau, Philip M. Carroll, and Thomas Carroll Burke, *Religion Under the State Constitutions* (1965), 101–107.

69. Luther Martin, *The Genuine Information* (1787), in Farrand, ed., *Records of the Federal Convention*, 3:227.

70. Madison, "Memorial and Remonstrance," para. 4.

71. Jefferson, "Notes on the State of Virginia," Query 17.

72. Constitution of New Jersey (1776), Art. XIX.

73. Delaware Declaration of Rights (1776), Sec. 3.

74. Maryland Declaration of Rights (1776), Sec. 33.

75. Virginia Declaration of Rights (1776), Art. 16.

76. Constitution of New York (1777), Art. XXXVIII.

77. Constitution of Massachusetts (1780), Part I, Art. 3, as amended by Art. XI.

78. See drafts in Appendix 1.

79. Martin Luther, *To the Christian Nobility of the German Nation* (1520), in *Three Treatises*, 2d rev. ed. (1986), 12, 16.

80. John Calvin, *Institutes of the Christian Religion* (1559), bk. 3., chap. 19.15; bk. 4., chap. 11.3; bk. 4, chap. 20.1–2.

81. John Milton, *Areopagatica and Other Political Writings of John Milton*, ed. John Alvis (1999), 111–112, 406–407; Milton, *Complete Prose Works of John Milton*, 7 vols., gen. ed. Don M. Wolfe (1953–1980), 1:476, 554, 6:798–799, 7:253–255, 262–268.

82. *The Complete Writings of Menno Simons, c. 1496–1561,* trans. L. Verduin, ed. J. C. Wenger (1984), 29, 117–120, 158–159, 190–206; *Biblical Concordance of the Swiss Brethren, 1540,* ed. C. A. Synder, trans. G. Fast and G. A. Peters (2001), 56–60.

83. *The Freeman's Remonstrance,* 5–8, 12. The metaphor is drawn from the recurrent biblical image of the marriage between Christ and the Church, Yahweh and the elect nation of Israel. See esp. Eph. 5:25–33.

84. See above pp. 26–27 and Daniel L. Dreisbach, *Thomas Jefferson and the Wall of Separation Between Church and State* (2002), 83–94; Philip Hamburger, *Separation of Church and State,* (2002), 55.

85. Locke, *Works,* 5:21.

86. Dreisbach, *Thomas Jefferson,* 79–82.

87. James Burgh, *Crito, or Essays on Various Subjects* (1767), 2:117–119 (emphasis removed).

88. Condorcet's notes on Voltaire, in *Oeuvres Completes de Voltaire,* 70 vols. (1784), 18:476; translated in Hamburger, *Separation of Church and State,* 60.

89. Williams, *Essential Rights and Liberties,* 46.

90. "To the Baptist Churches Belonging to the Philadelphia Association," in *Ratification of the Constitution by the States,* ed. John P. Kaminski et al. (2003), 19:332.

91. Tunis Wortman, *A Solemn Address to Christians and Patriots* (1800), in Sandoz, ed., *Political Sermons,* 1477, 1482, 1487–1488.

92. Ibid.

93. Ibid.

94. *Cato's Letters,* 2:469.

95. In Adams, *Works,* 3:447.

96. Quoted by Hamburger, *Separation of Church and State,* 81; see also New York Constitution, Arts. XXXVIII–XXXIX.

97. See John Witte, Jr., "'A Most Mild and Equitable Establishment of Religion': John Adams and the Massachusetts Experiment," *Journal of Church and State* 41 (1999): 213, 242ff.; Hamburger, *Separation of Church and State,* 79–88.

98. Letter to Jeremiah Moor (August 4, 1800), in *The Works of Thomas Jefferson*, ed. P. L. Ford, 12 vols. (1904–1905), 9:143. The Supreme Court used this same argument to outlaw a Tennessee constitutional prohibition on ministers serving in political office. See *McDaniel v. Paty*, 435 U.S. 618 (1978).

99. South Carolina Constitution, Art. XXI. See also New York Constitution, Arts. XXXVIII-XXXIX (1777); Delaware Constitution, Art. XXIX (1776), Maryland Constitution, Art. XXXVII (1776), North Carolina Constitution, Art. XXXI (1776). Among later constitutions, see Tennessee Constitution, Art. 8 (1796), struck down in *McDaniel v. Paty*, 436 U.S. 618 (1978).

100. See, e.g., *The Political Writings of William Penn*, 101, 112; James H. Hutson, *Forgotten Features of the Founding: The Recovery of Religious Themes in the Early American Republic* (2003), 133–153; Brian Tierney, "Religious Rights: A Historical Perspective," *Religious Human Rights: Religious Perspectives*, 38ff.

101. Williams, *Essential Rights and Liberties*, 7–8.

102. Charles James, ed., *Documentary History of Struggle for Religious Liberty in Virginia* (1971), 237–238.

103. Madison, "Memorial and Remonstrance," para. 2.

104. *The Writings of Thomas Jefferson*, ed. H. Washington, 9 vols. (1853–1854), 8:113 (emphasis added). The Washington edition of the letter inaccurately transcribes "legitimate" as "legislative." See a more accurate transcription in Dreisbach, *Thomas Jefferson*, 148.

105. Ibid.

106. Ibid., 25–54.

107. Quoted in Dreisbach, *Thomas Jefferson*, 152.

108. Ibid., 25–54, 129–33. See further below, pp. 92–95

109. Lambert, *The Founding Fathers*, 207–235.

110. Hamburger, *Separation of Church and State*, 244–247, 262–267, 305–308, 355–357, 391–399, 414–417, 445–446.

111. South Carolina Constitution (1778), Art. XXXVIII; see also Georgia's 1785 bill, "For the Regular Establishment and Support of the Public Duties of Religion," in *The Colonial Records of the State of Georgia*, ed. Allen D. Candler (1907), 19:395.

112. See Donald Drakeman, *Church, State, and Original Intent* (2010).

113. See entries under "establish" and "establishment" in John Andrews, *A Complete Dictionary of the English Language*, 4th ed. (1789); John Ash, *A New and Complete Dictionary of the English Language* (1775); Samuel Johnson, *A Dictionary of the English Language*, 4th ed. (1773); William Perry, *The Royal Standard English Dictionary*, 1st Am. ed. (1788); Thomas Sheridan, *A Complete Dictionary of the English Language*, 2d ed. (1789).

114. See T. Jeremy Gunn, *A Standard for Repair: The Establishment Clause, Equality, and Natural Rights* (1992), 46–47, 71–73.

115. Delaware Declaration of Rights (1776), sec. 3; Pennsylvania Declaration of Rights (1776), II.

116. Letter to the London Packet (June 3, 1772), in *The Papers of Benjamin Franklin*, ed. William B. Wilcox, 39 vols. (1976), 19:163–168, and in Kurland and Lerner, eds., *Founders' Constitution*, 5:58–60. Montesquieu had written similarly: "It is a principle that every religion which is persecuted itself becomes persecuting; for as soon as by some accidental turn it arises

from persecution, it attacks the religion which persecuted it; not as religion, but as tyranny." *Spirit of the Laws* (1748), bk. 12, chap. 9.

117. Thomas Paine, *Rights of Man* (1791), in *The Founders' Constitution*, 5:95–96.

118. For Edmund Randolph, see Elliot, ed., *Debates*, 3:208; 3:431. For Madison, see Elliot, ed., *Debates*, 3:330; for Zachariah Johnson, see 3:645–646.

119. Quoted in Chester J. Antieau, Arthur T. Downey, and Edward C. Roberts, *Freedom from Federal Establishment: Formation and Early History of the First Amendment Religion Clauses* (1964), 106.

120. New Jersey Constitution (1776), Art. XIX.

121. Elliot, ed., *Debates*, 1:328, 334.

122. See Appendix 1.

123. Thomas Jefferson, Letter to Rev. Samuel Miller (1808), in Kurland and Lerner, eds., *The Founders' Constitution*, 5:98–99.

124. Madison, "Memorial and Remonstrance," para. 5.

125. Letter to Robert Walsh (March 2, 1819), in Madison, *Writings,* 8:430–432 (spelling and punctuation modernized).

126. See Antieau et al., *Freedom from Federal Establishment*, 1–92; Michael W. McConnell, "Establishment and Disestablishment at the Founding," *William and Mary Law Review* 44 (2003): 2105–2181.

127. See Hutson, *Forgotten Features*, 111: "The white population of the United States 1790 has been estimated at 3,173,000. Of this, a thousand or so were Jews who lived in cities along the Atlantic seaboard. Muslims, Hindus, and Buddhists, could be counted on the fingers of one hand." Citing Henry Gemery, "The White Population of the Colonial United States," in Michael R. Haines and Richard H. Steckel, eds., *A Population History of North America* (2000), 150.

128. See, e.g., Delaware Declaration of Rights (1776), sec. 3; Constitution of Maryland, Declaration of Rights, XXXIII (1776); Constitution of South Carolina (1778), XXXVIII.

129. Declaration of Rights, XXXIII. This was outlawed by amendment, Art. XIII (1810). See Francis N. Thorpe, ed., *The Federal and State Constitutions*, 7 vols. (1909), 3:1189, 1705.

130. Letter to Edward Everett (March 19, 1823), in Madison, *Writings,* 9:126–127 (spelling and punctuation modernized). See comparable views in Madison's Letter to Edward Livingston (July 10, 1822), in Madison, *Writings,* 9:101–102.

131. Thomas Jefferson, "Freedom of Religion at the University of Virginia (Oct. 7, 1822)," in Padover, ed., *The Complete Jefferson,* 958.

4

Forging the First Amendment
Religion Clauses

Four views drove much of the early American experiment in religious liberty—
Puritan, Evangelical, Enlightenment, and Republican. Six principles of religious
liberty were held in common among them—liberty of conscience, free exercise of
religion, religious pluralism, religious equality, separation of church and state, and
disestablishment of a national religion. The First Amendment religion clauses, we
contend, can be rightly understood only in the context of this plurality of opinions
and panoply of principles.

In an effort to come to terms with the range of views on religious liberty in the
founding era, the two previous chapters touched on speeches and acts made in the
Continental Congress of 1774–1789, the Constitutional Convention of 1787, and
the First Congress of 1789. This chapter examines more carefully the work of these
federal bodies up to the final formulation of the First Amendment religion clauses
on September 26, 1789. The federal record in this early period is rather spare. We
quote extensively from what is said in the earliest federal records about religion and
religious liberty, look carefully at the various drafts of the religion clauses that were
proposed by the states and debated by the First Congress in 1788 and 1789, and
then sketch the range of plausible meanings that can be assigned to the final text of
the First Amendment: "Congress shall make no law respecting an establishment
of religion, or prohibiting the free exercise thereof."

Religion and the Continental Congress

The Continental Congress, comprised of delegates from the colonies, met for the
first time on September 5, 1774, to respond to the increasingly harsh economic
measures imposed by Great Britain.[1] Its second session, commencing on May 10,
1775, was devoted to coordinating the revolutionary war against Great Britain. It
was during this session that the Congress began to emerge in a new role—as the
provisional federal government of a budding nation, a status later confirmed by the

Articles of Confederation (1781) and continued (albeit with decreasing effectiveness) until 1789. The principal mandate of the Continental Congress was to deal with pressing military issues, interstate relationships, national commerce, foreign diplomacy, and the like. But in the course of its work from 1774 to 1789, it also issued a number of acts touching religion.

On the second day of its first session, September 6, 1774, the Continental Congress resolved to open its daily sessions with prayer. An Anglican priest began offering these prayers the next morning, along with Bible reading. He was, according to one representative, "a Gentleman of Sense and Piety, and a warm Advocate for the religious and civil Rights of America."[2] During the second session, on December 21, 1776, the Congress appointed two legislative chaplains, an Anglican priest and a Presbyterian pastor, who served until 1784, when replaced by two other chaplains appointed by the Congress.[3]

On July 29, 1775, the Congress created the Chaplain Corps of the Continental Army, and appointed and paid chaplains to serve in it. Both as general and as first president, George Washington was a firm supporter of these military chaplains, and issued several calls for Congress to increase the number of chaplains that served and sent out several orders for military personnel to make ample use of these chaplains' services.[4]

In the summer of 1775, the Continental Congress vetted the "Plan of Accommodation with the Parent State," a proposed negotiated compromise with Great Britain. It included a provision that, "No earthly legislature or tribunal ought or can of Right interfere or interpose in any wise howsoever in the religion and ecclesiastical concerns of the colonies." This "foolish religious business," as Gouverneur Morris described it, got nowhere.

> As the Inhabitants of the Continent are happily united in a political Creed, we are of Opinion that it would be highly imprudent to run the Risque of dividing them by the Introduction of Disputes foreign to the Controversy; especially as the Discussion of them can be attended with no one single advantage. They are Points about which Mankind will forever differ and therefore should always, and at least in Times like these be kept out of Sight. We are the more confirmed in these Sentiments by this circumstance, that both this and the former Congress have cautiously avoided the least Hint on Subjects of this Kind, all the members concurring in a Desire of burying all Disputes on ecclesiastical Points, which have for ages had no other Tendency than that of banishing Peace and Charity from the World.[5]

Despite Morris's warning against congressional involvement in "religious business," on June 12, 1775, the Congress issued the first of its four fast-day proclamations, urging a "day of publick humiliation, fasting, and prayer; that we may, with united hearts and voices, unfeignedly confess and deplore our many sins"; that we may "be ever under the care and protection of a kind Providence, and be prospered"; and "that virtue and true religion may revive and flourish throughout our land."[6] On November 1, 1777, the Congress issued the first of what would become annual Thanksgiving Day proclamations. This first proclamation was an overtly Trinitarian Christian statement, providing that "it is the indispensable Duty of all men to adore the superintending Providence of Almighty God; to acknowledge with Gratitude their Obligation to him for Benefits received, and to implore such farther Blessings as they stand in need of." The proclamation set aside a day each year of "solemn thanksgiving and praise":

> That at one Time and with one Voice, the good People may express the grateful Feelings of their Hearts, and consecrate themselves to the Service of their Divine Benefactor; and that, together with their sincere Acknowledgements and Offerings, they may join the penitent Confession of their manifold Sins, whereby they had forfeited every Favour; and their humble and earnest Supplication that it may please God through the Merits of Jesus Christ, mercifully to forgive and blot them out of Remembrance: That it may please him graciously to afford his Blessing on the Governments of these States respectively, and prosper the public Council of the whole: To inspire our Commanders, both by Land and Sea, and all under them, with that Wisdom and Fortitude which may render them fit instruments, under the Providence of Almighty God, to secure for these United States, the greatest of all human Blessings, Independence and Peace: That it may please him, to prosper the Trade and Manufactures of the People, and the Labour of the Husbandman, that our Land may yield its Increase: To take Schools and Seminaries of Education, so necessary for cultivating the Principles of true Liberty, Virtue and Piety, under his nurturing Hand; and to prosper the Means of Religion, for the promotion and enlargement of that Kingdom, which consisteth "in Righteousness, Peace, and Joy, in the Holy Ghost."[7]

Beyond issuing prayers, the Continental Congress took further steps to cultivate the moral and religious sentiments of the budding nation. In 1774, for example, Congress resolved to "encourage frugality, economy, and industry, and . . . discountenance and discourage every species of extravagance and dissipation, especially all horse-racing, and all kinds of gaming, cockfighting, exhibition of shews, plays, and other expensive diversions and entertainments."[8]

During the Revolutionary War against Great Britain, the Continental Congress passed a resolution to protect the conscientious objections of pacifists to participation in war. Various religious groups in the colonies—especially Quakers, Mennonites, Shakers, and Brethren—had professed pacifist scruples. The Congress accommodated them in a resolution of 1775 and urged them to assume noncombat duties instead: "As there are some people, who from religious principles, cannot bear arms in any case, this Congress intends no violence to their consciences, but earnestly recommend it to them, to contribute liberally in this time of universal calamity, to the relief of their distressed brethren, in the several colonies, and do all other services to their oppressed Country, which they can consistently [do] with their religious principles."[9]

The Continental Congress expressed frequent concern about their Catholic neighbors to the north in Quebec. Initially their views were hostile. In 1763, after the British-French war, Quebec had become a British colony. In the Quebec Act of 1774, the British Parliament had guaranteed to these new subjects "free exercise of the religion of the Church of Rome, subject to the king's Supremacy."[10] The Congress denounced this act as tantamount to "establishing the Roman Catholick religion" in a manner which is "dangerous in an extreme degree to the Protestant religion and to the civil rights and liberties of all America." It expressed "astonishment that a British Parliament should ever consent to *establish* in that country a religion that has deluged your island in blood, and dispersed impiety, bigotry, persecution, murder and rebellion through every part of the world." All such acts "are impolitic, unjust, and cruel, as well unconstitutional, and most dangerous and destructive of American rights."[11] If this new religious establishment in Quebec comes subject to "the designs of an ambitious and wicked minister," Alexander Hamilton declared breathlessly, "we may see an Inquisition erected in Canada, and priestly tyranny hereafter find as propitious a soil in America as it ever has in Spain or Portugal."[12] It is hard to read from the historical record whether this anti-Catholic tirade was genuine religious sentiment or only political concern about America's vulnerability to its strong Catholic neighbors in the French north and the Spanish south.

During the Revolutionary War with Britain, however, the Congress abruptly reversed its sentiments about its French Catholic neighbors, now for obvious political reasons. Congress sent two letters to their counterparts in Quebec. They urged them to cede from the British and join the American cause, enticing them with guarantees of religious freedom. To press their case, Congress also sent a distinguished delegation to the north with this instruction:

> You are further to declare that we hold sacred the rights of conscience and may promise to the whole people, solemnly in our name, the free and undisturbed exercise of their religion; and, to the clergy, the full, perfect, and peaceable possession and enjoyment of all their estates. That the government of everything relating to their religion and clergy, shall be left entirely in the hands of the good people of that province and such legislature as they shall constitute: provided, however, that all other denominations of Christians be equally entitled to hold offices and enjoy civil privileges and the free exercise of their religion and be totally exempt from the payment of any tythes or taxes for the support of any religion.[13]

Also during the revolutionary war, the Congress sought to encourage defection of German mercenaries who were fighting for Great Britain. It offered would-be defectors guarantees of liberty, security, and property. It also ordered all states to receive these soldiers, and ensure that they "be protected in the free exercise of their respective religions."[14]

On September 11, 1777, a narrow majority of the Congress voted to import 20,000 Bibles for distribution in the new states but did not follow through, largely due to a lack of funding. Instead, the Congress resolved tepidly on October 26,

1780: "That it be recommended to such of the States who may think it convenient for them that they take proper measures to procure one or more new and correct editions of the Old and New Testament to be printed and thus such states regulate their printers by law so as to secure effectively the said books from being misprinted."[15] Thereafter, the Congress also endorsed a privately funded translation of the Bible, directed the legislative and military chaplains to make use of it, and recommended "this edition of the Bible to the inhabitants of the United States."[16]

On November 15, 1778, the Congress approved the Articles of Confederation, which came into effect in 1781. A prior draft of the Articles, prepared principally by John Dickinson, had included a rather lengthy provision on religious liberty designed to bind the individual colonies and states:

> No person in any Colony living peaceably under the Civil Government, shall be molested or prejudiced in his or her person or Estate for his or her religious persuasion, Profession or practice, nor be compelled to frequent or maintain any religious Worship, Place of Worship, or Ministry, contrary to his or her Mind, by any Law or ordinance hereafter to be made in any Colony different from the usual Laws & Customs subsisting at the Commencement of this War—provided, that such person frequent regularly some place of religious Worship on the Sabbath; & no religious Persuasion or practise for the Profession or Exercise of which, persons are not disqualified by the present Laws of the said Colonies respectively, from holding any offices Civil or military, shall by any Law or Ordinance hereafter to be made in any Colony, be rendered a Disqualification of any persons profession or exercising the same from holding such offices, as fully as they might have done heretofore: nor shall any further Tests or Qualifications concerning religious persuasion, Profession or Practise, than such have been usually administered in the said Colonies respectively, be imposed by any Law or Ordinance hereafter to be made in any Colony; and whenever on Election or Appointment to any Offices, or any other occasions, the Affirmation of persons conscientiously scrupulous of taking an Oath, hath been admitted in any Colony or Colonies, no Oath shall in any such Cases be hereafter imposed by any Law or Ordinance in any such Colony or Colonies, it being the full Intent of these united Colonies that all the Inhabitants thereof respectively of every Sect, Society, or religious Denomination shall enjoy under this Confederation, all the Liberties and Priviledges [sic] which they have heretofore enjoyed with the least abridgement of their civil Rights for or on Account of their religious Persuasion, profession or practise.[17]

Had this article been enacted, it would have been a remarkable step on the path toward creating a national law on religious liberty. The Congress, however, rejected this article as too intrusive on local regulation of religion. The final Article III, much more cryptically, simply bound the states to "assist each other, against all force offered to, or attacks made upon them, or any of them, on account of religion."[18]

Four treaties adopted by the Congress included religious liberty clauses. The treaty with the Netherlands (1782) provided that "[t]here shall be an entire and perfect liberty of conscience allowed to the subjects and inhabitants of each party, and to their families, and no one shall be molested in regard to his worship, provided he submits, as to the public demonstration of it, to the laws of the country."[19] The language reappeared almost verbatim in a treaty with Sweden (1783). A 1785 treaty with Prussia provided: "The most perfect freedom of conscience and of worship is granted to the citizens or subjects of either party within the jurisdiction of the other, without being liable to molestation in that respect for any cause other than an insult on the religion of others."[20] The final peace treaty with England (1783) was also made "[i]n the name of the Most Holy and Undivided Trinity."[21]

The 1787 Northwest Ordinance, establishing a new territorial government for the midwestern frontier, set forth various "fundamental principles of civil and religious liberty," including: "No person, demeaning himself in a peaceable and orderly manner, shall ever be molested on account of his mode of worship, or religious sentiments"; and "Religion, morality and knowledge, being necessary to good government and the happiness of mankind, schools and the means of education shall forever be encouraged."[22]

The record of the Continental Congress includes other scattered acknowledgments and endorsements of public worship, Christian thanksgiving, Sunday observance, and confession of sin. The record is also amply peppered with genial references to and invocations of God and Christianity. The most famous of these divine invocations was the Declaration of Independence of 1776, with its references to "the Laws of Nature and Nature's God," "the Creator," "the Supreme Judge of the world," and "a firm reliance on the protection of Divine Providence."[23]

The 1787 Constitutional Convention

The United States Constitution—debated and drafted by the Constitutional Convention from May 25 to September 17, 1787—is largely silent on questions of religion and religious freedom. The preamble to the Constitution speaks generically of the "Blessings of Liberty." Article I, section 7 recognizes the Christian Sabbath: "If any Bill should not be returned by the President within ten days (Sundays excepted) after it shall have been presented to him, the Same shall be a Law." Article VI provides "no religious Test shall ever be required as a Qualification to any Office or public Trust under the United States." A reference to "the Year of our Lord" sneaks into the dating of the instrument. But nothing more. The "Godless Constitution" has been both celebrated and lamented ever since.[24]

The seeming impiety of the work of the 1787 Constitutional Convention must be understood in political context. It was commonly assumed at the convention that questions of religion and of religious liberty were for the states and the people to resolve, not the budding federal government. By 1784, eleven of the thirteen states had already crafted detailed constitutional provisions on religious liberty. The two remaining states, Rhode Island and Connecticut, had retained their colonial charters, which included religious liberty clauses. The mandate of the 1787 convention was to create a new national sovereign with enumerated powers and delineated procedures. Whatever was not specifically given to this new federal sovereign was to be retained by the sovereign states and the sovereign people.

Federal power over religion was not considered part of this new constitutional calculus. As James Madison put it to the Virginia ratification convention: "There is not a shadow of right in the general government to intermeddle with religion. Its least interference with it, would be a most flagrant usurpation."[25] James Iredell concurred in the North Carolina ratification convention, arguing that the federal branches of government "certainly have no authority to interfere in the establishment of any religion whatsoever, and I am astonished that any gentleman should conceive they have."[26]

Federal protection of religion was also considered beyond the mandate of the 1787 convention. Both the natural checks and balances inherent in the nation's religious pluralism and the new religious liberty provisions of the state constitutions were considered to be ample protection.[27] For the emerging federal constitution to guarantee religious and civil rights was viewed to be unnecessary, if not dangerous. James Wilson put the case famously in the Pennsylvania ratification convention:

> [A] bill of rights is neither an essential nor a necessary instrument in framing a system of government, since liberty may exist and be as well secured without it. But it was not only unnecessary, but on this occasion it was found impracticable—for who will be bold enough to undertake to enumerate all the rights of the people?—and when the attempt to enumerate them is made, it must be remembered that if the enumeration is not complete, everything not expressly mentioned will be presumed to be purposely omitted.[28]

Alexander Hamilton warned further in *Federalist* 84 that to specify federal rights was "not only unnecessary in the proposed Constitution, but would even be dangerous. They would contain various exceptions to powers not granted; and, on this very account, would afford a colorable pretext to claim more than was granted. For why declare that things shall not be done which there is no power to do?"[29]

Accordingly, the three weak attempts to introduce federal protections of religion and religious liberty into the new constitution were quickly quashed. Early in the convention debates, on May 29, 1787, Charles Pinckney of South Carolina submitted to the convention a draft constitution, which included a religion clause: "The Legislature of the United States shall pass no Law on the subject of Religion."[30] Although many of Pinckney's proposed provisions (including against religious oaths) helped shape the debates and the final form of the Constitution, his religious liberty clause was passed over without comment and evidently died silently. On September 12, five days before the conclusion of the convention, George Mason and Elbridge Gerry moved to designate a committee to attach a bill of rights to the largely completed Constitution. The motion failed, 10–0.[31] On September 14, James Madison and Charles Pinckney sought to ascribe to Congress a power "to establish an University, in which no preferences or distinctions should be allowed on account of religion."[32] The motion failed, 6–4.

Even Benjamin Franklin's motion to have the convention sessions open with prayer garnered virtually no support. On June 28, the elderly Franklin, exasperated by the casuistic debates in the convention to date, had issued a short sermon to his fellow delegates on the importance of prayer:

> [W]e have not hitherto once thought of humbly applying to the Father of lights to il-luminate our understandings. In the beginning of the Contest with G. Britain, when we were sensible of danger we had daily prayer in this room for the divine protec-tion. . . . And have we now forgotten that powerful friend? or do we imagine that we no longer need his assistance? I have lived, Sir, a long time, and the longer I live, the more convincing proofs I see of this truth—*that God governs in the affairs of men.* And if a sparrow cannot fall to the ground without his notice, is it probable that an empire can rise without his aid? We have been assured, Sir, in the sacred writings, that "except the Lord build the House they labour in vain that build it." I firmly believe this; and I also believe that without his concurring aid we shall succeed in this political building no better than the Builders of Babel: We shall be divided by our little partial local in-terests; our projects will be confounded, and we ourselves shall become a reproach and bye word down to future ages. And what is worse, mankind may hereafter from this unfortunate instance, despair of establishing Governments by Human Wisdom and leave it to chance, war and conquest.
>
> I therefore beg leave to move—that henceforth prayers imploring the assistance of Heaven, and its blessings on our deliberations, be held in this Assembly every morning before we proceed to business, and that one or more of the Clergy of this City be re-quested to officiate in that service.

Franklin's motion failed, the record reads, for fear it might "1. bring on it some disagreeable animadversions. & 2. lead the public to believe that the embarrass-ments and dissentions within the convention, had suggested this measure." More-over, another delegate pointed out, there were no funds to pay a chaplain to pray.[33]

The only proposal about religion to receive support was Charles Pinckney's pro-posal that religion not be considered a condition for federal office. On August 20, Pinckney had proposed a freestanding provision in the Constitution prohibiting re-ligious tests or qualifications for federal office.[34] On August 30, he moved to amend a clause specifying the oath of office with the words that would eventually find their way into Article VI of the Constitution: "but no religious test shall ever be required as a qualification to any office or public trust under the authority of the U. States." Only one delegate objected to the motion—not because he favored religious test oaths but because he thought "it unnecessary, the prevailing liberality being a suf-ficient security against such tests." Pinckney's motion, however, was seconded and passed, with one dissent.[35]

During the ratification debates and thereafter, the no religious test provision of Article VI was sometimes denounced as an invitation to "Papists" and "Mahome-tans," and even "infidels" and "pagans," to hold federal office. It was defended, as we saw, on principles both of liberty of conscience and equality of faiths before the federal law.[36] But in the 1787 convention, the almost casual passage of the prohibition against religious tests for federal office was testimony to the commonality of the assumption that religion and religious liberty were beyond the pale of federal authority.

Ratification and Proposed Amendments

The Constitutional Convention completed its draft Constitution on September 17, 1787. The Continental Congress approved it by unanimous vote on September 28 and sent it to the states for ratification. Article VII of the proposed Constitution required ratification by the "Conventions of nine States." The Constitution was ratified on July 2, 1788, when the ninth vote, from the New Hampshire ratification convention, was recorded.[37]

In these state ratification debates, the absence of a bill of a rights to the Constitution, particularly the lack of a religious liberty guarantee, was a point of considerable controversy. Thomas Tredwell's reservations, stated in the 1788 New York ratification convention, were typical: "I could have wished also that sufficient caution had been used to secure to us our religious liberties, and to have prevented the general government from tyrannizing over our consciences by a religious establishment."[38] Despite repeated assurances from the federalists that Congress could not and would not exercise power over subjects like religion that were not specifically enumerated in the Constitution, only four states would ratify the instrument without a federal bill of rights. The remaining states ratified the Constitution only on the condition that the first session of Congress would prepare a bill of rights to amend the Constitution. These states discussed and proposed provisions to be included in a federal bill of rights, including various religious liberty clauses.[39] We shall format these proposals in boldface type and number them in the order of their appearance. Appendix 1 to this volume lists all these proposals in order.

In early December 1787 the Pennsylvania ratification convention repeatedly discussed a proposed amendment on religious liberty. A strong federalist, Benjamin Rush, thought the Constitution was not only fine as it stood, but even a miracle: "the hand of God was employed in this work, as that God had divided the Red Sea to give passage to the children of Israel, or had fulminated the Ten Commandments from Mount Sinai."[40] A strong anti-federalist, William Findley, however, pressed for a strong religious liberty amendment to the federal constitution. On December 15, 1787, he proposed:

[1] **The rights of conscience shall be held inviolable; and neither the legislative, executive, nor judicial powers of the United States, shall have authority to alter, abrogate, or infringe any part of the constitutions of the several States, which provide the preservation of liberty in matter of religion.**[41]

Though the Pennsylvania convention ultimately did not propose this draft to the First Congress, Findley himself, as an elected representative to the First Congress, evidently discussed this proposal with fellow representatives, though nothing survives of their discussion save Findley's own recollections.[42]

On February 6, 1788, a minority faction of the Massachusetts ratifying convention proposed the following amendment:

[2] [T]hat the said Constitution be never construed to authorize Congress to infringe the just liberty of the press, or the rights of conscience.[43]

On April 21, 1788, a minority group in the Maryland ratification convention proposed two religious liberty amendments, neither of which was ultimately recommended by the convention, though, again, these views were known to the First Congress.

[3] That no persons conscientiously scrupulous of bearing arms, in any case, shall be compelled personally to serve as a soldier.

[4] That there be no national religion established by law; but that all persons be equally entitled to protection in their religious liberty.[44]

A majority of the Maryland ratification convention accepted the recommendation of a third proposal that protected the rights of conscience in oath swearing:

[5] That all warrants, without oath, or affirmation of a person conscientiously scrupulous of taking an oath, to search suspected places, or to seize any person, or his property, are grievous and oppressive. . . .

On June 21, 1788, New Hampshire proposed the following religious liberty amendment:

[6] Congress shall make no laws touching religion, or to infringe the rights of conscience.[45]

On June 26, 1788, Virginia—stating its concern "that no right of any denomination" may be violated and "among other essential rights, the liberty of conscience, and of the press, cannot be cancelled, abridged, restrained, or modified, by any authority of the United States"—proposed the following amendments:

[7] All warrants . . . to search suspected places, or seize any freeman, his papers or property, without information upon Oath (or affirmation of a person religiously scrupulous of taking an oath) of legal and sufficient cause, are grievous and oppressive . . . and ought not to be granted.

[8] That religion, or the duty which we owe to our creator, and the manner of discharging it, can be directed only by reason and conviction, not by force or vi-

olence, and therefore all men have an equal, natural and unalienable right to the free exercise of religion according to the dictates of conscience, and that no particular religious sect or society ought to be favored or established by law in preference to others.[46]

On July 26, 1788, New York proposed:

[9] That the people have an equal, natural, and unalienable right freely and peaceably to exercise their religion, according to the dictates of conscience; and that no religious sect or society ought to be favored or established by law in preference to others.[47]

On August 1, 1788, North Carolina—after resolving to protect the "great principles of civil and religious liberty" and expressing its concern "that the general government may not make laws infringing their religious liberties"[48]—repeated the Virginia provision (with only cosmetic changes in punctuation), prefaced by a conscientious objection clause:

[10] That any person religiously scrupulous of bearing arms ought to be exempted, upon payment of an equivalent to employ another to bear arms in his stead.[49]

Rhode Island repeated in full North Carolina's language in its proposed amendment, belatedly tendered on June 16, 1790, after the Congress had already prepared the Bill of Rights and sent it to the states for ratification.[50]

Drafting the First Amendment Religion Clauses

It was up to the First Congress to cull from these proposals, and the broader perspectives that they represented, a suitable amendment on religious rights and liberties. The record of its effort is considerably slimmer than is apt for such a momentous act. Neither the House nor the Senate kept an official record of its proceedings in this first year. The Senate met in closed session and merely kept a journal of brief minutes of its resolutions. The House debates are better preserved, for they were sometimes open to visitors. Much of what appears in the *Annals of Congress* for the first session of 1789, though, is drawn from the inexactly taken and transcribed notes of newspaper reporter Thomas Lloyd.[51] These minutes and notes include several drafts of the religion clauses that were considered intermittently between June 8 and September 26, 1789. They also include summaries, paraphrases, or quotations of a few of the House debates on August 15, 17, and 20. But for the critical stages of deliberation in late August and September 1789, when these various drafts and speeches were pressed into the final text of the First Amendment, the record is cryptic and conclusory—leaving courts and commentators ever since with ample room for speculation and interpolation. In the pages below, we quote all the surviving data from these debates.

On June 8, 1789, James Madison, representing Virginia in the House, now took up the call to help prepare a bill of rights to the United States Constitution. He reduced the multiple state proposals for religious rights provisions into two religion clauses. These he put to the House for consideration:

[11] **The civil rights of none shall be abridged on account of religious belief or worship, nor shall any national religion be established, nor shall the full and equal rights of conscience be in any manner, or any pretext infringed.**

[12] **No state shall violate the equal rights of conscience, or the freedom of the press, or the trial by jury in criminal cases.**[52]

The House agreed to give formal consideration to Madison's proposals in due course. But debate was postponed for several weeks as Congress devoted itself to the immediate task of organizing the new government.[53]

On July 21, again prompted by Madison, the House finally turned to Madison's proposals and appointed a committee comprised of one representative of each of the eleven states represented in the First Congress.[54] Madison, representing Virginia, was included. This committee of eleven put forward its proposed rights provisions on July 28, including three separate provisions on religion:

[13] **no religion shall be established by law, nor shall the equal rights of conscience be infringed.**

[14] **no person religiously scrupulous shall be compelled to bear arms.**

[15] **no State shall infringe the equal rights of conscience, nor the freedom of speech or of the press, nor of the right of trial by jury in criminal cases.**

The committee's report was tabled without any recorded discussion. On August 13, the House, sitting as a committee of the whole, took up the report, one provision at a time.

On August 15, the House reached the first of the three committee provisions on religion: "no religion shall be established by law, nor shall the equal rights of conscience be infringed." The House ultimately approved an amended version of the same. The full record of this debate (concluding with a modified provision) reads thus:

Mr. SYLVESTER had some doubts of the propriety of the mode of expression used in this paragraph. He apprehended that it was liable to a construction different from what had been made by the committee. He feared it might be thought to have a tendency to abolish religion altogether.

Mr. VINING suggested the propriety of transposing the two members of the sentence.

Mr. GERRY said it would read better if it was, that no religious doctrine shall be established by law.

Mr. SHERMAN thought the amendment altogether unnecessary, inasmuch as Congress had no authority whatever delegated to them by the constitution to make religious establishments; he would, therefore, move to have it struck out.

Mr. [Daniel] CARROLL. As the rights of conscience are, in their nature, of peculiar delicacy, and will little bear the gentlest touch of governmental hand; and as many sects have concurred in opinion that they are not well secured under the present constitution, he said he was much in favor of adopting the words. He thought it would tend more towards conciliating the minds of the people to the Government than almost any other amendment he had heard proposed. He would not contend with gentlemen about the phraseology, his object was to secure the substance in such a manner as to satisfy the wishes of the honest part of the community.

Mr. MADISON said, he apprehended the meaning of the words to be, that Congress should not establish a religion, and enforce the legal observation of it by law, nor compel men to worship God in any manner contrary to their conscience. Whether the words are necessary or not, he did not mean to say, but they had been required by some of the State Conventions, who seemed to entertain an opinion that under the clause of the constitution, which gave power to Congress to make all laws necessary and proper to carry into execution the constitution, and the laws made under it, enabled them to make laws of such a nature as might infringe the rights of conscience, and establish a national religion; to prevent these effects he presumed the amendment was intended, and he thought it as well expressed as the nature of the language would admit.

Mr. HUNTINGTON said that he feared, with the gentleman first up on this subject, that the words might be taken in such latitude as to be extremely hurtful to the cause of religion. He understood the amendment to mean what had been expressed by the gentleman from Virginia; but others might find it convenient to put another construction upon it. The ministers of their congregations to the Eastward were maintained by the contributions of those who belonged to their society; the expense of building meetinghouses was contributed in the same manner. These things were regulated by by-laws. If an action was brought before a Federal Court on any of these cases, the person who had neglected to perform his engagements could not be compelled to do it; for a support of ministers, or building of places of worship might be construed into a religious establishment.

By the charter of Rhode Island, no religion could be established by law; he could give a history of the effects of such a regulation; indeed the people were now enjoying the blessed fruits of it. He hoped, therefore, the amendment would be made in such a way as to secure the rights of conscience, and a free exercise of the rights of religion, but not to patronize those who professed no religion at all.

Mr. MADISON thought, if the word national was inserted before religion, it would satisfy the minds of honorable gentlemen. He believed that the people feared one sect might obtain a pre-eminence, or two combine together, and establish a religion to which they would compel others to conform. He thought if the word national was introduced, it would point the amendment directly to the object it was intended to prevent.

Mr. LIVERMORE was not satisfied with that amendment; but he did not wish them to dwell long on the subject. He thought it would be better if it was altered, and made to read in this manner, that **[16] Congress shall make no laws touching religion, or infringing[55] the rights of conscience.**

Mr. GERRY did not like the term national, proposed by the gentleman from Virginia, and he hoped it would not be adopted by the House. It brought to his mind some observations that had taken place in the conventions at the time they were considering the present constitution. It had been insisted upon by those who were called antifederalists, that this form of Government consolidated the Union; the honorable gentleman's motion shows that he considers it in the same light. Those who were called antifederalists at that time complained that they had injustice done them by the title, because they were in favor of a Federal Government, and the others were in favor of a national one; the federalists were for ratifying the constitution as it stood, and the others not until amendments were made. Their names then ought not to have been distinguished by federalists and antifederalists, but rats and antirats.

Mr. MADISON withdrew his motion, but observed that the words "no national religion shall be established by law," did not imply that the Government was a national one; the question was then taken on Livermore's motion, and passed in the affirmative, thirty-one for, and twenty against it.[56]

On August 17, the House came to the second provision on religion in the committee report: "no person religiously scrupulous shall be compelled to bear arms." The record of their debate, which ended inconclusively, reads thus:

Mr. GERRY—This declaration of rights, I take it, is intended to secure the people against the mal-administration of the Government; if we could suppose that, in all cases, the rights of the people would be attended to, the occasion for guards of this kind would be removed. Now, I am apprehensive, sir, that this clause would give an opportunity to the people in power to destroy the constitution itself. They can declare who are those religiously scrupulous, and prevent them from bearing arms. . . . Now, if we give a discretionary power to exclude those from militia duty who have religious scruples, we may as well make no provision on this head. For this reason, he wished the words to be altered so as to be confined to persons belonging to a religious sect scrupulous of bearing arms.

Mr. JACKSON did not expect that all the people of the United States would turn Quakers or Moravians; consequently, one part would have to defend the other in case of invasion. Now this, in his opinion, was unjust, unless the constitution secured an equivalent: for this reason he moved to amend the clause, by inserting at the end of it, "upon paying an equivalent, to be established by law."

Mr. SMITH, of South Carolina, inquired what were the words used by the conventions respecting this amendment. If the gentleman would conform to what was proposed by Virginia and Carolina, he would second him. He thought they were to be excused provided they found a substitute.

Mr. JACKSON was willing to accommodate. He thought the expression was, "No one, religiously scrupulous of bearing arms, shall be compelled to render military service, in person, upon paying an equivalent."

Mr. SHERMAN conceived it difficult to modify the clause and make it better. It is well known that those who are religiously scrupulous of bearing arms are equally scrupulous of getting substitutes or paying an equivalent. Many of them would rather die than do either one or the other; but he did not see an absolute necessity for a clause of this kind. We do not live under an arbitrary Government, said he, and the States, respectively, will have the government of the militia, unless when called into actual service; besides, it would not do to alter it so as to exclude the whole of any sect, because there are men amongst the Quakers who will turn out, notwithstanding the religious principles of the society, and defend the cause of their country. Certainly it will be improper to prevent the exercise of such favorable dispositions, at least whilst it is the practice of nations to determine their contests by the slaughter of their citizens and subjects.

Mr. VINING hoped the clause would be suffered to remain as it stood, because he saw no use in it if it was amended so as to compel a man to find a substitute, which, with respect to the Government, was the same as if the person himself turned out to fight.

Mr. STONE inquired what the words "religiously scrupulous" had reference to: was it of bearing arms? If it was, it ought so to be expressed.

Mr. BENSON moved to have the words "but no person religiously scrupulous shall be compelled to bear arms," struck out. He would always leave it to the benevolence of the Legislature, for, modify it as you please, it will be impossible to express it in such a manner as to clear it from ambiguity. No man can claim this indulgence of right. It may be a religious persuasion, but it is no natural right, and therefore ought to be left to the discretion of the Government. If this stands part of the constitution, it will be a question before the Judiciary on every regulation you make with respect to the organization of the militia, whether it comports with this declaration or not. It is extremely injudicious to intermix matters of doubt with fundamentals.

I have no reason to believe but that the Legislature will always possess humanity enough to indulge this class of citizens in a matter they are so desirous of; but they ought to be left for their discretion.

The motion for striking out the whole clause being seconded, was put, and decided in the negative—22 members voting for it, and 24 against it.[57]

Later that same day of August 17, the House debated the third of the provisions recommended by the committee: "no State shall infringe the equal rights of conscience, nor the freedom of speech or of the press, nor of the right of trial by jury in criminal cases." It approved a slightly amended version:

Mr. TUCKER.—This is offered, I presume, as an amendment to the constitution of the United States, but it goes only to the alteration of the constitutions of particular States. It will be much better, I apprehend, to leave the State Governments to themselves, and not to interfere with them more than we already do; and that is thought by many to be rather too much. I therefore move, sir, to strike out these words.

Mr. MADISON conceived this to be the most valuable amendment in the whole list. If there was any reason to restrain the Government of the United States from infringing upon these essential rights, it was equally necessary that they should be secured against the State Governments. He thought that if they provided against the one, it was as necessary to provide against the other, and was satisfied that it would be equally grateful to the people.

Mr. LIVERMORE had no great objection to the sentiment, but he thought it not well expressed. He wished to make it an affirmative proposition; [17] **"the equal rights of conscience, the freedom of speech or of the press, and the right of trial by jury in criminal cases, shall not be infringed by any State."**

This transposition being agreed to, and Mr. TUCKER's motion being rejected, the clause was adopted.[58]

Up to this point, the House had considered its rights amendments as individual provisions to be inserted at appropriate places in the body of the Constitution. On August 20, the House agreed to consolidate these multiple rights provisions, including those on religion, into a more systematic and uniform "supplement" to the Constitution—a separate bill of rights.[59] The three provisions on religion discussed to date were distilled into two provisions. The record of the debate (on August 20) on these two provisions is quite brief:

> On motion of Mr. AMES, the fourth amendment was altered so as to read: **[18]** **"Congress shall make no law establishing religion, or to prevent the free exercise thereof, or to infringe the rights of conscience." This being adopted, the first proposition was agreed to.**

> Mr. SCOTT objected to the clause in the sixth amendment, "No person religiously scrupulous shall be compelled to bear arms." He observed that if this becomes part of the constitution, such persons can neither be called upon for their services, nor can an equivalent be demanded; it is also attended with still further difficulties, for a militia can never be depended upon. This would lead to the violation of another article in the constitution, which secures to the people the right of keeping arms, and in this case recourse must be had to a standing army. I conceive it, said he, to be a legislative right altogether. There are many sects I know, who are religiously scrupulous in this respect; I do not mean to deprive them of any indulgence the law affords; my design is to guard against those who are of no religion. It has been urged that religion is on the decline; if so, the argument is more strong in my favor, for when the time comes that religion shall be discarded, the generality of persons will have recourse to these pretexts to get excused from bearing arms.

> Mr. BOUDINOT thought the provision in the clause, or something similar to it, was necessary. Can any dependence, said he, be placed in men who are conscientious in this respect: or what justice can there be in compelling them to bear arms, when, according to their religious principles, they would rather die than use them? He adverted to several instances of oppression on this point that occurred during the war. In forming a militia, an effectual defence ought to be calculated, and no characters of this religious description ought to be compelled to take up arms. I hope that in establishing this Government, we may show the world that proper care is taken that the Government may not interfere with the religious sentiments of any person. Now, by striking out the clause, people may be led to believe that there is an intention in the General Government to compel all its citizens to bear arms.

> Some further desultory conversation arose, and it was agreed to insert the words "in person" to the end of the clause; after which it was adopted. (This yielded **[19] "No person religiously scrupulous shall be compelled to bear arms in person."**)[60]

On August 22, these two provisions on religion, along with other amendments, were referred to a House style committee.[61] Two days later, the committee issued its final report. It included the first religion provision, which had been introduced by

Fisher Ames on August 20, but in a slightly revised version. It omitted the second provision without explanation. This final House version, sent to the Senate on August 25, read thus:

[20] **Congress shall make no law establishing religion, or prohibiting the free exercise thereof, nor shall the rights of conscience be infringed.**[62]

On September 3, the Senate took up debate of this religion clause proposed by the House. No record of their debate survives. The *Journal of the Senate* reports that a motion to adopt the House provision on religion was defeated, as was a later motion to strike it.[63] The journal then reports that three alternative drafts of the religion clauses were proposed and defeated:

[21] **Congress shall make no law establishing One Religious Sect or Society in preference to others, nor shall the rights of conscience be infringed.**[64]

[22] **Congress shall not make any law, infringing the rights of conscience, or establishing any Religious Sect or Society.**[65]

[23] **Congress shall make no law establishing any particular denomination of religion in preference to another, or prohibiting the free exercise thereof, nor shall the rights of conscience be infringed.**[66]

Although none of these versions passed, the Senate did agree to a fourth proposal on September 3:

[24] **Congress shall make no law establishing religion, or prohibiting the free exercise thereof.**[67]

Agreement on this clause, however, was short-lived. On September 9, the Senate passed a rather different version of the religion clause, now combined with clauses on free speech, press, and assembly.

[25] **Congress shall make no law establishing articles of faith or a mode of worship, or prohibiting the free exercise of religion,** or abridging the freedom of speech, or the press, or the right of the people peaceably to assemble, and petition to the Government for the redress of grievances.[68]

That same day, September 9, the Senate sent this final version to the House for approval.

The House rejected this version. A joint committee composed of three representatives and three senators was appointed to forge a consensus draft. Representing the House were three members of the original committee of eleven that had prepared the draft religion clauses of July 28—Madison; Roger Sherman, a Puritan from Connecticut; and John Vining, a Republican from Delaware. Representing the Senate were Oliver Ellsworth, a Republican from Connecticut; William Patterson, an Evangelical from New Jersey; and Charles Carroll, a Catholic from Maryland. No record of their debate survives.

On September 24, 1789, the joint committee reported the final text that came to be the First Amendment:

[26] **Congress shall make no Law respecting an establishment of Religion, or prohibiting the free exercise thereof.**[69]

On September 25, the Senate concurred in the House resolution to send the draft bill of rights, including this religion clause, to President Washington. It was sent the following day, and the president sent it to the states for ratification. The final vote needed for ratification, from Virginia, was recorded on December 15, 1791, rendering the amendments effective from that day forward.

"Original Intent": Interpreting the Final Text

We are now in position to see the challenge facing interpreters of these religion clauses: What is the original understanding of the First Amendment? Is there one interpretation, or many? Is it even useful to probe such questions? The final text of the First Amendment itself has no plain meaning. The congressional record holds no Rosetta stone for easy interpretation; there is no "smoking gun" that puts all evidentiary disputes to rest. Congress considered twenty-five separate drafts of the religion clauses (highlighted and numbered above)—ten different ones tendered by the states, ten debated in the House, five more debated in the Senate, and the final draft forged by the joint committee of the House and Senate. The congressional record holds no dispositive argument against any one of the drafts and few clear clues on why the sixteen words that comprise the final text were chosen.

A Thinner Reading

One plausible reading is that the final text of the religion clauses is a compromise agreement only on the outer boundaries of appropriate congressional action on religion. Congress may not prescribe religion. Congress may not proscribe religion. Nothing more and nothing less. To try to impute more meaning to the language is to overread the unreliable record of debates in the First Congress.

On this thinner reading, the First Amendment leaves open to later discussion and development which governmental bodies, besides Congress, might be bound by its terms. Earlier drafts of the First Amendment proposed by the state ratification conventions or debated in the First Congress had sought to bind "the national government" and even "the legislative, executive, and judicial powers of the United

States" (Draft nos. 1, 4, 11). Other drafts had tried to bind the states by name: "no state may infringe [or "violate"] the equal rights of conscience" (nos. 12, 15, 17). Other drafts had been written in the passive voice and were thus potentially applicable to all government officials: "no religion shall be established by law, nor shall the equal rights of conscience be infringed"; "the people have an equal, natural, and unalienable right freely and peaceably to exercise their religion according to the dictates of conscience" (nos. 1, 4, 8–11, 13–14, 19). But in several earlier drafts (nos. 2, 6, 16, 18, 20–25) and in the final text, "Congress" alone was singled out for special limitations on issues of religion in a way that no other amendment in the Bill of Rights seeks to do. Nothing is said about what state governments or the executive or judicial branch of the federal government can do. That can be read as a deferral of the question of whether the states and other branches of the federal government can be bound by the religion clauses. Or it can be read as settling the question: the use of the clear and certain language of "Congress" necessarily *excludes* other branches and levels of government from being bound. This interpretive question, we shall see, is now deeply dividing the United States Supreme Court.

On this reading, the First Amendment also leaves open to later discussion and development what government laws short of prescribing or proscribing religion are forbidden. Earlier drafts of the establishment clause had included more sweeping and exact language: Congress was not to "touch" or "favor" religion; not to give "preference" to any religious sect, society, or denomination; not to "establish" any articles of faith or mode of worship (nos. 6, 8–10, 16, 21–23, 25). Such provisions were left aside for the more blunt provision that Congress could not do anything that would point to or come too close to ("respect") an establishment of religion. It remains an open question whether the instrument outlaws congressional conduct favorable toward religion but not necessarily of a sort traditionally associated with an established religion.

Likewise, the various drafts of the free exercise clause had included more sweeping guarantees: Congress was not to "touch," "infringe," "abridge," "violate," "compel," or "prevent" the exercise of religion or the rights and freedom of conscience (nos. 2, 6, 11–13, 15–18, 20–23). Again, such provisions were left aside for a more blunt provision: Congress could not "prohibit" the free exercise of religion. It is an open question whether government laws and conduct short of outright prohibition of religious exercise are forbidden.

Such a thin reading of the religion clauses comports with the eighteenth-century ideal that the new Constitution is a blueprint of government, not a code of governmental conduct. The First Amendment simply sets the outer boundaries to appropriate congressional action—no prescription and no proscription of religion. But it leaves the middle way between these outer boundaries open to constitutional discussion and development. The founders knew that this middle way was not uncharted and that the discussion was not unprincipled. After all, the twenty-five earlier drafts of the religion clauses included five of the six main principles of religious liberty regularly discussed in the founding era. Concern for the liberty (or rights or scruples) of conscience appears in twenty drafts. Free exercise appears in nine drafts, religious equality in ten, religious pluralism in six, disestablishment in thirteen. (Conspicuously absent from all the drafts is the principle of separation of church and state.)

It is instructive, on this thinner reading, that Congress chose the terms "free exercise" and "establishment" to define the outer boundaries of proper congressional conduct. As we saw, these were the broadest terms at hand to describe the principles and province of religious liberty. "Free exercise" was at once a source and summary of the principles of "liberty of conscience," "religious equality," "religious pluralism," and "separation of church and state." "Non-" or "disestablishment" was broadly defined as a general guarantee of "religious equality," "liberty of conscience," and "separation of church and state." While the religion clauses set only outside limits to congressional action, the boundary terms of no establishment and free exercise embodied—indeed "incorporated"—within the First Amendment all six principles of religious liberty.

Thicker Readings

The record of the debates over the religion clauses can also support more nuanced interpretations. The temptation to self-serving present-mindedness increases, of course, as the interpretation thickens. But even a cautious reading of the spare record suggests a bit more about the original understanding of some of the words and phrases.

"Congress." The specification of "Congress" underscored the founders' general agreement that the religion clauses were binding not on the states but on the most dangerous branch of the new federal government, the Congress. This was the strong sentiment already in the Continental Congress, and it continued in the 1787 Constitutional Convention and the state ratification debates. It was repeated in the surviving speeches of Sherman, Livermore, Gerry, and Tucker in the House.

Three of the draft religion clauses submitted by the state ratification conventions had specified "Congress" (nos. 1–2, 6). Three other state drafts submitted in the summer of 1788 included general guarantees of religious liberty that could be read to bind both federal and state governments. In his June 8, 1789, consolidated draft, Madison had sought to accommodate both readings—by outlawing a "national" establishment and by prohibiting states from infringing the rights of conscience (nos. 11–12). This construction failed, despite Madison's two arguments for it in the August 15 debate. The original focus on "Congress" became the norm, with the original New Hampshire version successfully reintroduced in the House by Charles Livermore of New Hampshire (no. 16) as the template.

In his same June 8 draft, Madison had also included generic guarantees of religious liberty without specifying the government entity bound thereby—"the full and equal rights of conscience shall not be infringed" and "the civil rights of none shall be abridged on account of religion" (no. 11). Such provisions too died without explanation. By August 20, Fisher Ames's draft (no. 18) specified Congress alone, and the Senate held to this.

"Shall Make No Law." The phrase "shall make no law" is expressed in the future active imperative voice, as our grammar teachers would say. In eighteenth-century parlance, "shall," as opposed to "will," is an imperative; it is an order, rather than a prediction, about what Congress does in the future. "Shall" is so used fifteen times in the Bill of Rights alone. But why the construction "shall make no law," which is a phrasing unique to the First Amendment? Could it be that Congress could make no new laws on religion but could confirm laws that had already been made— before the First Amendment was passed, or by the Continental Congress before it?

Such a reading seems fanciful until we note an exchange in the House on September 25, 1787, the very day the House approved the final text of the religion clauses. Elias Boudinot of New Jersey, who chaired the recorded House debates on the religion clauses, announced that "he could not think of letting the session pass over without offering an opportunity to all the citizens of the United States of joining, with one voice, in returning to Almighty God their sincere thanks for the many blessings he had poured down upon them." He then moved that both houses of Congress request the president to set aside a day of "public thanksgiving and prayer, to be observed by acknowledging . . . the many signal favors of Almighty God." Aedanus Burke of South Carolina thought this too redolent of a military European custom, which made "a mere mockery of thanksgiving." Thomas Tucker, also of South Carolina, objected that "it is a business with which Congress ha[s] nothing to do; it is a religious matter, and, as such, is proscribed to us. If a day of thanksgiving must take place, let it be done by the authority of the several States; they know best what reason their constituents have to be pleased with the establishment of the Constitution." Roger Sherman countered that the tradition of offering such public prayers was "laudable," and after citing a few biblical precedents for it, declared the practice "worthy of Christian imitation on the present occasion." Boudinot defended his motion on grounds that it was "a measure both prudent and just" and quoted "further precedents from the practice of the late [Continental] Congress" to drive home his point. The motion passed in the House, and later also in the Senate.[70] President Washington set aside a Thanksgiving Day and gave a robust proclamation on October 3, 1789.

This was not the only inherited tradition touching religion that the First Congress confirmed and continued. On April 15, 1789, before deliberating the religion clauses, the Congress voted to appoint "two Chaplains of different denominations" to serve Congress, one in each house.[71] On April 27 the Congress ordered, relevant to the pending inauguration of President Washington: "That after the oath shall have been administered to the President, he, attended by the Vice President, and members of the Senate, and House of Representatives, proceed to St. Paul's Chapel, to hear divine service, to be performed by the Chaplain of Congress already appointed."[72] These chaplains served the Congress throughout the period of the debates on the religion clauses. On September 22, 1789, just as the joint committee was polishing the final draft of the religion clauses, Congress passed an act confirming their appointment and stipulating that the chaplains were to be paid a salary of $500 per annum.[73] Similarly, on August 7, 1789, after the committee of eleven had put to the House its three proposed religion clauses (nos. 13–15), the Congress reenacted without issue the Northwest Ordinance, with its two religion clauses: "No person, demeaning himself in a peaceable and orderly manner, shall ever be molested on account of his mode of worship, or religious sentiments"; and "Religion, morality and knowledge, being necessary to good government and happiness of mankind, schools and other means of education shall forever be encouraged."[74]

One cannot lean too heavily on this construction of the phrase "shall make no law." First, the congressional record is too blunt and cryptic to decide whether such a subtle play on words was deliberate. Second, remember that the First Congress served as both a legislature and a constitutional drafter in 1789. Its legislative acts were driven by the fleeting necessities of the time, its constitutional amendments by the enduring needs of the nation. The two kinds of acts should not be conflated. Nonetheless, the First Congress had little compunction about confirming and continuing the Continental Congress's tradition of supporting chaplains, prayers, Thanksgiving Day proclamations, and religious education. And during the 1790s and 1800s, the Congress also continued the Continental Congress's practice of including religion clauses in its treaties, condoning the American edition of the Bible, funding chaplains in the military, and celebrating religious services officiated by congressional chaplains—all with little dissent or debate. The ease with which Congress passed such laws gives some guidance on what forms of religious support the First Congress might have condoned.

"Respecting an Establishment of Religion." The phrase "respecting an establishment of religion" is decidedly unclear. Thirteen drafts of the religion clauses included references to the "establishment" of religion, but the only debate that has survived is the brief and inconclusive discussion of August 15 on the draft: "no religion shall be established by law" (no. 13). In eighteenth-century dictionaries, as we have already seen, to "establish" something meant "to settle firmly," "to fix unalterably," "to make firm," "to ratify," "to ordain," "to enact," "to set up," and to "build firmly" (p. 58). On this plain meaning, Congress was not permitted to "settle," "fix," "define," "ordain," "enact," or "set up" the nation's religious doctrines and liturgies, clergy and property, as Parliament had done for England and its colonies—and seven of the new American states were still doing per their own state constitutions.

But the final text of the First Amendment does not simply state that "Congress shall not establish religion" or "make laws establishing religion" or generically outlaw "a national establishment of religion"—as earlier drafts had done. The final wording is much more ambiguous: "Congress shall make no law respecting an establishment of religion." The important new word is "respecting." It does not appear in any of the twenty-five drafts of the First Amendment, but instead emerged, without explanation, in the final draft from the joint committee. We have no record of any debate regarding this word, and "respecting" is a studiously ambiguous term. It is variously defined in eighteenth-century dictionaries as: "to look at, regard, or consider"; to "heed or pay attention to"; "to regard with deference, esteem, or honor"; and to "expect, anticipate, look toward."[75]

One plausible reading of the final text is that Congress shall make no laws "respecting" a *state establishment* of religion. This would make the First Amendment a complement to the Tenth Amendment, which reserved to the states any powers not explicitly given to the Congress. In 1789, after all, seven states still had some form of religious establishment, which both their state legislatures and constitutional conventions defined and defended, often against strong opposition from religious dissenters. Moreover, Virginia had just passed Jefferson's bill "for the *establishment* of religious freedom," also against firm opposition, but now by defenders of the traditional establishment of Anglicanism. Having just defended their state establishments (of whatever sort) at home, the new members of Congress were not about to relinquish control of them to the new federal government. The first minority proposal from Pennsylvania stated the federalist concern directly: "neither the legislative, executive, nor judicial powers of the United States, shall have authority to alter, abrogate, or infringe any part of the constitutions of the several States, which provide the preservation of liberty in matter of religion" (no. 1). North Carolina too stated its concern "that the general government may not make laws infringing their religious liberties."[76] The Massachusetts and New Hampshire proposals zeroed in on Congress, the dangerous new lawmaking body, with New Hampshire stating bluntly: "Congress shall make no laws touching religion" (no. 6).

This federalist concern continued in the House debates. Several House members said they feared that Congress might pass laws that interfered in religious matters—particularly through the "necessary and proper clause" of Article I, which clause Madison signaled as the danger point in the August 15 debate. There was also some concern—reflected both in Huntington's second intervention on August 15 and in Benson's intervention on August 17—about state actions on religion being adjudicated in "federal courts." To be sure, the First Congress had explicitly rejected drafts of the religion clauses that bound the states directly as well as those that were cast in more general terms (not merely directed at "Congress") and thus potentially binding on the states. And the Tenth Amendment (which was under discussion in the Congress at the same time) guaranteed generally: "The powers not delegated to the United States by the Constitution . . . are reserved to the States respectively, or to the people." But perhaps on an issue as sensitive as religion, it was best to be triply sure—and explicitly outlaw any congressional interference in the states' establishment of religion or religious freedom. Perhaps, in the final House-Senate committee of six, it was the hard political issue of federal versus state power that was resolved by adding the curious phrase "respecting an establishment." Congress could simply make no law that "looked at," "regarded," or "paid attention to" a state establishment of religion—whether benignly or unfavorably.

This reading of the establishment clause, which is regaining momentum today under the inspiration of Justice Thomas of the United States Supreme Court,[77] would be considerably easier to press if the final draft said "a *state* establishment," rather than "an establishment." But since reference to "state establishments" had not appeared before in the drafts, perhaps the final committee thought it prudent to avoid introducing a new contested term so late in the debate—particularly given the squabbling over the term *"national* establishment" in the August 15 House debate. This federalist reading is how the language was sometimes defended in the state ratification debates over the draft Bill of Rights. As James Iredell put it to his fellow conventioneers in North Carolina: "Each state . . . must be left to the operation of its own principles" when it comes to religion.[78]

A second plausible reading is that Congress could neither establish religion outright nor make laws that would "point toward," "anticipate," or "reflect" such an establishment. On this reading, Congress could not pass a comprehensive new religion law defining the texts, doctrines, and liturgies of the nation's faith and/or governing religious polity, clergy, and property. Such a law, reflective of traditional English ecclesiastical laws, would clearly be unconstitutional. But that was not the founders' only fear, according to this reading. They also feared stepping on a slippery slope, or introducing "the nose of the camel in the tent," as Chief Justice Burger later put it.[79] Thus they prohibited Congress from making more discrete laws that might "respect"—point toward, anticipate, or reflect—such an establishment. The First Congress's concern was to prevent not only a single comprehensive law that established a national religion but also piecemeal laws that would move incrementally toward the same.

The establishment clause, on this reading, was not necessarily a prohibition against all laws "touching" religion, as some earlier drafts had indicated. After all, Congress had already passed several such laws—supporting chaplains, prayers, religious education, and Thanksgiving Day proclamations. Such laws presumably did not point toward or reflect an established religion but simply reflected commonplaces of the day about what was proper for the young nation. But the establishment clause was a rather firm barrier against a large number of laws touching religion that might move toward an establishment.

This reading, pressed most forcefully in recent years by Justice Souter of the Supreme Court,[80] turns on a crucial judgment about why the First Congress had rejected earlier drafts that were more specific about defining a religious establishment. On August 15, the House debated whether to outlaw "religious establishment" per se (no. 13). There seemed to be consensus on this, as Roger Sherman said early in the debate. The moment that the representatives began to specify what they meant by religious establishment, however, the conversation broke down. Gerry was concerned about establishing religious doctrines, Huntington about forced payments of religious tithes, Madison about compulsory worship of God and giving preeminence to one sect—all features of a traditional establishment of religion. The initial compromise was Livermore's clause that sought "no law touching religion" at all (no. 16). By August 20, the House had returned to the language that opened the August 15 debate:

"Congress shall make no law establishing religion" (no. 18). That was the language sent to the Senate. The Senate also could not nuance this "no establishment" formulation—failing to reach agreement on drafts that would outlaw the establishment of "one Religious Sect or Society" or of "articles of faith or a mode of worship" or that would outlaw the preference of one religious sect, society, or denomination (nos. 21–23, 25). On this second reading of the establishment clause, the word "respecting," therefore, becomes something of an umbrella term for these and other features of a religious establishment. Congress could not agree on what specifics of religious establishment to outlaw—and so it simply outlawed the establishment of religion altogether and anything that "pointed to" or "moved toward" the same.

On the first reading, the establishment clause is a limited prohibition against congressional interference with state control of religion. Read as a federalism clause, it leaves little guidance for what Congress might do at the federal level respecting (an establishment of) religion. On the second reading, the establishment clause is a comprehensive prohibition against any congressional inclination toward establishing religion. This leaves a little room for Congress to pass laws "touching religion," but not much—save maybe those legislative commonplaces from history that we saw. These two prominent readings of the phrase "respecting an establishment of religion" do not exhaust the possibilities, of course; they set the sharpest contrasts on an interpretive spectrum that offers a host of alternatives in between.

Among the more popular intermediate readings is that of "nonpreferentialism," which Chief Justice Rehnquist of the Supreme Court pressed.[81] The establishment clause, on this reading, simply outlaws preferential support for a "national religion" but allows for "nonpreferential" support for multiple religions. On this reading, the feature of "establishment" that concerned Congress most was not a grand establishment scheme as prevailed in English ecclesiastical law; that was clearly beyond the pale, and no one was seriously advocating this for America in the 1780s. Congress's real concern was to avoid official "preferences" for one religious sect, denomination, doctrine, or mode of worship that "reflected" (that sense of "respected") the old religious establishments which allowed only one faith per territory. Seven drafts of the religion clauses, including the penultimate one, sought to formulate the establishment clause this way by outlawing various types of "preferential" establishments by name (nos. 8–10, 21–23, 25). All of these drafts failed. But, the argument goes, Congress accomplished its goal of outlawing preferential support more efficiently by simply prohibiting laws against "an" establishment of this sort—rather than prohibiting laws against "the" establishment of religion altogether. On this formulation, Congress could certainly "touch religion"—rather generously in fact—so long as it did so in a way that would not prefer one religious sect or society above another. And Congress demonstrated what such nonpreferential support meant by appointing and funding chaplains from different denominations, supporting general "religious education," and condoning pious but nondenominational prayers and Thanksgiving Day proclamations.

This "nonpreferential" reading of the establishment clause, while plausible, relies heavily on Madison's rejected concern about "national establishment." It still does little to explain the insertion of the curious word "respecting," and uses a tertiary dictionary definition of "reflecting." It also relies heavily on a clever linguistic distinction between "an" and "the" establishment of religion—words on which the sloppy congressional record slipped more than once.[82]

"Or." Modern judges and jurists are still debating whether there is one religion clause or two—and whether they should actually be called "clauses" (given that they have no subjects or predicates) or more properly "guarantees." Modern jurists further debate whether, even if there are two clauses or guarantees, there is a necessary tension between them. The argument for tension runs thus: anytime government establishes or favors one religion, it of necessity impinges the freedom of all other religions to exercise their faith. In turn, anytime government gives special support to the free exercise of (one) religion, it of necessity has moved toward ("respected") the establishment (the favoring or preferring) of that (one) religion. The argument against tension runs like this: no establishment means that government may not evaluate, approve, or disapprove any religion, and free exercise means that individuals and groups are free to practice whatever religion they choose. The point of both "clauses" (to use the conventional language) is to leave the field of religion entirely free.

Little in the final text of the First Amendment, or in the debates surrounding its formation, resolves these modern controversies. But a bit of the modern controversy turns on how to read the word "or" that separates the establishment and free exercise language in the First Amendment. Is this a disjunctive "or" or a conjunctive "or," and is the "or" directed at "Congress" or at the "no law" part of the phrase: "Congress shall make no law respecting an establishment of religion, or prohibiting the free exercise thereof"? And also, what does the comma between "religion" and "or" signify?

This may look like hopelessly casuistic hairsplitting, but such are bread-and-butter questions for modern textual interpretation in the law, and both judges and jurists sometimes train this heavy hermeneutical machinery on the First Amendment. Two interpretations are equally plausible under this close linguistic parsing of the "or" and its anticipatory comma. If it is read as a disjunctive "or," then the emphasis is on two separate guarantees: Congress shall make no law that establishes religion, and Congress shall also make no law that prohibits religion. It is two separate clauses guaranteeing religious liberty—with the "or" modifying "Congress" and with the comma dividing what Congress may not do. If it is read as a conjunctive "or," then the emphasis is on the single guarantee that Congress may not make laws on religion. These laws may not establish religion or prohibit its exercise, and perhaps *a fortiori* everything in between. It is one clause guaranteeing religious liberty—with the "or" modifying the "law" that Congress is not empowered to make and the comma separating the two extreme kinds of laws that are forbidden.

"Prohibiting the Free Exercise Thereof." Although the origins of the establishment clause have long occupied commentators, the origins of the free exercise clause have come into prominent discussion only over the past two decades. A modern controversy has driven much of the new interest—the weakening of the free exercise clause in the Supreme Court case of *Employment Division v. Smith* (1990) and Congress's various legislative attempts to restore a more rigorous free exercise test. As with the establishment clause, the historical record regarding the free exercise clause does not resolve all modern questions. Indeed, in the case of the free exercise clause, the congressional record seems to raise as many questions as it answers.

First, as we noted in the "thinner" reading above, the free exercise clause merely outlaws congressional acts that "prohibit" the free exercise of religion. Earlier drafts had included more robust protections by disallowing laws that would "touch," "infringe," "abridge," "violate," "compel," or "prevent" the same. All these suggestions were replaced by the seemingly minimalist guarantee that Congress not "prohibit" the free exercise of religion.

Second, the free exercise clause is not matched by an explicit liberty of conscience clause. Twenty drafts of the religion clauses had included a provision protecting the liberty or rights of conscience—sometimes generally, and sometimes in specific areas only (religious scruples against bearing arms or swearing oaths). The final recorded House debates on August 20 show agreement on both such protections: "Congress shall make no law establishing religion, or to prevent the free exercise thereof, or to *infringe the rights of conscience*" (no. 18). And again, "no person *religiously scrupulous* shall be compelled to bear arms in person" (no. 19). The Senate included a guarantee to avoid infringing the rights of conscience in its first three drafts but then abruptly and permanently dropped any reference to rights of conscience at the end of September 3 (no. 24). We are left with the final spare free exercise clause.

Third, and importantly, Congress was simultaneously formulating and debating the free speech, free press, and free assembly clauses when it was creating the religion clauses. The House had combined the speech, press, and religion clauses already on July 28 (nos. 15, 17). The Senate combined these with the assembly clause on September 9 (no. 25), and thereafter they were all considered together. The House debates on these other First Amendment provisions make clear that religious speech, religious press, and religious assembly were covered by these three clauses.[83] Surely the free exercise clause was not intended to be merely redundant of these attendant clauses. But this leaves the question: what independent content (if any) is protected by the free exercise clause beyond free religious speech, free religious press, and free religious assembly?

To read the free exercise clause too minimally is hard to square with the widespread solicitude for rights of conscience and free exercise reflected in the First Congress's debates. Every one of the ten different state drafts of the religion clauses included such protections. For example, the Virginia and North Carolina drafts, as we saw, went on at length: "That religion, or the duty which we owe to our creator, and the manner of discharging it, can be directed only by reason and conviction, not by force or violence, and therefore all men have an equal, natural and unalienable right to the free exercise of religion according to the dictates of conscience" (no. 8). New York's draft was also effusive: "That the people have an equal, natural, and unalienable right freely and peaceably to exercise their religion, according to the dictates of conscience" (no. 9).

The August House debates that have survived echo a hearty support for the rights of conscience and free exercise. As we saw, Daniel Carroll spoke eloquently that "the rights of conscience are, in their nature of such peculiar delicacy, and will little bear the gentlest touch of government." Benjamin Huntington warned against anything "hurtful to religion" and hoped the "amendment would be made in such a way as "to secure the rights of conscience and a free exercise of the right of religion." Elias Boudinot gave the final resounding word of the House on August 20: "I hope that in establishing this Government, we may show the world that proper care is taken that the Government may not interfere with the religious sentiments of any person."

How does this enthusiasm for the rights of conscience and freedom of exercise from the states and First Congress square with the textually meager guarantee that "Congress shall make no law . . . prohibiting the free exercise" of religion?

One response is that the free exercise clause is somewhat less crabbed when read in eighteenth-century terms, rather than ours. In eighteenth-century parlance the word "prohibiting" was as much a synonym as a substitute for the terms "infringing," "restraining," or "abridging." As Michael McConnell has shown, dictionaries and political tracts of the day conflated these terms. To flip from one to the other, particularly in the charged political rhetoric of the First Congress, could have been driven more by aesthetics and taste than by substantive calculation.[84] This conflation of terms is evident in the original draft submitted by the Virginia ratification convention in the summer of 1788. In the preface to its proffered amendments, the Virginia convention cited its main concern—"that essential rights, the liberty of conscience, and of the press, cannot be cancelled, abridged, restrained, *or* modified, by any authority." Commenting on this passage in 1800, Madison argued that the point of listing all these verbs was simply to underscore "that the liberty of conscience and the freedom of press were equally and completely exempted from all authority whatever of the United States." Such rights, in Madison's view, were equally and completely protected by the First Amendment, despite its use of the alternative terms, "prohibiting" (free exercise) and "abridging" (free speech, press, etc.). To read the First Amendment otherwise would lead to silly results:

[I]f Congress may regulate the freedom of the press, provided they do not abridge it, because it is said only "they shall not abridge it," and is not said, "they shall make no law respecting it," the analogy of reasoning is conclusive that Congress may regulate and even abridge the free exercise of religion, provided they do not prohibit it; because it is said only "they shall not prohibit it," and is not said "they shall make no law respecting, or no law abridging it."[85]

Of course, one cannot lean too heavily on this construction since the primary meaning of "prohibit" in the eighteenth century was still to "forbid," "prevent," or "preclude." But awareness of the elasticity of the term in the day, when read with the inexactitude of the congressional record, helps explain the understanding(s) of the First Congress.

Moreover, the phrase "free exercise" in eighteenth-century parlance was both a source and a summary of a whole range of principles of religious rights and liberties. "Free exercise" did have a distinct meaning in the eighteenth century, as we saw earlier (pp. 45–46). It was conventionally understood to protect the religious speech, press, assembly, and other activities of individuals, and the actions respecting the religious property, polity, discipline, and clergy of religious groups.[86] But we also saw that "free exercise" was just as much an umbrella term that connoted protections of liberty of conscience, religious equality and pluralism, and (in some formulations) separation of church and state. In earlier drafts of the religion clauses, Congress sought to spell out these various principles separately—listing liberty of conscience twenty times, religious equality ten times, and religious pluralism six times. Perhaps in an attempt to avoid giving priority to any particular construction, Congress thought it best to use the generic term "free exercise" and leave its specific province open to ongoing constitutional development and application. This is a speculative reading, but certainly a plausible one even on the thin congressional record.

The record of the First Congress gives a better indication of why a specific clause on conscientious objection to bearing arms might have been excluded. The Continental Congress had included such a provision, as we saw, and several state constitutions did so as well. The North Carolina ratification convention had suggested in 1788 that such a provision be included (no. 10). The House committee of eleven had repeated it on July 28 (no. 14). The House debated the clause on August 17 and 20. It was clearly controversial—passing only 24–22 in the full House on August 20, before being silently dropped by the House style committee four days later. Both Gerry and Scott objected because such an open-ended clause might well be abused, with the military and the nation thereby imperiled. Both Scott and Jackson thought it unfair that "one part" of the nation "would have to defend the other in case of invasion." Chairman Boudinot ultimately carried the slender majority at that time with an impassioned speech: "what justice can there be in compelling them to bear arms, when, according to their religious principles, they would rather die than use them?"

The clause itself quietly disappeared after August 20, however—and this may be explained by the suggestions by three of the representatives that a legislative alternative should prevail rather than a constitutional provision. Sherman hinted at this by saying the clause was not "absolutely necessary." Scott said more explicitly that conscientious objection status was not a constitutional but a "legislative right." Benson elaborated this view, advising that such questions be left "to the benevolence of the Legislature," to the "discretion of the Government." "If this stands part of the constitution," Benson reasoned, "it will be before the Judiciary on every regulation you make with respect to the organization of the militia." This reading gained traction and the contentious issue of conscientious objection status in the military has remained almost consistently subconstitutional—handled by statute and regulation, rather than by direct free exercise inquiry, as we shall see.

Conscientious objection to military service was only one application of the broader principle of liberty of conscience, however. Another was the conscientious objection to oath swearing that was included in the Maryland and Virginia draft proposals (nos. 5, 7). This concern received no attention in the surviving congressional debates on the First Amendment. Perhaps the founders thought conscience claims concerning oaths were better left to Article VI of the Constitution, which explicitly outlawed religious test oaths for religious office. Or perhaps they thought this so obvious an application of liberty of conscience embedded within the notion of free exercise that it warranted no specific additional text of its own. These too are plausible readings, but nothing in the surviving record confirms that this was their intent.

Even if these two specific concerns about liberty of conscience—military service and oath swearing—were addressed, that still leaves unexplained why the First Amendment seems to leave other dimensions of liberty of conscience unprotected. Sixteen drafts of the religion clauses, after all, were concerned to guard generally against infringements of any rights of conscience. Before 1789, many founders, as we saw, were concerned to protect religious parties, particularly minorities, from obeying any laws that required them to do something or to forgo doing something that conflicted with a core dictate of conscience or a central commandment of their faith. Possibly the First Congress decided to leave all such conscience claims to the legislature, as they explicitly had done with the most contested claims of conscientious objection to military service. But that solution does not address concerns about the "tyranny of the majority," which Madison had signaled as the primary danger point: "In our Governments the real power lies in the majority of the Community, and the invasion of private rights is chiefly to be apprehended, not from acts of Government contrary to the sense of its constituents, but from acts in which the Government is the mere instrument of the major number of the constituents."[87] So, what in the First Amendment protected rights of conscience, including the right to be free from compliance with majoritarian laws that ran afoul of core claims of conscience?

A few interpreters have used clever wordplay to suggest that the First Amendment leaves it to Congress to protect these rights of conscience. While Congress could make no law "prohibiting the *free* exercise of religion," the argument goes, Congress did have power to make laws when the exercise of religion was not "free"—say, when a state government impeded a party's freedom to exercise its religion or conscience. That reading finds no support at all in the surviving record, and seems highly unlikely given the heavy federalist concerns that informed the First Amendment. A dominant stated concern of both the state ratification conventions and the first House of Representatives was to keep Congress from interfering in the states' treatment of religion. It strains credulity to say that, for all that stated federalist concern, the founders intended to sneak congressional power over state religions through such shrewd hair-splitting.

But one linguistic aspect of this reading is important, namely, that in the eighteenth century, the phrase "free exercise" was synonymous with the phrases "freedom to exercise," "freedom to practice" or "freedom to act out" or "on" one's religion as conscience demanded. The New York proposed draft, as we saw, spelled this out: "the people have an equal, natural, and unalienable right *freely and peaceably to exercise their religion*, according to the dictates of conscience" (no. 9). Casting the First Amendment free exercise clause as a right or "freedom to exercise" or "the freedom to act" peaceably in accordance with conscience might well allow one to read a general right to liberty of conscience into the free exercise clause. Moreover, it would allow one to read the right to liberty of conscience as the right to forgo an act per the dictates of conscience even if a general law might require it. Any lawyer in the eighteenth century would understand that freedom to act included the freedom to forgo an action. Think of the voluntary act requirement in criminal law: parties can be liable if they voluntarily act (in shooting someone), or if they voluntarily fail to act when they have a duty to act (in failing to rescue their spouse who has been shot). The First Amendment "free exercise" clause could be read analogously. It is the "freedom to exercise" one's religion, which consists of both acts and omissions, prescriptions and prohibitions, which the law must protect so long as they are "peaceable." This too is a speculative reading, not explicitly supported by the surviving record. But it offers another interpretation of why an explicit liberty of conscience clause was left out of the First Amendment, namely, that it is an inherent part of the free exercise clause.

This leaves two plausible readings of the place of the freedom of conscience in the First Amendment, both of which have ample champions today. One reading says that freedom of conscience is not a constitutional concern of the First Amendment, but a legislative concern to be addressed issue by issue, starting with conscientious objection to military service. A second reading says that freedom of conscience is an inherent part of the First Amendment free exercise clause, and federal courts must sometimes exempt minorities from compliance with general laws that violate the "dictates of conscience." Both readings are plausible on the original record of the First Amendment, but neither is dispositive.

"Of Religion." We would be remiss without some reflection upon the word "religion," for it forms the backbone of the clauses themselves—by explicitly modifying the establishment clause and implicitly modifying the free exercise clause. Nowhere is the word "religion" defined in the Constitution, and if we strictly observed original intent, much of what constitutes religion in the twenty-first century would be excluded from First Amendment protection. In the eighteenth century, the founders recognized and celebrated a plurality of Protestant Christian faiths. When pressed as to how much further to extend recognized religion and its attendant constitutional protection there was minor disagreement. Some set the legal line at Protestantism, others at Christianity in general (thereby including Catholics and Eastern Orthodox), and still others at theism (thereby including Jews, Muslims, and Deists). But no founders writing on religious rights and liberties argued seriously about extending constitutional protection to others by setting the line to include African or Native American religions, let alone nontheistic faiths such as Buddhism.

The First Congress did little more than repeat this conventional understanding of the term "religion." While the House debates repeated the general endorsement of a plurality of sects, societies, and denominations, they touched by name only

Quakers and Moravians. They did allude to a distinction between religion and non-religion, as they sought to reserve the protections of constitutional religious rights to the former only. In the House debates, Sylvester expressed concern about "abolishing religion altogether" by crafting too broad a disestablishment clause. Huntington wished "to secure the rights of conscience, and a free exercise of the rights of religion, but not to patronize those who professed no religion at all." Scott wanted to prevent misuse of the conscientious objection clause by "those who are of no religion." But the congressional record leaves little clue about precisely what constituted religion and nonreligion and where the line was to be drawn between them.

Summary and Conclusions

In Chapters 1–4, we have taken our stand with the founders in 1789 and looked backward to appreciate both the genesis and the genius of the American experiment in religious liberty. James Madison tells us what the founders saw and what they initially had in mind:

> In most of the governments of the old world, the legal establishment of a particular religion and without any, or with very little toleration of others, makes a pa[c]t of the political & civil organization; & there are few of the most enlightened judges who will maintain that the system has been favourable either to Religion or to government. Until Holland ventured on the experiment of combining a liberal toleration, with the establishment of a particular creed, it was taken for granted that an exclusive & intolerant establishment was essential, and notwithstanding the light thrown on the subject by the experiment, the prevailing opinion in Europe, England not excepted, has been that Religion could not be preserved without the support of Government, nor Government be supported witht. an established Religion, that there must be at least an alliance of some sort between them. It remained for North America to bring the great & interesting subject to a fair, & finally, to a decisive test.[88]

The "decisive test" of the American founders was to press the earlier European and colonial experiments with religious toleration and disestablishment to their theological and political conclusions. Theologians and jurists, believers and skeptics, churchmen and statesman alike all participated in this exercise—Puritans, Evangelicals, Republicans, and Enlightenment exponents most prominently and consistently. Their efforts, while often independent and wide-ranging, collectively yielded several "first principles" to guide the new American experiment—liberty of conscience, free exercise of religion, religious equality, religious pluralism, separation of church and state, and disestablishment at least of a national religion. These first principles, some of ancient Western vintage, were collectively called "the essential rights and liberties of religion."

These essential rights and liberties of religion came to fullest expression and experimentation in the eleven new state constitutions forged between 1776 and 1784. No state constitution embraced all six of these principles equally, nor did they always institute them without qualifications that we would regard as improper, if not unconstitutional, today. Most states retained some semblance of a traditional religious establishment—usually by favoring certain religious ceremonies and moral codes; sometimes by instituting religious tithes, taxes, and test oaths; and occasionally by condoning only certain modes and manners of religious worship and organization. Most states retained constraints on the free exercise of religion—usually by prohibiting breaches of the peace and public morality; and sometimes by curbing religious speech that was deemed blasphemous, religious assemblies that were considered dangerous, or religious allegiances that were judged unpatriotic, if not treasonous. Nonetheless, the state experiences and experiments with disestablishment of religion and separation of church and state, and the state protections of liberty of conscience, free exercise, and equality for a plurality of religions, were critically instructive.

These essential rights and liberties of religion were also incorporated into the First Amendment to the United States Constitution. The founders regarded religion as special. Drawing on their heritage and history, theology and politics, they did not leave the protection of religion to constitutional provisions of speech, press, or assembly. They singled out religion for special constitutional attention and assigned it a distinct place in the Bill of Rights. Today, the First Amendment is taken as the source and summary of much of the nation's law on religious liberty. We have thus taken the time to watch its birth carefully and parse its words closely, for those words will be our principal occupation for much of the remainder of the volume.

Importantly, however, in the founding era the First Amendment religion clauses were only a small part of the American experiment. The religion clauses bound only the national government (Congress). They set only hazy outer boundaries for constitutional congressional conduct respecting religion. These religion clauses were designed in part to legitimate, or at least to live off, the state constitutional guarantees of religious rights and liberties. The twin guarantees of no establishment and free exercise depended for their efficacy on each other and on other religious rights and liberties that the founders regarded as "essential." The guarantees of no establishment and free exercise standing alone—as they came to be during the 1940s when the Supreme Court "incorporated" these two guarantees into the due process clause of the Fourteenth Amendment—could legitimately be read to have multiple principles embedded, even incorporated, within them.

Indeed, it may not be too strong to say that the "first incorporation" of religious rights and liberties was engineered not by the Supreme Court in the 1940s but by the First Congress in 1789 when it drafted the First Amendment religion clauses. This "first incorporation"—if it can be so called—had two dimensions. First, the pregnant language that "Congress shall make no law *respecting an establishment* of religion" can be read as a confirmation and incorporation of prevailing state constitutional precepts and practices. Such state practices included "the slender establishments" of religion in New England and the southern states, which nonetheless included ample guarantees of liberty of conscience, free exercise, religious equality, religious pluralism, and separation of church and state. Such practices also included the "establishment of religious freedom" that had prevailed in Virginia since 1786. The First Amendment drafters seem to have contemplated and confirmed a plurality of constitutional constructions "respecting" religion and its establishment.

Second, the embracive terms "free exercise" and "establishment" can be read to incorporate the full range of "essential rights and liberties" discussed in the eighteenth century. The founders often used the term "free exercise" synonymously with liberty of conscience, religious equality, religious pluralism, and separation of church and state. They similarly regarded "nonestablishment" or "disestablishment" as a generic guarantee of liberty of conscience, religious equality, and separation of church and state. Read in historical context, therefore, the cryptic religion clauses of the First Amendment can be seen to "embody"—to "incorporate"—multiple expressions of the essential rights and liberties of religion.

Notes

1. See Derek H. Davis, *Religion and the Continental Congress 1774–1789: Contributions to Original Intent* (2000); James Hutson, *Church and State in America: The First Two Centuries* (2008), 95–138. For the record, see *Journals of the Continental Congress, 1774–1789,* ed. Worthing C. Ford et al., 34 vols. (1904–1937).

2. Davis, *Religion and the Continental Congress,* 73–75. The quote is from Samuel Ward's Diary, September 9, 1774, in *Letters of Members of the Continental Congress,* 1:55.

3. Ibid., 1:76.

4. *Journals of the Continental Congress,* 2:220; Davis, *Religion and the Continental Congress,* 80–83.

5. *Journals of the Continental Congress,* 2:87.

6. Ibid., 1:155–156.

7. Ibid., 9:855 (emphasis in original).

8. Ibid., 1:3; see Davis, *Religion and the Continental Congress,* 67, 175–198.

9. *Journals of the Continental Congress,* 2:18.

10. 14 Geo. III, c. 83.

11. *Journals of the Continental Congress,* 1:34–35, 66, 72, 88; see T. Jeremy Gunn, *A Standard for Repair: The Establishment Clause, Equality, and Natural Rights* (1992), 73–78.

12. *The Works of Alexander Hamilton,* ed. Henry Cabot Lodge, 12 vols. (1904), 1:1.

13. *Journals of the Continental Congress,* 4:217.

14. Ibid., 5:654.

15. Ibid., 18:979.

16. Ibid., 23:574.

17. Ibid., 5:547; see also Davis, *Religion and the Continental Congress,* 160–161.

18. *Journals of the Continental Congress,* 19:214.

19. Ibid., 24:67–80. See Madison's influence on this formulation in W. T. Hutchinson et al., eds., *The Papers of James Madison,* 17 vols. (1962), 6:57, 60.

20. *Journals of the Continental Congress,* 30:269–285.

21. Quoted by Anson P. Stokes and Leo Pfeffer, *Church, State, and Freedom in the United States,* rev. ed. (1975), 120.

22. *Journals of the Continental Congress,* 32:340. On various earlier drafts of the Northwest Ordinance with more expansive language on religious liberty, see Edwin S. Gaustad, *Faith of the Founders: Religion and the New Nation, 1776–1826,* 2d ed. (2004), 115–117, 151–156.

23. See various examples in Davis, *Religion and the Continental Congress,* 57–72, 95–116.

24. See Isaac Kramnick and R. Laurence Moore, *The Godless Constitution: The Case Against Religious Correctness* (1996).

25. Elliot, ed., *Debates,* 3:313.

26. Ibid., 4:197.

27. Ibid., 3:207–208, 313, 431.

28. *The Records of the Federal Convention of 1787,* ed. Max Farrand, 3 vols. (1911), 3:143–144.

29. Catherine Drinker Bowen, *Miracle at Philadelphia: The Story of the Constitutional Convention, May to September, 1787* (1966), 243–253.

30. Farrand, ed., *Records of the Federal Convention,* 1:23; 3:599.

31. Ibid., 2:587–588. The motion makes no express mention of religious liberty, however; when Mason later specified what rights he had in mind, he mentioned only liberty of press, jury trial, and protection against the military in peacetime. Ibid., 2:640.

32. Ibid., 2:616.

33. Ibid., 1:451–452 (emphasis in original). For recollections of this speech by other convention members, see documents in Farrand, ed., *Records,* 3:471–472, 479, 499, 531. See also Franklin's own reflections on this motion in Farrand, ed., *Records,* 3:296–297.

34. Ibid., 2:342.

35. Ibid., 2:468. Alexander Hamilton proposed a more expansive clause at the conclusion of the 1787 convention that was apparently never considered: "Nor shall any Religious Sect, or denomination, or religious test for any office or place, be ever established by law." Ibid., 3:617–630, at 628.

36. See above pp. 33 and 50, and Elliot, ed., *Debates,* 2:44, 119, 148–149, 199, 215; 3:207–208; 4:195–199.

37. Elliot, ed., *Debates,* 1:332.

38. Intervention on July 1, 1788, in Elliot, ed., *Debates,* 2:399.

39. We are omitting from analysis the repeated attempt by South Carolina, in the ratification and congressional debates, to have Article VI amended to read "no *other* religious test shall ever be required." Such an amendment would have allowed for introduction of religious oaths through the prior clause of Article VI binding all federal officials "by Oath or Affirmation to support the Constitution." The proposal received no support each time it was raised. See Elliot, ed., *Debates,* 1:325; Gales and Seaton, *Annals,* 1:807; *Journal of Senate,* 1:122.

40. John P. Kaminski et al., eds., *Commentaries on the Constitution: Public and Private* (1984), 3:47.

41. *The Freeman's Journal,* or the *North-American Intelligencer,* December 19, 1787, 1; *Providence Gazette and Country Journal,* January 19, 1788, 1.

42. See his reflections in William Findley, *Observations on "The Two Sons of Oil": Containing a Vindication of the American Constitutions, and Defending the Blessings of Liberty and Toleration Against the Illiberal Strictures of the Rev. Samuel B. Wylie* (1812). See further

background in Owen S. Ireland, *Religion, Ethnicity, and Politics; Ratifying the Constitution in Pennsylvania* (1995).

43. Reprinted in Dreisbach and Hall, eds., *The Sacred Rights of Conscience,* 415–416.

44. Elliot, ed., *Debates,* 1:553.

45. Elliot, ed., *Debates,* 1:326.

46. Ibid., 1:327; 3:591, 594.

47. Ibid., 1:328.

48. This is the language from the intervention by Henry Abbot about religious test oaths on July 30, 1788, in Elliot, ed., *Debates,* 4:191–192.

49. Ibid., 1:331, 4:244.

50. Ibid., 1:333–335. The Avalon Project collection of documents dates this ratification as May 29, 1790. http://avalon.law.yale.edu/18th_century/ratri.asp.

51. See Marion Timling, "Thomas Lloyd's Reports of the First Federal Congress," William and Mary Quarterly, 3d ser., 18 (1961): 519; James H. Hutson, "The Creation of the Constitution: The Integrity of the Documentary Record," *Texas Law Review* 65 (1986): 1.

52. Gales and Seaton, *Annals,* 1:451–452.

53. Ibid., 1:468.

54. The committee included John Vining of Delaware, Abraham Baldwin of Georgia, Roger Sherman of Connecticut, Aedanus Burke of South Carolina, Nicholas Gilman of New Hampshire, George Clymer of Pennsylvania, Elias Boudinot of New Jersey, and George Gales of Maryland.

55. *The Connecticut Journal,* August 26, 1789, 3; and *Massachusetts Spy,* or *The Worcester Magazine,* August 27, 1789, 2. Both report Livermore's motion thus, without the word "infringing": "The Congress shall make no laws touching the rights of religion, or the rights of conscience."

56. Gales and Seaton, *Annals,* 1:757–759.

57. Ibid., 1:778–780.

58. Ibid., 1:783–784.

59. Ibid., 1:795–796.

60. Ibid., 1:796.

61. Ibid., 1:808.

62. Linda DePauw et al., eds., *Documentary History of the First Federal Congress of the United States of America,* 14 vols. (1972), 3:159, 166.

63. *Journal of Senate,* 1:116–117.

64. Ibid., 1:116.

65. Ibid.

66. Ibid., 1:117.

67. Ibid.

68. Ibid., 1:129.

69. *Journal of Senate,* 1:145, 148; Gales and Seaton, *Annals,* 1:948.

70. Gales and Seaton, *Annals,* 1:949–950, 958–959.

71. Ibid., 1:18–19. See also *Journal of Senate,* 16 (reporting that the Senate voted for its chaplain on April 25, 1789); Gales and Seaton, *Annals,* 1:233 (recording that the House voted for its chaplain on May 1, 1789).

72. *Journal of Senate* (April 27, 1789), as reported in Gales and Seaton, *Annals,* 1:25. A slightly reworded version was passed in the House on April 29, 1789. Ibid., 1:241.

73. Ibid., 2:22–37; 1 Stat. 71.

74. Statutes, 1789, C. VIII, in *Documents of American History,* ed. Henry Steele Commager, 5th ed. (1949), 130–131. However, this does not appear in the Annals for August 7, 1789. See Gales and Seaton, *Annals,* 1:59–62, 710–714.

75. See entries for "respect" in the dictionaries listed in Chapter 3 n. 117. See also the early modern sources quoted in *Oxford English Dictionary* (1971) under "respect."

76. This is the language from the intervention by Henry Abbot about religious test oaths on July 30, 1788, in Gales and Seaton, *Annals,* 4:191–492.

77. See, e.g., *Elk Grove Unified School District v. Newdow,* 542 U.S. 1, 49 (2004) (Thomas, J., concurring).

78. Elliot, ed., *Debates,* 4:195.

79. *Walz v. Tax Commission,* 397 U.S 664, 678 (1972).

80. *Lee v. Weisman,* 505 U.S. 577, 612 (1992) (Souter, J., concurring); *Rosenberger v. University of Virginia,* 515 U.S. 819, 865 (Souter, J., dissenting).

81. See esp. *Wallace v. Jaffree,* 472 U.S. 38, 91 (1985) (Rehnquist, J., dissenting).

82. See, e.g., Gales and Seaton, *Annals,* 1:948, transcribing the final Senate version of the free exercise clause: "prohibiting a free exercise thereof." See also ibid., 1:451, 778–780, variously quoting Madison's call for disestablishment of "any" and "a" religion.

83. Philip Kurland and Ralph Lerner, eds., *The Founders' Constitution,* 5 vols. (1987), 5:111–208.

84. Michael W. McConnell, "Origins and Historical Understanding of Free Exercise of Religion," *Harvard Law Review* 103:7 (1990): 1486–1488. See entries under "prohibit" in dictionaries listed Chapter 3 n. 113.

85. Report on the Virginia Resolutions (January 1800), in Kurland and Lerner, eds., *The Founders' Constitution,* 5:141, 146–147.

86. The Congressional Record of 1790 includes an instructive anecdote illustrating the congressional presumption of the free exercise rights of the church and clergy. Medieval canon law had granted to clergy "privilege of forum" or "benefit of clergy"—the right of an ordained cleric to have any criminal case against him heard in a church court rather than in a civil court. This practice continued after the Reformation, in Catholic and in many Protestant polities alike, and was a familiar feature of American colonial law. See Richard Burn, *Ecclesiastical Law,* 6th ed., 4 vols. (1797), 1:185–192; George W. Balzell, *Benefit of Clergy in America and Related Matters* (1955). In an act of 1790, Congress provided: "That the benefit of clergy shall not be used or allowed, upon conviction of any crime, for which, by any statute of the United States, the punishment is or shall be declared to be death." Anson P. Stokes, *Church and State in the United States,* 3 vols. (New York, 1950), 1:492.

87. Letter to Thomas Jefferson (October 17, 1788), in Madison, *Writings,* 5:272.

88. Letter to Rev. Adams (1833), in Daniel L. Dreisbach, *Religion and Politics in the Early Republic: Jasper Adams and the Church-State Debate* (1996), 118 (paragraph breaks omitted).

5

Religious Liberty in the States Before 1947 and the Creation of a New National Law on Religious Liberty

For the first 150 years of the republic, principal responsibility for the American experiment in religious rights and liberties lay with the states. Eleven of the original thirteen states had state constitutions in place by 1784; Rhode Island and Connecticut continued to live by their colonial charters until 1819 and 1843. The First Amendment, by its terms, governed only "Congress." The Supreme Court, in its earliest cases, insisted that this language be read literally. "The Constitution makes no provision for protecting the citizens of the respective states in their religious liberties; this is left to the state constitutions and laws," the Court held in 1845.[1] There was an uncertain prospect at best, before the twentieth century, that the Court would incorporate the First Amendment religion clauses into the due process clause of the Fourteenth Amendment of 1868 and apply them to the states.[2] Congress repeatedly tried but failed to pass constitutional amendments and national laws on religious liberty applicable to the states and enforceable in the federal courts—most notably the Blaine Amendment to the United States Constitution that was only narrowly defeated.[3] Most questions of religious liberty were thus left to the states to resolve, each in accordance with its own state constitution.

This left a patchwork quilt of laws on religious liberty at the state level. But many state constitutions started with the six founding principles of religious liberty of the American experiment—liberty of conscience, free exercise, religious pluralism, religious equality, separation of church and state, and no establishment of religion. It was only after local state practices became increasingly discordant, and after state legislatures and courts began systematically abridging these essential rights and liberties of religion, especially for religious minorities, that the Supreme Court stepped in to create a more uniform national law of religious liberty.

In the landmark cases of *Cantwell v. Connecticut* (1940) and *Everson v. Board of Education* (1947), the Supreme Court applied the First Amendment religion clauses to state and local governments via the Fourteenth Amendment due process clause— thereby catalyzing the development of a national law on religious liberty, enforceable in the federal courts. This modern national law of free exercise and no establishment of religion, as developed by the Supreme Court, is the primary subject of the next six chapters. In this chapter, we survey state constitutional laws on religious liberty prior to 1947 and then analyze the Supreme Court's experiments with national religious liberty norms that eventually culminated in the incorporation of the First Amendment religion clauses into the Fourteenth Amendment due process clause.

State constitution making was a complex and shifting legal business from 1791 to 1947—with 135 different state constitutions featured. Only Massachusetts and New Hampshire retained their original constitutions of 1780 and 1784, respectively— albeit with many amendments. Each of the other original states created at least one new constitution after 1787—Georgia leading the way with eight new constitutions, the last ratified in 1945. Thirty-five new states joined the union in this period, each bringing its own constitution. Seventeen of these thirty-five new states retained their original constitutions; eighteen adopted at least one replacement constitution before 1947—Louisiana leading the way with ten, the last ratified in 1921.[4] Every such constitution empowered state courts to hear constitutional cases from its own citizens or subjects. Before 1947, thousands of cases came before these state courts raising questions of state power over religious matters or of religious freedom from an exercise of state power.

A comprehensive analysis of this state constitutional law on religious liberty— both on the books and in action—could easily fill several dozen thick volumes. We think it critical to the current understanding of the First Amendment to understand at least the basic patterns of religious rights and liberties protected formally in the final state constitutions adopted before 1947, the year that the establishment clause was incorporated against the states in *Everson*.[5] Focusing exclusively on the formal constitutional laws on the books, of course, deprives us from seeing trends in state constitutional cases on religious liberty and may understate the level of de facto protection or abridgement of religious liberty at the local level. But an overview of how the states understood and implemented basic principles of religious liberty allows us to assess what the Supreme Court retained, reformed, and rejected after 1947. Accordingly, our particular concern will be to watch the treatment of the six main principles of religious liberty forged in the founding period. Appendix 2 provides a table with state-by-state comparison of a number of salient provisions as they existed in each state constitution that was in effect in 1947.

Liberty of Conscience and Free Exercise

Forty-two of the forty-eight state constitutions in effect before 1947 (Hawaii and Alaska came later) had a general clause explicitly protecting the liberty and/or rights of conscience. Sometimes the language was direct and efficient, as in the 1851 Indiana constitution:

> All men shall be secured in the natural right to worship Almighty God according to the dictates of their own consciences. No law shall, in any case whatever, control the free exercise and enjoyment of religious opinions, or interfere with the rights of conscience. No preference shall be given, by law, to any creed, religious society or mode of worship; and no man shall be compelled to attend, erect or support any place of worship, or to maintain any ministry, against his consent. No religious test shall be required as a qualification for any office of trust or profit. . . . No person shall be rendered incompetent as a witness, in consequence of his opinion on matters of religion.[6]

Sometimes the language was more florid; for example, the 1843 Rhode Island constitution's paraphrase of Jefferson's Bill for the Establishment of Religious Freedom:

> Whereas Almighty God hath created the mind free; and all attempts to influence it by temporal punishments or burdens, or by civil incapacitations, tend to beget habits of hypocrisy and meanness; and whereas a principal object of our venerable ancestors, in their migration to this country and their settlement of this state, was, as they expressed it, to hold forth a lively experiment, that a flourishing civil state may stand and be best maintained with full liberty in religious concernments: We, therefore, declare that no man shall be compelled to frequent or to support any religious worship, place, or ministry whatever, except in fulfillment of his own voluntary contract; nor enforced, restrained, molested, or burdened in his body or goods; nor disqualified from holding any office; nor otherwise suffer on account of his religious belief; and that every man shall be free to worship God according to the dictates of his own conscience, and to profess and by argument to maintain his opinion in matters of religion; and that the same shall in no wise diminish, enlarge or affect his civil capacity.[7]

Six constitutions lacked an express liberty or rights of conscience clause— Alabama, Iowa, Maryland, Oklahoma, South Carolina, and West Virginia. Of these six constitutions, however, four expressly outlawed compulsory participation in, or support for, religion. Twenty-two states in all—including three from this list—had express clauses protecting those with religious scruples against bearing arms (which was important since state involvement in the military was still commonly assumed). The constitution of Oklahoma (1907), though lacking both a conscientious objection and a compulsory support clause, nonetheless provided: "Perfect toleration of religious sentiment shall be secured, and no inhabitant of the State shall ever be molested in person or property on account of his or her mode of religious worship; and no religious test shall be required for the exercise of civil or political rights."[8]

Only twenty-five state constitutions included an explicit free exercise clause. Of these, nine couched this as "the free exercise" or the "(free) enjoyment" of "religious profession," "religious sentiment," or "religious worship." Delaware and Vermont spoke of "the free exercise of religious worship" alone. Oregon and Indiana spoke of "the free exercise of religious opinion." Idaho spoke of "the free exercise of religious faith and worship." The remaining state constitutions had more open-ended free exercise clauses.

The relative rarity and restrictiveness of these free exercise clauses is explained in part by the detail of most state constitutional provisions on religion. Rather than using the umbrella term "free exercise," as the First Amendment does, most state constitutions spelled out the meaning of religious freedom in more detail. Twenty-nine state constitutions outlawed state coercion or compulsion in matters of religion, particularly compulsory attendance at religious worship or in religious exercises. Twenty-two state constitutions had explicit provisions exempting those with religious scruples from bearing arms.[9] Nineteen state constitutions explicitly outlawed mandatory payments of religious tithes, taxes, or other forms of compulsory support for religion; none, after 1833, required such support. Fifteen state constitutions provided in more general terms that a person's civil and political rights could not be affected or compromised by his or her religious beliefs or affiliations. Three states—Colorado, New Jersey, and Kentucky—specifically outlawed religious discrimination in public schools.

Religious test oaths for holding political office remained a highly contested issue among the states until finally outlawed by the United States Supreme Court in *Torcaso v. Watkins* (1961).[10] Twenty-four states explicitly banned religious test oaths for political or public office altogether; but of these states, six required that political officers believe in God. Seven state constitutions provided explicitly that the guarantees of religious freedom did not foreclose the state from administering religious test oaths. In practice, these latter six states plus the remaining states that lacked constitutional provisions on political test oaths generally continued to administer religious test oaths of varying rigor, at least for the governor.[11] Controversy over religious tests and oaths spilled over into other areas of public involvement too, as twenty-four state constitutions banned oaths and tests as a precondition to jury service and/or to be competent to testify in criminal and civil cases; two other states explicitly insisted that such tests could continue. Eight states also banned religious tests as a condition for voting in political elections.

A number of state constitutions, following eighteenth-century precedents, set firm limits on the rights of conscience and free exercise of religion. Seventeen constitutions indicated that these guarantees would not excuse "licentious" actions or conduct that violated the peace, safety, order, and/or security of the state. Two other states added "morals" to this list. Four states added that one person's exercise of religious rights could not violate "the natural, civil, or religious rights" of others.[12] Five Western states—Arizona, Montana, New Mexico, Idaho, and Utah—followed congressional mandates and explicitly foreclosed religious liberty protection to bigamy or polygamy. Every other state had criminal laws against polygamy, but their constitutions did not touch on the religious liberty implications of these laws.

Religious Pluralism and Equality

In the eighteenth century, religious pluralism was viewed as a critical constitutional condition for ensuring religious liberty. Religious pluralism, in the founders' view, served as a natural check on both the monopolistic inclination of any church and the establishment tendencies of any state. In the state constitutions of the nineteenth and early twentieth centuries, religious pluralism was more a sociological fact than a constitutional condition of religious liberty. Most state constitutions included clauses acknowledging the existence of confessional pluralism—the multiplicity of religious sects, societies, and/or denominations within the community. Most also included clauses acknowledging the existence of social pluralism—the multiple "institutions," "societies," "associations," and/or "corporations" that religious groups operated besides places of worship: lower schools, colleges, seminaries, charities, cemeteries, hospitals, asylums, poor houses, mission societies, religious clubs, and other such voluntary religious associations.

For states, more important than creating pluralism was maintaining equality among existing plural groups. Thirty-six state constitutions included affirmative guarantees of equality for these multiple religious institutions. Of these, thirty-two constitutions formulated this as a general "no preference" clause. The constitution of Arkansas (1874) had typical language: "Religion, morality and knowledge being essential to good government, the General Assembly shall enact suitable laws to protect every religious denomination in the peaceable enjoyment of its own mode of public worship . . . and no preference shall be given, by law, to any religious establishment, denomination or mode of worship above any other."[13] Seven state constitutions guaranteed "equality of faiths" before the law or "equal protection under the law" for all faiths. Eight state constitutions included compacts with the United States that guaranteed "a perfect toleration" of all religious sects and sentiments. And two early state constitutions (New Hampshire, 1784, and Connecticut, 1818), restricted their equality guarantee to "every denomination of Christians"—although in practice these provisions were extended to all theistic religious groups.[14]

Few state constitutions went beyond these general guarantees of equality to specify any affirmative constitutional rights of religious groups. The Delaware constitution guaranteed the "rights, privileges, immunities, and estates of religious societies."[15] Kansas included a right of religious groups to incorporate and to hold corporate property. Louisiana and Maryland protected the rights of religious trusts and charities to receive donations. Maine and Massachusetts provided that religious societies had freedom to enter contracts with their ministers. New Mexico explicitly protected the church authority's right to acquire and use sacramental wine. But most states left issues of particular religious group rights to statutory, rather than constitutional, formulation.[16]

Two pairs of state constitutions imposed explicit disabilities on religious bodies. Virginia and West Virginia banned the right of religious groups to organize themselves as corporations, thereby foreclosing to them the property, liability, inheritance, and tax advantages that attached to corporate status—prohibitions that remain to this day in West Virginia, though Virginia now allows for religious incorporation.[17] Maryland and Tennessee expressly prohibited clergy from holding political office— a prohibition later explicitly outlawed by the United States Supreme Court in *Mc-Daniel v. Paty* (1978).[18]

Separation of Church and State

While today the principle of separation of church and state is regarded as essential to American religious liberty, historically it was considered more dispensable. None of the twenty-five drafts of the First Amendment religion clauses from 1787 to 1789 included the principle, as we saw in Chapter 4, and that trend continued among the state constitutional drafters. Only the constitution of Utah (1896) included a general guarantee: "There shall be no union of Church and State, nor shall any church dominate the State or interfere with its functions." Congress had insisted on this provision before admitting the heavily Mormon territory of Utah to statehood.[19]

Although they did not use the language of separation of church and state, a number of state constitutions adopted some measure of this principle in the context of education and state funding. Thirty-five state constitutions insisted that state and local governments grant no funds to religious schools. Fifteen state constitutions insisted that state schools remain free from "sectarian influence" or from the control of religious officials and institutions. These provisions were motivated, in part, by the growing bias against emerging Catholic primary and secondary schools in the nineteenth century. These provisions also testified to the rapidly growing number and power of Baptists and Methodists who, following their eighteenth-century forebearers, urged a greater separation of church and state. And they were also part and product of the effort in the nineteenth century to create a "nonsectarian" "common school" movement.

A few constitutions included affirmative guarantees for religious education. The constitution of Missouri (1945) required that the Bible be taught in public schools. The constitutions of New York (1895) and New Jersey (1947) provided that "the legislature may provide for the transportation of children to or from any school or institution of learning."[20] Six other states repeated the platitudes of the Northwest Ordinance without additional commentary: "Religion, morality, and knowledge being necessary for good government and the happiness of mankind, schools and the means of education shall for ever be encouraged."

Twenty-nine state constitutions broadened their rule against state funding for religion to apply not only to religious schools but to all religious causes and institutions. The Nevada constitution (1864), for example, provided briefly: "No public funds of any kind or character whatever, State, county, or municipal, shall be used for sectarian purpose[s]."[21] Several states echoed the strong language of the 1870 Illinois constitution:

> Neither the General Assembly nor any county, city, town, township, school district or other public corporation shall ever make any appropriation or pay from any public fund

whatever, anything in aid of any church or sectarian purpose, or to help support or sustain any school, academy, seminary, college, university or other literary or scientific institution, controlled by any church or sectarian denomination whatever; nor shall any grant or donation of land, money or other personal property ever be made by the State or any such public corporation to any church or for any sectarian or religious purpose.[22]

Today, these state constitutional provisions against funding of religion are often called "state-Blaine" or "mini-Blaine" amendments, in reference to Representative Blaine's proposed amendment to the Constitution, narrowly defeated in Congress in 1875. Despite the moniker, a number of these state constitutional provisions against religious funding antedated Blaine's efforts by more than a decade and often used language quite different from the proposed federal amendment.

Today, these state constitutional provisions are also often described as the products of a growing anti-Catholic, and anticlerical, campaign by sundry nineteenth-century nativist groups—the American Protestant Association, the Know-Nothing Party, the Ku Klux Klan, the American Protective Association, the National Liberal League, the American Secular Union, the National Reform Association, and others.[23] While these and other groups gained ample rhetorical currency in the nineteenth century, their antireligious biases and legal influence on these state constitutional reforms should not be exaggerated. A number of the state constitutional delegates who sought to outlaw government aid to religion used familiar eighteenth-century Evangelical and Enlightenment arguments for separation of church and state that had little to do with anti-Catholicism or anticlericalism. Indeed, they were often made by clerics themselves. Moreover, their separationist arguments against government funding of religion were often coupled with separationist arguments for religious tax exemptions that would aid all religions. Thirty-three state constitutions exempted from general taxation all properties devoted to religious worship, religious charity, and religious education.[24] These new tax exemption provisions were not just attempts by religious bodies to seize indirect funding now that they lacked the political power to command direct funding. Rather, tax exemption provisions were often described as a better way to ensure nonpreferential state support to all religious organizations, rather than preferential support to religious groups that had the power to extract funding from the legislatures.

No Establishment of Religion

In the eighteenth century, as we have seen, the guarantee of no establishment of religion was broad and multilayered. At its core, this principle prohibited government from defining by law the religious doctrines, liturgies, texts, and traditions of a community. But as an umbrella term, the establishment clause outlawed governmental violations of several other principles of religious liberty—particularly liberty of conscience, religious equality, and separation of church and state (pp. 57–63).

Only seven state constitutions before 1947 included an explicit "no establishment" clause. The constitutions of New Jersey and Maine cast the clause thus: "[N]o subordination nor preference of any one sect or denomination shall ever be established by law." The constitutions of Iowa, Louisiana, South Carolina, and Utah simply emulated the First Amendment: "The General Assembly shall make no law respecting an establishment of religion." Only the Alabama constitution of 1901 had a direct and general guarantee: "[N]o religion shall be established by law."

This relative rarity of state "no establishment" clauses is explained in part by the pervasive religious pluralism among most of the states. Pluralism often made the establishment of one state religion too remote a prospect to outlaw. In the new, thinly populated western states, however, the threat of such a religious establishment was quite real. These states sought to avert this threat not by adopting a "no establishment" clause but by entering a compact with the United States that guaranteed a "perfect toleration" among all religious sects and sentiments.[25]

The relative absence of state no "establishment clauses" is also explained in part by the detail of state religious freedom guarantees. Most state constitutions, as we have seen, had lengthy provisions on liberty of conscience, free exercise of religion, and religious pluralism and equality. Most also respected the separation of church and state at least to the point of granting religious institutions their autonomy and equality, and in a number of states also by barring them from interfering in state education and from receiving state funds. Since these key features of traditional religious establishments had been expressly outlawed, a general "no establishment" clause was often considered unnecessary, if not dangerous.

The danger was that a general prohibition against establishment might conflict with other provisions in the state constitutions favorably touching religion. A good illustration of this comes from Massachusetts, usually described as the last state to disestablish religion by passing its famous Amendment XI of 1833. But this amendment actually said nothing about disestablishment. It simply replaced Article III of the original 1780 constitution, which had mandated payment of tithes and supports for religion. The 1833 amendment commended theistic religion while confirming the principles of religious equality and freedom of exercise. The full text of Amendment XI reads thus:

> As the public worship of GOD and instructions in piety, religion, and morality, promote the happiness and prosperity of a people, and the security of a republican government; therefore, the several religious societies of this commonwealth, whether corporate or incorporate, at any meeting legally warned and holden for that purpose, shall ever have the right to elect their pastors or religious teachers, to contract with them for their support, to raise money for erecting and repairing houses for public worship, for the maintenance of religious instruction, and for the payment of necessary expenses; And all persons belonging to any religious society shall be taken and held to be members, until they shall file with the clerk of such society, a written notice declaring the dissolution of their membership, and thenceforth shall not be liable for any grant or contract which may be thereafter made, and denominations, demeaning themselves peaceably, and as good citizens of the Commonwealth, shall be equally under the protection of the law; and no subordination of one sect or denomination to another shall ever be established by law.

The 1833 amendment left untouched many provisions in the Massachusetts constitution, still in place today, that commend religious ceremony and morality. The preamble, for example, refers to the constitution as "a covenant" or "compact" between the people and God:

> [T]he people of Massachusetts, acknowledging, with grateful hearts, the goodness of the great Legislator of the universe, in affording us, in the course of His providence, an opportunity, deliberately and peaceably, without fraud, violence, or surprise, of entering into an original, explicit, and solemn compact with each other; and of forming a new constitution of civil government for ourselves and Posterity; and devoutly imploring His direction in so interesting a design, do agree upon, ordain and establish the following *Declaration of Rights and Frame of Government.*

This is a classic covenant ceremony, rooted in the Hebrew Bible and in a New England tradition going back to the Mayflower Compact of 1620.

The moral implications of this covenant are set out elsewhere in the Massachusetts constitution. Article II of the Declaration of Rights states: "It is the right as well as the duty of all men in society, publicly, and at stated seasons to worship the SUPREME BEING, the great Creator and Preserver of the Universe." Article XVIII rendered adherence to moral duties integral to the character of public offices and public officials:

> A frequent recurrence to the fundamental principles of the constitution, and a constant adherence to those of piety, justice, moderation, temperance, industry, and frugality, are absolutely necessary to preserve the advantages of liberty, and to maintain a free government. The people ought, consequently, to have a particular attention to all those principles, in the choice of their officers and representatives: and they have a right to require of their lawgivers and magistrates an exact and constant observance of them, in the formation and execution of the laws necessary for the good administration of the commonwealth.

For, as Article VII added, "Government is instituted for the common good; for the protection, safety, prosperity, and happiness of the people."

Moral qualities were also regarded as essential ingredients of state-funded public education, and Chapter V of the Frame of Government explicitly named the same:

> [It is] the duty of Legislatures and magistrates in all future periods of this commonwealth to cherish the interests of literature and sciences, and all seminaries of them; . . . to encourage private societies and public institutions, rewards and immunities, for the promotion of [education]; . . . to countenance and inculcate the principles of humanity and general benevolence, public and private charity, industry and frugality, honesty and punctuality in their dealings; sincerity, good humor, and all social affections, and generous sentiments among the people.

Further, Chapter V confirmed and commended the incorporation of Harvard College, since "the encouragement of arts and sciences, and all good literature, tends to the honor of GOD, the advantage of the Christian religion, and the great benefit of this and the other United States of America." All these constitutional provisions remain in place in the Massachusetts constitution to this day.[26]

To be sure, the 1780 Massachusetts constitution was unusual in the rigor and detail of its continued endorsement of religion. And the thick religious language, crafted in the days of Puritan hegemony, might well have been tempered had the Massachusetts constitution been reissued by a more religiously heterogeneous nineteenth-century state convention. Nonetheless, this language attests to a pervasive understanding among the states about the salutary, even necessary, role of religion in public life.

Like Massachusetts, forty-three of the forty-eight state constitutions in place before 1947 included in their preamble some ceremonial expression of gratitude to "Almighty God" (or the "Supreme Legislator" or "Supreme Being" or "Supreme Ruler of the Universe" or "Sovereign Ruler of Nations"). Most of these preambles were a brief line or two, but several went on for a full paragraph. The New Jersey constitution of 1947, for example, which was the last constitution ratified in this period, provided: "We, the people of New Jersey, grateful to Almighty God for the civil and religious liberty which He hath so long permitted us to enjoy, and looking to Him for a blessing upon our endeavors to secure and transmit the same unimpaired to succeeding generations, do ordain and establish this Constitution."

Endorsements of religious morality also appear in some state constitutions. Connecticut, Delaware, and Maryland followed Massachusetts in providing that it was "the right as well as the duty of the person to worship Almighty God." The 1902 constitution of Virginia retained its original 1776 religious liberty clause with the concluding admonition that "it is the mutual duty of all to practice Christian forbearance, love, and charity towards each other."[27] Six state constitutions repeated the language that "religion, morality, and knowledge" are necessary for good government and the happiness of mankind. Three state constitutions made provisions for chaplains in prisons and the legislatures, and two others for observance of the Christian Sabbath and religious holidays.

Faith, Freedom, and the Frontier

The constitutional law on the books, of course, does not necessarily describe the law in action. But the provisions noted above of the state constitutions before 1947 give some indication of the prevailing pattern of religious rights and liberties among the states in the nineteenth century. The dominant pattern was that states sought to balance the general freedom of all private religions with the general patronage of one common public religion, and they increasingly relied on the frontier as a release valve for the tensions between this private religious freedom and public religious patronage.

On the one hand, state and local governments granted basic freedoms of conscience, exercise, and equality to most religious groups and religious practices (at least those that conformed with common culture and average temperament). Most religious individuals were granted rights to assemble, speak, publish, parent, educate, and travel on the basis of their religious beliefs. Most religious groups were generally afforded the rights to incorporate, hold property, receive private donations, enforce religious laws, and maintain buildings, schools, and charities for their voluntary members.

Many states, however, still dealt discriminately with religious minorities, particularly those of high religious temperature or low cultural conformity. The New England states, for example, continued to resist the missionary efforts of Catholics, Baptists, and Methodists, partly by routinely delaying delivery of their corporate charters, tax exemptions, and educational licenses. New York, New Jersey, and Pennsylvania were similarly churlish with Unitarians, Adventists, and Christian Scientists, often turning a blind eye to private abuses against them. Virginia and the Carolinas tended to be hard on conservative Episcopalians and upstart Evangelicals alike. Many southern states were notorious in their resistance to Catholic churches, schools, missions, and literature. Few legislatures and courts, outside of the main cities on the eastern seaboard, showed much respect for the religious rights of Jews or Muslims in the United States, let alone Native Americans or enslaved or emancipated African Americans.

On the other hand, state and local governments patronized a "public" religion that was generally Christian, typically Protestant in character. A "mass of organic utterances," as the Supreme Court later put it, attest to the typical features of this system.[28]

State and local governments endorsed religious symbols and ceremonies. "In God We Trust" and similar confessions appeared on governmental seals and stationery. The Ten Commandments and favorite Bible verses were inscribed on the walls of courthouses, public schools, and other public buildings. Crucifixes were erected in state parks and on statehouse grounds. Flags flew at half mast on Good Friday. Christmas, Easter, and other holy days were official holidays. Sundays remained official days of rest. Government-sponsored chaplains were appointed to the state legislatures, military groups, and state prisons, asylums, and hospitals. Prayers were offered at the commencement of each session of many state legislatures and at city council meetings. Thanksgiving Day prayers were offered by governors, mayors, and local officials. Election day sermons were offered, especially in rural and town churches, throughout the nineteenth century.

State and local governments also afforded various forms of aid to religious groups. Subsidies were given to Christian missionaries on the frontier. States and municipalities occasionally underwrote the costs of Bibles and liturgical books for poorer churches and donated land and services. Property grants and tax subsidies were furnished to Christian schools and charities. Special criminal laws protected the property, clergy, and worship services of the churches. Tax exemptions were accorded to the real and personal property of many churches, clerics, and charities. Tax revenues supported the acquisition of religious art and statuary for state museums and other public buildings.

State and local governments predicated some of their laws and policies on biblical teachings. Many of the first public schools and state universities had mandatory courses in the Bible and religion and compulsory attendance in daily chapel and Sunday worship services. Employees in state prisons, reformatories, orphanages, and asylums were required to know and teach basic Christian beliefs and values. Polygamy, prostitution, pornography, and other sexual offenses against Christian morals and mores were prohibited. Blasphemy and sacrilege were still prosecuted. Gambling, lotteries, fortune-telling, and other activities that depended on fate or magic were forbidden. In many jurisdictions, these and other laws were predicated on explicitly religious grounds. It was a commonplace of nineteenth-century American legal thought that "Christianity is a part of the common law."[29]

This prevalent pattern of balancing the freedom of all private religions with the patronage of one public religion worked rather well for the more religiously homogeneous times and towns of the early republic. The established public religion confirmed and celebrated each community's civic unity and confessional identity. It also set natural limits on both political action and individual freedom—limits that were enforced more by communal reprobation than by constitutional litigation.

One of the saving assumptions of this system was the presence of the frontier and the right to emigrate thereto. Religious minorities who could not abide a community's religious restrictions or accept its religious patronage were not expected to stay long to fight the local establishment as their European counterparts had done. They moved—or were moved, sometimes at gunpoint—to establish their own communities on the frontier, often on the heels of missionaries and schoolmasters who had preceded them. Mormons moved from New York to Ohio, to Missouri, to Illinois, before finally settling in Utah and thereafter colonizing Nevada, California, Idaho, and Wyoming. Catholics moved to California, the Dakotas, Illinois, Louisiana, Montana, Nevada, and New Mexico. Baptists and Methodists poured into the southern states from Georgia and Tennessee to Mississippi and Missouri. Free spirits escaped to the mountainous frontiers of Wyoming, Montana, Washington, and Oregon.[30]

The right—sometimes the duty—to emigrate was a basic assumption of the American experiment in religious liberty. Many first-generation Americans had left their European faith and territory to gain their freedom. Accordingly, they embraced the right to leave both figuratively and literally—to exit their faith, to abandon their blood and soil, to reestablish their lives, beliefs, and identities afresh—as a cardinal axiom of religious freedom. Escape to the frontier provided the release valve for the common state system of balancing freedom for all private religions with patronage of one public religion.

But the combination of increasing religious pluralism and the increasing population of the American frontier rendered this system harder to maintain. The Second Great Awakening of 1800–1860 introduced to the American scene a host of newly minted faiths—Adventists, Christian Scientists, Disciples of Christ, Holiness Churches, Jehovah's Witnesses, Mormons, Pentecostals, Unitarians, and Universalists. The Second

Great Awakening also fueled what Edwin Gaustad has aptly called "the reconquest" of the original eastern seaboard states by evangelical Baptists and Methodists as well as by Roman Catholics.[31] The American Civil War (1861–1865) permanently divided Lutherans, Presbyterians, and other denominations into northern and southern branches. The Thirteenth, Fourteenth, and Fifteenth Amendments (1865–1870) not only outlawed slavery but also liberated a host of long-cloaked African beliefs and rituals, some in pure African forms and others inculturated within various Christian traditions. After the 1840s, great waves of European emigration brought new concentrations and forms of Catholicism and Protestantism from Ireland, Germany, and Great Britain; at the same time, a host of Catholic believers were moving from Mexico. After the 1880s, fresh waves of emigrants from Eastern Europe and Russia brought new forms and concentrations of Catholicism, Judaism, and Orthodox Christianity. At the same time, a growing number of emigrants from across the Pacific introduced Buddhism, Confucianism, Hinduism, and other Eastern religions to the western states.

These movements of new inspiration, immigration, and invention radically recast the American religious map in the course of the nineteenth century—with the high number of Calvinist and Anglican churches from the early republic dramatically decreasing in percentage of overall adherents, overtaken primarily by precocious new forms of Evangelical Baptists and Methodists.

Table 5.1: Proportional Numbers of Mainline Churches, 1780–1900

	Anglican	Calvinist	Evangelical	Lutheran	Catholic
	percent	*percent*	*percent*	*percent*	*percent*
1780	14.8	50.2	16.7	8.7	2.1
1820	5.5	30.1	49.4	7.3	1.1
1860	4.1	18.6	61.2	4.1	4.9
1900	3.8	14.3	63.7	6.6	6.3

Table 5.1 shows the change over time in the relative numbers of the main founding churches: (1) Anglican (later called Episcopalian), (2) Calvinist (Congregationalist, Presbyterian, and Reformed), (3) Evangelical (mostly Methodist and Baptist), (4) Lutheran (Swedish, German, and Swiss), and (5) Roman Catholic.[32] Note the huge percentage increase in Evangelical churches and the corresponding drop in Calvinist and Anglican churches between 1780 and 1860. Throughout this period, Quakers remained a consistent minority, attracting 1–2 percent of the population. This chart does not do justice to variations within these broad categories or, importantly, to the varying forms of religion mentioned in the earlier paragraphs. By 1850 and increasingly thereafter, new religious groups became prominent—notably Adventists, Christian Scientists, Holiness Churches, Mormons, Pentecostals, Unitarians, and Universalists.

This radical reconfiguration of the American religious map in the course of the nineteenth century eventually challenged state constitutional patterns of religious liberty. State policies of patronizing a public religion became increasingly difficult to maintain with the growing pluralism of religion in the populace and the growing political strength of groups who opposed such policies. Many Evangelical churches, both Baptist and Methodist, and their exploding numbers of adherents insisted that states adhere more firmly to principles of no establishment of religion and separation of church and state; in a number of states, they gained the political power to revise the constitutions accordingly. Religious minorities in many communities—whether Protestant, Catholic, Orthodox, Jewish, Adventist, Holiness, Mormon, or other—also began to ally themselves in opposition to this system, particularly the patronage of a common Protestantism within the public schools, which became a great flashpoint of constitutional controversy. Some of these minority religious communities refused to conform or assimilate. Others refused to live or leave quietly. Still others began to crusade actively against the system.

When neither assimilation nor accommodation policies proved effective, state and local legislatures began to clamp down on these dissenters. At the turn of the twentieth century and increasingly thereafter, local officials began routinely denying Roman Catholics their school charters, Jehovah's Witnesses their preaching permits, Eastern Orthodox their canonical freedoms, Jews and Adventists their Sabbath day accommodations, and non-Christian pacifists their conscientious objection status. Private, nonstate persecution of religious minorities was on the increase in the late nineteenth and early twentieth centuries, and dissenters often failed to receive any meaningful relief from public authorities and officials.[33] As state courts and legislatures turned an increasingly blind eye to their plight, religious dissenters began to turn to the federal courts for relief, and the Supreme Court began to take notice.

Fundamental Religious Liberty and Incorporation

In several nineteenth-century cases, as we shall see, the Supreme Court had heard appeals from state cases raising issues of religious property and polity, Sabbath day observance, and oath swearing. Some of these cases involved citizens from two or more states and thus found their way into federal courts on "diversity jurisdiction" grounds. Some of these cases were appeals from state supreme court judgments that were considered violations of fundamental fairness. In all these cases, the Supreme Court applied federal common law rather than applying the First Amendment directly to the states.

Beginning in the 1920s and 1930s, however, the Supreme Court began to review state and local laws touching religion under an emerging standard of "fundamental liberty" and then "fundamental religious liberty." These cases first stated the concept of fundamental (religious) liberty in the abstract, then later tied it to the Fourteenth Amendment guarantee that "no state shall deprive any person of life, liberty, or property, without due process of law." The Supreme Court began to outlaw state laws touching religion because they violated the liberty guarantee of the Fourteenth Amendment.

The first reference to this standard of religious liberty as a "fundamental liberty" came in *Meyer v. Nebraska* (1923). The state of Nebraska, like several other states in the aftermath of World War I, began to clamp down on German Protestant immigrants, exposing them to increasingly onerous registration and taxation policies and often turning a blind eye to private violence against them. At issue in *Meyer* was a new state law that mandated English instruction in all grade schools. Teachers in private Protestant grade schools were convicted under this statute for allowing Bible stories to be read in German. The Supreme Court reversed the conviction, mostly on grounds of the rights of the parents to direct the education of their children. But the Court noted in passing that such an action also violated the Fourteenth Amendment due process clause that protected, among others, the defendant's right "to worship God according to the dictates of his own conscience."[34]

The Court touched on this standard again in *Pierce v. Society of Sisters* (1925). Oregon had passed a law mandating that all eligible students must attend public schools. The Oregon law, like that of many states at the time, was enacted, in part, to drive out of existence emerging Catholic and other private religious schools and to give new impetus to the development of public schools. The Society of Sisters, which owned and operated several private Catholic schools jeopardized by the new Oregon law, challenged this law as a violation of the right of the parents, children, schools, and schoolteachers alike. The Supreme Court struck down the Oregon law and upheld the rights of the parents and of the religious schools. Again, the Court offered a suggestive dictum about protecting the fundamental liberty interests at stake: "[R]ights guaranteed by the Constitution may not be abridged by legislation which has no reasonable relation to some purpose within the competency of the state. The fundamental theory of liberty upon which all governments in this Union repose excludes any general power of the state to standardize its children by forcing them to accept instruction from public teachers only." It also forecloses "unwarranted compulsion . . . over present and future patrons" of the religious schools.[35] These principles were echoed in two subsequent cases.[36]

In *Hamilton v. Regents of the University of California* (1934), the Court stated this principle of fundamental liberty more explicitly. State university students objected to mandatory ROTC training in violation of their conscientious scruples to participation in war or preparation for the same. One basis of their challenge was the explicit guarantee of "liberty" in the Fourteenth Amendment due process clause. Although the Court rejected the substance of the students' appeal, they did accept this constitutional basis for review. As Justice Butler put it for the Court: "There need be no attempt to enumerate or comprehensively to define what is included in the 'liberty' protected by the due process clause [of the Fourteenth Amendment]. Undoubtedly it does include the right to entertain the beliefs, to adhere to the principles, and to teach the doctrines" of a faith.[37] Justice Cardozo concurred in the result but added even more directly: "I assume for present purposes that the religious liberty protected by the First Amendment against invasion by the nation is protected by the Fourteenth Amendment against invasion by the states."[38]

Three years later, in *Palko v. Connecticut* (1937), Justice Cardozo sharpened this view of fundamental liberty. The due process clause of the Fourteenth Amendment, he argued, requires that all state and local governments must adhere to the "fundamental

principles of liberty and justice which lie at the base of all our civil and political institutions." An authoritative definition of these principles of liberty and justice is set forth
in the Bill of Rights attached to the United States Constitution. The first eight amendments of the Bill of Rights, by their terms, bind the federal government. But, as authoritative statements of fundamental principles of liberty, they might also be understood
to bind the states. The Court, in interpreting and applying the "liberty" provision of
the Fourteenth Amendment due process clause, may thus selectively apply various provisions of the federal Bill of Rights to test state and local ordinances. While the Court
did not, in that case, delineate which provisions were applicable to the states via the
Fourteenth Amendment, it indicated that it would look to rights "so rooted in the traditions and conscience of our people as to be ranked as fundamental."[39]

In *Lovell v. City of Griffin* (1938) and *Schneider v. Town of Irvington* (1939), the
Court selectively applied the free speech and free press clauses of the First Amendment to invalidate a series of municipal ordinances that prohibited the distribution
of religious literature. Freedoms of speech and press, Chief Justice Hughes declared
for the *Lovell* Court, are "among the fundamental personal rights" that neither federal nor state officials have power to abridge.[40]

In *Cantwell v. Connecticut* (1940), the Court for the first time applied the free
exercise clause to a local ordinance. In *Cantwell*, Jehovah's Witnesses had been convicted under a city licensing law. The law required all parties who wished to solicit
for "any alleged religious, charitable or philanthropic cause" to procure a license in
advance. Local administrators could deny a license to those whose cause did not
seem to be in good faith. The Witnesses were convicted for preaching and soliciting
without having procured such a license. They appealed, arguing, in the Court's
words, that the statute "was offensive to the due process clause of the Fourteenth
Amendment because, on its face and as construed and applied, it denied them freedom of speech and prohibited their free exercise of religion." With matter-of-fact
simplicity, the Court applied the free exercise clause to the local ordinance and held
for the Witnesses. Justice Roberts wrote for the *Cantwell* Court:

> We hold that the statute, as construed and applied to the appellants, deprives them
> of their liberty without due process of law in contravention of the Fourteenth Amend-
> ment. The fundamental concept of liberty embodied in that Amendment embraces
> the liberties guaranteed by the First Amendment. The First Amendment declares that
> Congress shall make no law respecting an establishment of religion or prohibiting the
> free exercise thereof. The Fourteenth Amendment has rendered the legislatures of the
> states as incompetent as Congress to enact such laws.[41]

Seven years later, in *Everson v. Board of Education* (1947), the Supreme Court
accepted a state taxpayer's challenge to a local law that reimbursed parents for transportation to religious schools. In its opinion upholding the law, the Court held that
the establishment clause applied to state and local governments as well the federal
government, via the Fourteenth Amendment due process clause. This time Justice
Black wrote more expansively for the majority:

The meaning and scope of the First Amendment, preventing establishment of religion or prohibiting the free exercise thereof, in the light of its history and the evils it was designed forever to suppress, have been several times elaborated by the decisions of this Court prior to the application of the First Amendment to the states by the Fourteenth. The broad meaning given the Amendment by these earlier cases has been accepted by this Court in its decisions concerning an individual's religious freedom rendered since the Fourteenth Amendment was interpreted to make the prohibitions of the First applicable to state action abridging religious freedom. There is every reason to give the same application and broad interpretation to the "establishment of religion" clause.[42]

Cantwell and *Everson* did more than incorporate the First Amendment free exercise and establishment clauses into the Fourteenth Amendment due process clause in order to make them binding on the states. These two landmark cases also restated the eighteenth-century founders' assumptions that these two First Amendment guarantees together embraced all six of the founding principles of religious liberty. The free exercise clause, the *Cantwell* Court declared, protects "[f]reedom of conscience and freedom to adhere to such religious organization or form of worship as the individual may choose." It "safeguards the free exercise of the chosen form of religion," the "freedom to act" on one's beliefs. It protects a "plurality of forms and expressions" of faith, each of which deserves equal protection under the law. "In the realm of religious faith, and in that of political belief," the Court wrote, "sharp differences arise."

But the people of this nation have ordained in light of history, that, in spite of the probability of the excesses and abuses, these liberties are, in the long view, essential to enlightened opinion and right conduct on the part of the citizens of the democracy. The essential characteristic of these liberties is, that under their shield many types of life, character, opinion and belief can develop unmolested and unobstructed. Nowhere is this shield more necessary than in our own country for a people composed of many races and of many creeds.[43]

Similarly, in *Everson,* the Court reiterated each of the first principles that the founders had incorporated into the establishment clause. "The 'establishment of religion' clause of the First Amendment means at least this," Justice Black wrote. No federal or state government (1) "can set up a church"—a violation of the core establishment principle; (2) "can force or influence a person to go or to remain away from church against his will or force him to profess a belief or disbelief in any religion"—a violation of liberty of conscience; (3) can "punish [a person] for entertaining or professing religious beliefs or disbeliefs, for church attendance or nonattendance"—a violation of both liberty of conscience and religious equality; or (4) "can, openly or secretly, participate in the affairs of any religious organizations or groups, or *vice versa*"—a violation of the principle of separation of church and state.[44] Justice Black also underscored the founders' principle of religious pluralism, declaring that government may not exclude "individual Catholics, Lutherans, Mohammedans, Baptists, Jews, Methodists, Nonbelievers, Presbyterians, or the members of any faith, *because of their faith, or lack of it,* from receiving the benefits of public welfare legis-lation."[45] Liberty of conscience, religious equality, religious pluralism, and separation of church and state were all considered part of the establishment clause in the Court's initial formulation.

From the 1940s to this day, various critics have complained that the Supreme Court's incorporation of the religion clauses into the due process clause runs counter to the text and intent of both the First and Fourteenth Amendments and represents a blatant federal judicial usurpation of the state's legislative prerogatives. This criticism is easier to press with respect to the First Amendment, which quite clearly and deliberately singled out Congress for a special prohibition and did not touch the states. It is harder to press with respect to the Fourteenth Amendment, whose drafters and ratifiers contemplated that its guarantees of "liberty" and "priv-ileges and immunities" would be expansively applied against the states by the federal courts and whose plain text seemingly indicates the same.

But, however such textual disputes are resolved, we believe that courts must honor not only the "original intent" of constitutional texts, but also the constitu-tional process of interpretation that the original constitutional text also contem-plated. It makes good sense, in our view, for a federal court to look first within the broader constitutional text itself for more specific understandings of what might be embodied within a general guarantee of "liberty." Freedom of religion, as well as freedoms of speech, press, and assembly have always been at the heart of American "liberty" and could thus be responsibly "incorporated" into the "liberty" guarantee of the Fourteenth Amendment. Moreover, given the way that the larger First Amendment text is written, it is no easier to "deincorporate" the religion clauses than it is to deincorporate the free speech, press, or assembly clause—and few critics go that far. The text reads: "Congress shall make no law respecting an establishment of religion, or prohibiting the free exercise thereof; or abridging the freedom of speech, or of the press; or the right of the people peaceably to assemble, and to pe-tition the Government for a redress of grievances." All these First Amendment free-doms, by their terms, bind Congress only.

We further believe that religious liberty is too precious a guarantee to be left vulner-able to the fleeting political fashions of a legislature or contingent upon a claimant's ge-ographical location. In our view, the federal courts, sometimes aided by Congress, should provide common and firm religious liberty protections for all American parties, no matter where they happen to reside or where they choose to file their lawsuit. We believe this is consonant with the founders' vision of a set of principles or conditions of religious liberty that all individuals or groups held in common, regardless of belief, locale, or particular persuasion. And the rise and size of the modern state only under-scores the need for a more unitary law. The need for firm and common laws on religious liberty, in the face of grim local bigotry at home and abroad, was also among the com-pelling reasons that led the Supreme Court in the 1940s to apply the religion clauses against the states. It was also the reason that America and the world embraced religious freedom in the 1940s as a universal and nonderogable human right of all persons—one of the famous "four freedoms" that Roosevelt championed to rebuke the horrific abuses inflicted on Jews and other religious minorities during World War II. We think this vision of a national theory of religious liberty remains an important aspiration for America, and we think the federal courts are in the best position to achieve it.

Summary and Conclusions

Cantwell and *Everson* fundamentally changed the landscape of American religious freedom. From 1787 to 1947, American religious liberty had proceeded on two constitutional tracks. On one track were individual state laws of religious liberty, created by state legislatures and interpreted by state courts in light of their own state constitutional provisions on religious liberty. These state constitutions offered their own blends of the founding principles of religious liberty and their own patterns of balancing public and private expressions of religion. Education and its funding was one of the main forums for contest, but dozens of other issues came before the state courts for resolution. Only rarely did Congress or the federal courts involve themselves in these local disputes.

On the other track were federal laws on religion, which Congress made and the federal courts interpreted in light of the First Amendment religion clauses. We shall see in succeeding chapters that before 1940 both the establishment clause and the free exercise clause offered litigants little relief. The Supreme Court heard its first free exercise case in 1879, and its first establishment clause case in 1899. In neither case, nor in any other case before 1940, did the Supreme Court find Congress to be in violation of the First Amendment religion clauses.

Cantwell and *Everson* changed everything. First, the Court merged these two constitutional tracks of cases, creating a single national law of religious liberty that was applicable to federal, state, and local governments alike. State constitutional laws on religion remained on the books, of course, and state courts still heard religious liberty cases arising under their state constitutions. But for the next half century, the growing majority of religious liberty cases were filed in the federal courts, and a growing number of state courts began to interpret their own state religious liberty provisions much as the federal courts interpreted the First Amendment. A uniform national law of religious liberty began to emerge. Second, the Court breathed new life into the free exercise and establishment clause cases. It provided heightened levels of scrutiny under both clauses and began to strike down offending state legislation. This triggered a small explosion of First Amendment litigation after the 1940s, with more than 160 cases reaching the Supreme Court. Of these Supreme Court cases fully 80 percent dealt with state and local government issues, and roughly half of the cases found constitutional violations. It is to that group of cases we now turn in succeeding chapters; the cases are summarized in tabular form in Appendix 3.

Notes

1. *Permoli v. Municipality No. 1 of New Orleans,* 44 U.S. (3 How.) 589, 609 (1845). See also *Barron v. Baltimore,* 32 U.S. (7 Pet.) 243 (1833) (holding that the Bill of Rights in general,

and the Fifth Amendment in particular, applied only to the national government); see also Joseph Story, *Commentaries on the Constitution,* 2d ed. (1851), 2:597.

2. For the unclear and conflicting evidence on originalism and the Fourteenth Amendment regarding the religion clauses, see, e.g., Akhil Reed Amar, *The Bill of Rights* (1998), 246–257; Russell A. Hilton, "The Case for the Selective Disincorporation of the Establishment Clause: Is *Everson* a Super-Precedent?" *Emory Law Journal* 56 (2007): 1701, 1715–1723; Vincent Phillip Munoz, "The Original Meaning of the Establishment Clause and the Impossibility of Its Incorporation," *University of Pennsylvania Journal of Constitutional Law* 8 (2006): 585, 632–636; Chester James Antieau, *The Original Understanding of the Fourteenth Amendment* (1981), 30–33. See further, pages 122–126.

3. The proposed Blaine Amendment read: "No state shall make any law respecting an establishment of religion, or prohibiting the free exercise thereof; no money raised by taxation in any state for the support of public schools, or derived from any public fund therefor nor any public lands devoted thereto, shall ever be under control of any religious sect or denomination; nor shall any money so raised or lands so devoted be divided between religious sects or denominations." The amendment proposed by Rep. Blaine in 1875 passed the House but was narrowly defeated in the Senate. 4 *Congressional Record* 5190 (1876). A furious lobbying effort in the 1880s and 1890s sought to resurrect this amendment, but in vain. See Alfred W. Meyer, "The Blaine Amendment and the Bill of Rights," *Harvard Law Review* 64 (1951): 939–945; F. William O'Brien, "The Blaine Amendment, 1875–1876," *University of Detroit Law Journal* 41 (1963): 137–205; O'Brien, "The States and 'No Establishment': Proposed Amendments to the Constitution Since 1789," *Washburn Law Journal* 4 (1965): 183–210 (listing 21 failed attempts to introduce such amendments to the United States Constitution). On the modern usages of the amendment, see Steven K. Green, "The Blaine Amendment Reconsidered," *American Journal of Legal History* 36 (1992): 38; and sources below at notes 21–25.

4. See *The Book of the States* (1972), 21; and Cynthia E. Browne, *State Constitutional Conventions* (1973), xxviii–xxix, for convenient tables. For multiple editions of these state constitutions, see Francis N. Thorpe, ed., *The Federal and State Constitutions,* 7 vols. (1909).

5. The provisions here under review are from the following state constitutions: Alabama (1901), I.3, IV.73, XI.217, XII.229, XIV.263; Arizona (1912), II.7, 12, IX.2, 10, XI.7; Arkansas (1874), II.24–26, XVI.5, XIX.1; California (1879), I.4, IV.22, 30, IX.8, 9, XIII.1.5; Colorado (1876), II.4, V.34, IX.7, 8, X.5, XVII.5; Connecticut (1818), I.3, 4, VII.1, 2, VIII.2; Delaware (1897), I.1, 2, VIII.1, IX.4, X.3, 4; Florida (1887), Decl, sec. 5; IX.1, XII.13, XIV.1; Georgia (1945), I.12–14, VII.4; Idaho (1890), I.4, VI.3, IX.5, 6, XIV.1, XXI.19; Illinois (1870), II.3, IX.3, XII.6; Indiana (1851), I.1–8, X.1, XII.6; Iowa (1857), I.3, 4, VI.2; Kansas (1861), Rights, sec. 7; VI.8, VIII.1, XI.1, XII.2, 3; Kentucky (1891), Rights, secs. 1, 5; Revenue, sec. 170; Education, sec. 189; Militia, sec. 220; Louisiana (1921), I.4, IV.8, 16, X.4, 8, XII.13, XIV.15; Maine (1820), I.3, VII.5, IX.1; Maryland (1867), Rights, Arts. 36–39; III.11; Massachusetts (1780), Part I, Arts. II, III, XVIII; Amendment XI (1833), XLVI (1917); Michigan (1890), II.3, 17; V.26, XI.1, XV.1; Minnesota (1857), I.16, 17, VIII.3, IX.1; Mississippi (1890), III.18, IV.66, VIII.208, XIV.265; Missouri (1945), I.5–7, III.38, IX.8, X.6; Montana (1889), III.4, V.35, XI.8, 9, XII.2, XIII.1; Nebraska (1875), I.4, VII.11, VIII.2; Nevada (1864), I.4, II.2, VIII.2; New Hampshire (1784), Part I, 4–6, 13; Part II, 83, 84; New Jersey (1947), I.3, 4, VIII.2; New Mexico (1912), II.11,

IV.31, VII.3, VIII.2, IX.14, XII.3, XX.13, XXI.1, 4; New York (1895), I.3, 11, VII.8, VIII.1, XI.4, XVI.1; North Carolina (1868), I.26, V.5, VII.8, IX.1, XII.1; North Dakota (1889), I.4, VIII.147, 149, 152, IX.159, XI.176, XII.185, XIII.188, XVI.203, XVII.211; Ohio (1851), I.7, VI.1, 2, VII.2; Oklahoma (1907), I.2, 5, II.5, X.6, 15, XI.5; Oregon (1859), I.1–6, X.2; Pennsylvania (1874), I.3, 4, III.17, 18, IX.1, X.2, XI.1; Rhode Island (1843), I.3; South Carolina (1895), I.4, X.1, 4, XI.9, XIII.1, XVII.4; South Dakota (1889), VI.3, VIII.16, XI.6, XV.7, XXII, XXVI.18; Tennessee (1870), I.3, 4, 6, 28; II.28, VIII.3, IX.1, 2, XI.15; Texas (1876), I.4–7, III.51, VII.5, VIII.2, XVI.47; Utah (1896), I.1, 4, III.1, 4, X.1, 12, 13, XIII.2; Vermont (1793), Rights, III, IX; II.64; Virginia (1902), I.16, IV.58, 59, 67, IX.141, XIII.183; Washington (1889), I.11, IX.4, X.6, XXVI.1, 4; West Virginia (1872), III.11, 15, VI.47, X.1; Wisconsin (1848), I.18, 19, X.3, 6; Wyoming (1890), I.18, 19, III.36, VII.8, 12, XV.12, XVI.6, XVII.1, XXI.25, 28.

The table in Appendix 2 summarizes these provisions. See analysis in Chester J. Antieau, Philip M. Carroll, and Thomas Carroll Burke, *Religion Under the State Constitutions* (1965); Carl Zollman, *American Church Law*, repr. ed. (1933); Michael S. Ariens and Robert A. Destro, *Religious Liberty in a Pluralistic Society*, 2d ed. (2002), 101–202.

6. Constitution of Indiana (1851), I.2–7 (deleting section numbers).

7. Constitution of Rhode Island (1843), Art. I.3.

8. Constitution of Oklahoma (1907), Art. I.2.

9. In addition, the Constitution of Florida (1887), Art. XIV.1 explicitly put questions of conscientious objection to the legislature. The rest of the states were silent on the subject.

10. 367 U.S. 488 (1961).

11. See details in Antieau, Carroll, and Burke, *Religion and the State Constitutions,* 100–119.

12. Constitution of Maryland (1867), Rights, Art. 36.

13. Constitution of Arkansas (1874), Art. II.24, 25.

14. Constitution of New Hampshire (1784), Part I, Art. 6, and Constitution of Connecticut (1818), Art. I.4, both repeating Constitution of Massachusetts (1780), Part I, Art. III. By Amendment XI (1833), the Massachusetts constitution rendered this as "all religious sects and denominations."

15. Constitution of Delaware (1897), Art. IX.4.

16. See generally Paul G. Kauper and Stephen B. Ellis, "Religious Corporations and the Law," *Michigan Law Review* 71 (1973): 1499.

17. Virginia Constution, Art. IV, Sec. 14 (as amended effective January 1, 2007); *Falwell v. Miller,* 203 F.Supp. 2d 624 (W.D. Va. 2002).

18. 435 U.S. 618 (1978).

19. Constitution of Utah (1896), Art. I.4. See below, pp. 140–143.

20. Constitution of New York (1895), Art. XI.4. See similarly Constitution of New Jersey (1947), Art. VIII., Sec. IV.3. Such policies of furnishing transportation to religious school children on public school buses were upheld as constitutional in *Everson v. Board of Education,* 330 U.S. 1 (1947).

21. Constitution of Nevada (1864), Art. XI.10.

22. Constitution of Illinois (1870), Art. VIII.3.

23. See Philip Hamburger, *Separation of Church and State* (2002); Hamburger, "Separation and Interpretation," *Journal of Law and Politics* 18 (2002): 7.

24. Twenty-seven of the thirty-three state constitutions that explicitly outlawed state funding of religion also explicitly authorized such exemptions, and the remaining seven states had strong statutory provisions in effect providing for the same. See Appendix 2.

25. These western states were Arizona, Idaho, Montana, New Mexico, North Dakota, South Dakota, Washington, and Wyoming. Congress generally included these religious liberty clauses, among others, in the enabling acts that allowed new states into the union. Such clauses were irrevocable without the consent of the Congress and the people of the states, and they remain in place today, albeit sometimes in new forms. See, e.g., 1953 amendment to the New Mexico compact, consented to by Congress, 67 Stat. 586, chap. 506.3. See further Robert F. Williams, *State Constitutional Law*, 2d ed. (1993), 76ff.

26. Reprinted with modernized spelling and capitalization in Thorpe, ed., *Federal and State Constitutions*, 3:1888.

27. Constitution of Virginia (1902), Art. I.16 (retained in the 1971 constitution).

28. *Church of the Holy Trinity v. United States*, 143 U.S. 457, 478 (1892).

29. The phrase was coined by Sir Matthew Hale in *Taylor's Case*, 1 Vent. 293, 86 English Reports 189 (K.B. 1676), and is repeated in several American tracts and cases. See, e.g., *The Works of James Wilson*, 2:671; and *Vidal v. Girard's Executors*, 43 U.S. (2 How.) 127, 198 (1844); see Stuart Banner, "When Christianity Was Part of the Common Law," *Law and History Review* 16 (1998): 27–62.

30. Edwin S. Gaustad, *Historical Atlas of Religion in America*, rev. ed. (New York, 1976).

31. Ibid., 42.

32. The figures that follow are drawn from the tables in Gaustad, *Historical Atlas*, 4, 42–44, which include actual numbers of churches. In calculating these percentages, we have simply totaled the number of churches in each table and divided the number of churches listed under each category against the total.

33. See, e.g., Shawn Francis Peters, *Judging Jehovah's Witnesses: Religious Persecution and the Dawn of the Rights Revolution* (2000), 1–18, 72–152.

34. 262 U.S. 390, 399 (1923).

35. 268 U.S. 510, 535 (1925).

36. *Farrington v. Tokushige*, 273 U.S. 284 (1927); *Cochran v. Louisiana State Board of Education*, 281 U.S. 370 (1930).

37. *Hamilton v. Board of Regents*, 293 U.S. 245, 262 (1934).

38. 293 U.S. 265 (1934) (Cardozo, J., concurring).

39. 302 U.S. 319, 325, 328 (1937).

40. 303 U.S. 444, 450 (1938). See also *Schneider v. Town of Irvington*, 308 U.S. 147 (1939).

41. 310 U.S. 296, 297, 300, 303 (1940).

42. 330 U.S. 1, 14–15 (1947).

43. *Cantwell*, 310 U.S. at 303–304, 310.

44. *Everson*, 330 U.S. at 15–16.

45. 330 U.S. at 16 (emphasis in original).

6

The Free Exercise of Religion

The incorporation of the First Amendment religion clauses into the Fourteenth Amendment due process clause in the 1940s shifted principal authority over the American experiment in religious liberty from the states to the federal courts. This shift did not foreclose the states from participation in the experiment. State and local legislatures have continued to issue numerous laws governing religious expression in public schools and the public square; the use, zoning, and taxation of religious property; the incorporation, regulation, and subsidization of religious nonprofit organizations, and much more. State courts have kept an ample docket of cases on religious liberty, adjudicating them under their own state constitutional and state statutory provisions on religion. But after the First Amendment religion clauses were made binding on the states in the 1940s, most laws in America that touched religion became subject to First Amendment influence, if not scrutiny. And until recently, most state courts tended to follow Supreme Court precedents when interpreting their state constitutional clauses on religious liberty.

This chapter analyzes the Supreme Court's interpretation and application of the First Amendment free exercise clause. First, we shall map the main shifts in doctrine in the Supreme Court's free exercise cases. Second, we shall analyze the Court's adjudication of various free exercise issues with a close analysis of the main cases. Third, and throughout, we shall watch the Court's treatment of the essential principles of religious liberty in these free exercise cases.

Two methodological notes relate to this chapter and the next five, all of which analyze the Supreme Court cases on religious liberty. First, Appendix 3 provides a detailed chronological table of all Supreme Court cases on religious liberty, including their citations and holdings. These chapters distill and quote from the cases, but we have not cluttered our analysis with detailed citations to the secondary literature or to the cases themselves.[1] We have, instead, provided a footnote at the conclusion of each case analysis that supplies a citation to the case, including the actual pages quoted. Readers are strongly encouraged to read the cases themselves, which can be readily downloaded, following the citations in Appendix 3.[2]

Second, we have divided the materials into manageably sized and thematically coherent chapters for easy use in the classroom and for casual reading. These chapters cover, respectively, the free exercise clause, the establishment clause, religion and public education, government and religious education, religion and public life, and religious organizations and the law. But it would be artificial and indeed impossible to cordon off free exercise and related free speech issues, which are the focus of this chapter, from later chapters. In the same way, establishment issues (the main focus of the next chapter) are not entirely absent from this chapter, nor other ones. This intermixing of First Amendment principles and values is inevitable, as religious liberty issues that come before the courts often raise both establishment and free exercise concerns. This underscores one of our themes in this volume—that courts and commentators often pigeonhole religious liberty disputes rather than assess issues using the full range of first principles of religious liberty discussed in earlier chapters.

Mapping Modern Free Exercise Doctrine

Free Exercise Rights Versus Governmental Power

At the heart of a free exercise case is a conflict between the exercise of governmental power and the exercise of a private party's religion. The private party challenges the exercise of governmental power as a violation of rights protected by the free exercise clause. The challenged governmental entity or officer can be at any level—federal, state, or local. The governmental action that is challenged can be executive, legislative, or regulatory in nature. But it must be governmental, not private, conduct at issue; there must be some form of "state action" to trigger a constitutional case. When one private party violates another private party's religious rights, such conduct is addressed by civil suits and/or criminal prosecution brought under federal and state statutes, not by constitutional litigation under the free exercise clause.

A free exercise claimant may be either a religious individual or a religious group. Their claim is that the law at issue infringes upon their beliefs of conscience. It inhibits their acts of worship or of religious speech, press, or association. It commands them to do something, or to forgo something, that conflicts with the demands of their individual conscience or collective faith. It discriminatorily singles out their activity, organization, or property for duties or exclusions that are not imposed on other individuals or groups similarly situated. In brief, government "prohibits" or unduly "burdens" the claimant's freedom to exercise religion.[3]

Free exercise claimants must meet the usual "justiciability" requirements for pressing any constitutional case against the government. The claimants must state an actual "case or controversy"—not an issue that has become moot or requests only an advisory opinion from the Court. They must have "standing" to bring the suit— showing an actual injury to themselves caused by the allegedly unconstitutional law and showing how removal of the law or exemption from compliance with it will grant them relief. They must raise a constitutional issue on which a court has actual "jurisdiction"—not a "political question" that is better addressed by other branches of government. These threshold requirements, which are the subject of an elaborate law on federal courts and constitutional litigation, can often raise complicated technical questions for parties to negotiate. A surprising number of cases are fumbled at this threshold level.[4] Nonspecialists should tread carefully when analyzing this part of the law.

In addition to meeting general "justiciability" requirements, free exercise claimants must demonstrate that it is their *religious* exercise that has been improperly burdened. In many instances, the religious qualities of the claim are easy enough to make out: a Jehovah's Witness is discriminately denied a license to preach; a Jewish officer is forbidden to wear his yarmulke on an air force base; a Muslim prisoner is kept from prayer at the appointed hour of the day or from collective Friday worship.[5] These are core free exercise cases involving religious individuals. A religious school is required to hire a teacher who does not share its faith; a religious crusade is fined for selling religious articles without collecting sales and use taxes; a Native American tribe is told that the National Forest Service will build a road through its sacred burial ground.[6] These are core free exercise cases involving religious groups. Sometimes religious parties also raise free exercise rights as a defense when government seeks to enforce laws of taxation, discrimination, labor, bankruptcy, health, child care, land use, historical preservation, and more that burden their religious exercise.[7]

In a number of other cases, however, a claimant's free exercise interest appears more attenuated: an applicant at a temporary agency refuses a job because it might require him to work on Sunday, his day for "rest" though not for worship. He claims unemployment compensation, is denied, and appeals.[8] A furniture store owner, who is a strict Saturday Sabbatarian, opens his store on Sunday in violation of Sunday blue laws that prohibit all but "necessary labor." He is fined and appeals, claiming that the law burdens his free exercise rights to observe his Saturday Sabbath.[9] A religious university discriminates against African American employees and students based on its understanding that the Bible requires that white and black races be kept separate. The school is stripped of its federal tax exempt status and appeals, claiming that its free exercise rights have been violated just because its beliefs are not popular.[10] In each of these cases, the religious interests may be perceived as core by those within the religion, but may be viewed as penumbral by courts and commentators outside that religion. In many of these cases, free exercise claimants will lose because courts judge that they have not pressed a serious enough religious interest, have not demonstrated a substantial enough burden on their religious exercise, or have not shown that their interest outweighs the government's. These different perspectives on what is core to religious practice and what more penumbral can lead to important differences in such cases.

Further complicating the analysis is the lack of singular definition of "religion" for free exercise purposes. Instead of defining religion, the Supreme Court has insisted that free exercise litigants make a "sincere" and "good faith" claim—even if it is inconsistent, incoherent, idiosyncratic, or newly acquired. In some cases, this sincerity test "cannot completely escape the distinctly bad aroma of an inquisition," in Ira Lupu's apt phrase,[11] as it can lead courts to inquire intrusively into the faith of a person or a group or play to their prejudices against unpopular or exotic religions.[12] But if the Court is to limit the reach of the free exercise clause to "religious" exercises only, and if it is to be protected from fraudulent or sham claims, some measured inquiry into the "religious" nature of claims seems unavoidable, especially for new religions. Few free exercise cases, however, are lost on this threshold inquiry. The federal courts have heard free exercise cases from Jews, Christians, Muslims, Hindus, Buddhists, and Confucians, as well as from Native American Indians and self-professed atheists, and from practitioners of various new and new age religions in America. In *Torcaso v. Watkins* (1961), the first Supreme Court case to uphold the free exercise rights of an atheist, the Court made clear that theists and nontheists alike should be included within the ambit of the First Amendment: "Among religions in this country which do not teach what would generally be considered a belief in the existence of God are Buddhism, Taoism, Ethical Culture, Secular Humanism and others."[13] New or newly arrived religions will often lose their free exercise claims, but they will rarely be denied their day in federal court.[14]

Resolving the Conflict

Assuming that the claimant can meet these threshold requirements to press a free exercise claim against the government, how does the Court resolve this basic conflict between government power and free exercise rights, both claims anchored in the Constitution? The Court has used two principal methods, which lead to two different ways to organize its free exercise cases.

One way is simply to balance juxtaposed constitutional claims, reach a judicious or pragmatic judgment, and then follow that reasoning and result in subsequent cases. Thin lines and then clusters of cases slowly emerge as the Court adjudicates cases with comparable facts and builds on its immediate factual precedents, even if it has to reach back several decades.[15] What sometimes tips the balance in favor of the government is the centrality of the government power being challenged. What sometimes tips the balance in favor of the free exercise litigant is the transparency of the religious discrimination at work in the challenged law.

Using this method, we find some clusters of cases that favor free exercise claimants and others that favor the government. A large cluster of cases from 1940 to 1992 upholds free exercise (and sometimes also free speech) rights to engage in religious worship, proselytism, publication, and other forms of religious expression. A small cluster of cases from 1963 to 1989 upholds free exercise rights to receive unemployment compensation by employees fired for religious reasons. A case cluster from 1981 to 2002 uses the free speech clause to grant religious claimants equal access to public forums open to nonreligious parties. Other cases, especially those involving central government power, go in the opposite direction. A thin cluster of cases from 1879 to 1990 rejects claims for free exercise exemption from criminal law. A thicker case cluster from 1918 to 1971 denies free exercise rights to conscientious objection status, leaving such issues to the legislature. Another cluster from 1982 to 1990 rejects claims to exemptions from taxation, social security, military dress, and prison regulations. A relatively consistent internal logic governs each of the factually connected clusters of cases, as we shall see. But it is harder to make out a common free exercise logic that applies across all these cases.

A second (and more commonly utilized) way to view the Court's adjudication of these cases is to examine its basic standard of review of the challenged law. The focus is not so much on the facts of the free exercise issue being litigated and its factually relevant precedents, but rather on the standard of review that the Court has adopted for all free exercise cases. On occasion, the Court will change the standard of review—sometimes in response to a shift in Court personnel or to the appointment of a new chief justice, sometimes in reaction to an extreme holding under the prior standard pressed by an overreaching litigant or an overindulgent Court.[16] But unless and until the Court changes the stated standard, all free exercise cases get the same review, regardless of the facts, the centrality of the government power being challenged, or even the transparency of the religious discrimination.

Defining general standards of review to resolve constitutional conflicts between powers and rights is not unique to the free exercise clause. The Supreme Court has engaged in this exercise in many cases arising under the Bill of Rights and the Fourteenth Amendment. Particularly in the past half century, the Court has developed three standards of review, from low-level to high-level scrutiny of the law that is challenged.

Under *low-level scrutiny*, the Court will uphold the challenged law if (1) it is in pursuit of a *legitimate governmental interest*, and (2) it is *reasonably related* to that interest. This test, often called the *rational basis test*, features high judicial deference to the legislature and other branches of government. It provides a loose safety net to protect parties against blatant governmental actions that yield patently discriminatory and arbitrary laws. But it gives little protection. Free exercise litigants rarely win under this standard.

Under *intermediate* or *heightened* scrutiny, the Court will uphold the challenged law if (1) it is in pursuit of an *important* or significant *governmental interest*, and (2) it is *substantially related* to that interest. This test, often called the *intermediate scrutiny test,* is not as deferential to the legislature. Courts will inquire more closely what the government is trying to achieve in passing this law, and whether it has taken sufficient steps to avoid burdening the religious interests of individuals and groups. Free exercise litigants and the government win comparable numbers of cases under this standard.

Under *high-level* or *strict scrutiny*, a Court will uphold the challenged law only if (1) it is in pursuit of a *compelling* or overriding *governmental interest,* and (2) it is *narrowly tailored* to achieve that interest, not intruding on the claimant's rights anymore than is absolutely necessary. This test, often called the *compelling state interest test,* involves close judicial inquiry into the purposes and provisions of the law (though judges sometimes divide on whether and how to read the legislative history alongside the actual text of the challenged law). This strict scrutiny test empowers a court to strike down the law altogether or to tailor it in a manner that will cause less harm to the claimant. In free exercise cases, strict scrutiny is not "strict in theory, but fatal in fact," as it is in some other areas of constitutional law.[17] Free exercise litigants win the majority of cases under this standard, but government can still win, especially if the case involves core governmental powers over taxation, crime, prisons, or the military.

This spectrum of standards of review provides a second picture of the Supreme Court's free exercise cases. Since its first free exercise case in 1879, the United States Supreme Court has ranged across the entire spectrum of review, with periodic watershed cases that shift the standard. Although not all free exercise cases fit on this spectrum, a good number of them do. By plotting them (see Figure 6.1), we can get a rough picture of the main shifts in the Court's application of the free exercise clause.

Because the remainder of the chapter undertakes a closer analysis of cases through a more "topical" method, we explicate these main shifts in free exercise law now to have this second map. In *Reynolds v. United States* (1879), its first free exercise case, the Supreme Court applied a very low level of scrutiny for cases dealing

Figure 6.1: Trends in Modern Free Exercise Law

Low Scrutiny	Heightened Scrutiny	Strict Scrutiny
legitimate interest rational link	important interest substantial link	compelling interest narrowly tailored
Reynolds (1879)		
	Cantwell (1940)	
		Sherbert (1963)
Smith (1990)		
		RFRA (1993)
		RFRA/*Boerne* (1997) [federal laws only]
	Watchtower (2002)	
		RLUIPA (2000)/ *Cutter* (2005) [federal and state laws]

with free exercise claims against the federal government. In reviewing these federal laws, the Court's only stated concerns were whether the laws were "authorized," "reasonable," and "general," and whether they properly reached the actions of the parties.[18] For the next sixty years, every Supreme Court application of this standard of review in free exercise cases resulted in a win for the government. Most lower federal court cases used the same standard with the same results.

In *Cantwell v. Connecticut* (1940), as we saw earlier (pp. 124–125), the Court applied the free exercise clause to state and local government for the first time. *Cantwell* also marked the first application of a heightened level of scrutiny for the entire class of free exercise cases. The Court cordoned off areas of religion that government could not regulate (unless they were clearly criminal): religious beliefs, worship, and assembly. Regulation of other religious conduct was "permissible" so long as it was by "general and non-discriminatory legislation" and did not "unduly infringe" upon this exercise.[19] Later cases explained that government could not infringe on religious conduct on "such slender grounds" as "rational basis" or other "modest estimates of governmental competence." Its law must "serve a significant governmental interest" to withstand free exercise scrutiny.[20] From 1940 to 1963, the Court applied this heightened scrutiny standard of review in both its free exercise and free speech cases, with the cases roughly evenly divided in holding for government and for the free exercise claimant. This standard of review continues to operate today in free speech cases involving religion, as the Court demonstrated most recently in *Watchtower Bible and Tract Society v. Village of Stratton* (2002). In later chapters, we shall also see this heightened scrutiny regime applied in a series of "equal access" cases from 1981 to 2002 brought principally under the free speech clause.

In *Sherbert v. Verner* (1963), the Court for the first time applied a strict scrutiny standard of review in a free exercise case. Rather than just requiring a law to be general (as the rational basis test required), or nondiscriminatory on religious grounds and not touching religious beliefs (as the intermediate scrutiny test required), the Court now required more. To pass strict scrutiny, a law must also (1) serve a compelling state interest, and (2) be narrowly tailored to achieve that interest with the least possible intrusion on free exercise rights.[21] Under this standard, the Court must review both the law in general and its particular application to the free exercise claimant. If the law in general does not meet these two criteria, it will be struck down. If the law in general meets these two criteria, but the particular application of the law to this free exercise litigant does not, the Court will uphold the law but grant the individual litigant an exemption from compliance with it. The Court has repeatedly said that such a judicially created exemption from a general law on behalf of a free exercise claimant does not constitute an establishment of religion. The Supreme Court used this strict scrutiny test of free exercise in ten cases after 1963, six times finding for the religious claimant, four times for the government.

In *Employment Division v. Smith* (1990), the Court formally rejected the strict scrutiny test of free exercise and adopted a lower-level scrutiny test. Building on a series of cases in the prior decade that had avoided application of the *Sherbert* strict scrutiny test, the *Smith* Court held that "the right of free exercise does not relieve an individual of the obligation to comply with a 'valid and neutral law of general applicability on the ground that the law proscribes (or prescribes) conduct that his religion prescribes (or proscribes).'"[22] Any law that is neutral and generally applicable is constitutional, said the Court, even if the law burdens a central aspect of the claimant's religion.[23] If a law is not neutral or not generally applicable, however, then government must justify that law by demonstrating that it furthers a compelling governmental interest and is narrowly tailored to achieve that interest. This latter caveat rendered the *Smith* test somewhat more protective of religious interests than the original 1879 *Reynolds* rationality test. Moreover, *Smith* did allow "hybrid rights claims" where free exercise rights were combined with free speech, equal protection, or other fundamental right claims to receive heightened and even strict scrutiny. But *Smith* nonetheless weakened the free exercise clause considerably.

The *Smith* case was widely denounced as a travesty to religious liberty. It set off a decade-long feud between Congress and the Supreme Court about the free exercise clause and the appropriate standard of review—and also about the institutional powers and competencies of the various branches of government. In direct reaction to *Smith*, Congress passed the Religious Freedom Restoration Act (RFRA) in 1993 to "restore the compelling state interest test" of *Sherbert* and its progeny.[24] In *City of Boerne v. Flores* (1997), however, the Supreme Court declared RFRA unconstitutional as applied to the states. Congress had passed RFRA using section 5 of the Fourteenth Amendment, which empowers Congress to "enforce" the liberty provisions of the amendment against state and local governments by "appropriate legislation." To the *Boerne* Court, Congress had overstepped the bounds of section 5 power. "Legislation which alters the meaning of the Free Exercise Clause cannot be said to be enforcing the Clause."[25] Because RFRA fundamentally changed the free exercise law by insisting on a certain standard of review, the Court held it unconstitutional as to state and local governments. With respect to free exercise claims against state and local laws, the *Smith* low-level scrutiny test again became the law and remains so. The *Boerne* case left RFRA untouched as applied to federal laws, on the argument that Congress could hold itself to higher standards of review when its own laws burdened the free exercise of religion. Federal courts have continued to apply RFRA against federal laws, and the Supreme Court endorsed this as recently as 2006.[26]

In a continued effort to strengthen religious liberty claims against state and local governments, Congress responded to *Boerne* in 2000 by passing the Religious Land Use and Institutionalized Persons Act (RLUIPA). For this law, Congress used its broader Article I powers over interstate commerce and over taxing and spending at the federal and state levels. It focused more narrowly on the religious rights of institutionalized persons in state-run prisons, hospitals, and other institutions, and the rights of religious property owners burdened by zoning and landmark laws. If parties covered by the statute prove that a federal or state law imposes a substantial burden on their religious exercise, RLUIPA mandates strict scrutiny of that law and, if it is necessary and possible, grants a claimant exemption from compliance with that law.[27]

This law was immediately challenged—not structurally, as RFRA had been, but as a violation of the First Amendment establishment clause. The argument was that Congress had unduly favored religious parties with special protections and procedures not available to nonreligious counterparts; that is, it had impermissibly favored religion over nonreligion. In *Cutter v. Wilkinson* (2005), a unanimous Court upheld the constitutionality of RLUIPA as applied to "institutionalized persons." The *Cutter* Court held that a legislature did not establish religion by creating narrowly tailored exemptions and procedures for parties whose religious interests and exercises are substantially burdened by general legislation. This holding was consistent with the Court's repeated earlier statements that it is not an establishment of religion for the judiciary or for the legislature to carve out narrow exemptions from compliance with general laws for free exercise parties.[28] The *Cutter* holding emboldened both Congress and state legislatures to pass or amend several statutes that now provide particular protections, exemptions, and immunities for religion, and institute heightened or strict standards of review to be applied when these statutory rights are violated. More than a dozen states now have their own state version of the Religious Freedom Restoration Act in operation that provides strict scrutiny of state and local laws that substantially burden the freedom to exercise one's religion.

All these shifts occasioned by the 1990 *Smith* case have complicated free exercise litigation considerably. A party whose religious exercise has been substantially burdened by the government now has a range of constitutional and statutory options to consider, and it makes a difference whether the law in question is a federal or a state law. Ironically, the First Amendment free exercise clause (unless made part of a "hybrid rights claim" with the free speech or equal protection clause) provides the *lowest* scrutiny and the *least* promising pathway to relief. The First Amendment free speech clause provides greater scrutiny and a higher probability of success. Federal and state statutes often provide the most stringent scrutiny and the likeliest recourse for religious liberty advocates. These litigation options are summarized in Figure 6.2. We shall return to this menu of options in the summary and conclusions of this chapter.

Figure 6.2: Standards of Review to Adjudicate Burdens on Religious Exercise

Government Entity Challenged	Scrutiny of Free Exercise Claims	Scrutiny of Free Speech Claims	Scrutiny of Hybrid Claims	Scrutiny of RFRA Claims	Scrutiny of RLUIPA Claims	Scrutiny in Other Statutes
Federal	Rational basis	Heightened	Heightened or Strict	Strict	Strict	Heightened or Strict
State	Rational basis	Heightened	Heightened or Strict	Not applicable	Strict	Heightened or Strict

The two readings above give us two pictures of the Court's modern free exercise doctrine—the first as a collection of case clusters, the second as a series of shifting standards of review. Both readings account for most of the free exercise cases of the modern era, but neither accounts for all of them and neither provides complete consistency. With our two maps in hand, we shall let the Supreme Court speak for itself. The remainder of this chapter works through the free exercise cases more or less chronologically, with an eye to testing whether the "cluster" perspective or the "standard of review" perspective offers a clearer picture. We will also watch closely as the Supreme Court wrestles with the other core principles of religious liberty— notably liberty of conscience and equality of a plurality of faiths before the law. In Chapter 11, we shall look separately at the Court's treatment of religious groups and see, especially, how the principle of separation of church and state has operated in that sphere.

Free Exercise and Polygamy (1879–1890)

The Court first applied the free exercise clause in *Reynolds v. United States* (1879).[29] In that case, and in a pair of cases in 1890, the Court used an extremely narrow reading of the free exercise clause to uphold congressional restrictions on individuals and groups that preached and practiced polygamy. Each case involved the Church of Jesus Christ of Latter-Day Saints—the LDS Church as it is often called today, or the Mormon Church as it was called in the nineteenth century. This was one of numerous new churches to emerge during the Second Great Awakening in the early nineteenth century. Its founder, Joseph Smith, had developed, under divine inspiration, a new Scripture to supplement the Christian Bible—the *Book of Mormon,* which he published in 1830. He had further developed a separate *Book of Commandments* in 1833, which described followers of the *Book of Mormon* as a new chosen people. The Mormon faith called for the formation of new communities centered on a temple, devoted to a common "Law of Consecration and Stewardship," and especially committed to mission. This faith also featured a number of novel teachings, such as the efficacy of proxy baptism for the dead, the preexistence of man, and a metaphysical materialism that stood in tension with the traditional biblical story of creation *ex nihilo.* Such novel teachings and practices, and the ardent advocacy of them by missionaries, soon led to severe repression of the Mormon Church. The church was driven from New York to Ohio, and then to Missouri and Illinois. After severe rioting and the murder of Joseph Smith and his brother in 1844, Mormon believers migrated to the American frontier under the leadership of Brigham Young; they settled in what soon became the Territory of Utah (1850).

Many new religious communities born of the Second Great Awakening were left to themselves. But the Mormon Church, even far away on the frontier, continued to attract attention. The seminal cause was an 1852 manifesto from the church leadership that commended polygamy. For one man to have several wives, the church taught, was an appropriate and biblical form of communal living. It also increased the opportunities for women to enjoy the spiritual benefits of marriage and motherhood. To set an example for the reticent, the church's leaders took several wives. They further reported that Joseph Smith and other church leaders had done the same in the 1830s and 1840s.

When Congress learned of this policy of polygamy, it responded with instant denunciation and a political crusade against the Mormon Church. Since Utah and some of the other western areas where the Mormons settled were still United States territories, Congress had general authority to pass laws regulating issues of marriage, family, and sexuality. Congress exercised this authority with increasing sternness against Mormon polygamous practices. An 1862 law made polygamy a federal crime in all United States territories, including Utah. An 1882 law disqualified polygamists, as well as men cohabiting with more than one woman, from holding political office, voting in elections, and sitting on juries. Related statutes required parties to swear oaths denying practice or advocacy of polygamy, and subjected them to close scrutiny for even suspected belief in polygamy. An 1887 law called for the complete forfeiture of the Mormon Church's property if it persisted in its preaching and practice of polygamy.[30] The Mormons repeatedly challenged technical aspects of these laws, appealing more than a dozen times to the Supreme Court, but to little avail.

Three of these Supreme Court cases directly challenged congressional laws as violations of the free exercise clause. In *Reynolds v. United States* (1879), a Mormon appealed a conviction under the criminal law against polygamy. In *Davis v. Beason* (1890), a Mormon appealed a conviction for false swearing of a mandatory oath renouncing polygamy.[31] In *Church of Jesus Christ of Latter Day Saints v. United States* (1890), the Mormon Church challenged the government's dissolution of its corporate charter and confiscation of its property.[32] In each case, the Mormon parties claimed that they had a free exercise right to participate in voluntary polygamy as their faith encouraged, and they thus sought exemptions from compliance with congressional law.

The Supreme Court quickly dispensed with the Mormons' free exercise arguments and held for Congress each time. In *Reynolds,* Chief Justice Waite took Jefferson's adage of "building a wall of separation between church and State . . . almost as an authoritative declaration of the scope and effect of the [rights that the first] amendment thus secured." The free exercise clause protects religious beliefs only and not religious actions, he argued. "Congress was deprived of all legislative power over mere opinion, but was left free to reach [religious] actions which were in violation of social duties and subversive of good order." The preaching and practice of polygamy were notorious examples of such subversive conduct.[33] The congressional power to pass general laws in promotion of the health, safety, welfare, and morality of the community, the Court continued in *Davis* (1890), could not be compromised by judicial creation of a free exercise exemption from these laws. To exempt Mormons from compliance with general laws, particularly criminal prohibitions against polygamy, Justice Field thundered for the Court, would "shock the moral judgment of the community . . . [and] offend the common sense of mankind."[34]

Justice Bradley drove home these sentiments in the Court's opinion in the 1890 *Latter Day Corporation* case: "The organization of a community for the spread and practice of polygamy is, in a measure, a return to barbarism. It is contrary to the spirit of Christianity and of the civilization which Christianity has produced in the Western world." It is a "sophistical plea" to claim free exercise protection for this "nefarious doctrine." Granting free exercise protection in this case would invite specious evasions of criminal law—even religious excuses for human sacrifice and suicide, the Court reasoned. "The state has a perfect right to prohibit polygamy, and all other open offenses against the enlightened sentiment of mankind, notwithstanding the pretense of religious conviction by which they may be advocated and practiced."[35]

In 1890, confronted with these political and legal realities, Wilford Woodruff, the presiding officer of the Mormon Church, issued a manifesto disavowing any further participation in polygamy and urging church members to follow. On October 6, 1890, a Mormon Church conference accepted the manifesto—although a small group of self-defined "Fundamentalist Mormons" broke off and have quietly maintained their polygamous practices to this day, each time losing their free exercise claims when prosecuted.[36] In response to the 1890 manifesto, Congress returned the Mormon Church's property in 1894. Utah became a state in 1896, and its new constitution prohibited polygamy and featured the only explicit clause on separation of church and state to appear among the state constitutions before 1947.[37] In time, the Mormon Church began to develop its distinctive ethical code, featuring abstinence from tobacco, alcohol, and caffeine, and strict codes for dress, diet, hygiene, and sexual practice. It also routinized its theology and practice of mission, becoming one of the fastest growing faiths in America and elsewhere.

These early cases on polygamy did little to embellish the meaning of the free exercise clause and in fact seemed to deprive it of any real value. The Court effectively reduced the free exercise clause to a minimalist guarantee of liberty of conscience alone—and even that was cast as a mere freedom to have one's belief or opinion, but not a protection against being forced to swear exculpatory oaths, give testimony adverse to one's religious beliefs, or have one's rights to jury trial, probate, voting, and the like denied if associated with Mormonism. The Court gave short shrift to free exercise arguments that individuals are entitled to preach or practice polygamy peaceably and privately, or even to associate with those suspected of the same. The free exercise clause, the Court held, protected religious opinions about polygamy but gave no protection to actions taken upon such beliefs by individuals or groups. Congress had power to regulate all such religious actions, and it had declared all such actions related to polygamy to be dangerous and criminal. Congress had power to incorporate the Mormon Church; it also had power to dissolve this corporation if it persisted in its crime. For the Court, this was the end of the matter, and it would entertain no free exercise claim to exemption from compliance with these laws. Very little in the text or the history of the free exercise clause supported such a narrow reading. Just how far this belief/action logic extended, and just how far

Congress's authority extended to trump free exercise complaints using criminal laws on subjects other than polygamy, the Court did not explain.

Free Exercise and Conscientious Objection (1918–1971)

In a series of cases after 1918, the Court used similar logic to address the free exercise claims of pacifists who claimed conscientious objection to war or to oaths supporting warfare. Belief in pacifism was constitutionally protected, the Court said repeatedly, but actions or omissions taken upon those beliefs were not. Congress had full power to decide whether and which pacifists might be excused from military preparation or participation, or from oaths attesting to the same. It was simply not "within the province of the courts to make bargains" with individuals whose religious scruples were not sufficiently respected by Congress.[38]

The first case concerned exemptions from the military draft. In *Arver v. United States* (1918), a pacifist challenged the Selective Draft Act in which Congress had granted conscientious objector status only to ordained ministers and theology students and to members of "any well recognized religious sect or organization whose existing creed or principles forbid its members to participate in war."[39] The petitioner contended that the Selective Draft Act violated both the free exercise and the establishment clauses by privileging religious pacifists over nonreligious pacifists and by preferring some religious pacifists over others like himself who were equally religious. The Court thought such arguments too far-fetched to merit analysis: "We pass without anything but statement the proposition that an establishment of a religion or an interference with the free exercise thereof repugnant to the First Amendment resulted from the exemption clauses . . . because we think its unsoundness is too apparent to require us to do more."[40]

In *United States v. Schwimmer* (1929) and *United States v. Macintosh* (1931), the Court denied relief to parties who were denied naturalized citizenship status solely because of their failure to swear an oath that they would take up arms in defense of the country. Schwimmer was a forty-nine-year-old, well-educated Hungarian woman who wrote and lectured on pacifism. Macintosh was a Baptist divinity professor at Yale and former military chaplain in the Canadian armed forces. Both were ineligible for the military under then current military draft laws. Both were otherwise eligible for citizenship. Both were willing to swear full allegiance to the nation but could not swear to bear arms in defense of the same because of their religious beliefs in pacifism. Both were denied citizenship and appealed to the Supreme Court, claiming free exercise defenses to the oath swearing. Both lost.

In *Schwimmer,* Justice Butler defended the military power of Congress as "a fundamental principle of the Constitution" and described pacifism as a danger to the same. "The common defense was one of the purposes for which the people ordained and established the Constitution," he wrote for the Court. "It empowers the Congress to provide for such defense, to declare war, to raise and support armies, to maintain a navy, to make rules for the government and regulation of the land and naval forces, to provide for organizing, arming and disciplining the militia." Pacifists can be dangerous, for they are "apt to be more detrimental than their mere refusal to bear arms. The fact that, by reason of sex, age, or other cause, they may be unfit to serve does not lessen their purpose or power to influence others."[41]

In *Macintosh,* Justice Sutherland, speaking for the Court, added that conscientious objection status was a legislative privilege, not a natural or constitutional right. The status "comes not from the Constitution, but from the acts of Congress. That body may grant or withhold the exemption as in its wisdom it sees fit." Moreover, it was for Congress, not for the individual subject, to judge the religious and moral propriety of the nation's military policy and the role of its citizens therein:

> We are a Christian people according to one another the equal right of religious free-
> dom, and acknowledging with reverence the duty of obedience to the will of God.
> But, also, we are a nation with the duty to survive; a nation whose Constitution con-
> templates war as well as peace; whose government must go forward upon the assump-
> tion, and safely can proceed upon no other, that unqualified allegiance to the nation
> and submission and obedience to the laws of the land, as well those made for war as
> those made for peace, are not inconsistent with the will of God.[42]

Chief Justice Hughes wrote a strong dissent in *Macintosh,* arguing that the Court had trespassed even the narrow view of liberty of conscience set out in the Mormon polygamy cases, as well as the policy reflected in the "no religious test oath" in Article VI. This argument failed to convince the *Macintosh* Court. It also failed to convince the Court in two subsequent cases in the next decade on the rights of religious pacifists. In both cases the Court held for Congress and denied the existence of a constitutional free exercise right to conscientious objection to military service or to oaths in support of the same.[43]

Fifteen years after *MacIntosh,* however, a 5–4 Court outlawed the imposition of military test oaths on applicants for naturalization. In *Girouard v. United States* (1946), a Canadian Seventh-Day Adventist applicant agreed to swear an oath pledging allegiance to the United States and fidelity to the Constitution. But he, like Schwimmer and MacIntosh, could not swear an oath that he would be "willing to take up arms in defense of this country." For "purely religious" reasons, he said, he could not bear arms but was willing to serve in a noncombatant role, like some 10,000 other Adventists who served in the military during World War II. He was refused naturalization, and appealed.

This time the Court reversed. "Refusal to bear arms is not necessarily a sign of disloyalty or a lack of attachment to our institutions," Justice Douglas wrote for the *Girouard* Court. "One may serve his country faithfully and devotedly, though his religious scruples make it impossible for him to shoulder a rifle." Moreover, refusal to swear an oath cannot alone be a disqualification for citizenship. After all, Article VI of the Constitution does not require citizens to swear an oath to hold federal office. Congress could not have meant to "set a stricter standard for aliens seeking admission to citizenship than it did for officials who make and enforce the laws of the nation and administer its affairs. It is hard to believe that one need forsake his religious scruples to become a citizen but not to sit in the high councils of state." *Schwimmer, Macintosh*, and their progeny, the Court concluded, "do not state the correct rule of law."[44]

While *Girouard* changed the laws of naturalization for those conscientiously opposed to swearing military oaths, it did not change the law with respect to conscientious objection to military service itself. To this day, such conscientious objection claims remain legislative, not judicial decisions. The Court consistently maintained this posture in a score of cases, the last issued in 1971, during the height of opposition to the military draft during the Vietnam War.[45] The Court has interpreted Congress's provision for pacifists generously, sometimes stretching statutory language near the breaking point to accommodate everyone claiming pacifism "by reason of religion and belief."[46] But the Court has never found a constitutional right to conscientious objection under the free exercise clause despite tempering its earlier opinions on naturalization oaths.

This cluster of cases on conscientious objection to military matters is more consistent with the original understanding of the First Amendment than the Court's churlish reading of the Mormon's free exercise claims to polygamy. As we saw, four drafts of the First Amendment religion clauses had included explicit conscientious objection clauses to military service, following in part precedents from the Continental Congress (pp. 100–102). But the proposal to include specific constitutional protections for pacifists in the Bill of Rights was perennially controversial and eventually dropped. The most persuasive argument against it came from Representative Benson in the House debate of August 17, 1789. Such questions, he said, must be left "to the benevolence of the Legislature" and to the "discretion of the Government." "If this stands part of the constitution, it will be before the Judiciary on every regulation you make with respect to the organization of the militia" (pp. 85–86). Although the Court made little reference to this history, its dismissive treatment of the claim of a free exercise right to pacifism seemed to be driven in part by this concern. The rights and limits of pacifism are for the legislature, not the courts.

Freedom and Equality of Religious Expression (1940–2002)

While conscientious objection may not have been at the core of the free exercise clause, freedom of religious expression certainly was. Both the eighteenth-century founders and nineteenth-century states, as we have seen, regarded freedom of religious speech, press, assembly, and other expressions of faith to be essential to religious liberty, and they took steps to protect them. The issue that emerged in the early twentieth century was whether the federal courts also should protect the freedom of religious expression under the free exercise clause.

This was, in part, a doctrinal issue. *Reynolds* and its progeny had stated that the free exercise clause protected religious beliefs, not religious acts. Religious expression was obviously an act, not just a belief. The federal courts could protect it under the free exercise clause only if the Supreme Court abandoned its earlier belief-act distinction. This was, in part, a political issue. In its earlier polygamy and conscientious objection cases, the Court had shown great deference to the legislature with only marginal judicial review. Moreover, most cases involving freedom of religious expression were being filed against state and local governments. The federal courts could intervene only if they had a valid constitutional basis for closer review, especially of state decisions. And this was, in part, a cultural issue. Most of the cases were raised by the indefatigable Jehovah's Witnesses—a newly prominent Christian missionary group, for whom strong religious preaching, proselytism, pamphleteering, and public demonstrations of biblical beliefs were vital exercises of faith. From the 1930s onward, the Witnesses had risen to loud prominence in public life, preaching the Gospel, knocking on doors, and denouncing traditional churches, states, and businesses alike as the "triple alliance of Satan." Annoyed by their messages and methods, many city, county, and state officials worked hard to keep them out or drive them away. The Witnesses filed scores of cases in the federal courts, claiming violations of their First Amendment free exercise and free speech rights.

In the landmark 1940 case of *Cantwell v. Connecticut,* the Supreme Court took firm control of these cases and welcomed the Witnesses and their free exercise claims. The *Cantwell* Court rejected the wooden "belief-act" distinction of its earlier polygamy cases. It applied the First Amendment free exercise clause to state and local governments via the Fourteenth Amendment due process clause. And it adopted a heightened standard of scrutiny to govern all cases involving freedom of religious expression. All forms of religious expression, "even if unpopular," Justice Roberts wrote for the *Cantwell* Court, are equally deserving of presumptive protection under the free exercise clause. But all forms of religious expression, even if purely motivated, "remain subject to regulation for the protection of society." Roberts laid out the standard to be applied henceforth in judging the constitutionality of these regulations under the free exercise clause:

> In every case the power to regulate must be so exercised as not, in attaining a permissible end, unduly to infringe the protected freedom. No one would contest the proposition that a State may not, by statute, wholly deny the right to preach or to disseminate religious views. Plainly such a previous and absolute restraint would violate the terms of the guarantee. It is equally clear that a State may by general and non-discriminatory legislation regulate the times, the places, and the manner of [religious expression] . . . without unconstitutionally invading the liberties protected by the Fourteenth Amendment. . . . No one would have the hardihood to suggest . . . that religious liberty connotes the privilege to exhort others to physical attack upon those belonging to another sect. When clear and present danger of riot, disorder, interference with traffic upon the public streets, or other immediate threat to public safety, peace, or order appears, the power of the State to prevent or punish is obvious. Equally obvious is it that a State may not unduly suppress free communication of views, religious or other, under the guise of conserving desirable conditions.[47]

These were the three keys to adjudicating free exercise cases on religious expression: (1) outright prohibitions and prior restraints on religious expression that effectively foreclosed religious expression were forbidden; (2) discriminatory regulations of religious expression were also forbidden; but (3) general regulations that properly protected public safety and security were permissible. The Court elaborated on these sentiments in a long series of cases after *Cantwell.*

The Court readily struck down outright prohibitions on religious proselytism and other forms of peaceable religious expression. In *Cantwell*, the Court held that merely unpopular preaching on the public streets could not be prohibited or punished as a breach of the peace. In *Jamison v. Texas* (1943) and *Martin v. Struthers* (1943), the Court struck down ordinances that prohibited distribution of religious pamphlets in the public square and door to door. "The state may prohibit the use of the streets for the distribution of purely commercial leaflets," Justice Black declared for the *Jamison* Court. But "they may not prohibit the distribution of handbills in pursuit of a clearly religious activity merely because the handbills invite the purchase of books for the improved understanding of the religion or because the handbills seek in a lawful fashion to promote the raising of funds for religious purposes."[48] Three years later, in *Marsh v. Alabama* (1946) and *Tucker v. Texas* (1946), the Court extended this ruling to company- and government-owned towns: per se prohibitions and criminal penalties levied on such religious expression violate the free exercise and free speech clauses.[49]

The Court also struck down taxing schemes on religious preaching and proselytizing as "prior restraints" on the freedom of religious expression. In the leading case, *Murdock v. Pennsylvania* (1943), a Jehovah's Witness challenged the constitutionality of a city ordinance that required all persons soliciting or selling goods to procure a license for a day, or for a one-, two-, or three-week period. Each license required payment of a fee, ranging from $1.50 for a day to $20 for three weeks—more than nominal fees by 1943 standards. Jehovah's Witnesses were convicted and fined for soliciting, distributing religious literature, and collecting donations in the town without a license. They appealed, arguing that this was a tax laid specifically on the exercise of their religion.

The *Murdock* Court agreed. "The hand distribution of religious tracts is an age-old form of missionary evangelism," Justice Douglas wrote for the Court. It "occupies the same high estate under the First Amendment as do worship in the churches or preaching from the pulpits. It has the same claim to protection as the more orthodox and conventional exercises of religion." The freedom to engage in such religious activity is "available to all, not merely to those who can pay their own way." The license fee imposed by the city "is a flat license tax, the payment of which is a condition for the exercise of these constitutional privileges. The power to tax the exercise of a privilege is the power to control or suppress its enjoyment. Those who can tax the exercise of this religious practice can make its exercise so costly as to deprive it of the resources necessary for its maintenance." The *Murdock* Court thus struck down this licensing scheme.[50] Three other early cases struck down comparable schemes, even with more nominal fees, that taxed the solicitation, distribution, and sale of religious literature and articles by Jehovah's Witnesses.[51]

Consistent with the dicta of *Cantwell,* the Court did allow general "time, place, and manner" regulations of religious expression—so long as they did not target religious expression per se and so long as local officials implementing the statute had clear standards for implementation and no discretion to discriminate on religious grounds. In *Cantwell,* the city licensing regulation failed because it targeted religion and gave officials discretion to deny licenses to unpopular religious applicants. In *Kunz v. New York* (1951), the denial of a license to a Baptist minister to preach in a public park was struck down because local officials had open discretion to deny licenses.[52] In *Niemotko v. State of Maryland* (1951), the denial of a permit to use a public park for "Bible talks" was struck down because the statute lacked clear criteria for such denials.[53] In *Fowler v. Rhode Island* (1953) an ordinance that prohibited religious speech but allowed for religious services in a public park was struck down because it discriminated on the basis of religion.[54]

In *Poulos v. New Hampshire* (1953), the Court upheld a municipal regulation of religious expression, and it used the case to underscore the kinds of regulation of religious expression that were permissible under the free exercise and free speech clauses. In *Poulos,* a New Hampshire town provided what the Court considered a properly "uniform, non-discriminatory, and consistent administration of . . . licenses for public meetings." Any parties intending to use public streets or parks for "theatrical or dramatic representation," "parades or processions," or "open air public meetings" were required to procure a license by written application in advance. A sliding fee of up to $300 would be charged for the license to pay for police protection, crowd control, and cleanup. Officials had no discretion to deny an application based on the nature of the applicant's activities. Parties would be fined if they failed to procure a license for such an occasion.

A group of Jehovah's Witnesses seeking to use the public park for a religious meeting challenged the statute. The Court upheld it as a valid regulation of religious expression. What impressed the Court was that "the state left to the licensing officials no discretion as to granting permits, no power to discriminate, no control over speech. . . . The ordinance merely calls for the adjustment of unrestrained exercise of religions with the reasonable convenience and comfort of the whole city." This was licit even in the face of strong claims to religious expression. Justice Reed wrote for the Court:

> The principles of the First Amendment are not to be treated as a promise that everyone with opinions or beliefs to express may gather around him at any public place and any time a group for discussion or instruction. It is a non sequitur to say that First Amendment rights may not be regulated because they hold a preferred position in the hierarchy of the constitutional guarantees of the incidents of freedom. This Court has never so held and indeed has definitely indicated the contrary. It has indicated approval of reasonable non-discriminatory regulation by government authority that preserves peace, order and tranquillity without deprivation of the First Amendment guarantees of free speech, press and the exercise of religion. . . . There is no basis for

saying that freedom and order are not compatible. That would be a decision of desperation. Regulation and suppression are not the same, either in purpose or result, and courts of justice can tell the difference.[55]

Several subsequent cases have upheld this standard, although increasingly on free speech grounds rather than explicitly through the free exercise clause. The Court's most recent application came in *Watchtower Bible and Tract Society v. Village of Stratton* (2002).[56] There the Court struck down a village ordinance that required all door-to-door solicitors and canvassers, including Jehovah's Witnesses, to obtain a permit in advance containing the licensee's name. Homeowners could register with the village and bar all solicitors, or they could select from a printed list those whom they wished to bar, including Jehovah's Witnesses, who were listed. The Witnesses objected to this ordinance both as a prior restraint on and discriminatory targeting of their proselytism activities in violation of their free speech and free exercise rights.

The *Watchtower* Court agreed. It recognized the "legitimate interests" a town may have to regulate solicitation, including the prevention of crime and fraud and the protection of privacy. However, the Court stressed that "our precedent is clear that there must be a balance between these interests and the effect of the regulations on First Amendment rights." The *Watchtower* Court struck the balance in favor of the Jehovah's Witnesses. The Court recognized the evangelists' religiously motivated desire for anonymity, and it found no evidence of crime or fraud in the record. Moreover, in the Court's judgment, the ordinance would have little to no effect on criminals who registered under a false name or knocked on doors for reasons not covered by the ordinance. The Court thus held that the ordinance was too broad in scope and insufficiently tailored to the government's stated interests to justify the burden it placed upon the Witnesses' free speech and free exercise rights.

The Court did uphold restrictions on religious expression that violated criminal laws. In *Chaplinsky v. New Hampshire* (1942), for example, the Court rejected the First Amendment claims of a Jehovah's Witness to be exempt from prosecution for breach of the peace. While standing on a busy public street, Mr. Chaplinsky denounced various government officials and police as "God damned racketeer[s]" and "damned Fascist[s]." Local police repeatedly warned him to desist. He persisted, and after unrest broke out he was arrested and charged with breaching the peace. He appealed, but the *Chaplinsky* Court rejected his claim. Just because his words may have been "religious in character" or inspiration, Justice Murphy wrote for the Court, that alone "would not cloak him with immunity."

> It is well understood that the right of free speech is not absolute at all times and under all circumstances. There are certain well-defined and narrowly limited classes of speech, the prevention and punishment of which have never been thought to raise any Constitutional problem. These include the lewd and obscene, the profane, the libelous, and the insulting or "fighting" words—those which by their very utterance

inflict injury or tend to incite an immediate breach of the peace. It has been well observed that such utterances are no essential part of any exposition of ideas, and are of such slight social value as a step to truth that any benefit that may be derived from them is clearly outweighed by the social interest in order and morality.[57]

Similarly in *Prince v. Massachusetts* (1944), the Court upheld a state criminal law against a Jehovah's Witness who was distributing religious literature on the public streets in the evening with her nine-year-old ward. Such distribution was in technical violation of a state criminal law against the use of child labor after certain hours. After ignoring several warnings by the police, the woman was arrested and fined for violating the statute. She appealed, claiming violation of both her and her ward's free exercise rights, as well as her parental rights to raise her ward in her own faith. She claimed further that the distribution of religious literature was not "labor" under the child labor statute but religious exercise under the First Amendment. The Court was impressed with the gravity of the state interest in protecting children, who had historically been abused in the workplace, despite the free exercise claims raised by the applicant. Justice Rutledge stated the "delicate balance" struck by the *Prince* Court:

> On one side is the obviously earnest claim for freedom of conscience and religious practice. With it is allied the parent's claim to authority in her own household and in the rearing of her children. The parent's conflict with the state . . . is serious enough when only secular matters are concerned. It becomes the more so when an element of religious conviction enters. Against these sacred private interests, basic in a democracy, stand the interests of society to protect the welfare of children. . . . [N]either rights of religion nor rights of parenthood are beyond limitation. Acting to guard the general interest in youth's well being, the state as *parens patriae* may restrict the parent's control by requiring school attendance, regulating or prohibiting the child's labor, and in many other ways. Its authority is not nullified merely because the parent grounds his claims to control the child's course of conduct on religion or conscience. . . . The right to practice religion freely does not include liberty to expose the community or the child to communicable disease or the latter to ill health or death.[58]

After such balancing, the Court applied the child labor statute literally and held for the state. With this precedent, it was very easy for the Court, a few years later, to affirm a lower court decision that a child of Jehovah's Witness parents could receive a necessary blood transfusion, despite the religious objection of conscientiously opposed parents.[59]

Liberty of Conscience and Free Exercise Exemptions (1943–1989)

At the heart of the principle of liberty of conscience is what the founders had called "the unalienable right of private judgment in matters of religion" (p. 42). This includes the freedom to choose or to change one's religious beliefs or practices without coercion or control by government, and without facing discrimination or penalties for the religious choices once made. It also includes the right to exemption from majoritarian laws that compel or forbid actions that contradict the "dictates of conscience." James Madison, as we have seen, understood the dangers of "tyranny of the majority" very well: "Wherever the real power in a Government lies, there is the danger of oppression. In our Governments the real power lies in the majority of the Community, and the invasion of private rights is chiefly to be apprehended, not from acts of Government contrary to the sense of its constituents, but from acts in which the Government is the mere instrument of the major number of the constituents." Religious exemptions from majoritarian laws are sometimes needed to protect the private rights of conscience of religious minorities, and such exemptions naturally flow from the principle of liberty of conscience.

The Supreme Court came only gradually to such an understanding in its interpretation of the free exercise clause. The Court's dicta in early cases before *Cantwell* seemed promising. In *Watson v. Jones* (1871), for example, Justice Miller had declared for a unanimous Court: "In this country the full and free right to entertain any religious belief, to practice any religious principle, and to teach any religious doctrine which does not violate the laws of morality and property, and which does not infringe personal rights, is conceded to all. The law knows no heresy, and is committed to the support of no dogma, the establishment of no sect."[60] But despite such suggestive dicta, the Court did little to protect liberty of conscience in these early free exercise cases. The polygamy cases from 1879 to 1890 upheld congressional laws that penalized Mormons for their polygamy and demanded from them all manner of confessions and exculpatory oaths. The early pacifism cases from 1918 to 1945 would hear nothing of a party's constitutional right to conscientious objection from military service or oaths—no matter how devout or developed a party's conscientious scruples. And, for all the promise that the 1946 *Girouard* case held out for protecting liberty of conscience through the no-religious test oath provision of Article VI, little came of this case thereafter.

This discordance of principle and practice continued in the early years after *Cantwell*. In *Cantwell* itself, Justice Roberts had declared confidently for the Court that the free exercise clause was "absolute" in forestalling "compulsion by law of the acceptance of any creed or the practice of any form of worship."[61] But in its very next case, *Minersville School Board v. Gobitis* (1940), decided two weeks later, the Court betrayed this very principle. The children of a Jehovah's Witness were expelled from a public school because they refused to salute the American flag or recite the Pledge of Allegiance. The Bible, in their understanding and that of their coreligionists, prohibited such acts as forms of false worship. To compel those acts, their parents argued, was a violation of the liberty of conscience. The Supreme Court disagreed. The purpose of the school policy was to promote national unity and loyalty, said the Court, not to institute a false form of worship. "To stigmatize legislative judgment in providing for this universal gesture of respect for the symbol of our national life in the setting of the common school as a lawless inroad on that freedom of conscience which the Constitution protects," Justice Frankfurter wrote for a divided Court, "would amount to no less than the pronouncement of pedagogical and psychological dogma in a field where courts possess no marked and certainly no controlling competence."[62]

Three years later, however, in *West Virginia State Board of Education v. Barnette* (1943), the Court directly overruled *Gobitis* and read the First Amendment free exercise clause to exempt parties from mandatory participation in a compulsory ritual to which they were conscientiously opposed. *Barnette* raised facts similar to those of *Gobitis:* Jehovah's Witness children were again expelled from public school for failing to salute the flag and recite the Pledge of Allegiance, and the families now faced fines if they persisted in their recalcitrance. While acknowledging the importance of teaching national loyalty and unity in public schools, the Court held that the compulsory participation in such civic ceremonies violated the liberty of conscience as embodied in the free exercise clause. As Justice Jackson wrote for the Court:

> If there is any fixed star in our constitutional constellation, it is that no official, high or petty, can prescribe what shall be orthodox in politics, nationalism, religion, or other matters of opinion or force citizens to confess by word or act their faith therein. If there are any circumstances which permit an exception, they do not now occur to us.[63]

Although in a pair of cases immediately thereafter the Court again stumbled on this principle of liberty of conscience, *Barnette* soon became the rule.[64]

The Court used this rule, as well as the earlier *Cantwell* dicta forbidding compulsory religious exercises, to reconsider the question of oath swearing outside the military context. In *Torcaso v. Watkins* (1961), the Court held that a professed atheist could not be required to swear an oath attesting to belief in God as part of his initiation into a state bureaucratic position.[65] "The Free Exercise Clause categorically forbids government from regulating, prohibiting, or rewarding religious beliefs as such," the Court later put it when summarizing the case.[66]

In *Sherbert v. Verner* (1963), the Court widened this understanding of liberty of conscience and belief while also introducing the strict scrutiny regime for application of the free exercise clause. Under this regime, the free exercise clause not only exempted conscientious parties from participation in oath swearing and other ceremonies that violated their conscientious beliefs but also could exempt them from adherence to other general laws and regulations that unduly burdened their consciences. In *Sherbert*, a Seventh-Day Adventist was discharged from employment and foreclosed from reemployment because of her conscientious refusal to work on Saturday, her Sabbath day. She was denied unemployment compensation from the state, for she had been fired for cause and was thus disqualified from the benefit. She appealed, arguing that the disqualifying provisions of the statute "abridged her right to the free exercise of her religion." If she exercised her religious right to Saturday Sabbatarianism, she would lose her civil right to a state benefit (unemployment compensation). If she was to receive her civil right to a state benefit, she would have to forgo her religious right to Saturday Sabbatarianism. Such a conflict, she argued, violated her free exercise rights.

The Supreme Court agreed. Justice Brennan wrote for the *Sherbert* Court: "To condition the availability of [state] benefits upon this appellant's willingness to violate a cardinal principle of her religious faith effectively penalizes the free exercise of her constitutional liberties."[67] Such a burden on her "sincere, and good faith" beliefs in Saturday Sabbatarianism could be justified only if the state could demonstrate that it was in pursuit of a "compelling state interest," was the "least restrictive alternative" for achieving that interest, and involved no religious discrimination. The state's unemployment compensation law failed under this strict scrutiny review. While the state was justified in protecting its unemployment benefits from fraudulent and undeserving claims, there was no evidence of fraud or lack of desert in this case. The state had simply not tailored its rules narrowly enough to accommodate all those whose religious scruples might require them to be excused from work. Further, the state accommodated Sunday Sabbatarians who were discharged from work but not Saturday Sabbatarians, making this an easy case of religious discrimination as well. The Court thus ordered Ms. Sherbert exempt from the general strictures on payment and entitled to unemployment compensation benefits.

In a concurring opinion in *Sherbert,* Justice Douglas made clear that this new regime of granting free exercise exemptions would need to become more commonplace as the nation's religions pluralized and its welfare laws proliferated:

> Religious scruples of Moslems require them to attend a mosque on Friday and to pray five times daily. Religious scruples of a Sikh require him to carry a regular or a symbolic sword. Religious scruples of a Jehovah's Witness teach him to be a colporteur, going from door to door, from town to town, distributing his religious pamphlets. Religious scruples of a Quaker compel him to refrain from swearing [an oath] and to affirm instead. Religious scruples of a Buddhist may require him to refrain from partaking of any flesh. The examples could be multiplied . . . to show that many people hold beliefs alien to the majority of our society—beliefs that are protected by the First Amendment but which could easily be trod upon under the guise of "police" or "health" regulations reflecting the majority's views.[68]

In a trio of cases in the 1980s, the Court extended *Sherbert*'s holding to other applicants for state unemployment compensation. *Thomas v. Review Board* (1981) involved a Jehovah's Witness who had individual scruples, not shared by fellow Witnesses, against production of hardware that would be used for military tanks.[69] *Hobbie v. Unemployment Appeals Commission of Florida* (1987) involved a new convert to Seventh-Day Adventism who began to insist on the right to observe her Saturday Sabbath.[70] *Frazee v. Illinois Department of Employment Security* involved a Christian party who refused a temporary position because it might require him to work on his Sabbath day of rest, though not of worship.[71] Each of these parties lost their employment. Each was denied unemployment compensation benefits on the general rule that they had been discharged for cause. Each successfully appealed to the Court for a free exercise exemption from this general rule and was found entitled to unemployment compensation. Neither the novelty nor the idiosyncrasy of a religious belief changed the core violation of the liberty of conscience. As Chief Justice Burger put it: "Where the state conditions receipt of an important benefit upon conduct proscribed by a religious faith, or where it denies such a benefit because of conduct mandated by religious belief, thereby putting substantial pressure on an adherent to modify his behavior and to violate his beliefs, a burden upon religion exists." This violates the liberty of conscience values of the free exercise clause and entitles the claimant to an exemption.[72]

In *McDaniel v. Paty* (1978), the Court pressed its concern for relieving the tension between juxtaposed religious and civil rights into the political sphere. The original constitution of Tennessee (1796) prohibited clergy from holding political office in the state. The purpose of this prohibition was "to assure the success of a new political experiment, the separation of church and state." A number of early state constitutions had included such clerical prohibitions, as we have seen (pp. 54–55). With the growing religious pluralism of their citizenry, however, most states had eventually rejected these provisions. Tennessee had not, and the state courts used this clerical exclusion provision to prevent an otherwise qualified Baptist minister from running for political office. He appealed, arguing a violation of his free exercise rights. The clerical prohibition posed a direct conflict between his free exercise rights to religious ministry and his civil rights to run for political office. The *McDaniel* Court agreed. Quoting both *Sherbert* and James Madison, the Court held that "the State is 'punishing a religious profession with the privation of a civil right.'" The Tennessee constitutional prohibition was struck down as a violation of the free exercise clause.[73]

In *Wisconsin v. Yoder* (1972), the Court extended this logic of free exercise exemptions to its furthest point. Wisconsin, like every other state, had mandatory school attendance rules. All able children were required to attend a public school or an accredited private school up to the age of sixteen. A group of Old Order Amish agreed to have their children educated through the eighth grade so that they could learn basic reading, writing, arithmetic, and other skills needed to survive in the world. But the Amish parents sought to withdraw their children from school thereafter—in part so they could be protected from the growing temptations of the world as teenagers, and in part so they could learn the agricultural, house holding, and other communal norms and habits that were central to the communitarian religious lifestyle of the Old Order Amish. Wisconsin refused to grant an exemption from its mandatory attendance rules. The Amish parents appealed, claiming violation of their free exercise rights.

The Supreme Court held for the Amish. The *Yoder* Court was impressed that the Amish "lifestyle," in Chief Justice Burger's words, was "not merely a matter of personal preference, but one of deep religious conviction, shared by an organized group, and intimately related to daily living" and that these "religious beliefs and attitudes towards life, family and home . . . have not altered in fundamentals for centuries." In the Court's view, compliance with the compulsory school attendance law "carries with it a very real threat of undermining the Amish community and religious practice as they exist today; they must either abandon belief and be assimilated into society at large, or be forced to migrate to some other and more tolerant region." The free exercise clause would not allow a state to force its citizens to choose between the duties and dictates of faith and the rights and benefits of citizenship. While Wisconsin's mandatory school attendance laws were perfectly constitutional as an exercise of state power, the application of those laws in this case was not. The free exercise clause exempted the Amish from full compliance with the laws, the Court held. And such an exemption does not constitute an improper establishment of religion.[74]

The *Yoder* Court was especially solicitous of the traditional religious communitarian practices of the Old Order Amish—much more solicitous than it would prove to be of traditional Jewish and Native American communal norms.[75] The *Yoder* Court was also especially deferential to the rights of parents to raise their children in their own faith, and to remove them from the temptations of the world. The case stands not only as one of the most expansive formulations of free exercise rights, but also as the landmark in the development of the homeschooling movement, which has become popular in many parts of the country and provides a third way, along with public schools and private schools, to meet mandatory school attendance laws.

Neutralizing the Free Exercise Clause (1982–1993)

From the 1940s to the 1980s, the Supreme Court read the free exercise clause in expansive terms. The clause protected the freedom of religious expression and further protected the attendant principles of liberty of conscience and equality of a plurality of faiths before the law. (We shall see in Chapter 11 that the Court also drew on the principle of separation of church and state to protect the free exercise rights of religious bodies.) The rigor and range of the Court's free exercise inquiry did not always bring victory to religious claimants. Free exercise claimants lost as many cases as they won in this period, particularly when they challenged central government powers over crime, taxation, and the military. But the free exercise clause, in these middle decades of the twentieth century, provided what *Cantwell* had first called for: "a multi-layered shield" to protect many forms and forums of individual and corporate religious life.

In the course of the 1980s, the Supreme Court gradually reduced the free exercise clause to a single and simple principle of neutrality. The Court's earlier concerns to protect the conscience of the religious individual and the autonomy of the religious group from state intrusions slowly fell aside. The Court's earlier decisions to strike down laws that imposed taxes or discriminatory restrictions on religious expression also fell aside. In a series of cases culminating in *Employment Division v. Smith* (1990), the Court systematically read each of these constitutive principles out of the free exercise clause, eventually reducing it to a single and simple guarantee of religious neutrality.

This new trend began in *United States v. Lee* (1982). This was another case involving the Old Order Amish. Mr. Lee employed fellow Amish to work on his farm and in his shop. In paying them, he deducted income taxes but not social security taxes. He believed it was "sinful" for the Amish "not to provide for their own elderly and needy," and he was "religiously opposed" to participation in the federal government's social security system. The Supreme Court accepted the "sincerity" of Lee's claim and acknowledged that the payment of social security taxes "interfere[d]" with his free exercise rights, but it nonetheless refused to grant him an exemption from compliance with social security regulations. Utilizing the strict scrutiny review then demanded by the free exercise clause, the Court found the massive and complex social security system to be constitutional. "Because the broad public interest in maintaining a sound tax system is of such a high order, religious belief in conflict with the payment of taxes affords no basis for resisting the tax. . . . When followers of a particular sect enter into commercial activity as a matter of choice, the limits they accept on their own conduct as a matter of conscience and faith are not to be superimposed on the statutory schemes which are binding on others in that activity."[76] The Court had held quite the opposite in *Sherbert* and its progeny, there allowing a person who chose to enter the workforce the right to superimpose her religious needs on the statutory scheme of unemployment compensation.

In *Goldman v. Weinberger* (1986), the Court carried this logic a step further, in the context of a military power case. In *Goldman*, the Court held that it was not a violation of the free exercise clause for the air force to prohibit a rabbi from wearing his yarmulke as part of his military uniform. The rabbi served as a psychologist in the mental health clinic of a military base. For him, wearing the yarmulke signaled both solidarity with the Jewish community and humility before God. For three years, he was accorded the "privilege" of wearing it while on base. But when he answered a subpoena to testify in a military court, he was challenged for wearing the yarmulke in violation of the military dress code. The 190-page code had numerous other exemptions for religious garb, including crucifixes, but yarmulkes were not mentioned and were therefore impermissible per the code. Rabbi Goldman sought a free exercise exemption from compliance with the code. It was refused, and he appealed. The Supreme Court refused to accommodate him. Free exercise rights are "severely diminished" on a military base, Justice Rehnquist wrote for the *Goldman* Court, in explaining its departure from the *Sherbert* strict scrutiny standard. Moreover, the requirements for military discipline and uniformity outweighed any countervailing religious interests—however ancient, deep-seated, and essential they might be.[77]

In *Bowen v. Roy* (1986), the Court pressed this concern for uniformity and neutrality from the military context back into the regulatory context, and now used *Goldman* as an authority to avoid use of the *Sherbert* strict scrutiny test. In *Bowen*, a Native American objected to having a social security number assigned to his daughter, arguing, in the Court's words, that "he must keep her person and spirit unique and that the uniqueness of the Social Security number as an identifier, coupled with the other uses of the number over which she has no control, will 'rob the spirit' of his daughter and prevent her from attaining greater spiritual power." He requested an exemption for his daughter, until she reached sufficient spiritual maturity at the age of sixteen. Although it acknowledged the sincerity and substance of the parent's claim, the Court found for the government. Chief Justice Burger's opinion for the Court was in striking contrast to his highly solicitous tone fourteen years earlier in *Wisconsin v. Yoder* (1972):

> Never to our knowledge has the Court interpreted the First Amendment to require the Government *itself* to behave in ways that the individual believes will further his or her spiritual development or that of his or her own family. The Free Exercise Clause simply cannot be understood to require the Government to conduct its own internal affairs in ways that comport with the religious beliefs of particular citizens. . . . Government meets its burden when it demonstrates that a challenged requirement for governmental benefits, neutral and uniform in its application, is a reasonable means of promoting a legitimate public interest.[78]

In *O'Lone v. Estate of Shabazz* (1987), the Court extended this logic to prison officials, holding that a change in prison policy that deprived Muslim inmates from attending Jumu'ah, their Friday collective worship service, did not violate their free exercise rights. The requirements for security, protection of other prisoners, and other "reasonable penological objectives," in the Court's view, outweighed the free exercise rights of the Muslim prisoners. Moreover, said the Court in quoting *Bowen v. Roy* and other precedents, it is wrong to impose a "special burden on prison officials to prove 'that no reasonable method exists by which [prisoners'] religious rights can be accommodated.'" So long as the prison's regulations are "neutral and reasonable," they pass constitutional muster.[79]

In *Lyng v. Northwest Indian Cemetery Protective Association* (1988), the Court extended this neutrality logic still further to uphold the discretionary actions of the United States Forest Service that threatened to "crush" a religion. The case involved whether the Forest Service could build a road in a national park directly through a sacred burial ground used for centuries by three Native American tribes. Various construction plans and environmental impact statements offered an alternative plan, but it would cost considerably more to go around the sacred site. The Forest Service chose the cheaper, more direct route through the sacred site, and the Native American tribes raised free exercise objections. The Court held for the government even while recognizing that the construction would "have severe adverse effects of the practice of their religion." Citing *Roy* and *O'Lone,* Justice O'Connor defended this holding with blunt textual literalism:

> The crucial word in the constitutional text is "prohibit": "For the Free Exercise Clause is written in terms of what the government cannot do to the individual." . . . However

much we might wish that it were otherwise, government simply could not operate if it were required to satisfy every citizen's religious needs and desires. A broad range of government activities—from social welfare programs to foreign aid to conservation policies—will always be considered essential to the spiritual well-being of some citizens, often on the basis of sincerely-held religious beliefs. Others will find the very same activities deeply offensive, and perhaps incompatible with their own search for spiritual fulfillment and with the tenets of their religion. The First Amendment must apply to all citizens alike, and it can give to none of them a veto over public programs that do not prohibit the free exercise of religion. The Constitution does not, and courts cannot, offer to reconcile the various competing demands on government, many of them rooted in sincere religious belief, that inevitably arise in so diverse a society as ours.[80]

Two years later, in *Jimmy Swaggart Ministries v. Board of Equalization of California* (1990), the Court continued its move to reduce free exercise to a neutrality principle only, as it upheld the retroactive imposition of sales and use taxes on the sale of religious articles by a religious ministry. Swaggart Ministries argued that the imposition of such taxes was a prior restraint on the exercise of its religion—which the Court had explicitly outlawed in *Murdock v. Pennsylvania* (1943) and its progeny. The Court distinguished these earlier cases rather tendentiously. The earlier cases, Justice O'Connor wrote for the Court, dealt with "prior" restraints on free exercise, not post hoc collections of taxes. (The Court said nothing about the future collection of such taxes on Swaggart Ministries.) The earlier cases addressed specific flat taxes on religious solicitation, said the Court, and not general state taxes imposed on all sales of goods. (The Court ignored that the earlier tax schemes were imposed on all solicitors, not just religious ministers, and in some schemes had sliding fee scales depending on the number of days the license was to be used.) The Court thus upheld the state tax because it was not "a flat tax, represents only a small fraction of any retail sale, and applies neutrally to all retail sales of tangible personal property." It also seemed important to Justice O'Connor that Swaggart Ministries had no substantial burden on its freedom to practice their ministry: "There is no evidence in this case that collection and payment of the tax violates appellant's sincere religious beliefs. . . . The only burden on appellant is the claimed reduction in income."[81]

The foregoing cases had, in effect, written out of the free exercise clause the multiple principles that had earlier informed the Court's free exercise opinions. *Bowen* and *Shabazz* undercut the Court's earlier solicitude for liberty of conscience. *Lee* and *Lyng* undercut the Court's concerns for the free exercise rights of religious groups. *Lyng, O'Lone,* and *Goldman* undercut the Court's earlier solicitude for the equality of a plurality of religious faiths, particularly the needs of religious minorities to be protected against general legislation. All these cases, most notably *Lyng* and *Swaggart,* reduced the Court's nuanced interpretations of the freedom of religious expression to a blunt inquiry into simple neutrality.

These cases may have, at the time, seemed isolated to their facts, in part since they often came down alongside other cases such as *Presiding Bishop v. Amos* (1987)[82] and *Frazee* (1989) that continued to apply the strict scrutiny standard introduced in the *Sherbert* case. But in 1990 the Supreme Court wove the holdings of these cases into an important, new, and narrow test to be used in future free exercise cases. In *Employment Division v. Smith* (1990), a Native American ingested peyote as part of the sacramental rite of the Native American church of which he was a member. Discharged from employment at a drug rehabilitation center because of this practice, he applied for unemployment compensation from the State of Oregon. He was denied on grounds that peyote ingestion was disqualifying criminal misconduct. Smith appealed, ultimately to the Supreme Court, claiming a violation of his free exercise rights. The *Smith* Court, led by Justice Scalia, held for the government. Smith argued that this was just another unemployment compensation case in the series from *Sherbert* to *Frazee*. If Frazee could get compensation for refusing to work on Sunday, his day of rest but not worship, Smith argued, surely he could get compensation for engaging in the arduous and ancient ritual of peyote ingestion. But the Supreme Court treated it as just another case where a religious party had sought free exercise exemptions from compliance with general criminal laws. The Court, Justice Scalia opined, had rejected claims for exemption from general criminal laws ever since the 1879 *Reynolds* case had rejected Mormon free exercise rights to be excused from polygamy crimes. Mr. Smith had been discharged for engaging in a major drug felony. Just as the free exercise clause would not protect him from prosecution, so the state unemployment compensation board should not pay him any benefits since he was fired for cause for criminal conduct.

The *Smith* Court did not end there, however. Justice Scalia, writing for the Court, reviewed and recast a host of earlier free exercise cases. While not explicitly overturning any prior cases, the Court substantially softened the *Sherbert* "compelling state interest" test and instructed lower courts thereafter to exercise much more restraint in granting free exercise exemptions. Some of the earlier cases, Justice Scalia wrote, like those on proselytism and education, were "hybrid rights" cases that combined free exercise concerns with those of free speech and parental rights. Such hybrid cases were properly accorded strict or heightened scrutiny. Some of the earlier cases dealt with coercion and control of religious beliefs and actions that clearly could still not be countenanced. "The government may not compel affirmation of religious belief, punish the expression of religious doctrines it believes to be false, impose special disabilities on the basis of religious views or religious status, or lend its power to one or the other side in controversies over religious authority or dogma. . . . It would doubtless be unconstitutional, for example, to ban the casting of 'statues that are to be used for worship purposes,' or to prohibit bowing down before a golden calf." Such cases, where religion was singled out for discrimination, were also correctly decided.

But what Justice Scalia gave with one hand in *Smith*, he took back with the other. For outside of cases featuring hybrid rights claims or explicit acts of religious discrimination, he substantially weakened the standard of review. Henceforth, "the right of free exercise does not relieve an individual of the obligation to comply with a 'valid and neutral law of general applicability.'"[83] Neutral, generally applicable laws are by definition constitutional under the free exercise clause—regardless of the nature of the state's interest and regardless of the burden cast upon a religious believer or body. Religious objections to such laws must be brought to the legislature, not to the courts. Only if the laws are not neutral or not generally applicable will the burden shift to the government to demonstrate that such seemingly discriminatory laws satisfy a compelling state interest and are the least restrictive alternative for achieving that interest. This holding effectively reduced the free exercise guarantee to the single principle of neutrality. And when coupled with Justice Scalia's insistence that any statute be judged only by its final words and not by its fuller legislative history, this holding meant that most well-crafted statutes would be free from free exercise challenge.

Smith did not leave free exercise litigants bereft of all constitutional protection from blatantly discriminatory laws, as the Court showed in its next free exercise case. *Church of Lukumi Babalu Aye, Inc. v. City of Hialeah* (1993) posed a free exercise challenge to a city ordinance that singled out local followers of the Santerian faith for special restrictions and penalties for engaging in the ritual slaughter of animals—a central practice of their faith. Even using the weaker free exercise test of *Smith*, the Court struck down the city ordinance, for it was neither a general law nor neutrally applied. Rather, it transparently targeted Santerian believers and their practices for special prohibitions, and such discrimination could not be justified by any compelling state interest.[84]

Free Exercise in the Age of Statutes

One of the ironies of the *Smith* case is that even as it weakened free exercise review, it has aided somewhat the cause of religious liberty. It has done so by pressing litigants and legislators to look elsewhere in the Constitution for fuller and firmer protection—with some notable successes. For example, despite *Smith,* religious liberty litigants have continued to find ample protection against religious discrimination under the First Amendment free speech clause, applied alone or along with a "hybrid" free exercise clause. The 2002 *Village of Stratton* case is a good example of this, as we have seen. Moreover, as we shall see in some detail in Chapters 8–9, religious liberty litigants have used the First Amendment free speech and establishment clauses and the Fourteenth Amendment equal protection clause together to create a whole series of precedents that grant religious parties equal access to government facilities, forums, and even funds available to nonreligious parties. These lines of argument are religious liberty by-products of the new clause shopping catalyzed by *Smith.* Such protections did not exist much before *Smith,* even when the Court was applying heightened or strict scrutiny.

Another irony of the *Smith* case is that statutes now provide considerably more protection for religious liberty than the First Amendment free exercise clause itself. •

In one sense, this is not so new and not so surprising. Before *Smith,* Congress and state legislatures had, according to one recent survey, passed two thousand special statutory and regulatory protections and exemptions for religion.[85] The Supreme Court had long viewed narrow and well-targeted provisions in legislation as suitable accommodations of religion that are neither mandated by the free exercise clause nor prohibited by the establishment clause.[86] We saw that in *Arver v. United States* (1918) and its progeny, where the Court upheld the Selective Service Act against charges of both establishment and free exercise violations (pp. 143–145). The Court has echoed this view many times, notably in the *Sherbert* line of cases, where the Court explicitly encouraged legislatures to accommodate the special religious interests of employees (pp. 152–155).

Since the early 1980s, however, Congress and state legislatures have passed aggressive new statutes to offset the Court's narrowing of free exercise protections. Following *Goldman v. Weinberger* (1986), for example, Congress in 1988 amended the military dress code to allow yarmulkes: "a member of the armed forces may wear an item of religious apparel while wearing the uniform of the member's armed force."[87] Similarly, following *Employment Division v. Smith* (1990), the State of Oregon amended its criminal code to allow peyote to be ingested as part of a Native American religious ceremony. Such statutory fixes are precisely what the Court sought to foster in these cases, it seemed—leaving exemptions to the legislatures rather than the courts. Subsequent challenges of these new statutes as forms of religious establishment have failed.

These early statutory responses to controversial cases were only the start. Since the 1990 *Smith* case, Congress has passed some two hundred federal statutes or statutory amendments designed to provide new protections, exemptions, privileges, immunities, benefits, and treatments for religious parties, often including strict scrutiny regimes for their enforcement.[88] The new statutes include not only the quite visible enactments of RFRA (1993) and RLUIPA (2000) that we saw earlier, or the International Religious Freedom Act (1998) that we shall see (pp. 270–271). Beyond these, and largely unnoticed by the public and largely unchecked by the courts, is a sprawling network of special religious rights that have been quietly stitched into federal laws governing all manner of subjects—laws of evidence and civil procedure, taxation and bankruptcy, disability, labor, employment, unions, civil rights, interstate commerce, ERISA, workplace, military, immigration and naturalization, food and drugs, prisons, hospitals, land use, and much more. And federal laws are only one part of this statutory network. State, county, city, and village laws also create sundry special religious rights for some of these same topics, as well as for local issues like property tax, zoning, nonprofit organizations, education, charity, and the like. Parties seeking freedom to exercise their religion today are often better served by pressing their claims under one of these federal or state statutes than by filing a constitutional case in federal court.

Not all statutes favoring or protecting religion have been sustained against establishment clause challenges, as we shall see.[89] Nor have all statutes proved equally effective. For example, in an attempt to grant protections to the religious rights of Native

Americans, who had fared poorly in the courts even before *Bowen, Lyng,* and *Smith,* Congress passed the American Indian Religious Freedom Act (AIRFA) in 1978. The act was only a resolution—not a statute with specific rights and duties set forth. Nonetheless, AIRFA provided: "It shall be the policy of the United States to protect and preserve for American Indians their inherent right of freedom to believe, express, and exercise the traditional religions of the American Indians . . . including but not limited to access to sites, use and possession of sacred objects, and the freedom to worship through ceremonials and traditional rites."[90] The Native American claims at issue in *Bowen, Lyng,* and *Smith* all fell easily within the preferred policy of AIRFA. The Court could have used the language of the act as a basis for extending free exercise protections to these claims, without undue worry of creating precedents for numerous new non-Native American claims. The Court chose instead to dismiss the act with wooden language, declaring in *Lyng:* "Nowhere in the law is there so much as a hint of any intent to create a cause of action or any judicially enforceable individual rights."[91]

In 1993 Congress passed a statute that did "create a cause of action and judicially enforceable individual rights"—the Religious Freedom Restoration Act (1993), designed to offset the *Smith* Court's narrow neutrality reading of the free exercise clause. But in the *City of Boerne v. Flores* (1997), as we saw, the Court struck down RFRA as a violation of section 5 of the Fourteenth Amendment. Congress responded with the Religious Land Use and Institutionalized Persons Act (2000), which is much narrower in scope and based on much broader constitutional powers. *Cutter v. Wilkinson* (2005) upheld this law against an establishment clause challenge, thereby encouraging further legislation in protection of religious liberty.

Summary and Conclusions

It must be said in conclusion that neither statutory nor free speech protections of religious liberty can ultimately substitute for a more rigorous free exercise clause. To be sure, the development of these doctrines testifies both to the ingenuity of litigants and legislators and also to the flexibility of the constitutional process to accommodate the pressing spiritual needs of citizens. And to be sure, the development of these doctrines has provided some religious minorities with forms and forums of relief hitherto foreclosed to them.

These can only be temporary refuges for religious liberty, however. Speech is only one form of religious exercise; equality is only one principle that the free exercise clause protects. Even generously defined, "speech" cannot embrace many forms of individual and corporate religious exercise—from the silent meditations of the sages to the noisy pilgrimages of the saints, from the corporate consecration of the sanctuary to the ecclesiastical discipline of the clergy. Even expansively interpreted, "equality" cannot protect the particular and special needs of religious individuals and religious groups. These needs were traditionally protected by the principles of liberty of conscience and traditionally reflected in the exemptions and exclusions countenanced and created by the free exercise clause.

Likewise, statutory provisions cannot substitute for constitutional principles of free exercise. It is an elementary but essential political reality that statutes generally privilege the views of the majority, not the minority. They are passed by elected officials who must be as vigilant in reflecting popular opinion as protecting constitutional imperatives. Even salutary laws that protect religious practice are tenuous, for they are passed by a political majority and can just as easily be retracted by a new majority. The free exercise clause, by contrast, is designed to protect the needs of the minority as much as the majority. Its provisions are enforced by appointed officials who must be more vigilant about protecting constitutional imperatives than reflecting popular opinion. The free exercise clause is designed to provide remedies for individuals and groups with insufficient political strength to have their religious views or practices reflected in or protected by statutes.

The original vision of the founders was that religion was special and that it was deserving of special protection. The founders thus placed the free exercise clause alongside the free speech, press, and assembly clauses to provide religious claimants with a special pathway to relief. They incorporated within this free exercise clause the principles of liberty of conscience, freedom of religious expression, religious equality and pluralism, and separation of church from the state. Both individuals and groups were thus protected in their most fundamental religious rights. One need not necessarily endorse a jurisprudence of originalism to embrace this multi-principled reading of the free exercise clause. This was, after all, the vision articulated by the Supreme Court in *Cantwell v. Connecticut* (1940), the case that opened the modern era of free exercise jurisprudence. And this was the Court's vision of the free exercise clause for more than forty years thereafter.

To date, the majority of the Supreme Court has shown little willingness to overturn the 1990 *Smith* case. Therefore, further free speech and statutory protections of religious liberty must be vigilantly pursued in the short term, along with more rigorous state constitutional laws. At the same time, religious claimants should continue to press their free exercise cases in federal courts, inviting the Supreme Court slowly to draw the sting from *Smith* and isolate it, even if not explicitly overturn it.

Notes

1. For excellent recent volumes that include analysis of the most relevant literature, see Kent Greenawalt, *Religion and the Constitution: Free Exercise and Fairness* (2006); Douglas Laycock, *Collected Writings on Religious Liberty*, 4 vols. (2010–).

2. Reliable websites offering complete and searchable judicial opinions include http://supreme.lp.findlaw.com/ and www.law.cornell.edu/supct/.

3. See Ira Lupu, "Where Rights Begin: The Problem of Burdens on the Free Exercise of Religion," *Harvard Law Review* 102 (1989): 933.

4. See, e.g., *Diffenderfer v. Central Baptist Church*, 404 U.S. 412 (1972) (a case arguing for property tax exemption for religious uses was rendered moot by a change in statute); *Bender v. Williamsport Area School District*, 475 U.S. 534 (1986) (school board member has no

standing, in his capacity as a parent, to appeal a board decision affecting the religious rights of his child in the school).

5. See *Cantwell v. Connecticut,* 310 U.S. 296 (1940); *Goldman v. Weinberger,* 475 U.S. 503 (1986); and *O'Lone v. Estate of Shabazz,* 482 U.S. 342 (1987), respectively.

6. See *National Labor Relations Board v. Catholic Bishop of Chicago,* 440 U.S. 490 (1979); *Jimmy Swaggart Ministries v. Board of Equalization of California,* 493 U.S. 378 (1990); and *Lyng v. Northwest Indian Cemetery Protective Association,* 485 U.S. 439 (1988), respectively.

7. See many examples in William Bassett, *Religious Organizations and the Law* (1998 with updates); James A. Serritella et al., eds., *Religious Organizations in the United States: A Study of Identity, Liberty, and Law* (2006). See further below, pages 253–259.

8. *Frazee v. Illinois Department of Employment Security,* 489 U.S. 429 (1989).

9. *Braunfeld v. Brown,* 366 U.S. 599 (1961). We deal with this case in Chapter 10, page 225.

10. *Bob Jones University v. United States,* 461 U.S. 574 (1983). We deal with this case in Chapter 11, pages 257–258.

11. Lupu, "Where Rights Begin," 954.

12. See *United States v. Ballard,* 322 U.S. 78 (1944) (allowing for jury instruction questioning the sincerity of claimant's "I Am" religion).

13. *Torcaso v. Watkins,* 367 U.S. 488, 495, n. 11 (1961).

14. It is not just religious minorities that lose free exercise claims. In fact, an exhaustive empirical study found that Catholics and Baptists performed especially poorly in free exercise claims brought between 1986 and 1995. Gregory C. Sisk et al., "Searching for the Soul of Judicial Decision-Making: An Empirical Study of Judicial Decision-Making," *Ohio State Law Journal* 65 (2004): 491.

15. See, e.g., *Jimmy Swaggart Ministries v. Board of Equalization of California,* 493 U.S. 378, 385ff. (1990), distinguishing at length *Murdock v. Pennsylvania,* 319 U.S. 105 (1943) and its progeny to uphold collection of taxes on sales of religious articles. See also *Employment Division v. Smith,* 494 U.S. 872, 879–880 (1990), reaching back to *Reynolds v. United States,* 98 U.S. 145 (1879) and *Prince v. Massachusetts,* 321 U.S. 158 (1944) to uphold application of a criminal law against free exercise objection.

16. For example, one can view *Sherbert v. Verner,* 374 U.S. 398 (1963), which generously upheld the Sabbatarian interests of a Seventh-Day Adventist, as a direct rebuke to *Braunfeld v. Brown,* 366 U.S. 599 (1961) and three other cases during the 1961 term in which the Court dealt churlishly with Jewish Sabbatarianism. In that same term, the Court had upheld the conscientious objection rights of an atheist: *Torcaso v. Watkins,* 367 U.S. 488 (1961). Similarly, one can view *Employment Division v. Smith,* 494 U.S. 872 (1990) as a direct rejoinder to the extreme application of its unemployment compensation precedents the year before in *Frazee v. Illinois Department of Employment Security,* 489 U.S. 429 (1989).

17. Greenawalt, *Religion and the Constitution,* 215.

18. *Reynolds v. United States,* 98 U.S. 145, 166–167 (1879); *Davis v. Beason,* 133 U.S. 333, 345–348 (1890).

19. 310 U.S. 296, at 303–304.

20. *West Virginia State Board v. Barnette,* 319 U.S. 624, 639 (1943); *Heffron v. International Society for Krishna Consciousness,* 452 U.S. 640, 649 (1981).

21. 374 U.S. 398 (1963).

22. *Smith,* 494 U.S. at 879.

23. *Smith,* 494 U.S. at 886–887.

24. 42 U.S.C. secs. 2000bb to 2000b–4.

25. 521 U.S. 507, 519 (1997).

26. *Gonzales v. O Centro Espirita Beneficiente Uniao Do Vegetal,* 546 U.S. 418 (2006).

27. 42 U.S.C.A. secs. 2000cc-2000cc5.

28. 544 U.S. 709 (2005). See further below n. 86.

29. 98 U.S. 145, 164 (1879).

30. 12 Stat. 501–502 (1862); 22 Stat. 30–32 (1882); *Congressional Record* 18, no. 585–593 (January 1887). Other laws are quoted and analyzed in *Murphy v. Ramsey,* 114 U.S. 15 (1885) and *Cannon v. United States,* 116 U.S. 55 (1885). See detailed study in Sarah Barringer Gordon, *The Mormon Question: Polygamy and Constitutional Conflict in Nineteenth-Century America* (2002).

31. 133 U.S. 333, 341–342 (1890).

32. 136 U.S. 1 (1890) and the companion case *Romney v. United States,* 136 U.S. 1 (1890). *Murphy v. Ramsey,* 114 U.S. 15, 45 (1885), upheld various laws disenfranchising known and suspected bigamists against challenges that the laws violated their more general "constitutional rights and liberties." In defense of the laws, Justice Matthews wrote: "For, certainly, no legislation can be supposed more wholesome and necessary in the founding of a free, self-governing commonwealth . . . than that which seeks to establish it on the basis of the idea of the family, as consisting in and springing from the union for life of one man and one woman in the holy estate of matrimony; the sure foundation of all that is stable and noble in our civilization; the best guarantee of that reverent morality which is the source of all beneficent progress in social and political improvement."

33. *Reynolds,* 98 U.S. at 164.

34. *Davis,* 133 U.S. at 336–337, 341–342.

35. *Latter Day Corporation,* 136 U.S. at 48–50.

36. See *Cleveland v. United States,* 329 U.S. 14 (1946); and John Witte, Jr., "The Legal Challenges of Religious Polygamy in the USA," *Ecclesiastical Law Journal* 11 (2009): 72.

37. Constitution of Utah (1896), Art. I, Sec. 4; Art. III.

38. *United States v. Macintosh,* 283 U.S. 605, 626 (1931).

39. 40 Stat. 76, 78 (1917).

40. 245 U.S. 366, 389–390 (1918). See similar results in *Eagles v. Samuels,* 329 U.S. 304 (1946); *Eagles v. Horowitz,* 329 U.S. 317 (1946).

41. *United States v. Schwimmer,* 279 U.S. 644, 650–651 (1929).

42. *Macintosh,* 283 U.S. at 624–625.

43. *United States v. Bland,* 283 U.S. 636 (1931); *Hamilton v. Regents of the University of California,* 293 U.S. 245 (1934); see also *In re Summers,* 325 U.S. 561 (1945).

44. 328 U.S. 61, 64–66, 69 (1946).

45. See Appendix 3. The most recent cases were *Gillette v. United States,* 401 U.S. 437 (1971) and *Clay v. United States,* 403 U.S. 698 (1971).

46. See *United States v. Seeger,* 380 U.S. 163 (1965); *Welsh v. United States,* 398 U.S. 333 (1970).

47. *Cantwell v. Connecticut*, 310 U.S. 296, 304, 308 (1940).

48. 318 U.S. 413–414 (1943); 319 U.S. 105, 110 (1943).

49. 326 U.S. 501 (1946); 326 U.S. 517 (1946).

50. 319 U.S. 105, 108–109, 111–112 (1943).

51. See *Jones v. Opelika [II]*, 319 U.S. 103 (1943), overruling *Jones v. Opelika [I]*, 316 U.S. 584 (1942); *Largent v. Texas*, 318 U.S. 418 (1943); *Follett v. McCormick*, 321 U.S. 473 (1944).

52. 340 U.S. 290 (1951).

53. 340 U.S. 268 (1951). See similar result in *Saia v. New York*, 334 U.S. 558 (1948).

54. 345 U.S. 67 (1953).

55. 345 U.S. 395, 398–408 (1953). See also *Cox v. New Hampshire*, 312 U.S. 569 (1941).

56. 536 U.S. 150 (2002).

57. 315 U.S. 568, 571–572 (1942).

58. 321 U.S. 158, 165–167 (1944).

59. *Jehovah's Witnesses v. King County Hospital*, 390 U.S. 598 (1968).

60. *Watson v. Jones*, 80 U.S. (13 Wall.) 679, 728 (1871).

61. *Cantwell*, 310 U.S. at 303.

62. *Minersville School District v. Gobitis*, 310 U.S. 586, 594, 597–598 (1940).

63. *Barnette*, 319 U.S. at 642.

64. *United States v. Ballard* (1944); *In re Summers*, 325 U.S. 561 (1945).

65. *Torcaso v. Watkins*, 367 U.S. 488 (1961).

66. *McDaniel v. Paty*, 435 U.S. 618, 626 (1978) (citing *Torcaso v. Watkins*).

67. *Sherbert*, 374 U.S at 401, 406.

68. *Sherbert*, 374 U.S. at 411 (Douglas, J., concurring).

69. 450 U.S. 707 (1981).

70. 480 U.S. 136 (1987).

71. 489 U.S. 829 (1989).

72. *Thomas v. Review Board*, 450 U.S. at 717–718. This same principle had earlier been denied to Jewish groups who sought free exercise exemptions from Sunday blue laws. See below, pages 224–225.

73. *McDaniel v. Paty*, 435 U.S. 618, 622–626 (1978).

74. 406 U.S. 205, 216–218 (1972).

75. Compare *Yoder* to the Court's much more dismissive treatment of the unusual religious, cultural, and linguistic needs of Hasidic Jews in *Kiryas Joel Village School District v. Grumet*, 512 U.S. 687 (1994). In *Kiryas Joel*, the Court struck down the state's creation of a single public school district within an exclusively Satmar Hasidic community as a violation of the establishment clause. See also the Native American cases—*Bowen v. Roy, Lyng v. Northwest Indian Cemetery Association*, and *Employment Division v. Smith*—discussed below, pages 156–160, 278–279.

76. 455 U.S. 252, 259, 261–262 (1982).

77. 475 U.S. 503 (1986).

78. 476 U.S. 693, 696, 699, 707–708 (1986).

79. 482 U.S. 342, 350, 352 (1987).

80. 485 U.S. 439, 447, 451–452 (1988).

81. 493 U.S. 378, 389, 391 (1990).

82. 483 U.S. 327 (1987). See discussion in Chapter 11.

83. *Smith,* 494 U.S. at 872, 877–879.

84. 508 U.S. 520 (1993). We take up the Court's final free exercise case, *Locke v. Davey,* 540 U.S. 712 (2004), in Chapters 8–9. Interestingly, it was only Justices Scalia and Thomas, in dissent in that case, who thought that a state scholarship scheme that excluded only "theology majors" from eligibility rendered the law "non-neutral."

85. See James J. Ryan, "*Smith* and the Religious Freedom Restoration Act," *Virginia Law Review* 78 (1992): 1407, 1445; Douglas Laycock, "Regulatory Exemptions of Religious Behavior and the Original Understanding of the Establishment Clause," *Notre Dame Law Review* 81 (2006): 1793, 1837ff.

86. In *Zorach v. Clauson* 343 U.S. 306, 313–314 (1952), for example, the Court upheld a local statute allowing religious students release time to attend religious classes off the school's premises—calling this a "suitable accommodation . . . to spiritual needs" rather than an establishment of religion. In *Walz v. Tax Commission,* 397 U.S. 664 (1970), the Court sustained a state tax exemption of church property against a taxpayer challenge that this was an establishment of religion. In *Transworld Airlines v. Hardison,* 432 U.S. 63 (1977), the Court upheld Title VII provisions that required employers to make "reasonable accommodations" to their employees' religious needs. In *Presiding Bishop v. Amos,* 483 U.S. 327 (1987), the Court sustained a 1972 amendment to the Civil Rights Act that exempted religious organizations from the general prohibition against religious discrimination. Several lower federal courts have further sustained, against establishment clause challenges, provisions in the federal Fair Housing Act that allow religious organizations to favor their own coreligionists and state laws that allow religious schools and charities to favor their own coreligionist pupils and patrons. The Court said the same in a series of equal access cases discussed in the next chapters (pp. 198–204): legislative accommodations and provisions for religion are not violations of the establishment clause.

87. 10 U.S.C. sec. 774 (2009).

88. See the six-part exposé by Diana Henriques, "As Exemptions Grow, Religion Outweighs Regulation," *New York Times,* October 8–December 10, 2006. See further the sources cited in note 7 above and analysis of new legislation in the periodical *Church Law and Tax Report.*

89. See, e.g., *Estate of Thornton v. Caldor, Inc.,* 472 U.S. 703 (1985) (striking down statute that gave employees a categorical right not to work on their Sabbath); *Texas Monthly, Inc. v. Bullock,* 489 U.S. 1 (1989) (striking down special state tax exemption for sale of religious periodicals); *Kiryas Joel Village School District v. Grumet,* 496 U.S. 226 (1990) (striking down creation of public school district that followed boundaries of religious village).

90. 42 U.S.C. sec. 1996 (1978).

91. *Lyng,* 485 U.S. at 455.

7

Modern Establishment Law
Mapping the Doctrinal Terrain

One of the most distinctive principles of the American constitutional experiment in religious liberty is the prohibition on establishments of religion. From the fourth to the eighteenth century, as we have seen, the dominant assumption in the West was that each polity would have one form of Christianity established by law. The state afforded this established religion special patronage and protection. It accorded the established clergy special privileges and prerogatives. It collected special tithes and donations in support of the established church. And it defined by law the religious canons, doctrines, liturgies, symbols, and texts to be used in the community. In earlier centuries, religious nonconformists were sometimes persecuted as pagans or heretics; in the course of the sixteenth and seventeenth centuries, some came to be tolerated. But those who worshiped outside the established church were still, by definition, second-class citizens with a variety of disabilities and special burdens imposed upon them, and with their social standing at the mercy and caprice of state officials.

The 1791 First Amendment, as we have seen, rejected this traditional law of religious establishments at the national level, and by 1833 every state had rejected formal state religious establishments as well. Disestablishment of religion, many founders argued, was ultimately the best way to protect all the essential rights and liberties of religion. Disestablishment kept government from coercively prescribing forms of religious belief, doctrine, and practice at the cost of the principles of liberty of conscience and freedom of exercise. It kept government from singling out certain religious beliefs and bodies for preferential treatment at the cost of the principle of equality for a plurality of faiths. And it kept government from influencing religious bodies, or from coming under their influence, at the cost of the principle of separation of church and state. The 1947 *Everson* case repeated these basic correlative principles when it incorporated the First Amendment establishment clause into the Fourteenth Amendment due process clause and applied it to state and local governments. In more than fifty subsequent cases, the Supreme Court worked to give concrete meaning and discrete application to this multiprincipled guarantee of no establishment of religion.

This chapter maps the Supreme Court establishment clause cases, using the Court's own shifting terminology, which partially repeats the traditional principles of religious liberty but also introduces new terms. The Court's establishment clause cases are even more confusing than the free exercise cases reviewed in Chapter 6. This makes the establishment map offered here even more complicated than the free exercise map set out in the last chapter. We will thus take our time in this chapter describing the various doctrinal shifts and juxtaposed approaches developed by the Court, after first laying out the basic steps in bringing an establishment clause case.[1]

Most of the Supreme Court establishment clause cases concern three broad issues. First, what is the place of religion in public schools—whether religious teachers, texts, teachings, symbols, ceremonies, or prayers? Second, what is the place of government in religious schools—particularly in regulating, funding, facilitating, or cooperating with religious schools or with the activities of religious school teachers, students, or parents? And third, what is the place of religion in public life and public policy—in particular, may government fund, maintain, or display religious texts, ceremonies, and symbols; and may government use religious officials, institutions, or personnel in discharging its political tasks?

While it is hard to see a consistent logic or logical development across these three main lines of cases, a more coherent logic governs each line of cases when considered separately. Moreover, the First Amendment free speech clause and attendant concerns for equality play a critical role in the first two lines of cases on education, and that development deserves close attention. Rather than trying to cram all this into one long, convoluted chapter, we shall treat these three lines of cases in three separate shorter chapters that follow this one. In Chapter 10 we shall use the summary and conclusions section to revisit the bigger picture of establishment clause jurisprudence today.

Bringing an Establishment Clause Case

At the heart of an establishment case is a claimant's challenge that the government has made a law establishing religion or "respecting" the same. The challenged government entity or official can be at the federal, state, or local level. The law at issue can involve the exercise of executive or legislative authority, or the application of administrative rules and regulations. The challenge posed by an establishment clause litigant is that the government has improperly funded, supported, or endorsed religion. It has improperly coerced parties to participate in religious worship, indoctrination, or education. It has made improper use of religious sanctuaries, symbols, or services. It has improperly allied itself with religious causes, clerics, or corporations. It has discriminately favored or preferred some religious interests, individuals, or institutions over others. In brief, government has taken one or more steps down the road toward the establishment of religion.

Parties who file establishment clause cases must meet the usual "justiciability" requirements that we reviewed in the last chapter on free exercise claims (pp. 131–134). They must press a case that is "ripe" and not "moot" or theoretical. They must state an actual "case or controversy" over which the federal court has jurisdiction. And they must have "standing" to bring their suit.

The Supreme Court, however, has softened some of these threshold "justiciability" requirements for establishment clause cases. In free exercise and other constitutional cases, we saw in the last chapter, the Court read the "case and controversy" rules strictly: "It is a fundamental rule of judicial restraint, that this Court will not reach constitutional questions in advance of the necessity of deciding them."[2] But in modern establishment cases, the Court has not always shown such restraint. In *Epperson v. Arkansas* (1968), for example, a public school teacher challenged a state criminal law that prohibited the teaching of evolution in a public school or state university. The textbook the school had assigned for the course had included a section on evolution, and the teacher feared criminal prosecution. Even though the law had not yet been enforced against the teacher, and a case was thus arguably not yet "ripe," the *Epperson* Court addressed the constitutional issue. It found that the state law violated the establishment clause because the teacher "faced at least a literal dilemma" of whether the state law had indirectly established the teaching of creationism alone.[3] In *Zobrest v. Catalina Foothills School District* (1993), the Court again relaxed the case and controversy rule, but this time to find no constitutional violation. A student attending a religious high school challenged a state decision not to afford him disability services. The case below turned largely on interpretation of applicable state and federal disability statutes. On appeal, the student raised the question whether state-funded disability services in a religious high school would constitute an establishment of religion. Four dissenters argued that the Court "should vacate and remand this case for consideration of various threshold questions, statutory and regulatory, that may moot the constitutional question."[4] The *Zobrest* majority judged otherwise: "The fact that there may be buried in the record a nonconstitutional ground for decision is not by itself enough to invoke this rule."[5]

Not only "case and controversy" rules but also "standing" rules were, until recently, more relaxed in establishment clause cases. The Court's traditional standing rules for all constitutional cases, formulated in 1923, required that any claimant "must be able to show that he has sustained or is in immediate danger of sustaining some direct injury as a result of the statute's enforcement and not merely that he suffers in some indefinite way in common with people generally."[6] In its early establishment cases, the Court applied this traditional standing rule, sometimes rejecting establishment clause cases on that ground.[7] In *Abington Township v. Schempp* (1963), however, the Court declared that "the requirements for standing to challenge state action under the Establishment Clause, unlike those relating to the Free Exercise Clause, do not include proofs that particular *religious freedoms* are infringed."[8] More importantly, in *Flast v. Cohen* (1968), the Court held further that federal taxpayers could challenge any government programs that involved taxing and spending in aid of religion. This case opened federal courts to a flood of establishment cases filed by federal taxpayers.[9]

Defenders of these relaxed standing rules argued that the establishment clause needed a large group of willing and permissible litigants for it to be an effective restraint on government. "History makes it clear," Justice Brennan argued, "that the federal taxpayer is a singularly 'proper and appropriate party to invoke a federal court's jurisdiction' to challenge a federal bestowal of largesse as a violation of the Establishment Clause. Each, and indeed every, federal taxpayer suffers precisely the same injury: . . . a continuing and intolerable burden on his pocketbook, his conscience, and his constitutional rights."[10] Critics countered that such permissive standing rules effectively empowered a single secular party to "veto" popular laws touching religion that caused him or her only tangential injury. These criticisms became more pointed in the 1980s and 1990s, after the Court began holding that the free exercise clause does not grant individual exemptions from neutral and generally applicable laws (pp. 155–160). It was no small irony that a secular claimant could use the establishment clause to overturn a carefully calibrated local law that happened to touch religion too favorably,[11] but a religious claimant could not use the free exercise clause to claim an individual exemption from a discretionary regulatory decision that happened to "virtually destroy" its religion.[12]

Perhaps because of this irony, the Court has tightened standing rules in more recent establishment clause cases. In *Valley Forge Christian College v. Americans United for Separation of Church and State* (1982), the Court held that a religious liberty organization by itself lacked standing to file an establishment case on grounds of "a generalized interest of all citizens in constitutional governance." It could bring an action only if it could show a redressable injury to itself or to one of its members.[13] In *Elk Grove Unified School District v. Newdow* (2004), the Court held that a noncustodial father had no standing to challenge his daughter's voluntary recitation in public school of the Pledge of Allegiance, with its "one nation under God" language that the plaintiff considered a form of religious establishment.[14] And in *Hein v. Freedom from Religion Foundation, Inc.* (2007), a plurality of the Court held that a federal taxpayer lacked standing to challenge decisions about how to implement an executive order creating a faith-based initiatives program. Taxpayers, the plurality held, had standing to challenge only legislative actions that used federal tax funds. The concurring justices in *Hein* wanted to overturn *Flast v. Cohen* altogether and thereby deny taxpayers special standing to challenge either legislative or judicial actions under the establishment clause.[15] Most recently, in *Salazar v. Buono* (2010), a majority of the Court agreed that a former employee had standing to challenge a private cross display in a national park, but divided on whether he had standing to challenge the private transfer of that cross and surrounding land designed to remedy any establishment clause problem. The case was remanded.[16]

The result of these tighter standing requirements is that the litigants lost their cases and the challenged government practices were upheld—though on procedural grounds rather than substantive grounds. Some have accused the Court of avoiding hard substantive issues by such procedural maneuvers; others allege that the standing doctrine itself, in such cases, effectively functions in a substantive manner since it is so outcome-determinative. Regardless of the validity of these arguments, tighter standing rules necessarily mean fewer litigants to press establishment clause cases. This is important to bear in mind as we review the substance of establishment clause jurisprudence in these chapters and watch the numbers of cases fall off sharply in the past decade.

As the foregoing cases illustrate, standing and other justiciability questions are even more complex and more volatile under the establishment clause than they are under the free exercise clause. Here again, nonspecialists must tread very carefully in analyzing these technical issues or contemplating a lawsuit.[17]

Mapping the Establishment Clause Cases

In Chapter 6, we mapped the Court's free exercise cases using the techniques of factual clustering and shifting standards of review (pp. 134–140). These two methods, which helped to map much modern free exercise law, avail us rather little in mapping modern establishment law. The only factual cluster in which the Court has kept a steady line of logic concerns the role of religion in public education; even in this cluster, the Court's rationale of late has begun to shift. The only formal standard of review the Court has developed is the so-called *Lemon* test of 1971. But the Court has repeatedly modified, ignored, and decried this test—although lower courts still use it readily and it seems to be making a comeback among at least some of the justices on the Supreme Court.

In its establishment cases, the Court has developed a number of unique, and sometimes sharply juxtaposed, approaches. From 1947 to the mid-1980s, these approaches were: (1) "separationism," (2) "accommodationism," and (3) "neutrality." Since the mid-1980s, the Court has added several new formulas: (4) "endorsement," (5) "coercion," and (6) "equal treatment." For each formula, one or more justices has offered lengthy historical and jurisprudential apologias. But history has also become a "wild card" in modern establishment cases, occasionally used on its own to uphold a particular practice. This has introduced, in effect, a seventh approach, "history or tradition."

In Figure 7.1, we provide a rough picture of these approaches as they emerged chronologically, citing the main cases that introduced them. In the sections that follow, we analyze and illustrate how each approach has been used to decide whether a challenged governmental action constitutes an establishment of religion. The three chapters that follow will analyze these cases in more detail and put them in a larger doctrinal framework. Our interest here is simply to have a map of the various approaches and some preliminary understanding of the tensions among them.

Separationism

A key principle at work in modern establishment law is the separation of church and state. This principle has firm historical roots, especially in the writings of

Figure 7.1: Trends in Modern Establishment Law

Likely Finding of Establishment		Likely Finding of No Establishment
Separationism		Accommodationism
McCollum (1948)		*Zorach* (1952)
	Wholesome Neutrality	
	Schempp (1963)	
Strict Neutrality		Benevolent Neutrality
Lemon (1971)		*Walz* (1970)
Aguilar (1985)		*Mueller* (1983)
Texas Monthly (1989)		*Kendrick* (1988)
		History
		Marsh (1983)
	Endorsement	
	Mergens (1990)	
Strict Neutrality	No Coercion	
Kiryas Joel (1994)	*Weisman* (1992)	
	Equal Access/Treatment	
	Rosenberger (1995)	
	Good News Club (2001)	
Strict Neutrality Revived		Benevolent Neutrality Revived
McCreary (2005)		*Zelman* (2002)
		Van Orden (2005)

eighteenth-century Enlightenment and Evangelical groups. They called on religious and political authorities to end their alliances and rivalries, to distinguish their forms and functions. The state, they argued, should not give special aid, support, privilege, or protection to religious doctrines or groups through special tax appropriations or government donations of land and goods. The state should not predicate its laws on religious premises or direct them to religious purposes. The state should not draw on the services of religious groups or seek to interfere in their order, organization, or orthodoxy. Religion should be left alone to flourish in the conscience of each individual and in the voluntary assemblies that individuals convene.

Enlightenment formulations of this separationist doctrine emphasized the need to protect politics and the state from the intrusions and undue influence of religion and the church. Evangelical formulations emphasized the need to protect religion and the church from the intrusions and undue control of politics and the state. Both views were united, however, in opposing the traditional entanglements of religion and politics and the traditional alliances of church and state—even though they did not always view separation as an establishment clause issue, as we have seen. Both views had a formidable influence on the development of eighteenth-century state and federal laws on religious liberty. Both came to special prominence in some states during the later nineteenth and early twentieth centuries—particularly in state constitutional provisions prohibiting governmental aid to religious causes and religious aid to public schools (pp. 26–33).

The Supreme Court's first modern articulation of this separationist doctrine was offered by Justice Black in *Everson v. Board of Education* (1947):

> The "establishment of religion" clause of the First Amendment means at least this: Neither a state nor the Federal Government can set up a church. Neither can pass laws which aid one religion, aid all religions, or prefer one religion over another. Neither can force nor influence a person to go or to remain away from church against his will or force him to profess a belief or disbelief in any religion. No person can be punished for entertaining or professing religious beliefs or disbeliefs, for church attendance or non-attendance. No tax in any amount, large or small, can be levied to support any religious activities or institutions, whatever they may be called, or whatever form they may adopt to teach or practice religion. Neither a state nor the Federal Government can, openly or secretly, participate in the affairs of any religious organizations or groups, or vice versa. In the words of Jefferson, the clause against establishment of religion by law was intended to erect "a wall of separation between church and state."[18]

In later cases, Justice Black stressed that "a union of government and religion tends to destroy government and to degrade religion." "Religion is too personal, too sacred, [and] too holy, to permit its 'unhallowed perversion' by a civil magistrate."[19] Religion is also too powerful, too sinister, and too greedy to permit its unhindered pervasion of a civil magistracy. "[T]he same powerful religious propagandists" who are allowed to make inroads on the state and its laws, Justice Black wrote, "doubtless will continue their propaganda, looking toward complete domination and supremacy of their particular brand of religion. And it is nearly always by insidious approaches that the citadels of [religious] liberty are more successfully attacked."[20] "The First Amendment has erected a wall of separation between church and state. That wall must be kept high and impregnable. We could not approve the slightest breach."[21]

Separationist logic found its strongest and most consistent application in a long series of cases outlawing religious officials, texts, ceremonies, and symbols from public schools. Separationism also influenced other areas of government and religion, notably in cases dealing with tax support and tax exemption for religious organizations and religious causes.[22] Until 1971, separationist logic was applied directly. Since then, it has often expressed itself in a "separationist reading" or "strict neutrality reading" of the *Lemon* test (discussed below).

Accommodationism

Just as separationists are, in some ways, the modern heirs of the Enlightenment and Evangelical founders, so accommodationists are the modern heirs of Puritan and Civic Republican founders. Both Puritans and Civic Republicans, as we have seen, argued that every polity must support some form of public religion, some common morals and mores to undergird and support the plurality of protected private religions. Both groups supported state-appointed chaplains for the legislature, military, and prison; state sanctions against blasphemy, sacrilege, and iconoclasm; state administration of tithe collections, test oaths, and clerical appointments; and state sponsorship of religious schools, charities, and other societies. Puritan exponents of this accommodationist doctrine were inclined to a more specifically Christian public religion, while Civic Republicans were less denominationally rigorous. Puritan exponents tended to be more churlish in their toleration of private religions that strayed from the mainstream, while Civic Republicans were generally more charitable to all peaceable religions. Both formulations had a formidable influence on state and federal constitution making in the eighteenth century and on both state and federal constitutional decisions in the nineteenth and early twentieth centuries.

The Court's first modern formulation of this accommodationist doctrine came in *Zorach v. Clauson* (1952), which upheld the constitutionality of granting students release time from public schools to attend religious education or services. Justice Douglas wrote for the Court:

> We are a religious people whose institutions presuppose a Supreme Being. We guarantee the freedom to worship as one chooses. We make room for as wide a variety of beliefs and creeds as the spiritual needs of man deem necessary. We sponsor an attitude on the part of government that shows no partiality to one group and that lets each group flourish according to the zeal of its adherents and the appeal of its dogma. When the state encourages religious instruction or cooperates with religious authorities by adjusting the schedule of public events to sectarian needs, it follows the best of our traditions. For it then respects the religious nature of our people and accommodates the public service to their spiritual needs. To hold that it may not would be to find in the Constitution a requirement that government show a callous indifference to religious groups. That would be preferring those who believe in no religion over those who do believe. Government may not finance religious groups nor undertake religious instruction nor blend secular and sectarian education nor use secular institutions to force one or some religion on any person. But we find no constitutional requirement which makes it necessary for government to be hostile to religion and to throw its weight against efforts to widen the effective scope of religious influence. The government must be neutral when it comes to competition between sects. It may not thrust any sect on any person. It may not make a religious observance compulsory. It may not coerce anyone to attend church, to observe a religious holiday, or to take religious instruction.[23]

Later formulations of this accommodationist doctrine counseled against overzealous applications of separationist logic.[24] To restrict all religious exercises in the public school and public square, Justice Stewart wrote, can be viewed "as the establishment of a religion of secularism, or at the least, as government support of beliefs of those who think that religious exercises should be conducted only in private."[25] Justice Rehnquist added: "The 'wall of separation between church and state' is a metaphor based on bad history, a metaphor that has proved useless as a guide to judging." The establishment clause was designed only to prohibit government "from asserting a preference for one religious denomination or sect over others." It does not mandate "government to be strictly neutral between religion and irreligion, nor does the Clause prohibit Congress or the States from pursuing legitimate secular ends through non-discriminatory sectarian means."[26]

Accommodationists share much common ground with separationists. Both forbid formal government alliances with religious groups. Both forbid government coercion of religious teaching or observance. Both agree that a plurality of religions must stand equal before the law. Both agree that government must not discriminate on religious grounds. But separationists and accommodationists also differ at crucial points. Separationists forbid any government aid to religion; accommodationists allow aid that is equally or nonpreferentially distributed among religions. Separationists forbid any government participation in religious worship, education, or charity. Accommodationists allow such participation so long as citizens are not coerced into participation. Separationists forbid religious and political institutions from cooperating; accommodationists allow for such cooperation in the delivery of charity, education, and other social services.

Accommodationist logic found its strongest hold in some of the Court's pre-*Everson* cases on the place and role of government in religious schools. The Court repeated the logic and holdings of these cases a few times after *Everson,* although these early cases stood in tension with the Court's more dominant separationist tendencies in dealing with questions of religion and education. Since the mid-1980s, this accommodationist logic has returned in the form of a "benevolent neutrality" reading of the *Lemon* test and in cases upholding various legislative accommodations and uses of religious services and symbols. It has also recurred in the Court's solicitude toward government cooperation and even funding of faith-based organizations on an equal basis with other groups.

Neutrality

After a generation of vacillation between these juxtaposed separationist and accommodationist formulas, the Supreme Court in the early 1960s sought a middle way between them. In both its separationist and accommodationist opinions in these early years, the Court spoke intermittently about the need for government to adhere to a policy of religious "neutrality." Separationists tended to formulate this as government neutrality between religion and nonreligion, accommodationists as merely governmental neutrality among religions. But they held this concern for neutrality in common.

Beginning in the early 1960s, the Court made neutrality itself a new operative principle of establishment. Strict separation between church and state, the Court argued, is impossible in today's society in which government plays such a pervasive role in day-to-day affairs, even if it might have been possible in the eighteenth century. But evenhanded accommodation and acknowledgment of religion is similarly impossible in today's religiously heterogeneous society, even if it could have been permitted in the more religiously homogeneous eighteenth century. "Wholesome 'neutrality,'" Justice Clark announced for the Court in *Abington Township School District v. Schempp* (1963), is now the watchword. The establishment clause forbids the exercise of "all legislative power respecting religious belief or the expression thereof." Hereafter, if the stated purpose or primary effect of a law "either is the advancement or the inhibition of religion then the enactment exceeds the scope of legislative power as circumscribed by the Constitution."[27]

In *Walz v. Tax Commission* (1970) and *Lemon v. Kurtzman* (1971), the Court sharpened this "neutrality" approach into a formal three-pronged test. In order to pass constitutional muster, Chief Justice Burger wrote in both cases, a challenged law must (1) have a secular purpose, (2) have a primary effect that neither advances nor inhibits religion, and (3) foster no excessive entanglement between church and state. Incidental religious "effects" or modest "entanglements" of church and state are tolerable. But defiance of any of these three criteria is constitutionally fatal. The "three main evils," Burger declared in *Walz*, are "sponsorship, financial support, and active involvement of the sovereign in religious activity." These are categorically forbidden. But beyond that, the "line of separation, far from being a 'wall,' is a blurred, indistinct and variable barrier depending on all the circumstances of a particular relationship."[28]

From the start, this three-part test, later conventionally known as the *Lemon* test, proved amenable to both accommodationist and separationist readings. Despite its seeming formalism, the test left wide room for interpretation. The "secular purpose" of a statute could be determined alternatively by its plain words alone or by a full review of its legislative history.[29] The "primary effect" of the statute could be determined from the perspective of the plaintiff alone or by a full inquiry into the law in action. Whether an "entanglement" between church and state proved "excessive" depended on what Chief Justice Burger called "all the circumstances of a particular relationship." In the hands of skillful counsel, the *Lemon* test was subject to a variety of readings and applications.

In *Walz v. Tax Commission* (1970), which was the first case to name these three necessary prongs of analysis, the Court gave the test an accommodationist reading and upheld a state law granting tax exemption to properties devoted to religious, charitable, or educational uses. "The course of constitutional neutrality in this area cannot be an absolutely straight line," Chief Justice Burger wrote for the *Walz* Court. "The general principle" is that "we will not tolerate either governmentally established religion or government interference with religion. Short of those expressly proscribed government acts, there is ample room for play in the joints productive of a *benevolent neutrality* which will permit religious exercise to exist without sponsorship and without interference." Neutrality demands that we outlaw "the kind of involvement that would tip the balance toward government control of churches or government restraint on religious practice."[30] A general state policy of granting tax exemptions for church properties, alongside exemptions for charities, schools, and other public institutions, involves no such government control or restraint of the religious bodies that are so exempted. To the contrary, it reflects a spirit of benevolent neutrality toward religion, and also ensures the separation of church and state. It is not a religious establishment, the Court held.

This "accommodationist reading" of the *Lemon* test fell into desuetude for much of the 1970s and early 1980s. But it began to reappear in the Court's cases on government and religious education, beginning with *Mueller v. Allen* (1983).[31] A fuller exposition came in *Bowen v. Kendrick* (1988), which upheld federal funding of Catholic counseling centers for pregnant teenagers, in implementation of the Adolescent Family Life Act.[32] Some of these sentiments also inform the Court's reasoning in *Zelman v. Simmons-Harris* (2002) that upheld the funding of religious schools through state vouchers voluntarily expended by parents in a private school of their choice.[33]

In *Lemon v. Kurtzman* (1971) itself, the Court gave the three-part test a separationist reading and struck down a state policy that reimbursed religious schools for some of the costs of teaching secular subjects that the state prescribed. The challenged state policy was limited to religious schools that served students from lower-income families. Reimbursements were allowed only for clearly specified secular subjects and were limited to 15 percent of the costs. The Court declared that this policy fostered an "excessive entanglement between church and state." The Catholic schools in question were notably religious, staffed by ordained nuns, and populated principally by Catholic students. "[A] dedicated religious person, teaching at a school affiliated with his or her faith and operated to inculcate its tenets, will inevitably experience great difficulty in remaining religiously neutral." This will require the state to maintain a "comprehensive, discriminating, and continuing state surveillance . . . to ensure that these restrictions are obeyed and the First Amendment otherwise obeyed." This is precisely the kind of excessive entanglement between church and state that the establishment clause outlaws, said the Court.[34]

This "separationist reading" of the *Lemon* test guided most of the Court's establishment cases for the next fifteen years—in cases on the place of religion in public schools, on the place of government in religious schools, and sometimes on the place of religion in public life. In the 1980s, the Court's most forceful expositions came in *Wallace v. Jaffree* (1985), which outlawed moments of silence in public schools, and in *Texas Monthly v. Bullock* (1989), which outlawed state tax exemptions for the sale of religious periodicals alone.[35] This separationist reading of *Lemon* was dormant for a time, as the Court developed alternative approaches to the establishment clause. But in *McCreary County v. ACLU* (2005), a plurality of the Court used a strict separationist reading of the *Lemon* test to strike down a Ten Commandments display on a county courthouse.[36]

After years of using the *Lemon* test selectively, the Court reformulated it, at least for cases challenging the constitutionality of government aid to religion. As we just saw, *Lemon* required that challenged government aid programs (1) have a secular purpose, (2) have a primary effect that neither advances nor inhibits religion, and (3) do not foster an excessive entanglement between church and state. In *Agostini v. Felton* (1997), the Court distilled *Lemon* and its progeny into a two-pronged inquiry: (1) "whether the government acted with the purpose of advancing or prohibiting religion," and (2) "whether the aid has the effect of advancing or inhibiting religion." The second inquiry into the religious effect of the government action, the Court further held, should be guided by whether the government action (a) results in governmental indoctrination of religion, (b) defines its recipients with reference to religion, or (c) creates an excessive entanglement between government and religion.[37] The *Agostini* test, as it came to be called, was intended to be a less rigorous constitutional inquiry than the traditional *Lemon* test, and less amenable to strict separationist readings. Significantly, by rendering "excessive entanglement" merely one evidentiary factor among others used to assess the overall religious effect of a governmental program (rather than using entanglement as a separate inquiry), *Agostini* has allowed for greater cooperation between religious and political officials in discharging social and educational services funded by the government. Close entanglement of government and religious officials could be permitted so long as its primary effect does not advance religion.

The *Agostini* Court used this newly revised test to overturn *Aguilar v. Felton* (1985).[38] *Aguilar* was a controversial case that had enjoined state educators from using religious school buildings to deliver federal remedial educational services to poor children because such use fostered an excessive entanglement between church and state. The *Agostini* Court held, instead, that the mere presence of state educators delivering these remedial services at religious schools was not per se unconstitutional. The inquiry was not whether there was simply an "excessive entanglement" of government and religion, but whether such entanglement evinced the fatal effect of advancing religion. The Court found no such impermissible religious effect and thus lifted the injunction against the use of religious schools for delivery of Title I services to eligible indigent students.

In *Mitchell v. Helms* (2000),[39] a plurality of the Court used this same *Agostini* reformulation of the *Lemon* test to uphold a federally funded program that enabled states to lend educational materials directly to both public and private religious schools to implement "secular, neutral, and ideological programs." The *Mitchell* Court similarly overruled two earlier cases, *Meek v. Pittinger* (1975)[40] and *Wolman v. Walter* (1977),[41] that had read the *Lemon* test more strictly to outlaw "direct aid" to religious schools.

The increasingly wide disparities of logic and results in the Court's cases in the later 1970s and 1980s undercut the very rationale for devising the *Lemon* test in the first place—to provide a more predictable middle way between separationism and accommodationism. Since the mid-1980s, therefore, individual justices have begun to experiment with alternative approaches to establishment. Five such approaches have appeared—endorsement, coercion, strict neutrality, equal treatment, and history or tradition. No one approach has consistently captured a majority of the Court, but each has attracted considerable support among the justices, and each has led the Court in at least one recent case.

Endorsement

The endorsement approach to the establishment clause was largely the creation of Justice O'Connor, and this approach may well have ended with her retirement in 2005 as there is no obvious champion for it on the current Court. The establishment clause, Justice O'Connor argued, forbids governmental endorsement or disapproval of religion. "We live in a pluralistic society. Our citizens come from diverse religious traditions or adhere to no particular religious beliefs at all."[42] "[G]overnment may generally not treat people differently based on the God or gods they worship, or don't worship."[43] It may not "make adherence to religion relevant to a person's standing in the political community. Direct government action endorsing religion or a particular religious practice is invalid under this approach because it 'sends a message to nonadherents that they are outsiders, not full members of the political community, and an accompanying message to adherents that they are insiders, favored members of the community.'"[44]

Government accommodations of religion, if applied without discrimination for or against any one religious person or group, are acceptable, Justice O'Connor continued. "What makes accommodation permissible, even praiseworthy, is not that the government is making life easier for some particular religious group as such. Rather, it is that the government is accommodating a deeply held belief."[45] This fosters equal protection for all, religious and nonreligious alike.[46]

Justice O'Connor applied this endorsement reasoning in more than a dozen opinions after 1984. It found its strongest expression in Justice O'Connor's plurality opinion for the Court in *Board of Education v. Mergens* (1990), where the Court upheld the constitutionality of the Equal Access Act.[47] It also informed Justice Blackmun's opinion in *County of Allegheny v. ACLU* (1989), in which the Court struck down a Christmas display in a county courthouse.[48] It was invoked again by Justice Stevens in the majority opinion of *Santa Fe Independent School District v. Doe* (2000), striking down a state policy of allowing student-led invocations at public high school football games.[49] The endorsement test drove the plurality opinion of *Mitchell v. Helms* (2000) that allowed federal funding of the secular services in all high schools, including religious schools.[50]

When a government displays religious symbols prominently on its own buildings, that signals endorsement, Justice O'Connor has argued.[51] But when government accommodates private religious displays in public parks and squares, that does not signal endorsement. Governmental programs that give religious students equal access to state funding or facilities, or that support the secular functions of religious organizations, or that accommodate the special core needs of religious individuals or groups are all necessary protections against outright hostility to religion. But equality and accommodation become impermissible endorsement when the boundary of a public school district follows exactly the boundary of an exclusively religious community. In such an instance, religion does affect a person's standing in the political community.

No Coercion

Justice Kennedy has occasionally lifted up "coercion" as a central concern of the establishment clause. In his view, "government may not coerce anyone to support or participate in any religion or its exercise; and it may not, in the guise of avoiding hostility or callous indifference, give direct benefits to religion in such a degree that it in fact 'establishes a religion or religious faith, or tends to do so.'"[52] The establishment clause is designed to protect liberty of conscience and the autonomy of religious groups, Justice Kennedy has argued, and not to purge the public square or public policy of all religion. "[P]reservation and transmission of religious beliefs and worship is the responsibility and a choice committed to the private sphere, which itself is promised freedom to pursue its mission."[53] "Government policies of accommodation, acknowledgement or support for religion are an accepted part of our political and cultural heritage" and should be maintained in a pluralistic manner.[54] Only where such accommodations of religion effectively coerce public participation in religious exercises such as prayer or merge "political and religious lines" and institutions should they be struck down.[55] These latter policies invariably invite the kind of religious stigmatizing that impairs true liberty of conscience and autonomy of religious governance. Parties might choose to participate in the prayer or abide by the religious line drawing not out of voluntary conviction but because of the civil and social advantages attached to them, and this would run afoul of establishment concerns.

A majority of the Court used this coercion test in *Lee v. Weisman* (1992) to outlaw prayers at a public middle school graduation ceremony. In this case, the school principal engaged a local rabbi to offer the prayers—instructing him to be "nonsectarian" and furnishing him with published guidelines to illustrate an appropriate prayer. The graduation ceremony took place on public school grounds. Students were not required to participate in either the ceremony or the prayer, but most did. Speaking for the *Weisman* Court, Justice Kennedy found the state's action doubly coercive. The state was dictating to the rabbi the content of his prayer, and it was also coercing all students to participate in its recitation. Although he adduced earlier cases that outlawed prayer in schools, Justice Kennedy did not dwell on their separationist reasoning. He did not apply the *Lemon* test, but he explicitly rejected the recommendation of both parties and the dissent to bury it.[56] Instead, he held that a strong line of cases prohibiting prayer in public schools controlled this situation, that the driving force behind those prior cases was to avoid religious coercion, and that the practice of such prayers at graduation ceremonies thus violated the establishment clause.

This concern to avoid coercion of religion was also at work in *Santa Fe Independent School District v. Doe* (2000), which outlawed student prayer at public high school football games.[57] Inquiries into coercion, of course, are also pertinent to the free exercise clause via the underlying principle of liberty of conscience that holds the two clauses together. When government mandates certain religious activities, it not only establishes that religion contrary to the establishment clause but also violates the free exercise rights of those who are compelled to participate in those activities.

Strict Neutrality

According to Justice Souter, the endorsement approach is too unpredictable, and the coercion approach is too narrow to outlaw more subtle forms of religious discrimination or favoritism that are forbidden by the establishment clause. Under this view, the establishment clause mandates "governmental neutrality"—both *among* religions and *between* religion and nonreligion. While the *Lemon* test can be a helpful guide to finding neutrality, as Justice Souter demonstrated in *McCreary County v. ACLU* (2005), it is not a dispositive method for judging whether government has acted neutrally.

Justice Souter has used his neutrality approach to challenge various governmental accommodations of religion or cooperation with religious officials in the public school or the public square, for such actions favor religion over nonreligion.[58] Religiously neutral policies that afforded an incidental benefit to religious beliefs or bodies were acceptable. Governmental programs that supported secular institutions along with religious institutions delivering secular services were also acceptable—so long as there is "a searching enquiry to ensure that the institution kept the secular activities separate from its sectarian ones, with any direct aid flowing only to the former and never the latter." Direct government funding of any religious activities was "categorically prohibited," however, for taxpayers either of different or nonreligious persuasion cannot be forced to pay for the religious activities of another.[59]

Justice Souter's neutrality approach carried a plurality of the Court in *Kiryas Joel Village School District v. Grumet* (1994). That case outlawed New York's creation of a new public school district that followed exactly the boundaries of a Hasidic Jewish community. The state had created this special school district in order to offer handicapped students in the Hasidic community the remedial services mandated by federal and state law, without forcing these students into the gentile world. All students in these remedial programs were Hasidic, and the school officials could respect the community's religious laws, particularly those mandating separate sex education. Writing for the Court, Justice Souter held that this policy violated the establishment clause. It favored religious over nonreligious students. It subordinated and delegated the state's educational responsibility to the religious leadership and preferences of the community. Both features of the program were impermissible under the neutrality required by the establishment clause.[60]

This strict neutrality logic was also at work in Justice Souter's plurality opinion in *McCreary County v. ACLU* (2005), which struck down a county's display of the Ten Commandments on its courthouse wall. Souter insisted on looking beyond the stated cultural and historical purpose of the display, and behind the final display in which the Decalogue was buffered with various secular documents. The first county display included the Decalogue alone and had a stated purpose of promoting Christian ethics. All this, to him, betrayed a sectarian rather than a secular purpose, and religious favoritism rather than strict neutrality.[61] It is not clear whether Justice Souter's departure from the Court in 2008 will signal the end to this test. Both Justice Stevens and Justice Ginsburg have regularly signed onto his opinions, and they may well continue this approach.

Equal Treatment/Evenhanded Neutrality

Yet another approach to the establishment clause is called "equal treatment," "equal access," and sometimes "evenhanded neutrality." This approach, pressed especially by Justices Thomas and Scalia, overlaps heavily in terminology with the neutrality approach and is somewhat consistent with the endorsement approach and *Agostini*'s reformulated *Lemon* test. But whereas Justice Souter's formulation of neutrality *forbids* government funding or alliances with religion, equal treatment exponents *allow* such funding and alliances so long as nonreligious parties that are similarly situated receive comparable treatment.

Equal treatment of religion, of course, is no recent invention and is no monopoly of the establishment clause. Already in *Bradfield v. Roberts* (1899), its first establishment clause case, the Court upheld a federal grant to a religious hospital alongside others.[62] In *Everson*, despite strong separationist language, the Court upheld school bus transportation for religious students alongside nonreligious students; it did the same for loans of textbooks.[63] It upheld construction grants to religious schools and religious charities as part of broader programs that fund nonreligious institutions as well.[64] It upheld tax exemptions to church properties alongside those of schools, charities, and other associations.[65] And the Court has said that it is not an establishment of religion for religious workers to receive the same access to unemployment compensation benefits afforded other workers.[66] The Court's rationale for such earlier holdings, however, was usually not clearly stated in explicit terms of "equality" or "equal treatment." Instead it talked of legislative religious accommodation, protections of free exercise, expressions of benevolent neutrality, or suitable means of implementing secular policy.

In recent cases, however, the Court has said more explicitly that religious institutions and individuals are not "disabled by the First Amendment" from equal access to forums open to others, or from equal participation in government programs in which nonreligious parties participate.[67] Thus in *Capitol Square v. Pinette* (1995) the Court upheld the private display of a cross in a public square that was "open to all on *equal terms*."[68] In *Rosenberger v. University of Virginia* (1995), the Court upheld the equal access of a voluntary religious student group to state university funding for its publications, which was available to more than one hundred similarly situated nonreligious student groups.[69] And in *Good News Club v. Milford Central School* (2001), the Court insisted that religious groups be given equal access to public school classrooms that were open to other groups offering extracurricular instruction in civics.[70]

In the plurality opinion of *Mitchell v. Helms* (2000) and in the majority opinion of *Zelman v. Simmons-Harris* (2002), the Court cast these concerns of equal treatment into a new two-step inquiry into "evenhanded neutrality." A court must inquire whether a challenged statute is (1) religiously neutral on its face and (2) religiously neutral in its application. This second prong was explicitly intended to invoke the same concerns for religious indoctrination, line drawing, or excessive entanglement that had informed the *Agostini* test.

This latest neutrality-as-equality formulation of the establishment clause is a close cousin to the free exercise formulation of neutrality in *Smith* and its progeny. It is no coincidence that Justice Scalia has been the leading architect of both formulations. Under the *Smith* test, as we saw, a challenged law will satisfy the free exercise clause if it is (1) neutral and (2) generally applicable. Under the *Zelman* test, a law will satisfy the establishment clause if it is (1) neutral on its face and (2) neutral in application. There is certainly some distinction between these two inquiries, especially in their second prongs. But they run closely parallel. Such parallels suggest that this establishment clause test will help the Court achieve what many justices have long coveted: a more integrated jurisprudence of the First Amendment religion clauses. But the cost of this kind of formulation would be a substantial weakening of both the establishment and free exercise clauses.

History and Tradition

In a few recent cases, the Court has used tradition or history to uphold a practice against establishment clause challenge, disregarding the *Lemon* test and all other approaches in the process. The Court had used arguments from history and tradition a few times before, as part of broader rationales for upholding religious tax exemptions and Sabbath Day laws.[71] In *Marsh v. Chambers* (1983), however, this argument from tradition became the exclusive basis for upholding a state legislature's practice of funding a chaplain and opening its sessions with his prayers. Writing for the *Marsh* Court, Chief Justice Burger defended such practices as a noble survival of the traditional public role of religion in American life and law:

> In light of the unambiguous and unbroken history of more than 200 years, there can be no doubt that the practice of opening legislative sessions with prayer has become part of the fabric of our society. To invoke Divine guidance on a public body entrusted with making the laws is not, in these circumstances, an "establishment" of religion [but] simply a tolerable acknowledgement of beliefs widely held among the people of this country. . . . "[W]e are a religious people whose institutions presuppose a Supreme Being."[72]

Similarly in *Van Orden v. Perry* (2005), a plurality of the Court led by Chief Justice Rehnquist upheld a forty-year-old display of the Decalogue on the state capitol grounds in Texas. It helped that the monument had been privately donated, that it was one of thirty-eight other markers on the capitol, and that it was not in a prominent location. But what also impressed the Court was that old religious displays like this are part of our "American heritage," and part of "the fabric of American society." Maintaining these old public displays of religious symbols on government land democratically recognizes and represents that "religion has been closely identified with our history and government" and that Americans are "religious people, whose institutions presuppose a Supreme Being."[73]

Summary and Conclusions

Endorsement, coercion, strict neutrality, equal treatment, and history: these are the five main alternative approaches that the Court has recently imported into its establishment clause calculus, alongside its traditional separationist, accommodationist, and *Lemon* neutrality approaches. All five of these recent approaches have aimed to replace the *Lemon* neutrality test and to nuance the underlying separationist and accommodationist approaches that antedated and animated the *Lemon* test. None of these approaches has, as yet, commanded a consistent majority of the Court, and none has interred the *Lemon* test entirely. Absent clear direction, lower federal courts thus generally continue to start with the three-part *Lemon* inquiry into whether a challenged statute has a secular purpose, has a primary effect that neither advances nor inhibits religion, and fosters no excessive entanglement between church and state. Lower courts may modify this inquiry per *Agostini*, but also may feel compelled to make arguments based on coercion, endorsement, and other grounds. Increasingly, some federal courts are going their own way in adjudicating establishment cases, without much interference from the Supreme Court.

All this has left the future of establishment clause jurisprudence difficult to predict. The recent appointments of Justice Alito in place of Justice O'Connor and Justice Sotomayor in place of Justice Souter compound the unpredictability. The emerging trend, however, is that the establishment clause, like the free exercise clause, is becoming weaker and therefore less attractive to religious liberty litigants. Justice Alito, for example, has already authored two opinions in establishment clause cases to date. Both soften the establishment clause and hold for the government.[74] Five times since 1994, Justice Thomas has repeated his call for the Court to selectively deincorporate the establishment clause by restricting its application to the federal government (to "Congress") alone, thereby leaving the states free to operate under their own state constitutions. The Court's recent tightening of standing requirements in establishment cases (leaving fewer litigants to challenge laws) suggests further that the Supreme Court may be slowly pulling back from its ambitious disestablishment agenda of the 1960s to 1980s.

Notes

1. For further guidance, see Kent Greenawalt's excellent overview in *Religion and the Constitution: Establishment and Fairness* (2008).

2. *Zobrest v. Catalina Foothills School District*, 509 U.S. 1, 24 (O'Connor, J., dissenting), quoting *Three Affiliated Tribes of Fort Berthold Reservation v. Wold Engineering, P.C.*, 467 U.S. 138, 157 (1984). See also *McCollum v. Board of Education*, 333 U.S. 203, 232, 235 (Jackson, J., concurring) (expressing doubt whether the Court had jurisdiction over a local case involving religious instruction in public schools, and urging the Court to devise strict limits to jurisdiction over these cases).

3. 393 U.S. 97, 100 (1968).

4. *Zobrest*, 504 U.S. at 24 (O'Connor, J., dissenting).

5. Ibid., 8.

6. *Frothingham v. Mellon*, 262 U.S. 447 (1923).

7. See, e.g., *Doremus v. Board of Education*, 342 U.S. 429 (1952).

8. *Abington Township School District v. Schempp*, 374 U.S. 203, 224, n. 9 (1963) (emphasis added).

9. *Flast v. Cohen*, 392 U.S. 83 (1968). See also *Larson v. Valente*, 456 U.S. 228 (1982).

10. *Valley Forge Christian College v. Americans United for Separation of Church and State*, 454 U.S. 464, 509–510 (Brennan, J., dissenting) (references omitted).

11. See esp. *Kiryas Joel Village School District v. Grumet*, 114 S.Ct. 2481 (1994); *Aguilar v. Felton*, 473 U.S. 402 (1985); *Grand Rapids School District v. Ball*, 473 U.S. 373 (1985).

12. *Lyng v. Northwest Indian Cemetery Protective Association*, 485 U.S. 439, 451 (1988).

13. 454 U.S. 464, 487 (1982). See also *Karcher v. May*, 484 U.S. 72 (1987) (state legislators cannot appeal an establishment case involving a moment of silence law for which they voted, but which the legislature has chosen not to appeal).

14. 542 U.S. 1 (2004).

15. 551 U.S. 587 (2007).

16. __ U.S. __ (slip opinion) (April 28, 2010).

17. See Ira C. Lupu and Robert W. Tuttle, "Ball on a Needle: *Hein v. Freedom from Religion Foundation, Inc.* and the Future of Establishment Clause Adjudication," *Brigham Young University Law Review* (2008): 115.

18. *Everson*, 330 U.S. 1, 15–16 (1947).

19. *Engel v. Vitale*, 370 U.S. 421, 430–432 (1962).

20. *Board of Education v. Allen*, 392 U.S. 236, 251–252 (Black, J., dissenting).

21. *Everson*, 330 U.S. at 18.

22. See *Walz v. Tax Commission*, 397 U.S. 664 (1970); *Texas Monthly v. Bullock*, 489 U.S. 1 (1989).

23. 343 U.S. 306, 312–314 (1952).

24. *Engel v. Vitale*, 370 U.S. at 421, 445–446 (Stewart, J., dissenting).

25. *Schempp*, 374 U.S. at 313 (Stewart, J., dissenting).

26. *Wallace v. Jaffree*, 472 U.S. 38, 107, 113 (Rehnquist, J., dissenting).

27. *Schempp*, 374 U.S. at 222.

28. *Lemon v. Kurtzman*, 403 U.S. 602, 612–614 (1973), quoting in part, *Walz*, 397 U.S. at 670, 674–675. See also Burger's comments in *Tilton v. Richardson*, 403 U.S. 672, 677 (1971).

29. Compare, e.g., *Wallace v. Jaffree* (1985) (offering a searching inquiry into legislative history) with *Mueller v. Allen*, 463 U.S. 388 (1983) (spurning an inquiry into the motives of the legislature or the history of the statute).

30. *Walz*, 397 U.S. at 669–670 (emphasis added).

31. 463 U.S. 388 (1983).

32. 487 U.S. 589 (1988).

33. 536 U.S. 639 (2002).

34. *Lemon*, 403 U.S. at 619–620, 622.

35. 472 U.S. 38 (1985) and 489 U.S. 1 (1989), respectively.

36. 545 U.S. 844 (2005).

37. 521 U.S. 203 (1997).

38. 473 U.S. 402 (1985), overruled by *Agostini v. Felton*, 521 U.S. 203, 235 (1997).

39. 530 U.S. 793 (2000).

40. 421 U.S. 349 (1975), overruled by *Mitchell v. Helms*, 530 U.S. at 808.

41. 433 U.S. 229 (1977), overruled by *Mitchell v. Helms*, 530 U.S. at 808.

42. *Allegheny County v. American Civil Liberties Union*, 492 U.S. 573, 627 (O'Connor, J., concurring).

43. *Kiryas Joel*, 512 U.S. at 714–715 (O'Connor, J., concurring).

44. *Wallace*, 472 U.S. at 69 (O'Connor, J., concurring).

45. *Kiryas Joel*, 512 U.S. at 714–715 (O'Connor, J., concurring).

46. *Board of Education v. Mergens*, 496 U.S. 226, 248–250 (1990).

47. Ibid.

48. 492 U.S. 573 (1989).

49. 530 U.S. 793 (2000).

50. 530 U.S. 290 (2000).

51. *Allegheny County*, 492 U.S. at 623–637 (O'Connor, J., concurring).

52. 492 U.S. 659 (Kennedy, J., concurring in judgment in part, dissenting in part).

53. *Lee v. Weisman*, 505 U.S. 577, 586–587, 592–594 (1992).

54. *Allegheny County*, 492 U.S. at 657 (Kennedy, J., concurring in judgment in part, dissenting in part).

55. *Kiryas Joel*, 512 U.S. at 722 (Kennedy, J., concurring).

56. *Weisman*, 505 U.S. at 587, 589–592.

57. 530 U.S. 290 (2000).

58. See Souter's illustrations in *Lee v. Weisman*, 505 U.S. at 618–619 (Souter, J., concurring); *Kiryas Joel*, 512 U.S. at 701–703.

59. *Rosenberger v. University of Virginia*, 515 U.S. 819, 863 (Souter, J., dissenting).

60. *Kiryas Joel*, 512 U.S. at 694–701.

61. 545 U.S. 844 (2005).

62. *Bradfield v. Roberts*, 175 U.S. 291 (1899).

63. *Everson v. Board of Education*, 330 U.S. 1 (1947); *Board of Education v. Allen*, 392 U.S. 236 (1968).

64. See, e.g., *Tilton v. Richardson*, 403 U.S. 672 (1971); *Roemer v. Board of Public Works*, 426 U.S. 736 (1976); *Bowen v. Kendrick*, 487 U.S. 589 (1988).

65. *Walz v. Tax Commission*, 397 U.S. 664 (1970).

66. See *Sherbert v. Verner*, 374 U.S. 398, 409–410 (1963) (defending the free exercise exemption on grounds of neutrality but explicitly forgoing analysis of the equal protection

issue); repeated in *Thomas v. Review Board*, 450 U.S. 707, 719–720 (1981); *Hobbie v. Unemployment Appeals Commission*, 480 U.S. 136, 144–145 (1987).

67. Quoting *Bowen v. Kendrick*, 487 U.S. at 609.

68. *Capitol Square Review and Advisory Board v. Pinette*, 515 U.S. 753, 768 n. 3 (1995).

69. 515 U.S. 819 (1995).

70. 533 U.S. 98 (2001).

71. See *Walz v. Tax Commission*, 397 U.S. 664 (1970); *McGowan v. Maryland*, 366 U.S. 420 (1961).

72. *Marsh v. Chambers*, 463 U.S. 783 (1983), quoting, in part, *Zorach v. Clauson*, 343 U.S. 306 (1952).

73. 545 U.S. 677 (2005).

74. *Hein v. Freedom From Religion Foundation*, 551 U.S. 587 (2007); *Pleasant Grove v. Summum*, 129 S.Ct. 1125 (2009).

8

Religion and Public Education

No Establishment of Religion, but Equal Access for Religion

More than two-thirds of the Supreme Court establishment clause cases concern religion and education. One set of cases—the subject of this chapter—concerns the place of religion in public education. These cases fall into two phases. From 1948 to 1987, the Court applied a consistent separationist logic, using the establishment clause to ban religious teachers, texts, teachings, prayers, ceremonies, and symbols from public grade schools and high schools. Young, impressionable students who are required by law to attend school cannot risk being coerced by religion, the Court reasoned. Students and teachers could pursue their private religious exercises away from the school and could be released to do so.

In a second phase, beginning in 1981 and escalating after 1990, the Court used a new "equal access" logic to give religious parties equal access to public school facilities, forums, and funds that were made available to like-positioned nonreligious parties. This line of cases, grounded especially in the free speech clause, allowed religious students and others to use public school classrooms and other facilities outside of formal instructional time to engage in voluntary religious activities. Granting religious parties such equal access rights was not considered to be an establishment of religion but a vindication of the equality of all parties before the law.

Viewed collectively, these two lines of cases provide that religion still has no place in the public school when class is in session, but voluntary religious expression by students is permissible before, between, and after classes. To the dismay of some, mandatory group prayer and Bible reading as religious exercises in public schools have no foreseeable chance of being reinstated. To the dismay of others, various religious exercises and practices by the students themselves are not only permissible in public schools but must often be accommodated. These two lines of cases sometimes come close to colliding. The controversial cases concern one-time school activities like graduation ceremonies or sports events, with courts dividing on whether

191

those are more akin to classroom experiences that must be off-limits to religion or limited public forums in which discrimination against religion is forbidden.

Separationist Cases (1948–1987)

It is no surprise that the Court used a strict separationist reading of the establishment clause in its first modern cases on religion and public education. Between 1848 and 1921, as we have seen, thirty-five state constitutions banned government funding and other material support for religious schools. Fifteen state constitutions insisted further that state schools remain free from "sectarian influence" or from the control of religious officials and institutions (pp. 114–115). At the turn of the twentieth century, various religious groups led countercampaigns to reinvigorate traditional forms and forums of religion in public schools—calling for the enhancement of biblical teaching, the appointment of Christian teachers, and the expansion of religious ceremonies and symbols. This countercampaign led a few states to amend their state constitutions to require biblical and moral instruction and to provide aid to religious schools and their students. In response, however, various religious and nonreligious groups pushed back, filling the state courts with controversial and well publicized cases.

One such case was the famous 1925 *Scopes* monkey trial in Tennessee, which featured the spectacle of two giants, William Jennings Bryan and Clarence Darrow, fighting valiantly over the place of creation and evolution in the public school. Bryan, three-time presidential candidate, defended creationism as "inerrant fact" and denounced evolution as "atheistic fiction." Darrow, the famous lawyer representing the new ACLU, insisted that evolution was "scientific fact" and creationism "obsolete myth." Bryan won the argument. But the 1925 *Scopes* case was a storm signal of many battles to come over the place of religious teachings and texts in public schools.[1]

After 1947, the Supreme Court took firm control of these controversies and systematically barred religion from the public schools. In its early cases, the Court developed a general logic about religion and public education that it carried forward in its opinions and in public opinion for the next half century. The public school, the Court reasoned, is one of the most visible and well-known arms of the state in any community. A primary purpose of the public school is to stand as a model of constitutional democracy in the local community and to provide a vehicle for the communication and demonstration of democratic values and abilities to its students. The state compels its students to attend school until the age of sixteen, and these students are perforce young and impressionable. As a consequence, the public schools must cling closely to core constitutional and democratic values. One such core value is the separation of church and state taught by the establishment clause. Some relaxation of constitutional values, even establishment clause values, might be possible in other public contexts—where mature adults can make informed assessments of the values being transmitted. But no such relaxation can occur in public schools, with impressionable young people who are compelled to be there. In public schools, the constitutional values of strict separation of church and state must be vigorously protected.

The case that opened this series was *McCollum v. Board of Education* (1948). Pursuant to state law, a local public school board adopted a "release time" program for students in grades four through nine. For thirty to forty-five minutes once a week, students were released from their regular classes to participate in religious classes, if their parents consented to their participation. These classes were held on public school grounds during the regular public school hours. Students could choose among three such religious classes, taught respectively by qualified Protestant, Catholic, or Jewish teachers. These religious teachers were not employed by or paid for by the school, though they were approved by its superintendent. Students whose parents did not consent to their participation continued their "secular studies"—usually as a study break in the library—during this release time period.

A parent of one student challenged the release time program as a violation of the establishment clause. The *McCollum* Court agreed. Writing for the majority, Justice Black declared that this was precisely the kind of conflation of church and state that the establishment clause was designed to outlaw—using "tax-supported property for religious instruction and the close cooperation between school authorities and the religious council in promoting religious education."

> The operation of the State's compulsory education system thus assists and is integrated with the program of religious instruction carried on by separate religious sects. Pupils compelled by law to go to school for secular education are released in part from their legal duty upon the condition that they attend the religious classes. This is beyond all question a utilization of the tax-established and tax-supported public school to aid religious groups to spread their faith. And it falls squarely under the ban of the First Amendment [that] . . . had erected a wall of separation between Church and State.[2]

In a strongly worded concurrence, Justice Frankfurter underscored the importance of rigorous application of the principle of separation of church and state in the realm of public education. After lamenting that public schools of late had become "hostage" to "sectarian control," Justice Frankfurter wrote:

> Separation means separation, not something less. Jefferson's metaphor in describing the relation between Church and State speaks of a "wall of separation," not of a fine line easily overstepped. The public school is at once the symbol of our democracy and the most pervasive means for promoting our common destiny. In no activity of the State is it more vital to keep out divisive influences than in its schools, to avoid confusing, not to say fusing, what the Constitution sought to keep strictly apart. "The great American principle of eternal separation"—Elihu Root's phrase bears repetition—is one of the vital reliances of our Constitutional system for assuring unities among our people stronger than our diversities. It is the Court's duty to enforce this principle in its full integrity.[3]

In *Engel v. Vitale* (1962), the Court extended this separationist reasoning to outlaw prayers in schools—one of the main icons of the earlier Evangelical efforts to restore religion in the public schools and a source of cultural controversy, both in that day and still today. The State Board of Regents of New York had adopted a nondenominational prayer to be recited by public school teachers and their students at the commencement of each day: "Almighty God, we acknowledge our dependence upon Thee, and we beg Thy blessings upon us, our parents, our teachers, and our Country." Students who did not wish to participate in the prayer could remain silent or be excused from the room during its recitation. The parents of ten students challenged both the state's creation of the prayer and its use in the public school classroom. The *Engel* Court agreed that these violated the establishment clause. Again Justice Black wrote for the majority:

> It is no part of the business of government to compose official prayers for any group of the American people to recite as part of a religious program carried on by government. . . . There can be no doubt that New York's state prayer program officially establishes the religious beliefs embodied in the Regents prayer. . . . Neither the fact that the prayer may be denominationally neutral nor the fact that its observance on the part of the students is voluntary can serve to free it from the Establishment Clause. . . . When the power, prestige, and financial support of government is placed behind a particular religious belief, the indirect coercive pressure upon religious minorities to conform to the prevailing officially approved religion is plain.

Such a mandatory prayer in schools is unconstitutional, Justice Black concluded. It violates the "first and most immediate" principle of the establishment clause: "a union of government and religion tends to destroy government and to degrade religion."[4]

In *Abington Township School District v. Schempp* (1963), the Court extended this reasoning to outlaw Bible reading in the public schools.[5] Following general state law, a local public school district mandated that each school open its day with the reading of ten Bible verses. Either a teacher or a student who volunteered would read the text. Each reader was permitted to choose the text of the day. No commentary or discussion of the Bible reading was allowed. In some schools, a common Bible reading was broadcast throughout the school; in other schools, the reading was done in individual classrooms. In some schools, this reading was followed by public recitation of the Lord's Prayer and the Pledge of Allegiance. Students whose parents did not consent could again refuse to participate or leave the room during these religious exercises.

After the precedent of *Engel,* the *Schempp* Court easily found these facts to be a violation of the establishment clause, even though again this issue was highly controversial. The policy in question, Justice Clark wrote for the Court, was a state-mandated, overtly religious exercise aimed at impressionable youths who were required to be in school; further, there was no realistic opportunity for the average student to forgo participation. "[I]t is no defense that the religious practices here may be relatively minor encroachments on the First Amendment. The breach of neutrality that is today a trickling stream may all too soon become a raging torrent." Justice Clark emphasized that to ban religion from the public school was not to ban it from society altogether:

> The place of religion in our society is an exalted one, achieved through a long tradition of reliance on the home, the church, and the inviolable citadel of the individual heart and mind. We have come to recognize through bitter experience that it is not within the power of government to invade that citadel, whether its purpose or effect be to aid or oppose, to advance or retard. In the relationship between man and religion, the state is firmly committed to a position of neutrality.[6]

Responding to Justice Stewart's sharply worded dissent that the Court's purported neutrality toward religion effectively established "secularism" as the religion of the public school, Justice Clark offered a conciliatory word about the objective value and use of religion in public education, provided it was not for mandatory religious practice or recitation:

> We agree of course that the State may not establish a "religion of secularism" in the sense of affirmatively opposing or showing hostility to religion. . . . We do not agree, however, that this decision in any sense has that effect. In addition, it might well be said that one's education is not complete without a study of comparative religion or the history of religion and its relationship to the advancement of civilization. It certainly may be said that the Bible is worthy of study for its literary and historic qualities. Nothing we have said here indicates that such study of the Bible or of religion, when presented objectively as part of a secular program of education, may not be effected consistently with the First Amendment.[7]

While *Schempp* narrowly permitted objective instruction of religious topics in appropriate public school classes, later cases made clear that symbolic expressions of religion in general were not welcome nor was the science classroom an appropriate place for religious instruction. In *Stone v. Graham* (1980), the Court struck down a state statute that authorized the posting of a plaque bearing the Ten Commandments on the wall of each public school classroom. The plaques were donated and hung by private groups in the community. There was no public reading of the commandments nor any evident mention or endorsement of them by teachers or school officials. Each plaque also bore a small inscription that sought to immunize it from charges of religious establishment: "The secular application of the Ten Commandments is clearly seen in its adoption as the fundamental legal code of Western Civilization and the Common Law of the United States."

Using a separationist reading of the *Lemon* test, the Court struck down these displays as violations of the establishment clause. The per curiam opinion held that the statute mandating the Decalogue display had no "secular legislative purpose" but was instead "plainly religious." The Ten Commandments are sacred in Jewish and Christian circles, the Court reasoned, and they command "the religious duties of believers." It made no constitutional difference that the Ten Commandments were passively displayed rather than formally read aloud or that they were privately donated rather than purchased with state money. The mere display of the Decalogue in the public school classroom served only a religious purpose and was thus per se unconstitutional.[8]

In *Edwards v. Aguillard* (1987), the Court pressed this logic further to strike down a Louisiana law requiring a "Balanced Treatment for Creation-Science and Evolution-Science in Public School Instruction." The law mandated that a public school teacher could not teach "evolution-science" without teaching "creation-science" and vice versa. Teachers were not required to teach a theory of origins at all, but if they did, they had to give equal time to "the scientific evidence" for both evolutionary and creationist accounts of origins. The stated legislative purpose of the law was "to promote academic freedom" by allowing teachers and students to explore evidence of various theories of origins, including theories rooted in the Bible.

The *Edwards* Court declared the act unconstitutional. After rehearsing the legislative history at length, the Court concluded that the Louisiana law had no real secular purpose but was a thinly veiled attempt to import religious teachings into the public school curriculum, and precisely at a place where religion was least appropriate—the science classroom. The law evinced a "discriminatory preference for the teaching of creation and against the teaching of evolution," Justice Brennan wrote for the Court. Its "preeminent purpose" was "clearly to advance the religious viewpoint that a supernatural being created humankind. The term 'creation science' was defined as embracing this particular religious doctrine. . . . In this case, the purpose of the Creationism Act was to restructure the science curriculum to conform with a particular religious viewpoint." This was not a proper objective teaching of religion but rather an unconstitutional establishment of religion. Evolutionary theory is scientific, the Court said, and creationism is religious. The two cannot be mixed, not even under the guise of "equal time," at least in the science classroom of the public school.[9]

In *Wallace v. Jaffree* (1985), the Court extended the firm prohibition against prayer in schools to ban moments of silence as well. At issue in the case was a state statute that authorized a moment of silence at the beginning of each school day for "meditation or voluntary prayer." Upon reviewing the legislative history, the Court found that the statute revealed no secular purpose but instead betrayed a transparent "legislative intent to return prayer to the public schools." "The addition of 'or voluntary prayer'" to the statute, Justice Stevens wrote for the Court, "indicates that the State intended to characterize prayer as a favored practice. Such an endorsement is not consistent with the established principle that Government must pursue a course of complete neutrality toward religion."[10]

In more recent cases, the Court has extended this prohibition on prayer and other religious activities from daily classrooms to one-time public school graduation ceremonies and school sporting events as well. The logic of these more recent cases, however, has shifted from preserving the principle of separation of church and state to promoting the principle of liberty of conscience, and protecting parties from state coercion and endorsements of religion. As we have seen, protecting each person's liberty of conscience has long been one of the stated reasons for separating church and state, and indeed was the fundamental ground on which Thomas Jefferson had called for a "wall of separation" between church and state.

The principle of liberty of conscience was prominent in the case of *Lee v. Weisman* (1992), which outlawed prayers at a public middle school graduation ceremony. Consistent with state policy, the public middle school principal engaged a local rabbi to offer the prayers—instructing the rabbi to be "nonsectarian" and furnishing him with published guidelines that illustrated an appropriate prayer. The graduation ceremony took place on public school grounds. The prayer followed immediately after the public recitation of the Pledge of Allegiance, with all participants and graduates already standing. Although students were not required to participate in the graduation ceremony or listen to the prayer, most did. One of these graduating middle school students, through her parents, challenged the constitutionality of this practice.

The *Weisman* Court found the state's action doubly coercive. The state was impermissibly dictating to the rabbi the content of his prayer, and it was also effectively coercing all students to participate in its recitation. This was a clear violation of the establishment clause and its constituent principle of liberty of conscience, the Court concluded. Justice Kennedy wrote for the majority:

> The undeniable fact is that the school district's supervision and control of a high school graduation ceremony puts public pressure, as well as peer pressure, on attending students to stand as a group, or at least maintain respectful silence during the Invocation and Benediction. The pressure, though subtle and indirect, can be as real as any overt compulsion. . . . *[F]or the dissenter of high school age, who has a reasonable perception that she is being forced by the State to pray in a manner her conscience will not allow, the injury is no less real. . . .* [T]he embarrassment and the intrusion of the religious exercise cannot be refuted by arguing that these prayers, and similar ones said in the future, are of a *de minimis* character. To do so would be an affront to the Rabbi who offered them and to all those for whom the prayers were an essential and profound recognition of divine authority. And for the same reason, we think that the intrusion is greater than the two minutes or so of time consumed for prayers like these. Assuming, as we must, that the prayers were offensive to the student and the parent who now object, the intrusion was both real and, in the context of a secondary school, a violation of the objector's rights.[11]

In *Santa Fe Independent School District v. Doe* (2000) the Court held that a student's liberty of conscience rights must be protected at other school-sponsored events as well. The issue in *Santa Fe* was the traditional Texas state practice of offering prayers or invocations at public high school football games. The local school district had instituted a new "Prayer at Football Games" policy that authorized public high school students to participate in a two-step referendum. Students first voted whether "invocations" should be given at the school's football games; 91 percent of the students voted in favor. Students then elected one of their peers to deliver such invocations for all home football games that year. The stated purpose of the pregame invocation was "to solemnize the event, to promote good sportsmanship and student safety, and to establish the appropriate environment for the competition." A group of students and their parents brought suit, alleging that the district's policies and practices constituted an establishment of religion.

The Court agreed and declared this policy and practice unconstitutional. Justice Stevens, writing for the majority, reiterated the principle from *Lee v. Weisman* that "at a minimum, the Constitution guarantees that government may not coerce anyone to support or participate in religion or its exercise." The Court was not convinced that the private student speech in this context lacked governmental coercion. The invocations were "authorized by a government policy . . . on government property at government-sponsored school-related events," and attendance was mandatory for some students (including cheerleaders, band members, and football players). The Court further rejected an attempt to characterize the student election process as a "circuit-breaker" to the constitutional challenge. "[F]undamental rights may not be submitted to vote; they depend on the outcome of no elections." And the Court attached no significance to calling these "invocations" rather than "prayers," or to the new practice of using religiously inclusive and denominationally softened language. A prayer by any other name is still a prayer, the Court concluded, and prayers at public school events are not constitutionally permissible.

Not only was the *Santa Fe* policy an unconstitutional coercion of religion in violation of the principle of liberty of conscience; it was also an impermissible state endorsement of religion masquerading as a concern for the student's freedom of speech: "The District . . . asks us to pretend that we do not recognize what every High School student understands clearly—that this policy is about prayer. The District further asks us to accept what is obviously untrue: that these messages are necessary to 'solemnize' a football game and that this single-student, year-long position is essential to the protection of student speech. We refuse to turn a blind eye to the context in which this policy arose, and that context quells any doubt that this policy was implemented with the purpose of endorsing school prayer." And while the principle of equal access (discussed below) is important, the Court made clear in *Santa Fe* that such an "equality" principle cannot ultimately trump establishment clause concerns of no-coercion and separationism when countermajoritarianism is at work: "[T]he fact that only one student is permitted to give a content-limited message suggests this policy does little to 'foste[r] free expression.'"[12]

Equal Access Cases (1981–2001)

The foregoing line of establishment clause cases on the place of religion in the public schools—from *McCollum* (1948) to *Santa Fe* (2000)—is among the Court's most consistent applications of the First Amendment religion clauses. The results have been unwavering: religion is not permitted in the public school during instructional time or at school-sponsored events, save as an object of study in an appropriate course. The reasoning has been largely consistent as well: separation of church and state must be maintained in the public school, among other things to protect the liberty of conscience of the students from governmental coercion into religious expression or more subtle endorsements of it.

These public school cases, while widely applauded and applied, have not been without criticism. Some critics, particularly of the Court's early cases, have lamented the Court's removal of religion from public schools, and have worked persistently to return prayer and other traditional religious activities to the classroom. These groups are often conservative Christians pressing the broader thesis that America was founded as a Christian nation and must democratically reflect this in its political institutions, including its state schools. A second group of critics, building on Justice Stewart's dissent in *Schempp,* have charged the Court with establishing secularism in the public school under the guise of neutrality; these critics charge that the purportedly secular, rational, and scientific instruction of the public school is just as loaded with values and just as dependent on myths and metaphors as traditional forms of religion. The secular/sectarian line-drawing in these cases (as well as in the government and religious school cases in the next chapter) is too simplistic, they say. A third group of critics, including some education and child development specialists, have charged that the policy of quarantining public school students from religion harms rather than helps in cultivating the very democratic values and abilities the Court is trying to protect. Religion is not like alcohol that is to be avoided until adulthood, they argue, but is a powerful and perennial force in society, whether for good or ill, and every budding democratic citizen needs to learn to deal with it responsibly. Such groups have thus developed a number of ambitious curricular forums that seek to introduce religion judiciously into the public school curriculum in appropriate courses. Finally, some critics have charged that the Court has used the establishment clause to quash free exercise and free speech rights. Why should teachers, students, and parents be muzzled in their religious expression as a condition for participating in the state-mandated activity of education, they ask? Some critics add an economic argument: the religious rights of the poor suffer disproportionately, since only well-to-do students can afford to attend private schools that do not muzzle their religious expression.[13]

Particularly these latter two arguments—concerning the need to educate students about religion and to protect the student's rights to religious expression—have helped to drive the development of a new line of equal access cases. The principal logic of these cases is that religious students and other parties must be given equal access to facilities, forums, and even funds that the public school makes available to similarly positioned nonreligious parties. These cases have not directly changed or challenged the rule that religion is not allowed in the public school classroom during instructional time. But they have allowed for private religious exercises on school grounds outside of formal instructional time, as well as for extracurricular education on school premises even if it is religiously motivated and inspired. These cases were at first grounded variously in the free speech, free exercise, and equal protection clauses, but are now largely a staple of free speech jurisprudence. They first began in the public university and then worked their way into the public high school and eventually into the public grade school as well.

The opening equal access case was *Widmar v. Vincent* (1981). The state University of Missouri had a policy of opening its facilities after school hours to voluntary student groups pursuing extracurricular activities. More than one hundred student groups organized themselves one year, each paying a modest fee of $41 per semester to offset the university's extra costs for use of its space.[14] A voluntary group of Christian students, called Cornerstone, was organized for private religious devotion and charity. The group sought access to the university facilities that year, which had been granted to them the past four years. This year, however, Cornerstone was denied access when the university applied its written policy that its buildings and grounds were not to be used "for purposes of religious worship or religious teaching." Cornerstone appealed, arguing that this policy of exclusion violated their free exercise, free speech, and equal protection rights. The university countered that it had excluded the group based on a compelling state interest to maintain the "strict separation of church and state" as both the First Amendment and the state constitution required.

The *Widmar* Court found for the religious student group. Drawing on free speech precedents, the Court held that the state had created a limited public forum by opening its facilities to voluntary student groups and activities. Once opened, religious groups must be given "equal access" to that forum. The university could close its extracurricular student activities program altogether, with no harm to any students' First Amendment rights. But the university could not discriminate on religious grounds once the forum was established. "These are forms of speech and association protected by the First Amendment," Justice Powell wrote for the *Widmar* Court. "In order to justify discriminatory exclusions from a public forum based on the religious content of the group's intended speech" the university must withstand strict scrutiny by showing that "its regulation is necessary to serve a compelling state interest and that it is narrowly drawn to achieve that end." In the Court's view, a generic desire to maintain a strict separation of church and state was not a sufficiently compelling state interest to justify such overt religious discrimination. The religious groups would enjoy only "incidental benefits" from using the forum, the Court determined. The values of "equal treatment and access" for religious groups thus outweighed the hypothetical dangers of a religious establishment. The university's discriminatory rule could not stand.[15]

The *Widmar* Court explicitly limited its holding to the public university, since university students, unlike public high school and grade school students, were more mature and discerning and were not required by compulsory school attendance to be there. The following week, the Court let stand a circuit court opinion that refused to extend the *Widmar* holding into public high schools.[16] In response, Congress passed the Equal Access Act of 1984, which extended to public high schools that received federal funding the *Widmar* principle of equal access. Any high school that opened its facilities to some students for voluntary after-school activities would have to give religious students equal access to these facilities as well, the act provided. The religious students' activities, however, had to be completely voluntary and free from school endorsement or faculty participation. When a public high school began implementing the Equal Access Act, a group of students, through their parents, challenged the act itself as a violation of the establishment clause.

In *Board of Education v. Mergens* (1990), the Court upheld the Equal Access Act, finding it a proper protection against religious discrimination rather than an improper form of religious establishment. Justice O'Connor wrote for the Court, arguing that the act satisfied both the traditional *Lemon* test and her own endorsement test:

> Congress' avowed purpose—to prevent discrimination against religious and other types of speech—is undeniably secular. Even if some legislators were motivated by a conviction that religious speech in particular was valuable and worthy of protection, that alone would not invalidate the Act, because what is relevant is the legislative *purpose* of the statute, not the possible religious *motives* of the legislators who enacted the law.

Moreover, the primary effect of the statute was not to advance or endorse religion, but to protect the principle of equality rights of religious students against state discrimination.

> [T]here is a crucial difference between *government* speech endorsing religion, which the Establishment Clause forbids, and *private* speech endorsing religion, which the Free Speech and Free Exercise Clauses protect. We think the secondary school students are mature enough and are likely to understand that a school does not endorse or support student speech that it merely permits on a nondiscriminatory basis.[17]

In *Lamb's Chapel v. Center Moriches Union Free School District* (1993), the Court extended the constitutional equal access principle, via the free speech clause, to other religious groups besides students. A local school board, pursuant to state policy, opened its school facilities during nonschool time for various "social, civic, recreational, and political uses" by voluntary groups in the community. This program was a form of community outreach as well as a source of revenue for the school. The school board policy stated explicitly, however, that the "school premises shall not be used by any group for religious purposes." Lamb's Chapel, an evangelical church group, twice applied for use of the facilities to show a film series that discussed family values from a traditional Christian perspective. Their applications were denied. They appealed, arguing that such exclusion violated their free speech rights.

The *Lamb's Chapel* Court agreed. Relying on *Widmar* and other free speech cases, the Court found that Lamb's Chapel had been discriminatorily denied access to this limited public forum. Again, the school district's concern for protecting against the establishment of religion was not considered a sufficient reason for denying equal access to this religious group. As Justice White put it for the Court:

> The film series involved here no doubt dealt with a subject [namely, family values] otherwise permissible, . . . and its exhibition was denied solely because the film series dealt with the subject from a religious standpoint. The principle that has emerged from our cases "is that the First Amendment forbids the government to regulate speech in ways that favor some viewpoints or ideas at the expense of others."[18]

In *Rosenberger v. University of Virginia* (1995), a sharply divided Court extended this equal access principle to more direct funding. The Court held that a voluntary group of religious students in a state university was entitled to the same funding made available to nonreligious student groups. The University of Virginia encouraged student groups to organize themselves for extracurricular activities. Each student group was required to petition for the right to be recognized as such a group, and once organized it could apply for funds from a general student activity fund to facilitate their activities. The funds could be used for a variety of purposes, including the costs of printing and distributing the group's literature. All such funds were to be paid to outside contractors. In the year in question, 118 groups received funds, and 15 were denied funds. One of the groups denied funds was a religious student group that printed an overtly religious newspaper, *Wide Awake: A Christian Perspective at the University of Virginia.* They were denied on grounds that the student activity fund could not be used for "religious activities"—defined in the school's regulations as "any activity 'that primarily promotes or manifests a particular belief in or about a deity or an ultimate reality.'" The student group appealed, arguing that such discriminatory treatment violated their free speech rights.

The *Rosenberger* Court agreed. The state university policy, Justice Kennedy wrote for the Court, improperly "selects for disfavored treatment those student journalistic efforts with religious editorial viewpoints." The denial of funding to this otherwise qualified student group "is based upon viewpoint discrimination not unlike the discrimination the school district relied upon in *Lamb's Chapel* and that we found invalid." The constitutional principle of equal access applies as much to state university funding as to state university facilities, the Court held.

> Vital First Amendment speech principles are at stake here. The first danger to liberty lies in granting the State the power to examine publications to determine whether or not they are based on some ultimate idea and if so for the State to classify them [as religious]. The second, and corollary, danger is to speech from the chilling of individual thought and expression. That danger is especially real in the University setting, where the State acts against a background and tradition of thought and experiment that is at the center of our intellectual and philosophic tradition. . . . For the University, by regulation, to cast disapproval on particular viewpoints of its students risks the suppression of free speech and creative inquiry in one of the vital centers for the nation's intellectual life, its college and university campuses.[19]

In a sharply worded dissent, Justice Souter, joined by three others, argued that the Court had used the equal access principle of the free speech clause to undermine a cardinal principle of the establishment clause. "Using public funds for the direct subsidization of preaching the word is categorically forbidden under the Establishment Clause, and if the Clause was meant to accomplish nothing else, it was meant to bar this use of public money."[20] Government funding of religion has long been a sensitive topic in American history—as old as James Madison's famous *Memorial and Remonstrance Against Religious Assessments* in Virginia and as recent as the controversies surrounding the funding of religious charities through the federal "faith-based initiatives" program. Nonetheless, the *Rosenberger* majority held that equal access concerns outweighed funding concerns, at least in that case.

In *Good News Club v. Milford Central School* (2001), the Court again upheld the equal access principle in the face of countervailing establishment concerns, now for the first time in a public grade school. Authorized by state statute, a local school district enacted a policy for local residents to use local public school facilities after school hours, among other things, for "instruction in any branch of education, learning, or the arts" and for "social, civic and recreational meetings." The policy, however, prohibited use of the facilities by any group "for religious purposes," lest the school district violate federal and state prohibitions on the establishment of religion. Local representatives of the Good News Club, a private Christian organization that instructed six- to twelve-year-old children in Christian morality and practice, sought permission from the school district to hold weekly after-school meetings in the cafeteria of a public elementary school. The lesson plans indicated that these meetings would include adult-led prayers, the collective singing of religious songs, and the children's recitation of Bible verses. The school superintendent concluded that this would constitute use of the public school facilities for "religious purposes" and thus denied the group access to the school facilities. Good News Club appealed, arguing that this was religious viewpoint discrimination in violation of its free speech rights.

The *Good News* Court agreed. Writing for a plurality, Justice Thomas made clear that the school district was not obliged to create this "limited public forum," but once it did, any restriction had to be viewpoint-neutral and reasonable in light of the forum's purpose. The Good News Club's intended use met this forum's broadly stated purpose of facilitating "instruction in any branch of education, learning, or the arts." "[S]peech discussing otherwise permissible subjects cannot be excluded from a limited public forum on the ground that the subject is discussed from a religious viewpoint." The Court stated that the Good News Club's storytelling and prayers were no more religious in content than the *Wide Awake* articles protected in *Rosenberger* or the family values film protected in *Lamb's Chapel*. The Court noted further that "for purposes of the Free Speech Clause . . . we can see no logical difference in kind between the invocation of Christianity by the Club and the invocation of teamwork, loyalty, or patriotism by other associations to provide a foundation for their lessons." Accordingly, the Court held that denying Good News Club's application violated its equal access rights guaranteed under the free speech clause.

Moreover, the *Good News* Court held that this free speech protection of equal access rights outweighed the school district's concerns to avoid an establishment of religion. "The Good News Club seeks nothing more than to be treated neutrally and given access to speak about the same topics as are other groups. Because allowing the Club to speak on school grounds would ensure neutrality and not threaten it, Milford [School District] faces an uphill battle in arguing that the Establishment Clause compels it to exclude the Good News Club." Both Justice Thomas writing for the plurality and Justice Scalia writing in concurrence found unpersuasive the school's arguments that the club's use of its facilities would constitute a form of coercion, endorsement, or indoctrination of religion that violated the establishment clause.[21]

Three dissenting justices complained that the Good News Club's activities constituted overt "religious proselytizing" rather than simple moral instruction from a "religious viewpoint." Justice Souter accused the majority of ignoring the reality that the Good News Club intended to use the public school forum for an "evangelical service of worship calling children to commit themselves in an act of Christian conversion," and not for mere discussion of secular subjects from a Christian point of view. The Court's holding effectively "stand[s] for the remarkable proposition that any public school opened for civic meetings must be opened for use as a church, synagogue, or mosque."[22]

Critics of *Good News Club* have also focused on the mixed messages of such afterschool programs for grade school children. Young students, they charge, are simply not able to distinguish between the club's religious inspiration and its purported neutral moral instruction, especially when it takes the form of memorizing Bible verses and singing adult-led Christian songs. Young students are also not able to distinguish between what the school teaches and what the Club teaches. Both sets of teachers are adults with authority, both are operating in the school building, and both are offering instruction on what a child should read, say, and do. How are six- or seven-year-olds supposed to make the fine distinctions between the motivation and content of a teaching, or between mandatory instruction at school and optional "noninstruction" on school grounds but after official school hours? How are they to discern that the public school itself is not giving them religious instruction even if they are getting religious instruction in a public school? State university students can certainly make these distinctions and judgments, as *Rosenberger* assumed. Perhaps even public high school students can, but not first- or second-grade students, critics contend. Lower federal courts, while upholding *Good News Club,* have been sensitive to these hard questions and thus have worked hard to avoid using *Good News Club* as a stepping-stone to revisiting the release time program of religious instruction introduced in *McCollum,* the 1948 case that opened the Court's modern religion in public school cases.

Summary and Conclusions

The Supreme Court's religion and public school cases have long been its best known offerings, both in America and around the world. Its landmark cases are still taught in public school classes in history, civics, and American government, and they have shaped the religion-free curricular and educational experience of many citizens to-day. Because separation of church and state logic was in its zenith when most of to-day's opinion leaders were in public school, many of them continue to believe that the wall of separation metaphor is the sole and salutary source and summary of American religious liberty.

"Metaphors in law are to be narrowly watched," Justice Benjamin Cardozo once warned, "for starting as devices to liberate thought, they end often by enslaving it."[23] So it has been with the metaphor of a wall of separation. This metaphor has held pop-ular imagination so firmly that many have not noticed that separation of church and state is no longer the only principle governing public schools. The principle of sepa-ration still has its place in the public school, in part as a way of protecting the liberty of conscience of vulnerable students. Religious teachers, texts, prayers, symbols, and ceremonies remain formally forbidden from the public school during instructional time, save as subjects to be studied in appropriate classes like literature or history. But before, between, and after class, voluntary religious activities by students, parents, and outsiders alike are now permitted on public school grounds that open themselves up to other activities. For the Court, granting religious actors and activities equal access to public school forums, facilities, and even funds made available to everyone else is not just a gesture of fairness but a mandate of the principle of religious equality.

Notes

1. See Noah Feldman, *Divided by God: America's Church-State Problem and What We Should Do About It* (2005), 135–149; Edward J. Larson, *Summer for the Gods* (1997).

2. 333 U.S. 203, 209–211 (1948).

3. 333 U.S. 231 (Frankfurter, J., concurring).

4. 370 U.S. at 421, 430–432.

5. 374 U.S. 203 (1963). *Schempp* also involved a companion case, *Murray v. Curlett.* The Court, in a per curiam opinion, extended the *Schempp* holding in *Chamberlain v. Public In-struction Board,* 377 U.S. 402 (1964).

6. 374 U.S. 203, 221, 226 (1963).

7. 374 U.S. 225 (1963).

8. 449 U.S. 39, 40–41 (1980).

9. 482 U.S. 578, 591–593 (1987).

10. 472 U.S. 38, 59–60 (1985).

11. 505 U.S. 577, 593–594 (1992) (emphasis added).

12. 530 U.S. 290, 298, 302–303, 306, 309 (2000).

13. See analysis of the relevant literature and cases in Kent Greenawalt, *Does God Belong in Public Schools?* (2005). The First Freedom Forum, directed by Charles Haynes, provides highly valuable insights and materials on religion and education.

14. The Court later upheld the constitutionality of charging these flat fees, even to religious groups, finding no prior restraint on free exercise of religion. See *Board of Regents of University of Wisconsin System v. Southworth,* 529 U.S. 217 (2000); see also *Jimmy Swaggart Ministries v. Board of Equalization of California,* 496 U.S. 226 (1990) (discussed on page 257).

15. 454 U.S. 263, 270, 273 (1981).

16. *Brandon v. Bd. of Educ. of Guilderland Central School Dist.*, 635 F.2d 971 (2d Cir. 1980), *cert. denied,* 454 U.S. 1123 (1981).

17. 496 U.S. 226, 248–250 (1990).

18. 508 U.S. 384, 387, 394 (1993).

19. 508 U.S. 819, 831–832, 836–837 (1995).

20. 508 U.S. 868 (Souter, J., dissenting).

21. 533 U.S. 98, 112–114 (2001).

22. 533 U.S. 139 (Souter, J., dissenting).

23. *Berkey v. Third Ave. Ry. Co.*, 155 N.E. 58, 94 (N.Y. Ct. App. 1926).

9

Government and Religious Education
Accommodation, Separation, and Equal Treatment

The place of religion in public schools, discussed in Chapter 8, is one set of issues the Court addressed under the establishment law. The role of government in private religious schools, the subject of this chapter, is the other set of issues.[1] These latter issues, particularly the question of government funding and support for religious schools, were hotly contested in the states long before *Everson*. Between 1848 and 1921, thirty-five states, as we have seen, passed state constitutional amendments that barred state funding of religious schools, although tax exemptions for these schools continued (pp. 114–115). And in some states, various anti-Catholic and self-professed "secularist" groups pushed hard to eliminate religious schools altogether and to give public schools a monopoly on education. This movement drew the attention of the Supreme Court before *Everson*. The Court struck down several measures against private religious schools as violations of "fundamental liberty" (pp. 122–123); after *Everson,* the Court wove these precedents into its interpretation of the establishment clause.

The Supreme Court's cases on the role of government in religious education fall into three main phases: (1) an accommodationist phase from 1908 to 1971 that allowed for the coexistence and cooperation of public schools and religious schools; (2) a strict separationist phase from 1971 to 1986 that called for strict separation between religious schools and the state, including a ban on government aid to religious schools, students, teachers, and parents; and (3) an equal treatment phase from 1986 onward that restored some of the pre-1971 law on grounds of equal protection and equal treatment of religious and nonreligious parents, students, and teachers.

207

Accommodationist Cases (1908–1986)

Already before *Everson,* the Court had repeatedly countenanced general protection and support for religious schools, basing its decisions on general principles of liberty and fairness, and applying federal common law rather than the First Amendment directly. In *Quick Bear v. Leupp* (1908), the Court upheld the allocation of federal funds to Catholic schools that offered education to Native Americans.[2] In *Meyer v. Nebraska* (1923), the Court held that states could not forbid religious schools from teaching or reading the Bible in a foreign language.[3] In *Pierce v. Society of Sisters* (1925), the Court held that a state government could not mandate that all students attend public schools; religious schools were a viable alternative form of education.[4] In *Farrington v. Tokushige* (1927), the Court held that states could not impose unduly intrusive and stringent accreditation and regulatory requirements on religious and other private schools.[5] In *Cochran v. Louisiana State Board of Education* (1930), the Court held that a state policy of supplying textbooks to all students could supply them to religious school students too.[6]

These early cases, and their amplification in the lower federal courts, provided the foundation for a general accommodationist logic about the place of government in religious schools that emerged in the Court's cases after 1947. Public schools are only one form of lower education in this country, the Court argued; religious schools provide a valuable and viable alternative. While the First Amendment establishment clause generally bans religion from public schools, the First Amendment free exercise clause generally protects religion in private schools, allowing parents and children to pursue education in their own religious tradition.

It is no violation of the free exercise clause, the Court continued, for states to require private religious schools to meet accreditation requirements and be subject to general state standards of educational quality and governance. Nor is it a violation of the free exercise clause for states to impose instructional and testing requirements in reading, writing, and arithmetic, or in civics, geography, and science. Children who graduate from religious schools cannot be handicapped in their abilities and capacities as budding democratic citizens and productive members of society. Private schools are perfectly free to teach those secular subjects with the religious perspective they deem appropriate. They are perfectly free to supplement this core secular instruction with religious courses and other religious activities. But if religious groups wish to participate in education, they must play by everyone else's rules respecting the "secular" aspects of their education.

In turn, it is no violation of the establishment clause for private religious schools to receive the same general forms of government support that are given to public schools to meet secular educational requirements. This can include funds to build, furnish, and equip gymnasiums, libraries, or laboratories, or to support instruction in natural science, foreign languages, physical education, or comparable secular topics. Nor is it a violation of the establishment clause for public and private school children alike to receive school bus transportation, math textbooks, science equipment, or testing materials that support the secular dimensions of their education.

Religious schools and their students are just as entitled to general support for the secular aspects of their education as public schools and their students. After all, both sets of students are responding to the state's mandatory school attendance laws and prescribed curricular requirements.

The first case that pressed this accommodationist logic was *Everson v. Board of Education* (1947), despite its famously sweeping dicta about separation of church and state. In this case, pursuant to state law, a local school district reimbursed the bus transportation costs incurred by parents who sent their children to private schools, including religious schools. A local taxpayer challenged this policy as a violation of the establishment clause—a form of tax appropriation in support of religious education. The *Everson* Court disagreed. It was no establishment of religion for states to provide school bus transportation or bus fare to religious and public school children alike. Nor would it be an establishment to furnish religious and public schools alike with the same fire, police, sewage, utility, and other basic municipal services. "[C]utting off church schools from these services, so separate and indisputably marked off from the religious function, would make it far more difficult for the schools to operate," Justice Black wrote. "But such obviously is not the purpose of the First Amendment. The Amendment requires the State to be neutral in its relations with groups of religious believers and non-believers; it does not require the state to be their adversary. State power is no more to be used so as to handicap religions than it is to favor them."[7]

The Court struck a similar tone in *Board of Education v. Allen* (1968). The State of New York had a policy of lending prescribed textbooks in science, mathematics, and other "secular subjects" to all students in the state, whether attending public or private schools. Many of the private school recipients of the textbooks attended religious schools. A taxpayer thus challenged the policy as a violation of the establishment clause. Relying on the 1930 *Cochran* case, the Court upheld this state policy, emphasizing that it was the students and parents, not the religious schools, who directly benefited from this policy. "Perhaps free books make it more likely that some children choose to attend a sectarian school," Justice White wrote for the Court, "but that was true of the state-paid bus fares in *Everson,* and does not alone demonstrate an unconstitutional degree of support for a religious institution."[8]

The Court continued this accommodationist tone in a trio of cases upholding the payment of government construction grants and revenue bonds to religious colleges and universities.[9] In *Tilton v. Richardson* (1971), the Court rebuffed a challenge to a federal grant program that supported construction of library, science, and arts buildings at four church-related colleges. The grants were made as part of the federal Higher Education Facilities Act (1963), which sponsored new college and university buildings throughout the nation. Chief Justice Burger wrote for the plurality: "The Act itself was carefully drafted to ensure that the federally-subsidized facilities would be devoted to the secular and not the religious functions of the recipient institution."[10] This feature, together with the reality that most funding was directed to state, not religious, universities and colleges was sufficient to ensure their constitutionality. In *Hunt v. McNair* (1973), the Court upheld a state program of funding the construction of "secular" buildings at various state universities, including a religiously chartered college, by issuing secured state bonds that had to be repaid eventually. The *Hunt* Court was convinced that the state program had the secular purpose of enhancing the education of youth, did not have the primary effort of advancing religious education, and could be administered with minimal enough contacts between officials of the state and of the religious school.[11] And again in *Roemer v. Maryland Public Works Board* (1977), the Court upheld a state construction grant program that aided five church-related schools among its seventeen grant recipients. Writing for the *Roemer* Court and citing *Tilton* and *Hunt,* Justice Blackmun counseled against too zealous an application of the principle of separation of church and state, given the reality and reach of the modern welfare state:

> A system of government that makes itself felt as pervasively as ours could hardly be expected never to cross paths with the church. In fact, our State and Federal Governments impose certain burdens upon, and impart certain benefits to, virtually all our activities, and religious activity is no exception. The Court has enforced a scrupulous neutrality by the State, as among religions, and also as between religious and other activities, but a hermetic separation of the two is an impossibility [and] it has never been required. . . . [R]eligious institutions need not be quarantined from public benefits that are neutrally available to all. . . . Just as *Bradfield [v. Roberts* (1899)] dispels any notion that a religious person can never be in the State's pay for a secular purpose, so *Everson* and *Allen* put to rest any argument that the State may never act in such a way that has the incidental effect of facilitating religious activity.[12]

Separationist Cases (1971–1985)

While the Court's accommodation and funding of religious colleges continued into the 1970s, it ended abruptly in 1971 for religious grade schools and high schools. Using the three-part *Lemon* test, the Court adopted a firm policy against governmental aid to religious schools and against cooperation between religious and public schools, teachers, students, and programs. Parents and students deserve a clear choice between state-funded public schools and privately funded religious schools, the Court reasoned. The more clearly the operations and officials of these two schools are separated, and the more cleanly the religious schools are cut off from state funding, the better it is for all parties and for the establishment clause values that protect them. Public schools can stand on their own without the risks of undue religious influence or mixed messages to their students. Religious schools can stand on their own without the dangers of unwelcome political interference by or undue financial dependence upon the state.

In *Lemon v. Kurtzman* (1971) the Court struck down two state policies that supported religious grade schools catering to low-income children. One state's policy paid these private school teachers up to 15 percent of their salaries for teaching state-prescribed secular courses such as mathematics, foreign languages, natural sciences, and physical education. Another state's policy reimbursed the private schools themselves for up to 15 percent of the cost of the teachers' salaries, textbooks, and instructional materials for teaching these same courses. Both state policies catered to private schools that served students from lower-income families. Both insisted that the private schools or their teachers receive no more funding than their public school counterparts. Both insisted that state funds be used only to teach the secular subjects mandated by the state, using the same textbooks and materials used in the public schools.

Some 96 percent of the private schools that received state aid under these policies were religious schools, and of these the vast majority were Catholic. Taxpayers challenged the programs as violations of the establishment clause. The *Lemon* Court agreed, declaring that each policy fostered an "excessive entanglement between church and state," a fatal violation of the third prong of the *Lemon* test. The Catholic schools in question were notably religious, Chief Justice Burger wrote for the Court—closely allied with nearby parish churches, filled with religious symbols, and staffed primarily by nuns who were under "religious control and discipline." "[A] dedicated religious person, teaching at a school affiliated with his or her faith and operated to inculcate its tenets, will inevitably experience great difficulty in remaining religiously neutral." The teacher will be tempted to teach secular subjects with a religious orientation in violation of state policy. And the religious school or its teacher may well be tempted to direct government funds to other courses or use textbooks and materials different from those in the public school. "A comprehensive, discriminating, and continuing state surveillance will inevitably be required to ensure that these restrictions are obeyed and the First Amendment otherwise obeyed." This is precisely the kind of excessive entanglement between church and state that the establishment clause outlaws.

Distinguishing the Court's earlier religious school cases that taught accommodation, Chief Justice Burger acknowledged that these cases "do not call for total separation between church and state; total separation is not possible in an absolute sense. Some relationship between government and religious organizations is inevitable. Fire inspections, building and zoning regulations, and state requirements under compulsory school-attendance laws are examples of necessary and permissible contacts. . . . [T]he line of separation, far from being a 'wall,' is a blurred, indistinct, and variable barrier depending on all the circumstances of a particular relationship." But in this case, the states' policies of giving tax money to private schools and then scrupulously supervising the many religious schools that used the money clearly crossed the line into a forbidden zone of religious establishment, however blurry that line might be.[13]

Lemon left open the question of whether the state could give aid directly to religious students or to their parents—as the Court had allowed in earlier cases. Two years later, the Court closed this door tightly in the name of separation of church and state. In *Committee for Public Education v. Nyquist* (1973) and *Sloan v. Lemon* (1973), the Court struck down state policies that allowed low-income parents to seek reimbursement from the state for some of the costs of religious school tuition. *Nyquist* further struck down a state policy that allowed low-income parents to take tax deductions for the costs of sending their children to nonpublic schools—even though the parents complained of having to pay both state property taxes in support of public schools they did not use, and private tuition for the religious schools that their children attended. In *Nyquist,* Justice Powell characterized such policies as just another "of the ingenious plans of channelling state aid to sectarian schools." Responding to the state argument that "grants to parents, unlike grants to [religious] institutions, respect the 'wall of separation' required by the Constitution," Justice Powell declared for the *Nyquist* Court that "the effect of the aid is unmistakeably to provide desired financial support for non-public, sectarian institutions." This violates the second prong of the *Lemon* test that outlaws any policy whose primary effect is to advance religion. And it violates "the principle of total separation of Church and State. The core of that principle, as stated [by Madison] is that 'no man shall be compelled to frequent or support any religious worship, place, or ministry whatsoever.'"[14]

Lemon also left open the question of whether the state could give textbooks, educational materials, or other aid to religious schools for the teaching of mandatory secular subjects, or the administration of state-mandated tests and other programs. The Court struck down most such policies, save the lending of secular textbooks, which had been upheld in the 1930 *Cochran* case and again in the 1968 *Allen* case. In nine increasingly technical cases, from 1973 to 1985, the Court held that states could not reimburse religious schools for most costs incurred to administer standardized tests or to prepare mandated state records[15]—although the "actual costs" for certain tests could be recouped.[16] States could loan textbooks on secular subjects to religious schools, but not if those schools discriminated on racial grounds.[17] States could not loan or furnish religious schools with various supplies and films, and various counseling and other personnel, even if those were mandated by state policy.[18] States could not use public school teachers to hold remedial educational programs to indigent children in classrooms leased from religious schools.[19] And states could not lend public school personnel to teach remedial and enrichment courses in religious schools.[20] Justice Rehnquist summarized the prevailing establishment clause law as of 1985:

> [A] State may lend to parochial school children geography textbooks that contain maps of the United States, but the State may not lend maps of the United States for use in geography class. A State may lend textbooks on American colonial history, but it may not lend a film of George Washington, or a film projector to show it in history class. A State may lend classroom workbooks, but may not lend workbooks in which the parochial school children write, thus rendering them nonreusable. A State may pay for bus transportation to religious schools, but may not pay for bus transportation from the parochial school to the public zoo or natural history museum for a field trip. A State may pay for diagnostic services conducted in the parochial school but therapeutic services must be given in a different building; speech and hearing "services" conducted by the State inside the sectarian school are forbidden, but the State may conduct speech and hearing testing inside the sectarian school. Exceptional parochial school students may receive counseling, but it must take place outside of the parochial school, such as

in a trailer parked down the street. A State may give cash to a parochial school to pay for administration of State-written tests and State-ordered reporting services, but it may not provide funds for teacher-prepared tests on secular subjects. Religious instruction may not be given in public school, but the public school may release students during the day for religion classes [in the sectarian school], and may enforce attendance of those classes with its truancy laws.[21]

The final case in this line of separationist treatment of religious schools was *Aguilar v. Felton* (1985). The case involved the constitutionality of New York City's program that sent public school teachers into religious schools to offer remedial services to disadvantaged students or those with special educational needs. The remedial services in question were authorized and funded by Congress in the Elementary and Secondary Education Act (1965), known as the Title I program. The act established detailed standards for student eligibility and for the exclusively secular education that could be offered to eligible students. More than 20,000 students in Catholic, Jewish, Protestant, and other religious schools in the city annually availed themselves of these Title I services. Lacking sufficient space in existing public buildings and lacking sufficient land to build new public buildings adjacent to religious schools, New York City had chosen to offer the Title I services on site to eligible religious school students. State-funded public school teachers with materials were sent into the religious schools to teach the eligible religious school students. Field supervisors were sent out monthly to ensure compliance with the law and to confirm that the Title I funds were directed to remedial, not religious, education in these schools. The program operated for nineteen years without raising constitutional issues.

Local taxpayers, however, eventually challenged the program as a violation of the establishment clause. Why should government funds be used to pay for the deficiencies of a religious education that the Title I program remedies, the plaintiffs charged? And what are public school teachers doing teaching in religious schools, when religious school teachers are banned from teaching in public schools? The *Aguilar* Court agreed. Though "well-intentioned," Justice Brennan wrote for the Court, the program again fosters an excessive entanglement between church and state, akin to what the Court had outlawed in *Lemon*. The religious schools receiving the Title I instructors are "pervasively sectarian," having as a "substantial purpose, the inculcation of religious values." Because of this, "ongoing inspection is required to ensure the absence of a religious message. In short, the scope and duration of New York's Title I program would require a permanent and pervasive State presence in the sectarian schools receiving aid." This, Justice Brennan concluded, is precisely the kind of excessive entanglement between church and state that the establishment clause outlaws.[22]

Four justices wrote bitter dissents in *Aguilar*. Justice Rehnquist charged that the Court "takes advantage of the 'Catch 22' paradox of its own creation, whereby aid must be supervised to ensure no entanglement, but the supervision itself is held to cause an entanglement."[23] Justice O'Connor denounced the majority opinion as "wooden," "formalistic," and "lacking in common sense." In the nineteen years of the program, she wrote, "there has never been a single incident in which in a Title I instructor 'subtly or overtly' attempted to 'indoctrinate the students in particular religious tenets at public expense.'" The real losers, she wrote, are disadvantaged children who happen to live "in cities where it is not economically or logistically feasible to provide public facilities for remedial education adjacent to the parochial school. . . . For these children, the Court's decision is tragic."[24]

In *Agostini v. Felton* (1997), the Court overruled *Aguilar.* Writing for the *Agostini* Court, Justice O'Connor declared that the mere presence of a state supervising employee in a religious institution is not the kind of "symbolic union of church and state" that violates the excessive entanglement prong. Moreover, not "all government aid that directly aids the educational functions of religious schools is invalid." The *Aguilar* Court had been "unduly zealous and mechanical" in its application of the *Lemon* test, the *Agostini* Court concluded. In particular, it had used the "excessive entanglement prong" to enforce a form of separationism that could not be squared with other constitutional values. Children in religious schools are just as entitled to Title I benefits as children in public schools. They cannot be denied these benefits simply for the sake of upholding "the abstract principle" of separation of church and state.[25]

Equal Treatment Cases (1983–2004)

The *Agostini* case was part and product of a series of cases in which the Court undid some of its earlier separationist logic as applied to religious schools and (uncharacteristically) reversed three of its firmest separationist cases.[26] The core holdings of the separationist cases from 1971 to 1985 were not changed: government was still not permitted to directly fund, endorse, or cooperate in the core religious teachings of religious schools. But in several recent cases, the Court has upheld various government programs that grant to religious students or their parents the same general benefits afforded to others. The common rationale of these cases is that students and their parents must be protected in their choice to attend religious schools— even if this leads to indirect government funding of the religious education they choose. Applying the principle of separation of church and state too zealously intrudes on these parties' liberty of conscience and equal protection rights to choose between religious and public education. It is thus no violation of the establishment clause, the Court concluded, for a statute to give equal treatment to religious and nonreligious schools, parents, students, and teachers in the distribution of general educational benefits and services.

The first case to press this new equality logic was *Mueller v. Allen* (1983). A Minnesota law allowed parents of private school children to deduct the cost of "tuition, transportation, and textbooks" from their state income tax. Ninety-five percent of the private school children in the state attended religious schools, and most of their parents claimed this tax deduction. A state taxpayer challenged the law as an establishment of religion and an open defiance of the Court's holding in the 1973 *Nyquist* case that had struck down another such state tax deduction policy as "an ingenious scheme" of indirectly funding religious schools.

The *Mueller* Court upheld the state tax law, using the *Lemon* test. The tax deduction policy easily satisfied the first and third prongs of *Lemon,* Justice Rehnquist wrote for the Court. The statute had a secular purpose of fostering quality education for all, which "may be discerned from the face of the statute." Moreover, the law did not foster an entanglement between church and state. The "more difficult" question was whether the law met the second prong of the *Lemon* test or betrayed a "primary effect of advancing the sectarian aims of the non-public schools"—the principal ground on which the *Nyquist* Court had struck down an earlier state tax deduction policy. The *Mueller* Court distinguished *Nyquist* rather tendentiously. The saving features of this new state tax law, Justice Rehnquist argued, were that this was a deduction for costs for education, not just religious education; that it allowed deductions for the costs of "private" education, not "nonpublic" education; and that the deductions for religious education allowed by this law were sufficiently diluted by the many other tax deductions allowed for medical, charitable, and other causes. The *Nyquist* Court had characterized all such arguments as "ingenious schemes." The *Mueller* Court found that these features sufficiently "reduced the Establishment Clause objections" to the law. The state's aid to sectarian schools, Justice Rehnquist concluded, "becomes available only as a result of numerous, private choices of individual parents of school-age children." This saved it from constitutional infirmity. If the state was willing to forgo tax revenue by granting these tax deductions to its citizens, Justice Rehnquist added, signaling his neofederalist allegiance, the First Amendment gives state taxpayers little ground to object.[27]

In *Witters v. Washington Department of Services for the Blind* (1986), the Court upheld a state program that furnished aid to a visually impaired student attending a Christian college. The program provided funds "for special education and/or training in the professions, business or trades" for the visually impaired. Money was to be paid directly to eligible recipients, who were entitled to pursue education in the professional schools of their choice. Mr. Witters's condition qualified him for the funds. His profession of choice was the Christian ministry. He sought funds to attend a Christian college in preparation for the same. The state agency denied funding, on grounds that this was a direct funding of religious education prohibited by *Lemon* and its progeny.

The *Witters* Court disagreed. Applying the *Lemon* test, the Court found the policy, and its application to Mr. Witters, to be constitutional. The policy served a secular purpose of fostering educational and professional choice for all, including the handicapped. It involved no entanglement of church and state. Its primary effect was to facilitate this student's professional education, which happened to be religious. This "is not one of 'the ingenious plans' for channeling state aid to sectarian schools that periodically reach this Court," Justice Marshall wrote for the Court. "It creates no financial incentive for students to undertake sectarian education. It does not provide greater or broader benefits for recipients who apply their aid to religious education. . . . In this case, the fact that aid goes to individuals means that the decision to support religious education is made by the individual not by the State."[28]

In *Zobrest v. Catalina Foothills School District* (1993), the Court extended this logic from a college setting to a high school setting. Both federal and state disability acts required that a hearing-impaired student be furnished with a sign language interpreter to accompany him or her to classes. The state furnished the interpreter at its own cost. Mr. Zobrest's hearing impairment qualified him for an interpreter's services. He had gone to public elementary school and received these services on site without issue. But now, like his siblings, he had enrolled in a Catholic high school. The state refused to furnish him with an interpreter on the grounds that this would violate the *Lemon* rule disallowing direct state aid to a religious school. Moreover, the state argued, the presence of a state-employed interpreter in a Catholic high school would foster an excessive entanglement between church and state. Following *Mueller* and *Witters,* the *Zobrest* Court upheld the act as "a neutral government program dispensing aid not to schools but to handicapped children." "If a handicapped child chooses to enroll in a sectarian school," Chief Justice Rehnquist wrote for the Court, "we hold that the Establishment Clause does not prevent the school district from furnishing him with a sign-language interpreter."[29]

In *Agostini v. Felton* (1997), as we saw earlier, the Court extended this logic from the high school to the grade school, and extended its services from a single disabled student to a whole class of students with statutory rights to remedial services. State-funded teachers now could enter religious grade schools to teach remedial Title I programs to religious students who were eligible for them. *Agostini* accomplished this critical step not only by reversing *Aguilar v. Felton* but by introducing a softer test than the *Lemon* test. Like the *Lemon* test, the *Agostini* test still required that the statute have a secular purpose, which the Court found easily here. But *Agostini* narrowed the evidence that could be used to assess whether the primary effect of the statute was to advance or inhibit religion, and it eliminated a separate inquiry into "excessive entanglement." In judging the statute's "primary effect," *Agostini* provided that courts could consider only whether the state had engaged in undue religious indoctrination, religious line drawing, or religious entanglement. Other evidence was not unavailing. And "entanglements" of religious and political officials were fatal only if their primary effect was to advance religion. There was no evidence at all of religious indoctrination and line drawing in this case, the Court concluded. And what little "entanglement" actually existed between religious and political officials ensured that there was no advancement of religion in the delivery of Title I services. The Title I program in religious grade schools was thus no establishment of religion.[30]

In *Mitchell v. Helms* (2000), the Court extended *Agostini* to uphold the constitutionality of direct government aid to religious schools in support of the secular dimensions of their education. The federal Education Consolidation and Improvement Act (1981) channeled federal funds to state and local education agencies for the purchase of educational materials, books, science equipment, and the like. The act permitted states to loan such materials directly to public and private grade schools and high schools, provided that the state retained ownership of these materials and provided that the recipient schools used them only for programs that were "secular, neutral, and nonideological." The amount of aid received by each participating school depended on the number of students it matriculated. In this case, Louisiana followed the federal act in distributing materials and equipment to public and private schools within various school units in the state. In one such school unit, some 30 percent of the aid was allocated to private schools, most of them Catholic. The aid was used only for "secular, neutral, and nonideological" programs. Local taxpayers brought suit arguing that such "direct aid" to such "pervasively sectarian" schools constituted an establishment of religion.

The *Mitchell* Court disagreed, and held the aid program constitutional both on its face and as applied in this case. Both the plurality and concurring opinions found that the federal act did not have the primary effect of advancing religion. They both used the new *Agostini* formula: there was no governmental indoctrination of religion because the aid was "offered to a broad range of groups or persons without regard to their religion" and was used for "secular, neutral, and nonideological programs." The act did not draw lines between religious and nonreligious recipients; all accredited public and private schools and students were eligible. And there was no entanglement between religious and governmental officials in the administration of the program that served to advance religion. Accordingly, the Court upheld the act. It further overruled two earlier cases that had struck down similar state aid programs that distributed materials directly to religious schools. The separationist principles at work in these two cases, the *Mitchell* Court concluded, had become "unworkably rigid."[31]

In *Zelman v. Simmons-Harris* (2002) a narrowly divided Court upheld the constitutionality of a state school voucher program, now using neutrality and equal treatment logic alone. At issue was Ohio's school voucher program, which Ohio had adopted to address a "crisis of magnitude" in the Cleveland public schools. The program allowed parents to leave their children in their current public school or enroll them in another public school or private school (whether religious or nonreligious) in another school district. For parents who chose to place their children in a private school, the state provided a voucher that they had to deliver to the school to help defray tuition costs. These parents were further required to make a small copayment, with the fee graduated according to their economic means. Private schools that participated in the program were not permitted to engage in racial, religious, or ethnic discrimination, but they were not required to change their curriculum to accommodate these students. The value of the voucher and copayment together were less than half of the usual tuition rates normally charged by these private schools. During the year at issue, fifty-six private schools participated in the voucher program, forty-six of them religiously affiliated. More than 96 percent of the students who participated in the voucher program chose to enroll in the private religious schools, even though several of the nonreligious private schools were physically closer to their homes. Almost all the private religious schools required their voucher students to participate in overtly religious instruction and activities just like every other student in their school. A taxpayer filed suit, arguing that this was direct state funding of the core sectarian education of religious schools in violation of the establishment clause.

The *Zelman* Court upheld the voucher program. It concluded easily that there was no dispute that the program was enacted for a "valid secular purpose of providing educational assistance to poor children in a demonstrably failing public school system." The Court's principal focus was whether the Ohio program had the "effect" of advancing religion in violation of the establishment clause. Citing *Mueller, Witters,* and *Zobrest*, and specifically limiting *Nyquist*, Chief Justice Rehnquist wrote that:

> where a government aid program is *neutral* with respect to religion, and provides assistance directly to a *broad class of citizens*, who, in turn, direct government aid to religious schools wholly as a result of their own genuine and independent *private choice*, the program is not readily subject to challenge under the Establishment Clause. A program that shares these features permits government aid to reach religious institutions only by way of the deliberate choices of numerous individual recipients. The incidental advancement of a religious mission, or the perceived endorsement of a religious message is reasonably attributable to the individual, not the government, whose role ends with the disbursement of the funds (italics added).

The *Zelman* Court found that the Ohio voucher program was one of "true private choice" that was neutral to religion and thus constitutional. As in *Mitchell*, the majority stressed that there was a broad range of educational choices and the program did not define its recipients by reference to religion. Moreover, there were no financial incentives for parents to choose a religious school. Rather, there were disincentives since the parents' copayments to send students to religious schools were higher. There were also no financial incentives for religious schools to cooperate, for they received only a portion of the government assistance that public community and magnet schools received, and considerably less than the full tuition that they would have charged to any other student.[32]

Justice Souter dissented, denouncing the majority's "even-handed" neutrality approach. Joined by Justices Ginsburg, Stevens, and Breyer, he accused the majority of applying its "twin standards of neutrality and free choice" in a way that rendered them meaningless: "the espoused criteria of neutrality in offering aid, and private choice in directing it, are shown to be nothing but examples of verbal formalism." Most significant to Souter were the facts that the private schools predominated the program and that 96.6 percent of the voucher money went to religious schools offering overtly religious instruction. For Souter, these statistics revealed that the program was not neutral, and that parents did not in fact have a "true private choice." Instead, these statistics confirmed that the voucher program betrayed the central aim of the establishment clause so well expressed by James Madison: to ensure that "the minds of men always be wholly free" and "to save religion from its own corruption" through dependence on government money. In Souter's view, "the reality is that in the matter of [religious] education aid the Establishment Clause has largely been read away."[33]

In *Locke v. Davey* (2004), however, the last in this series of education cases, the Court made clear that establishment clause concerns were not entirely "read away." The State of Washington established a Promise Scholarship Program for highly promising college-bound students of limited economic means. The program set clear criteria requiring high grades and low family income. Scholarship recipients were free to use their scholarship at any accredited college or university, including those that were religiously chartered. But the program rules explicitly stated that the student could not pursue a major in theology. Davey met all the eligibility criteria and received a scholarship. He chose to attend Northwest College, an accredited college affiliated with the Assemblies of God Church that teaches a liberal arts curriculum from a Christian perspective. Davey declared a double major in business and pastoral ministry. Because of this latter interest, the state withdrew his scholarship.

Davey appealed, arguing that the state's scholarship rules unfairly targeted religion majors for special exclusion in violation of the principle of neutrality demanded by both the free exercise and the establishment clauses. Moreover, it forced him to choose between two rights: if he accepted the scholarship, he could not be a theology major; if he became a theology major, he had to give up his scholarship. This was an open violation of his free exercise rights. The state countered that it was not obstructing Davey's free exercise rights but merely refusing to pay for them: why should the "free" exercise of religion need to be "subsidized" by the state? Moreover, the state said it had a compelling reason to deny funding because its own state constitution required that "[n]o public money or property shall be appropriated for or applied to any religious worship, exercise, or instruction, or the support of any religious establishment."

The *Locke* Court agreed with the State of Washington and found no violation of Davey's free exercise rights. Writing for the majority, Chief Justice Rehnquist characterized this as a case that involves the "play in the joints" between the free exercise and establishment clauses. The free exercise clause does not require the state to pay for Davey's scholarship, any more than the establishment clause prevents the state from doing so. Distribution of scholarship money was a state legislative decision, and the state's decision to exclude theology majors from funding cast only "a relatively minor burden" on students. Eligible students could still go to any accredited college, including a religious college. They could still take any courses, including religion and theology courses. They simply could not be theology majors. This is not the kind of facial discrimination that requires inquiry into a compelling state interest or least restrictive alternative, the *Locke* Court concluded. It is a sensible, neutral, and generally applicable law that states are fully empowered to make and enforce.[34]

Narrowly read, the *Locke* case simply reiterates the traditional assumption that equal access, protection, and treatment of religious and nonreligious education is permissible under the establishment clause. In all the equal treatment cases we have just seen—from *Witters* in 1986 to *Zelman* in 2002—the religious party's claims are based on federal or state statutes. The Court repeatedly upheld these statutes when their application was challenged as a violation of the establishment clause. Allowing religious parties to avail themselves of the same statutory rights and benefits available to everyone else is no establishment of religion, the Court consistently concluded.

This is a narrower constitutional logic than prevailed in the equal access cases on the place of religion in public schools that we saw in Chapter 8. In all those cases—from *Widmar* in 1981 to *Good News Club* in 2001—the Court held that the equal access of religious parties to public school forums was not only permissible under the establishment clause but was also mandated by the free speech clause. The results of these two lines of cases are largely the same: religious and nonreligious parties get equality under the law with no establishment clause violation. But the logic is different. Religious parties claiming equal access in public schools are constitutionally entitled to this equal treatment under the free speech clause. Religious parties claiming equal treatment in religious schools, however, are only statutorily entitled to this equal treatment under applicable federal or state statutes. But what the legislature gives by statute, it can also take back by statute.

It was precisely this vulnerability to legislative change that led Davey to press his case as a First Amendment violation. But he made two moves at once in pressing his case, and that may have been his undoing. First, he sought to make equal treatment a constitutional right for students whether they attended a public or a private school. But second, he sought to make such equal treatment a free exercise right, rather than a free speech right. Had the Court taken this second step, it could have radically changed its prevailing free exercise law as it had been settled by the 1990 *Smith* case (pp. 159–160). The *Locke* Court would have none of it. Buoyed by its neofederalism, the Court left it to the state legislature to decide whether to give, condition, or withhold its funding to religious students. Here, the legislature had applied its own state constitutional prohibition on funding of religious education as narrowly as possible—allowing students to spend their state scholarship funds at religious universities and to take religion courses, but just not to become religion majors at religious universities. This was a sensible and well tailored application of state constitutional law, the Court concluded, and certainly permissible under the First Amendment.

Summary and Conclusions

In developing its two lines of establishment cases on education over the past century—one on religion in public schools, the second on government in religious schools—the Supreme Court has gradually worked out a middle way between the extreme demands of early separationists and accommodationists. While government has the power to mandate education for children, the Court has held, parents have the right to choose between public and private school education for their children—and government may now facilitate that choice through tax deductions, scholarships, and even vouchers. While the First Amendment forbids most forms of religion in public schools, it protects most forms of religion in private schools—even if those involve teachings and practices that are far removed from the cultural mainstream. While the First Amendment prohibits government from funding the core religious activities of private schools, it permits support of the secular aspects of religious education, delivery of general governmental services to religious schools, and provision of remedial, disability, and other social welfare services to religious school students. While the First Amendment forbids public school teachers from overt religious expression at school, it permits public school students to engage in private religious expression, and further requires religious students and others to get equal access to public school facilities, forums, and even funds that are open to their nonreligious peers.

These First Amendment cases have not always followed clean logical lines. The Supreme Court has sometimes digressed and occasionally reversed itself—more so in the government and religious education cases than in any other area of religious liberty law. Several of the Court's religion and education cases have featured brilliant rhetorical and judicial fireworks in majority and dissenting opinions as the Court has occasionally shifted into a new understanding of the demands of the First Amendment. Part of this back-and-forth is typical of any constitutional law in action. "Constitutions work like clocks," American founder John Adams once put it. To function properly, their pendulums must swing back and forth, and their mechanisms and operators must get "wound up from time to time."

The Court's cases on religion and public education swung from strict separationism to equal access. The controversial 1985 *Wallace* case, outlawing even moments of silence in public schools, was the likely tipping point. The 2001 *Good News Club* case, authorizing a grade school extracurricular program heavy on religion, might well become the stopping point to this equal access logic. The Court's cases on government in religious education cases swung from accommodation to separation to equal treatment. The controversial 1985 *Aguilar* case that cut 20,000 students from remedial education helped catalyze the emergence of equal treatment cases. The controversial 2002 *Zelman* voucher case that allowed state money to be used even for "sectarian education" might well become the stopping point—if the logic of *Locke v. Davey* gains momentum.

Since the *Locke* case in 2004, the Supreme Court has not taken a case on religion and education—leaving a series of sometimes sharply juxtaposed separationist, accommodationist, and equality precedents to guide the lower courts. This is a surprising hiatus, given how central these religion and education issues have been in the modern era since *Everson*. Part of this quietude may be a reflection of the Court's gradual weakening of the establishment clause altogether. Part of it may reflect the Court's satisfaction that, for now, these religion and education issues are better left to Congress and the states to resolve, consistent with a century-long record of Court rulings. But the dockets of lower federal courts are still teeming with controversial cases on religion and education, and it can't be long before the Court takes on another case in this perennially contested arena.

Notes

1. Except when quoting, we use the generic term "religious school." The conventional term "parochial" school has a deprecatory connotation in common parlance and when used properly means "parish" school. This term is also not inclusive enough, since it does not cover the range of Jewish, Muslim, Protestant, and other schools affiliated with religious groups. The other conventional term, "sectarian school," is even more deprecatory, even in technical parlance, and we have sought to avoid it as well.

2. 210 U.S. 50 (1908).

3. 262 U.S. 390 (1923).

4. 268 U.S. 510 (1925).

5. 273 U.S. 284 (1927).

6. 281 U.S. 370 (1930). See further discussion of these cases above, pages 122–124.

7. *Everson v. Board of Education,* 330 U.S. 1, 16, 18 (1947).

8. 392 U.S. 236, 243–244 (1968).

9. Respectively, *Tilton v. Richardson,* 403 U.S. 672 (1971); *Hunt v. McNair,* 413 U.S. 734 (1973); *Roemer v. Maryland Public Works Board,* 426 U.S. 736 (1976).

10. 403 U.S. 672, 679–682 (1971).

11. 413 U.S. 734 (1973).

12. 426 U.S. 736, 746 (1977).

13. 403 U.S. at 619–620, 622 (1971).

14. *Committee for Public Education v. Nyquist,* 413 U.S. 756, 783, 785 (1973).

15. *Levitt v. Committee for Public Education,* 413 U.S. 472 (1973); *New York v. Cathedral Academy,* 434 U.S. 125 (1977).

16. *Committee for Public Education v. Regan,* 444 U.S. 646 (1980).

17. *Norwood v. Harrison,* 413 U.S. 455 (1973); see also *Wolman v. Walter,* 433 U.S. 229 (1977), overruled by *Mitchell v. Helms,* 530 U.S. 793 (2000).

18. *Meek v. Pittinger,* 421 U.S. 349 (1975), overruled by *Mitchell v. Helms,* 530 U.S. 793 (2000); for exceptions, see *Wolman v. Walter* (1977), also overruled by *Mitchell v. Helms* (2000).

19. *Aguilar v. Felton,* 473 U.S. 402 (1985), overruled by *Agostini v. Felton,* 521 U.S. 203 (1997).

20. *Grand Rapids School District v. Ball,* 473 U.S. 373 (1985).

21. *Wallace v. Jaffree,* 482 U.S. 38, 110–111 (Rehnquist, J., dissenting).

22. 473 U.S. 402, 411–413 (1985).

23. 473 U.S. 420–421 (Rehnquist, J., dissenting).

24. 473 U.S. 402, 424, 431 (O'Connor, J., dissenting).

25. *Agostini,* 521 U.S. at 206.

26. *Meek v. Pittinger,* 421 U.S. 349 (1975) and *Wolman v. Walter,* 433 U.S. 229 (1977), both overruled by *Mitchell v. Helms,* 530 U.S. 793, 808 (2000); *Aguilar v. Felton,* 473 U.S. 402 (1985), overruled by *Agostini v. Felton,* 521 U.S. 203, 235 (1997).

27. 463 U.S. 388, 394–399 (1983).

28. 474 U.S. 481, 488 (1986).

29. 509 U.S. 1, 13–14 (1993).

30. *Agostini,* 521 U.S. at 206.

31. 530 U.S. 793, 810 (2000).

32. 536 U.S. 639, 652 (2002).

33. 536 U.S. 688–689 (2002).

34. 540 U.S. 712, 718–719 (2004).

10

Religion and Public Life

More than two-thirds of the Supreme Court's establishment cases since *Everson* have involved religion and education. Piecemeal reading of these education cases can lead a casual reader to despair. But a chronological reading, with a focus on emerging thematic patterns, shows more gradual and predictable developments, as we saw in Chapters 8–9.

It is harder to discern predictable patterns in the Court's other modern establishment clause cases. We already saw some of this unpredictability as we reviewed the Court's shifting approaches to the establishment clause (in Chapter 7). We shall see more of this unpredictability in some of the cases concerning the use, funding, and regulation of religious organizations (in Chapter 11). In this chapter, we wade through a convoluted set of cases that raised two loaded questions: (1) what role may religious officials, ceremonies, and symbols play in public life? and (2) to what extent may government recognize, support, fund, house, or participate in these forms and forums of religious expression?

Cases raising these questions poured into the lower federal courts after *Everson* rendered the establishment clause applicable to state and local governments. Litigation groups like the ACLU, Americans United for Separation of Church and State, and the Anti-Defamation League filed many of the lawsuits. Their efforts were complemented, if not catalyzed, by the nation's growing countercultural movements in the 1960s (think of the hippie movement, Woodstock, the Vietnam War protests), by a growing antireligious sentiment in the American academy in the 1970s (think of the "God is dead" movement and the Marxist critiques of religion), and by the rise of religious and cultural minorities whose views found too little place in majoritarian policies and practices. Cultural critics and constitutional litigants challenged a number of admixtures of religion and government—including governmental funding and use of chaplains in state legislatures and elsewhere; the presence of religious language, art, and symbols on government stationery and seals and in public parks and government buildings; the purchase and display of religious art, music, literature, and statuary in state museums; governmental recognition of Christian Sundays and holidays; and others.

Few of these establishment cases made much headway in the lower federal courts before the 1980s, and the Supreme Court repeatedly refused to hear these cases on appeal, save a small cluster of cases on Sabbath day legislation in 1961. After 1980, however, the Court heard several cases on state-funded legislative chaplains and state-supported displays of religious symbols. These cases divided (and continue to divide) the Court deeply, yielding wildly discordant approaches to the establishment clause and bitter dissenting opinions from several of the justices, notably Justices Scalia, Souter, and Stevens.

Sabbath Day Rules (1961)

In 1961 the Supreme Court heard four cases in a row challenging traditional state rules protecting the Christian Sabbath day.[1] In all four cases, the Court found no violation of the First Amendment. The first case, *McGowan v. Maryland* (1961), was dispositive on the establishment clause question. Like most states, Maryland maintained "Sunday blue laws" that prohibited any labor and commerce on Sunday that was not considered "necessary" or "essential." Of course, farmers could milk their cows; pharmacies could dispense their medication; and fire, police, medical, and other such necessary services could remain open. But most commercial, recreational, and other laborious activities were to be closed on Sunday, unless they fit into one of the "myriad exceptions" in the statute. McGowan worked at a general department store that fit no such exception, but nonetheless remained open for business. Charged with a misdemeanor, he challenged the blue laws as a violation of his equal protection, due process, and First Amendment rights. In particular, he argued that these laws constituted an establishment of the Christian Sabbath. Their purpose, McGowan charged, was "to facilitate and encourage church attendance," "to induce people with no religion or people with marginal religious beliefs to join the predominant Christian sects," and "to aid the conduct of church services and religious observance of the sacred day."

The *McGowan* Court disagreed. While "undeniably religious in origin," Chief Justice Warren concluded for the Court after a lengthy historical rehearsal, these Sunday blue laws have now developed sufficient "secular justifications" to pass constitutional muster. These blue laws are no longer complemented by compulsory church attendance laws, tithe payment laws, and other traditional features of a Christian legal establishment, the Court noted. Rather, the blue laws provide a regular and uniform day of wholesome rest and leisure for workers and their families, some of whom may choose to go to church. Providing one day off each week caters to the "improvement of the health, safety, recreation and general well-being of our citizens" and accords with numerous other workplace regulations (like wage and hour controls) that protect laborers from exploitation. That this uniform day of rest happens to fall on "Sunday, a day of particular significance for the dominant Christian sects, does not bar the State from achieving its secular goals. To say that the States cannot prescribe Sunday as a day of rest for these purposes solely because cen-

turies ago such laws had their genesis in religion would give a constitutional interpretation of hostility to the public welfare rather than one of mere separation of
church and State."[2]

The Court upheld the constitutionality of Sunday blue laws even when Orthodox Jewish merchants coupled charges of religious establishment with charges of
free exercise violation. In *Braunfeld v. Brown* (1961), a Jewish furniture and clothing
merchant was convicted of a misdemeanor for operating on Sunday in violation of
Pennsylvania's blue laws. He challenged the constitutionality of these laws, noting
that Jewish law required him to be closed on Saturday while state law required him
to be closed on Sunday. This not only put him at a competitive disadvantage as a
merchant, but it also burdened the free exercise of his religion. Why couldn't he be
open on Sunday like so many other "non-necessary" merchants who had been given
exceptions in the statute? And why should Jews and others with different or with
no Sabbatarian restrictions be prohibited from shopping at his store on Sunday?
The *Braunfeld* Court was not convinced. It repeated its *McGowan* holding that Sunday blue laws were not an establishment of religion. Further, it found no violation
of Braunfeld's free exercise rights, since the law regulated only his store hours and
not his religious practices. There was at best only an "indirect burden" on Braunfeld's religion, the Court concluded, and the free exercise clause could not be used
to excuse a party from compliance with general criminal laws.[3] The Court concluded the same in *Gallagher v. Crown Kosher Supermarket* (1961) when a kosher
store operator, selling exclusively to an Orthodox Jewish clientele, was arrested for
opening on Sunday. Again, the Court held that the law was regulating only the
store's commercial activity, not its religious provisioning—and nothing in the First
Amendment prohibits such regulations.[4]

These Sabbath day cases were widely denounced as a travesty against religious liberty. The Court had failed to deal directly with the obvious reality that the Sunday
laws were born of Christian inspiration and retained Christian import for the vast
majority of citizens. Cloaking a religious rest day in secular rationales struck many
as subterfuge. Even worse, the Court had failed to give even the slightest accommodation to the freedom of conscience, exercise, and equality claims of the Jewish merchants in question—even though the legislatures had already accommodated all
manner of commercial, recreational, and sporting enterprises by exempting them
from Sunday blue laws. *Gallagher* was particularly troubling in this regard, for in that
case a Jewish merchant merely wanted an exemption for Sunday opening so that his
exclusively Jewish clients could keep kosher. To add further insult, this same Court,
less than a month later, exempted an atheist from swearing an oath to God in order
to get a nonpaid notary public job with the state.[5] It was perhaps these Sabbath day
cases, more than any others, that prompted the Court two years later to issue *Sherbert
v. Verner,* another Saturday Sabbatarian case, with its strict scrutiny regime for free
exercise claims. Even without prompting from the courts, most state and local governments gradually did away with these discriminatory Sunday blue laws, or at least
built into these laws new legislative exemptions for Saturday Sabbatarians.

Legislative Chaplains (1983)

The Court offered a variant on *McGowan*'s argument from secularized tradition in *Marsh v. Chambers* (1983), which upheld the constitutionality of state legislative chaplains. The State of Nebraska had employed legislative chaplains from the time of its founding. For the prior sixteen years, it had consistently reappointed a Presbyterian minister as its legislative chaplain. He was paid a modest salary by the state, had an office in the state capitol building, and opened each state legislative session with prayer. His prayers were ecumenical but Judeo-Christian in tone. Legislators were free to skip these opening prayers but few did. A state legislator and taxpayer challenged the practice as a violation of the establishment clause.

The federal court of appeals had found this to be an easy violation of all three prongs of the 1971 *Lemon* test (which, of course, had not yet been formulated when the 1961 Sabbatarian cases had reached the Court). The policy of maintaining a legislative chaplain, the court of appeals found, had an overtly religious purpose, had the primary (indeed exclusive) effect of advancing religion, and was the most obvious case possible of excessive entanglement between religious and state officials.

In *Marsh v. Chambers,* however, the Supreme Court reversed and upheld the practice. Ignoring the *Lemon* test, the *Marsh* Court instead appealed to the "unique history" of legislative chaplains in the United States, which began with the Continental Congress in 1774. The Court was particularly impressed that the very Congress that had drafted the First Amendment establishment clause in 1789 had also authorized the reappointment of two congressional chaplains at a substantial rate of pay and with comparable duties to pray at the opening of legislative sessions. The Court was also impressed that most other states had employed legislative chaplains throughout their history. "Standing alone," Chief Justice Burger wrote for the *Marsh* Court, "historical patterns cannot justify contemporary violations of constitutional guarantees, but there is far more here than simply historical patterns. In this context, historical evidence sheds light not only on what the draftsmen intended the Establishment Clause to mean, but also on how they thought that Clause applied to the practice authorized by the First Congress—their actions reveal their intent." The pervasive and perennial practice of maintaining legislative chaplains was evidence that this practice was not an establishment of religion but a commonplace of American politics. "[T]here can be no doubt that the practice of opening legislative sessions with prayer has become part of the fabric of our society," and it is therefore not an establishment of religion.[6]

Justice Brennan wrote a firm dissent in the *Marsh* case, castigating the majority for ignoring the settled three-prong test of *Lemon* and betraying the nation's elementary principles of separation of church and state. Brennan also reminded his fellow justices of *Stone v. Graham* (1980), where, a mere three years earlier, a unanimous Court had used the *Lemon* test to strike down the private display of the Ten Commandments in public high schools. If a passive, privately donated display of a religious text presented as a moral code is an establishment of religion, as the *Stone*

Court had said, then surely this state-subsidized, overtly religious verbal message regularly delivered in the very seat of state government must constitute an establishment of religion also. Had the Court applied the *Lemon* test, as it had consistently done in its other establishment cases since 1971, this would have been an easy case of a religious establishment, Justice Brennan concluded.[7]

Religious Symbols (1984–2010)

The next year, in *Lynch v. Donnelly* (1984), the Court did use the *Lemon* test along with its argument from secularized tradition but again found no establishment of religion. The issue in *Lynch* was the constitutionality of a government display of a crèche, or manger scene. For forty years, officials in Pawtucket, Rhode Island, had coordinated with local merchants to put up a large Christmas display in a private park in the heart of the downtown shopping area. The display had many typical holiday decorations—stuffed animals, toys, striped poles, a Santa Claus house, a sleigh and reindeer, cardboard carolers, colored lights, a "Season's Greetings" sign, and more. Embedded in this large display was a manger scene that depicted the Bible's account of the birth of Christ. It included figurines of Mary, Joseph, and baby Jesus in a manger, surrounded by animals, shepherds, wise men, and angels. The crèche occupied about 10 percent of the total holiday display space and constituted 15 percent of all the figurines. The city had purchased the crèche forty years before for $1,365, and had since stored and maintained it at little cost. Local taxpayers challenged the display as a violation of the establishment clause.

The *Lynch* Court upheld the display, with Chief Justice Burger again writing for the majority. "There is an unbroken history of official acknowledgment by all three branches of government of the role of religion in American life," Chief Justice Burger wrote, repeating his *Marsh* argument from tradition and now giving an ample list of illustrations to show how the crèche and other religious symbols had long been embedded in American culture and experience. But Chief Justice Burger pronounced another reason to uphold this display as he expressly worked through the three *Lemon* criteria. The crèche, while of religious significance to Christians, was merely a "passive" part of "purely secular displays extant at Christmas." Much like the Sabbath laws at issue in *McGowan*, the crèche had taken on secular civic purposes and become embedded in the fabric of society.[8] Government acknowledgments of religion—like the crèche, like legislative prayers, and like the "In God We Trust" motto on coins— are not per se unconstitutional, Justice O'Connor added in concurrence. Instead, they serve "the legitimate secular purposes of solemnizing public occasions, expressing confidence in the future, and encouraging the recognition of what is worthy of appreciation in society."[9] The primary effect of displaying the crèche as part of the broader holiday display is not to advance the Christian religion, Chief Justice Burger continued, but to "engender a friendly community spirit of good will" that "brings people into the central city, and serves commercial interests and benefits merchants." Governmental participation in and support of such "ceremonial deism" is not a form of excessive entanglement with religion and cannot be assessed by "mechanical logic" or "absolutist tests" of establishment. "It is far too late in the day to impose a crabbed reading of the Establishment Clause on the country."[10]

Five years later, in *Allegheny County v. ACLU* (1989), the Court offered a much closer, if not "crabbed," reading of the establishment clause to outlaw a public holiday display that ran six weeks from Thanksgiving into the new year. This display was located in the county courthouse near the "grand staircase," a heavily trafficked area for the many people who used the county's offices for licensing, registration, litigation, and the like. A crèche occupied almost the entire display and featured the same biblical figurines displayed in *Lynch*. The tallest figurine was an angel holding a trumpet that bore a clearly visible sign: "Gloria in excelsis Deo" ("Glory to God in the highest"), the Latin words of a familiar Christmas carol. The crèche had been donated by a lay Catholic group, as indicated by a small sign. The county had surrounded the display with a small white fence, flanked by two small pine trees with red bows and lined with red and white poinsettias. During the three weeks before Christmas, the county had invited local high school choirs to sing carols at the crèche during lunchtime, dedicating the musical offerings to world peace and soldiers missing in action. Local taxpayers brought suit.

The *Allegheny* Court struck down this crèche display as a violation of the establishment clause. Justice Blackmun wrote for the plurality, noting that this display was on a prominent piece of government land, and not in a private park (as the *Lynch* display had been). This display was almost exclusively religious in content, and not buffered by ample secular accoutrements of comparable size and genre. And this display carried a single, undiluted verbal message—enjoining viewers to give "Glory to God in the highest." Taken together, Justice Blackmun concluded, these factors had the fatal effect of primarily advancing or endorsing the Christian religion to the exclusion of all other forms of faith.

The same *Allegheny* Court, however, upheld the public display of a menorah, the eight-armed candleholder symbolizing the Jewish holiday of Hanukkah. The menorah in question was an abstract eighteen-foot design, privately owned but erected and maintained by the county. It was displayed at a lesser used entrance to the same courthouse, alongside the city's forty-five-foot decorated Christmas tree, which had been labeled "A Salute to Liberty." Given its less prominent placement on government land, its abstract design, its proximity to the larger "Salute to Liberty" tree, its lack of verbal religious messages, and its use of a symbol (a menorah) that has both religious and cultural connotations, this display was constitutionally acceptable, Justice Blackmun concluded. The Court did not address the discordance of upholding a menorah while outlawing a crèche at the same courthouse, but seemed to suggest that each case turned on the context and the characterization of the religious symbol.[11]

How to characterize a religious symbol arose again six years later in *Capitol Square v. Pinette* (1995). For more than a century the State of Ohio had opened a ten-acre square around the state capitol building for public gatherings and displays of various sorts. Parties who wished to use the square had to obtain a free license from the state.

In December the state invited the community to erect various unattended displays in this square. The state put up its own Christmas tree and licensed a local rabbi to put up a menorah. But the state denied a license to the Ku Klux Klan to put up its signature Latin cross. The KKK appealed, charging the state with viewpoint discrimination in violation of its free speech rights. The state countered that to allow the KKK to display its cross next to the state capitol would constitute an establishment of religion, and an odious political form of religion at that.

The *Pinette* Court upheld the free speech rights of the KKK and found no establishment clause violation. "A free-speech clause without religion would be Hamlet without the prince," Justice Scalia wrote for the plurality. The state has created an open public forum in its capitol square, and it cannot discriminatorily exclude religious speech from this forum unless it has a compelling reason to do so. Merely seeking to avoid an establishment of religion is generally not a sufficiently compelling reason to justify religious discrimination, the Court concluded, citing *Widmar* and *Lamb's Chapel,* the two equal access cases we saw earlier (pp. 200–202). Moreover, the Latin cross is only a private expression of religion, and no reasonable person would assume that the state had erected or condoned it—especially since the KKK would prominently label the cross as its own. Unlike the single crèche display at the grand staircase in *Allegheny,* this display would be one of several in a public forum that was open to anyone who wished to apply. Justice Scalia thus thought this case was like *Widmar,* which had required a state university to give equal access to a private student prayer meeting alongside other extracurricular student activities.[12]

Justice Thomas concurred in the case, arguing not only that the Latin cross was a form of private expression but that it was not even religious. For the KKK, "[t]he erection of such a cross is a political act, not a Christian one." Its depiction is deeply offensive, given the nation's history of slavery and the KKK's history of racism. But even offensive speech deserves free speech protection.[13]

The Court's conflicting messages and methods of dealing with public displays of religion became even more confusing after its two cases on the constitutionality of Ten Commandments displays on government land. In *McCreary County v. ACLU* (2005) and in *Van Orden v. Perry* (2005), announced back-to-back on the same day, two sharply divided courts struck down one Decalogue display but left another standing. In *McCreary,* Justice Souter, writing for the majority, used a strict *Lemon* analysis to strike down the display, with *Stone v. Graham* as the strongest precedent. In *Van Orden,* Chief Justice Rehnquist, writing for the plurality, ignored *Lemon* and instead used a soft history argument to uphold the display, with *Lynch v. Donnelly* as the strongest precedent. The cases featured long and bitter dissents by Justices Scalia and Stevens and a cacophony of concurring and dissenting opinions by other justices. The practical difference in outcome on the Court was attributable to Justice Breyer, who joined the majority in *McCreary* and joined in the decision (but not the plurality opinion) in *Van Orden.* In his concurrence in *Van Orden,* Justice Breyer described it as a "difficult borderline case" that called for "the exercise of legal judgment."[14]

McCreary County v. ACLU concerned a Kentucky county's new display of the Ten Commandments (or Decalogue) on a prominent wall in its courthouse. Initially the county ordered the Decalogue to be hung by itself. When the ACLU brought suit, the county ordered that the Decalogue be retained but had other governmental documents put around the display. The county's new order stated that "the Ten Commandments are codified in Kentucky's civil and criminal laws"; that they were put up "in remembrance and honor of Jesus Christ, the Prince of Ethics"; and that the "Founding Fathers [had an] explicit understanding of the duty of elected officials to publicly acknowledge God as the source of America's strength and direction." Almost all the surrounding governmental documents chosen for the display had the religious language in them highlighted.

As the case proceeded through the courts, the county ordered a third display, but without repealing its prior two orders. Now the Decalogue on display was expanded to include the full verses from Exodus 20, not just a summary as in the prior exhibits. It was flanked by nine other documents of comparable size, including the Magna Carta, the Declaration of Independence, the Bill of Rights, and the Mayflower Compact, with more neutral language in these documents highlighted. The collection as a whole was entitled "The Foundations of American Law and Government Display." Each document had a comparable-length description of its historical and legal significance. The Ten Commandments bore this description:

> The Ten Commandments have profoundly influenced the formation of Western legal thought and the formation of our country. That influence is clearly seen in the Declaration of Independence, which declared that "We hold these truths to be self-evident, that all men are created equal, that they are endowed by their Creator with certain unalienable Rights, that among these are Life, Liberty, and the pursuit of Happiness." The Ten Commandments provide the moral background of the Declaration of Independence and the foundation of our legal tradition.

The entire exhibit was displayed on the wall of a heavily trafficked hallway in the county courthouse. The county had initiated and paid for the displays.

The *McCreary* Court struck down this display as a violation of the establishment clause. Its fatal feature, in the Court's judgment, was that it lacked a genuine secular purpose, as both *Lemon* and *Stone* had required. The Decalogue is "a pervasively religious text" with a clear religious message, Justice Souter wrote, even if this text may have had legal or political uses in the past. The county's stated legislative purpose in putting up the display was to "honor Christ," the "Prince of Ethics." "The original text viewed in its entirety is an unmistakably religious statement dealing with religious obligations and with morality subject to religious sanction. When the government initiates an effort to place this statement alone in public view, a religious object is unmistakable." That was fatal in *Stone,* and it was fatal here.

The county's clumsy attempts to dilute this religious message by relabeling the Decalogue as a moral code, and by displaying other political documents with their religious passages prominently highlighted, only compounded its constitutional error in the eyes of any "reasonable observer," Justice Souter continued. The purported secular purposes of the county's final display "were presented only as a litigating position" and did little to offset the offending religious purpose that had informed the first display and the county's actions throughout the lawsuit. A genuine attempt by government to cure an unconstitutional condition could certainly pass muster under the establishment clause, the *McCreary* Court concluded, but there was no such genuine attempt here. Viewed as a whole and over time, the county's actions constituted an establishment of religion.[15]

In *Van Orden v. Perry,* issued two hours after *McCreary,* the Court took a very different approach. This case concerned a six-foot stone monument of the Decalogue on the state capitol grounds in Austin, Texas. The Decalogue had been privately donated forty years before by a voluntary civic group, the Fraternal Order of Eagles. It was one of thirty-eight historical markers and monuments on a twenty-two-acre state capitol campus. It was located near a lesser sidewalk that connected the state capitol building with the state supreme court building. Van Orden, a state taxpayer who had regularly used the law library for six years, challenged the Decalogue display as a form of religious establishment.

The *Van Orden* Court upheld the display. "Our cases, Januslike, point in two directions," Chief Justice Rehnquist wrote candidly for the plurality. One set of cases "acknowledges the strong role played by religion and religious traditions throughout our Nation's history." "The other face looks toward the principle that governmental intervention in religious matters can itself endanger religious freedom." The *Van Orden* Court followed the first line of cases, citing *McGowan, Marsh,* and *Lynch,* and declaring the *Lemon* test "not useful" in this case. The Decalogue is clearly a religious text with a religious message, the Court made clear. But "simply having religious content or promoting a message consistent with a religious doctrine does not run afoul of the Establishment Clause." The Decalogue, like many other religious texts and symbols on federal, state, and local government lands, is also part of "America's heritage, part of the fabric of American society." Its public display on government land democratically recognizes and represents that "religion has been closely identified with our history and government" and that America has "a religious people, whose institutions presuppose a Supreme Being." Moreover, this Decalogue display was privately donated. It stood unchallenged for forty years. It was a merely "passive" display that anyone could easily avoid while walking the state capitol grounds. And its message was buffered by the thirty-seven other monuments and markers on the same government land, most decidedly secular. If this display is unconstitutional, Chief Justice Rehnquist wrote, then hundreds of other religious displays—and maybe even the religious statutes of Moses and Mohammed on a frieze in the Supreme Court building—must come down. That surely was neither the intent nor the import of the First Amendment establishment clause.[16]

After such a remarkably discordant pair of cases, it was surprising to most observers that the Supreme Court, in *Pleasant Grove City v. Summum* (2009), was unanimous in upholding the constitutionality of a Ten Commandments monument on government land. The monument had been privately donated forty years earlier by the same Fraternal Order of Eagles that we saw in *Van Orden*. It was one of a dozen old signs and markers in a city park in Utah. A new religious group, Summum, sought permission to erect a monument bearing its seven principles of faith in the same park. The city refused, so Summum sued under the First Amendment. It charged the city with violating the free speech clause by discriminating against its seven principles. It also threatened to charge the city with violating the establishment clause by displaying the Ten Commandments alone. This left the city with a hard choice: take down the Ten Commandments or put up the seven principles.

The *Pleasant Grove* Court held for the government. The Court treated the Ten Commandments monument as a form of permissible government speech. A government "is entitled to say what it wishes," Justice Alito wrote for the Court, and it may select and reflect certain views in favor of others. It may express its views by putting up its own tax-paid monuments or by accepting monuments donated by private parties (whose contents it need not fully endorse). In this case, city officials had earlier accepted a Ten Commandments monument on grounds that it reflected the "[a]esthetics, history, and local culture" of the city. The free speech clause does not give a private citizen a "heckler's veto" over that old decision by the city. Nor does it compel the city to accept every privately donated monument once it has accepted the first. Government speech is "not bound by the free speech clause," the Court concluded, nor is it subject to judicial second-guessing under the First Amendment. Government officials are "accountable to the electorate" for their speech, and they will be voted out of office if their views cause offense.

It helped the *Pleasant Grove* Court that there were a dozen monuments in the city park, only one of which was religious in content. It also helped that the Decalogue here was a forty-year-old monument that had never been challenged before. Such facts allowed some of the justices to agree that the display did not constitute an establishment of religion. But the case turned on a characterization of the Ten Commandments monument as a form of government speech—not as a secularized icon of ceremonial deism or as a religious symbol sufficiently buffered by secular equivalents. The *Pleasant Grove* Court did not deny or dilute the religious qualities of the Ten Commandments. Instead, it left it to elected government officials to decide how to reflect and represent the views of the people, including their religious views. And it left it to the people to debate and decide whether the government's representation of their views was adequate or outmoded. Courts could certainly step in if the government coerced citizens to accept the religious views on these symbols, or if the government's speech violated privacy, endangered society, or violated the constitution. But a merely passive display of a generic religious text was not nearly enough to trigger federal judicial intervention.[17]

The Supreme Court tested the limits of this government-speech logic in *Salazar v. Buono* (2010). The case concerned a challenge to a seven-foot cross displayed prominently in the Mojave National Preserve in California. The cross had been donated and erected in 1934 by a private group, the Veterans of Foreign Wars (VFW), as a memorial to fallen American soldiers. The cross stood alone, clearly visible on the horizon; a small sign at the base indicated that the VFW had donated it. A few years earlier, a Buddhist group had sought to place a shrine near the cross, but the government had denied the application. A former park worker then brought suit under the establishment clause, challenging the constitutionality of the cross display. A federal district found the cross to be an unconstitutional endorsement of religion in violation of the establishment clause and ordered it removed. The Ninth Circuit Court of Appeals affirmed. Congress responded by declaring the cross a national war memorial, and conveying a small parcel of the park land with and around the cross to a private party, in exchange for a nearby private tract of land that was added to the national park. The same plaintiff, Buono, returned to the district court challenging the constitutionality of the private sale. Citing *McCreary*, the district court declared this attempted constitutional cure a "sham," and repeated its order that the cross be removed. The Ninth Circuit again affirmed. The government appealed to the Supreme Court, challenging Buono's standing rights and the propriety of the court's injunction, and arguing that this privately-donated cross was a suitable war memorial for fallen soldiers that was permissible under the establishment clause

A narrow 5–4 plurality of the *Buono* Court, led by Justice Kennedy, reversed the Ninth Circuit's decision and remanded the case to the district court for further proceedings. Observers had expected the Court to return to *Pleasant Grove* and decide whether this privately-donated cross in a federal park, like the privately-donated Decalogue in a city park, would be viewed as a constitutionally permissible form of government speech. Unlike *Pleasant Grove,* there were no nearby secular buffers to offset the religious message, but here the cross was a non-verbal symbol, its location was much more remote, and it had stood almost twice as long without challenge. The six fractured opinions in *Buono,* however, focused largely on Buono's standing rights, the constitutionality of Congress's private land sale, and the district court's authority to enjoin it.

Writing for himself and two others, Justice Kennedy concluded that Buono had standing both to press his original case that challenged the constitutionality of the cross display on federal land and to press his subsequent case that challenged the federal land sale. But Kennedy was not convinced that the district court had jurisdiction to extend its original injunction against the cross to enjoin the congressional act authorizing the land sale. The decision to enjoin the land sale required a separate constitutional inquiry whether Congress had truly violated the establishment clause, not just a simple judgment that its act was a "sham" designed to "evade" the first injunction. Congress had tried to resolve a "dilemma" created by the district court, Kennedy concluded: "It could not maintain the cross without violating the injunction, but it could not remove the cross without conveying disrespect for those the cross was seen as honoring. . . . Deeming neither alternative to be satisfactory, Congress enacted the statute here at issue." The district court would now have to judge Congress's actions on the merits. In its judgment, the district court would have to take into account the reality that while the cross was "certainly a Christian symbol," it had not been erected in the park "to promote a Christian message" or to "set the imprimatur of the state on a particular creed. Rather those who erected the cross intended simply to honor our Nation's fallen soldiers." The district court would further have to recognize that "[t]ime also has a played a role" and "the cross and the cause it commemorated had become entwined in the public consciousness" and part of "our national heritage." Justice Kennedy thus reversed the order enjoining the land transfer and remanded the case to the district court to judge the constitutionality of Congress's act on the merits and in light of these factors.

Joining the plurality, Justice Alito thought the case was sufficiently developed for the Supreme Court itself to make that constitutional judgment—and in favor of the government. The cross had been privately donated to honor the nation's war dead (just like crosses in government cemeteries everywhere), it had stood without challenge for seventy years, and it was an utterly remote corner of a desert park "seen by more rattlesnakes than humans." Also joining the plurality, Justices Scalia and Thomas thought that Buono lacked standing to seek an injunction of the land sale and the district court lacked power to issue the injunction. Buono is asking a federal court to prevent the display of a small cross on private land, they concluded; this leaves no constitutional question to resolve.

That characterization missed the constitutional point, Justice Stevens wrote in dissent, joined by three others including new Justice Sotomayor. The issue is whether the original display of the cross violates the establishment clause, and whether Congress's actions in response to the district court order can be seen as an "evasion"—much like the government's actions in the *McCreary County* case, which had been judged unconstitutional. Justice Stevens concluded that both the purpose and effect of the land transfer statute was to endorse religion in violation of the establishment clause. In a separate dissent, Justice Breyer concluded that the district court did have power to enjoin the land transfer, making unnecessary any further inquiry into establishment clause issues.[18]

This thirty-year line of religious symbolism cases—from *Stone v. Graham* (1980) to *Salazar v. Buono* (2010)—has easily been the least steady of the Court's establishment clause cases. Many of these cases turn heavily on the facts and how these facts are characterized. Many feature widely discordant opinions, sometimes cast in rhetorically bombastic terms. Government officials often seem rightly bewildered about the constitutional limitations or permissions granted by the Court. Lower courts sometimes struggle to cobble together a coherent analysis from the Court's cases in this arena, and often struggle to predict what the Court might do next. And private citizens can seemingly all find a case to defend and another to decry. The Court itself still seems a long way from creating a new concordance of its discordant precedents. There are only a few rules of thumb to guide litigants and lower courts in these matters. Four are worth mentioning here—with the caveat that while each might be useful, none is dispositive.

First, older religious displays and practices tend to fare better than newer displays, particularly if they have not faced much constitutional challenge before. Even if the original inspiration for the old display or practice was religious, its long-standing presence in public life seems to imbue it with a kind of cultural and constitutional imprimatur. In the Court's view, it has become a part of American culture, society, and democracy—and is thus unlikely to be a fateful first step toward an establishment of religion. Sometimes the Court has stated that any offending religious meaning the display or practice may have had has now been lost; it is now either a civic symbol devoid of religious content or a generic symbol that evinces "ceremonial deism." Other times the Court has worked harder to acknowledge the ongoing religious nature and content of the symbol for many citizens. Moreover, if establishment clause litigants sit on their rights too long, those rights tend to get less deference when they are finally exercised. Older religious displays and practices were at issue in *McGowan, Marsh, Lynch, Van Orden, Pleasant Grove,* and *Buono,* and the government won each time. Newer displays were at issue in *Stone, Allegheny,* and *McCreary,* and the government lost each time.

The law recognizes both the power and the pressure of time in other areas. For example, the power of time can be seen in historical preservation and zoning rules that "grandfather" various older (religious) uses of property that do not comport with current preferred uses. It can also be seen in private property laws of "adverse possession": an open, continuous, and notorious use of property eventually will vest in the user. When applied to religious symbolism cases, these legal ideas leave older displays more secure but new displays more vulnerable. The law further recognizes the pressure of time in its rules of pleading and procedure. In order to promote finality and prevent stale claims, legislatures set statutes of limitations on many claims. The common law has long done the same through its equitable doctrine of "laches," which similarly penalizes parties for sitting too long on their rights. While the law does not set statutes of limitations on constitutional cases, of course, and the Court has never explicitly invoked laches, the idea seems to influence the Court. "If a thing has been practiced for two hundred years by common consent," especially at the local level, Justice Holmes once wrote, "it will need a strong case for the Fourteenth Amendment to affect it."[19]

Second, how the symbol or practice is labeled or characterized can be critical to a case. *Stone* and *McCreary* characterized the Decalogue as a religious symbol and struck it down; *Van Orden* and *Pleasant Grove* characterized it as an historical marker and let it stand. *Lynch* labeled the crèche a holiday display with commercial value and let it stand; *Allegheny* labeled the crèche a depiction of the Christmas story and struck it down. *Pinette* called the Latin cross a form of private expression protected by free speech clause; *Pleasant Grove* called the Decalogue a form of government speech immune from the speech clause. *Lynch* labeled the secular decorations around the crèche an effective buffer; *McCreary* regarded the secular documents around the Decalogue as fraudulent camouflage. For *Stone,* labeling the Decalogue as a moral code was viewed as a subterfuge belied by the imperative tone of the Commandments. For *Allegheny,* labeling a forty-five-foot county Christmas tree as "A Salute to Liberty" was sufficient constitutional cover for placement of a menorah. *Allegheny* treated as constitutionally fatal two signs at the crèche bearing the imperative "Gloria in excelsis Deo" and "Donated by the Holy Name Society." *Van Orden* thought a small sign, "Donated by the Fraternal Order of Eagles," offset any constitutional offense to a six-foot Decalogue with imperatives like "Thou shalt have no other gods before me." *Buono* thought a privately-donated Latin cross on federal land was a suitable memorial for fallen soldiers. The characterization of the symbol or practice can be key to its constitutional fate.

The Court uses characterization similarly in some of its First Amendment cases dealing with education, as we saw in the prior two chapters on religion and education. For example, *Widmar* and *Rosenberger* said the prayer meetings and evangelical publications in question were religious activities and thus could not be discriminated against for free speech purposes. *Lamb's Chapel* and *Good News Club*, by contrast, labeled the group's activities as acceptable educational programs that were only religiously inspired. School officials in *Weisman* and *Santa Fe* tried to label their prayers as ceremonial "invocations" permissible under the establishment clause, but they got nowhere. The *Mueller* tax deductions for children's religious textbooks and the *Zelman* vouchers for religious education, however, were upheld in part because they were treated as state taxing and spending decisions.

Third, geographical location can also be important. Government-sponsored displays on private property, as in *Lynch*, get more deference than private displays on government property, as in *Stone* and *Allegheny*. Displays in prominent places on government properties, like the grand staircase in *Allegheny* or the main hallway in the *McCreary* courthouse, are more suspect than those in less conspicuous places, like the secondary entrance in *Allegheny*, the small city park in *Pleasant Grove*, or the remote national park in *Buono*. Location is not dispositive of the establishment clause question, as litigants in *Pinette* and *Marsh* found out; there, religious activities and displays on the steps and in the very chamber of the state capitol were upheld. But location is a factor in some cases and can play a key role if it strongly influences whether citizens are actually or effectively forced to observe or participate in the religious exercise. That smacks of coercion and leads the Court to find a violation of the establishment clause, as in *Stone* and in the prayer in public school cases.

A fourth factor is whether the religious symbol or practice is offset by secular symbols or practices. Particularly when government sponsors or houses religious symbols on its property, they are best offset by nonreligious symbols of comparable size, weight, and genre. *McCreary* makes clear that a court can (and sometimes will) second-guess the government when the court suspects subterfuge. But lower courts have generally been sympathetic with government officials who try to balance religious and nonreligious messages in their public display. In assessing the balance, they will make rough judgments whether the messages of the offsetting symbols are of comparable genre; whether the religious qualities are obvious or more abstract; and whether the religious symbol is suitable or unsuitable for the government forum. For example, a Renaissance "Madonna with Child" may be fine in the foyer of the state museum but not in the entrance to the state capitol. This, like all these rules of thumb, merely reiterates that context matters.

Summary and Conclusions

In 1986 distinguished constitutional historian Leonard Levy wrote: "The Court has managed to unite those who stand at polar opposites on the results that the Court reaches; a strict separationist and a zealous accommodationist are likely to agree that the Supreme Court would not recognize an establishment of religion if it took life and bit the Justices."[20] In the quarter century since Levy wrote, the Court's establishment law has become a bit more coherent, particularly if the two sets of religion and education cases are read chronologically and along thematic lines, as we have done. But if they are viewed laterally across all the Court's establishment cases at any given time—especially in active years like 1961, 1971, 1983–1987, or 2000–2002—Levy's judgment is hard to resist. Few areas of law today are so riven with wild generalizations and hairsplitting distinctions, so given to grand statements of principle and petty applications of precept, so rife with selective readings of history and inventive renderings of precedent. Few areas of law hold such a massive jumble of juxtaposed doctrines, methods, and rules, particularly in the religion and public life cases. Even a sympathetic reader of the Court's modern establishment law is tempted to apply to it the definition that Oliver Wendell Holmes Jr. once applied to the common law: "chaos with an index."

It is therefore apt, in this context, to be reminded of the founders' original vision of the establishment clause. In the founders' view, the establishment clause complemented the free exercise clause in the protection of religious liberty. The free exercise clause outlawed government *proscriptions* of religion—actions that unduly burdened the conscience, restricted religious expression and action, discriminated against religion, or invaded the autonomy of churches and other religious bodies. The establishment clause outlawed government *prescriptions* of religion—actions that unduly coerced the conscience, mandated forms of religious expression, discriminated in favor of religion, or improperly allied the state with churches or other religious bodies. The free exercise clause and the establishment clause thereby provided complementary protections to the first principles of the American experiment—liberty of conscience, freedom of religious expression, equality of plural faiths before the law, and separation of church and state. In *Everson,* the Court repeated each of these principles of religious liberty as it opened the modern era of establishment clause jurisprudence, and in later cases the Court drew at least some of them into its calculus.

The Court has shown some concern for the principles of liberty of conscience and freedom of expression in its modern establishment clause cases. The Court's opinion in *Lee v. Weisman,* which barred a rabbi's invocation at a public middle school graduation ceremony, was overt about protecting both the student's conscience from "coercion" and the rabbi's prayer from the dictates of the school principal. This concern also animated some of the other cases on religion in public schools: young, impressionable students compelled to be in school cannot be coerced into religious activities and ceremonies. Concern for conscience also informed the Court's religious symbolism cases in *Allegheny* and *McCreary:* those who use the county courthouse to get their mandatory licenses or answer their mandatory subpoenas cannot be forced to read a prominent sign in the court that orders them to give "Glory to God in the Highest" or "Remember the Sabbath day, to keep it holy." But concern for liberty of conscience escaped the Court altogether in its cavalier dismissal of the Jewish Sabbatarian claims that Sunday blue laws constitute an establishment of religion (or at least infringe the claimant's free exercise rights). And outside of the *Mueller* tax deduction case and the *Zelman* school voucher case, the Court has given short shrift to arguments about the ample burden imposed on parents who must pay property taxes to support the secularized public schools they cannot abide plus pay private tuition to send their children to religious private schools that better suit their religious convictions.

The Court has also shown concern for religious equality and nondiscrimination in its modern establishment clause cases. Particularly noteworthy is the series of equal access, equal treatment, and equal protection cases that treated religions and nonreligions equally in their use of public forums, facilities, and funds, each time finding no establishment of religion in so doing. Also notable are the Court's repeated holdings that narrowly tailored judicial or legislative exemptions to accommodate the unique religious needs of individuals or groups do not constitute an establishment of religion. The Court has shown that exempting religiously motivated behavior from general laws and regulations is not an establishment of religion, but a neutral way of ensuring equality for all. And further notable are the Court's efforts to ensure that all peaceable religious communities are permitted to establish their own schools and charities, to display their own religious symbols and ceremonies in open public forums, and, we will discuss in the next chapter, to resolve their own internal religious disputes without state interference.

Separation of church and state has been the most important and original principle of religious liberty at work in the modern establishment cases, and it remains essential to maintain today. As we saw in the foregoing chapters and will see again in Chapter 11 on religious organizations, government officials have no constitutional business interfering in the internal affairs of peaceable and voluntary religious groups. Religious officials have no constitutional business converting the offices of government into instruments of their mission and ministry. Government has no business funding, sponsoring, or actively involving itself in the core religious exercises of a particular religious school, group, or official. Religious groups, in turn, have no business drawing on government sponsorship or funding for their core religious activities. Nor do religious groups have any constitutional business insisting that government cede or delegate to them some of the core political responsibilities. All such conduct violates the principle of separation of church and state and should be outlawed by the establishment clause.

But a categorical insistence on the principle of separation of church and state, along the lines of many of the Court's establishment cases in the 1970s and 1980s, has proved unworkable. James Madison warned already in 1833 that "it may not be easy, in every possible case, to trace the line of separation between the rights of Religion and the Civil authority, with such distinctness, as to avoid collisions & doubts on *unessential points*."[21] This caveat has become even more salient today. The modern welfare state, and now the modern security state, for better or worse, reaches deeply into virtually all aspects of modern life—through a vast network of laws and regulations on education, charity, welfare, family, child care, health care, construction, zoning, workplace, taxation, and more. Madison's solution was "an entire abstinence of the Government from interference [with religion] in any way whatever, beyond the necessity of preserving public order, & protecting each sect against trespasses on its legal rights by others."[22] This traditional understanding of a minimal state role in the life of society in general, and of religious bodies in particular—however alluring it may be in theory—is no longer realistic in practice.

It is thus even more imperative today than in Madison's day that the principle of separation of church and state not be pressed to reach the "unessentials," as Madison called them. It is one thing for the Court to outlaw daily Christian prayers and broadcasted Bible readings from the public school, quite another thing to ban moments of silence and private displays of the Decalogue in the same schools. It is one thing to bar direct tax support for religious education, quite another thing to bar tax deductions for parents who wish to educate their children in the faith. It is one thing to prevent government officials from delegating their core police powers to religious bodies, quite another thing to prevent them from facilitating the charitable services of voluntary religious and nonreligious associations alike. It is one thing to outlaw governmental prescriptions of prayers, ceremonies, and symbols in public forums, quite another thing to outlaw governmental accommodations of private prayers, ceremonies, and symbols in public forums. To press separationist logic too deeply into "unessentials" unduly "trivializes" the place of religion in public and private life, as Stephen Carter has argued.[23] Moreover, it also trivializes the power of the Constitution, converting it from a coda of cardinal principles of national law into a codex of petty precepts of local life.

Too zealous an interpretation of the principle of separation of church and state also runs afoul of other constitutive principles of the establishment clause—particularly the principles of liberty of conscience and religious equality. The Court must be at least as zealous in protecting religious consciences from secular coercion as protecting secular consciences from religious coercion. The Court should be at least as concerned to ensure the equal treatment of religion as to ensure the equality of religion and nonreligion. It is no violation of the principle of separation of church and state when a legislature or court accommodates judiciously the conscientious scruples of a religious individual or the cardinal callings of a religious body. It is also no violation of this principle when government grants religious individuals and institutions equal access to forums, facilities, or funds that are open to nonreligionists similarly situated. To do otherwise is, indeed, to move toward what Justice Stewart once called "the establishment of a religion of secularism."[24]

Notes

1. The Supreme Court heard eight earlier cases on Sabbath day issues. The most important are *Soon Hing v. Crowley*, 113 U.S. 703 (1885), which upheld a local Sunday law as a

day of rest from labor, not as a promotion of religion, and *Petit v. Minnesota,* 177 U.S. 164 (1900), which held that there was no right for a barber to be included among necessary workers permitted to work on Sunday.

2. 366 U.S. 420, 444–446 (1961).

3. 366 U.S. 599, 606 (1961).

4. 366 U.S. 617 (1961). See also *Two Guys from Harrison-Allentown v. McGinley,* 366 U.S. 582 (upholding a Sunday blue law).

5. *Torcaso v. Watkins,* 367 U.S. 488 (1961).

6. *Marsh v. Chambers,* 463 U.S. 783, 790–792 (1983). For the Court of Appeals opinion, see 675 F.2d 228 (8th Cir. 1982).

7. *Marsh v. Chambers,* 463 U.S. at 796 (Brennan, J., dissenting).

8. *Lynch v. Donnelly,* 465 U.S. 668, 680–686 (1984).

9. 465 U.S. 693 (O'Connor, J., concurring).

10. 465 U.S 685, 687 (1984).

11. 492 U.S. 573 (1989).

12. 515 U.S. 753, 760 (1995).

13. 515 U.S. 770 (Thomas, J., concurring).

14. 545 U.S. 677, 700 (Breyer, J., concurring in the judgment).

15. 545 U.S. 844, 847–848 (2005).

16. 545 U.S. 677, 678, 683, 686–687, 690 (2005).

17. 555 U.S. __, 129 S.Ct. 1125, 1132 (2009).

18. __ U.S. __ (slip opinion) (April 28, 2010).

19. *Jackman v. Rosenbaum,* 260 U.S. 22, 31 (1922).

20. Leonard W. Levy, *The Establishment Clause: Religion and the First Amendment* (1986), 163.

21. James Madison, Letter to Rev. Adams (1833), in Daniel L. Dreisbach, *Religion and Politics in the Early Republic: Jasper Adams and the Church-State Debate* (1996), 120 (emphasis added).

22. Ibid.

23. Stephen L. Carter, *The Culture of Disbelief: How American Law and Politics Trivializes Religious Devotion* (1993).

24. *Abington Township School District v. Schempp,* 374 U.S. 203, 313 (1963) (Stewart, J., dissenting).

11

Religious Organizations
and the Law

As we have seen, courts and commentators frequently break the First Amendment into two parts—free exercise and no establishment—rather than viewing the religion provisions of the First Amendment as working together, animated by the underlying six principles of religious liberty. Creating a dichotomy creates disparate lines of cases and masks the important fact that there are three areas for constitutional investigation rather than only two. The first two are, of course, the free exercise and establishment cases explored in Chapters 6–10. The third area is less explicitly textual but historically and structurally quite plain: the notion that there must be space between religious *organizations* and the civil government. Some issues relating to group rights of religious organizations are easily categorized as free exercise or establishment claims. But some free exercise or establishment claims pose particular problems when they deal with religious organizations rather than religious individuals. And still other issues touching group rights lack an easy fit within the constructs of the two clauses.

Sometimes issues involving religious organizations plainly relate to matters of legislative grace, or "benevolent neutrality" toward religion, as the Court has called it. The Court first spoke explicitly of a space between the free exercise clause and the establishment clause—in which the legislature may choose to grant deference to religion—in a case involving a tax exemption for a religious organization. In *Walz v. Tax Commission* (1971), Chief Justice Burger wrote: "[T]here is room for play in the joints productive of a benevolent neutrality which will permit religious exercise to exist without sponsorship and without interference."[1] Prudential concerns should lead legislatures to favor the collective exercise of conscience through associations, since they are healthy for both the individual involved and, generally, for the state.[2] The Court has drawn on this benevolent neutrality toward religious organizations, this "play in the joints" between what the free exercise clause requires and the establishment clause forbids, to uphold not only religious tax exemptions, but also direct

241

funding of religious organizations that assist civic life in charitable ways. Nonetheless, even benevolent neutrality has limits, and the Court has held that the government may not cede its core powers entirely to a religious organization.

More than just permitting legislative accommodations to include religious organizations, though, the Constitution requires that religious organizations have affirmative space to carry out their unique mission. This is partly because the organization is the place where individuals manifest their own free exercise rights.[3] But an organization is more than a mere aggregation of individuals and, for many religious adherents, has important communal components that cannot be realized independently.[4] The Supreme Court held in *Boy Scouts v. Dale* (2000) that a state may not inhibit an organization's right to associate for expressive purposes by dictating what persons should be acceptable as members. In *Dale*, the Court held that the Boy Scouts of America could set its own terms of membership and exclude an openly gay assistant scoutmaster and that the state could not interfere.[5] If freedom of expressive association attaches in this way to a nonreligious organization like the Boy Scouts, it surely must be at least that expansive for religious organizations—and more so, given the explicit textual protection for religion. Indeed, as we saw in *Pierce v. Society of Sisters* (1925) and its progeny, the Court historically has upheld religious group rights in various contexts, recognizing the "fundamental right of religious schools to exist and to educate children in the faith without undue state interference" and, more recently, determining that the National Labor Relations Act should not be interpreted to grant jurisdiction over a Catholic school's teachers so as to avoid implicating serious constitutional questions.[6]

In addition to encompassing corporate free exercise rights, the First Amendment embraces the principle of separation of church and state, which has long been understood to protect religious organizations from the state, not just the state from religious organizations. Western thought has long included the notion that the state and religious organizations, whether cast as two powers, two swords, or otherwise, each have legitimate claims over their adherents (even when the boundaries and jurisdictions of such claims remain disputed). Despite the strong pull of corporate free exercise rights and the separation of church and state, however, the Court has thus far failed to articulate a deep and broad-based theory of corporate free exercise (and religious associational) rights.[7]

In this chapter we provide an overview of the constitutional issues and challenges facing religious organizations. We first explore various organizational structures of religious groups. We then focus on intrachurch property disputes, which have given rise to more than a dozen Supreme Court cases. The cases are important in their own right and frequently provide the framework in which other church organizational issues are litigated. In these cases, we see that the Court has treated religious organizations on an equal footing with nonreligious organizations (1815–1914), has granted religious organizations greater deference than normally accorded to other groups (1872–1976), and, more recently, has attempted to move toward a principle of "neutral principles of law" (1979–). We then look briefly at other areas of overlap between religious organizations and civil law including taxation, employment, and law, including tort liability.[8]

Religious Polity and Structures

Religious groups organize themselves in two important ways simultaneously. First, religious groups voluntarily structure themselves internally (their "polity") in ways that conform to their religious beliefs or desires—or simply accord with what they think is effective operation. Second, religious groups are required to structure themselves in a legally sanctioned form to enjoy the benefits of legal status. These forms often overlap, but they are not the same, and this sometimes causes problems. Because these religious and legal organizational structures form an important background for understanding the emerging constitutional doctrine, we explain them here in broad strokes.

Religious Structures

Polity generally refers to the manner in which individual believers form a religious body.[9] This body has structures of governance, formation, and decision-making that are established by the religious believers, and more often than not these organizational structures derive from religious beliefs or texts. That is, the manner in which a group organizes itself is itself often a matter of theology.

Since the nineteenth century the Supreme Court has suggested that there are two forms of religious bodies: congregational and hierarchical. Congregational churches are autonomous local entities that are not subject to any higher authority. They operate by majority vote of the members, or some other mechanism established for self-governance. Hierarchical churches are "those organized as a body with other churches having similar faith and doctrine with a common ruling convocation or ecclesiastical head."[10]

While these categories of congregational and hierarchical fit well if applied to frontier Baptist congregations or Roman Catholic dioceses, they do not apply as well to many other religious bodies, some 40 percent of which self-describe as having different organizational forms—whether presbyterian, connectional, or a continuum of other types.[11] Nor do these basic categories of polity constructed a century ago in a predominantly Christian environment necessarily fit well in a society with an increasing plurality of religions and religious beliefs.

Legal Structures

Religious groups need proper legal status to enter binding contracts, to sue and be sued, to hold real property, and to limit their liability—and these rights are established by state law generally. States may restrict religious bodies from forming particular legal statuses, but the constitutional limits of these restrictions have not been widely tested. The West Virginia state constitution, for example, does not allow religious corporations, largely for historical reasons. Virginia had the same limitation until 2007.[12] In those states religious entities may incorporate only under general nonprofit organization statutes, seemingly ameliorating some of the harsher (and possibly unconstitutional) effects of those state constitutional provisions. By contrast, some states have specific forms of religious corporation status, which might eventually raise establishment clause concerns. New York, for example, has separate statutory incorporation provisions for dozens of religious denominations.[13] One of the underlying tensions regarding legal structures is the extent to which the state is defining and shaping the religious structure—or merely reflecting (poorly) the preexisting religious structure.

Religious bodies tend to organize themselves in certain ways.[14] (1) One method, which was more common in the past, is to form an unincorporated association. Such associations typically could not hold property, enter contracts, or sue or be sued at common law. Typically trustees hold property for the benefit of the organization. Some religious groups still use this organizational form, usually governed by articles of association and bylaws that are not filed with a secretary of state. These organizations may disdain any governmental control or contact at all. (2) Many religious organizations today form a nonprofit corporation under relevant state statutes. Such corporations have a constitution or bylaws and membership filed with the state; they also have directors or trustees to act for the corporation, but the corporation itself holds all property. The Model Nonprofit Corporation Act provides a handy framework that religious entities can adapt as desired. This model works best for congregational type organizations. (3) A different form is the corporation sole. This is a one-person corporation and vests full power of the corporation (including property ownership rights) in the individual holding a particular office. (4) Alternatively, religious organizations may form express trusts which have legal trustees who are appointed to hold and care for property directly.

A religious organization has a constitutional right to define itself as a legal entity, but the boundaries of that right are ill defined and therefore are subject to great variation and depend heavily on legislative grace. Because the outcomes of legal cases often turn on these legal structures and civil court interpretations of internal religious structure, such structures become quite important. Ideally, religious organizations would have ample legal forms to use to attain their goals, and legal structures and religious structures would be appropriately aligned. But the ideal is not always realized.

Religious Property Disputes

The Supreme Court's earliest cases on religion, beginning in 1815, were based on federal common law, not on the First Amendment directly. Most of these early cases involved disputes over church property. Two clear, though discordant, themes emerge from these church property cases. In one line of cases, the Court has held that religious groups must be treated equally with other legal associations, and subject to generally applicable legal principles to resolve disputes. In a second line of cases, the Court has held that religious groups must be treated differently from other organizations, and the courts must be diligent to avoid deciding matters of disputed doctrine. Courts thus frequently give substantial deference to decisions by internal religious bodies. These juxtaposed approaches have resulted in a hodgepodge of approaches to intrachurch disputes, which turn variously on the religious organizational structure, legal organizational structure of the divided church, and the proclivities of the state.

Equal Treatment (1815–1914)

The Court's first religion case, *Terrett v. Taylor* (1815), nicely illustrates the first theme. In *Terrett*, the Supreme Court declared null and void an 1801 Virginia act that rescinded the corporate charter of the Episcopal Church issued in 1776 and that required the church to sell its vacant glebe lands and turn over the proceeds to the poor. The act, even if consistent with the constitution of Virginia, Justice Story wrote for the Court, violated "fundamental principles of natural justice." Religious groups, like all other legal associations, must be allowed to retain a corporate charter once lawfully given and use their properties in any lawful manner they deem apt, without undue interference by the state.[15]

In a series of cases at the end of the nineteenth century, the Court was asked to intervene in the corporate property rights of the Harmony Society, a communitarian Christian group. Four separate times the court declined to do so, consistently turning to principles of contract and association. The Harmony Society was an intensely communitarian sect of German Anabaptist origin and orientation, which had adopted a policy and practice of holding all property in common. Members were expected to give up their private property and accept a new ethic and biblical practice of communal sharing and caring.[16] Most parties signed a document to this effect upon joining the group, laying the groundwork for later judicial determinations of contractual consent. In the disputes that reached the Court, former members or their heirs sought to recover the private property they had contributed to the organization, but the Court rejected each request.

In the first case, *Goesele v. Bimeler* (1852), the heir of a community member brought an action against the society. The heir sought a partition of property so that he could obtain the private property contributed by his ancestor. The Court made short work of the case, noting that the ancestor had signed articles of association not once but twice, each time acknowledging the communitarian nature of property. The heir contended that the leader of the movement, Joseph Bimeler, was guilty of fraud meriting the Court's disapproval, but the Court instead recited Bimeler's industrious, ethical nature and concluded that he was an honest man who was wrongly impugned by the lawsuit.[17]

Four years later the Court heard *Baker v. Nachtrieb* (1856), in which a disgruntled community member tried to regain what he had contributed to the Harmony Society. Once again, he charged the leader of this community (George Rapp) with malfeasance and various character flaws. The Court quoted the articles of association, which noted that upon joining the group "each individual is to be considered to have finally and irrevocably parted with all his former contributions . . . and [s]hould any individual withdraw from the Society, or depart this life, neither he . . . nor his representatives . . . shall be entitled to demand an account of said contribution. . . . " Despite this agreement, Rapp paid the plaintiff $200 when he left the community; the plaintiff had accepted the $200 and signed a document disavowing any further claim. This was effectively a contractual release and the Court would not contravene it or permit Rapp to be discredited.[18]

In *Speidel v. Henrici* (1887), a former member again tried to gain assets from the society. This allegation blatantly charged George Rapp with fraud, alleging that Rapp "falsely and fraudulently" persuaded his followers to obtain eternal salvation by surrendering their earthly property and by following Rapp "as their apostle." In a cursory opinion, the Court noted that the plaintiff had "allowed the avails of his work to become part of the common fund" but then failed to complain about it for fifty years after leaving the society. "If he ever had any rights, he could not assert them after such a delay," wrote Justice Gray. The claim was barred by laches.[19] The Court was asked to rule on the assets of the Harmony Society once again in *Schwartz v. Duss* (1902). Descendants of former members of the society sought a distribution of property, claiming that the society had been dissolved since the trustees were no longer pursuing the original purposes of the charter of the organization. The Court noted that the plaintiffs were never members of the society and that their ancestors had signed documents adopting communal property ownership. Further, the society had not dissolved by consent of the remaining members or the misuse of trust funds, and thus the society prevailed again.[20]

The rationale undergirding these cases was articulated clearly in a 1914 case. In *Order of St. Benedict v. Steinhauser* (1914), a monastic order that practiced community property claimed title to the estate of a deceased member. The executor of the estate objected, claiming that the monastic order had no legitimate claim, and if it did, such a claim was contrary to public policy. The executor contended that the decedent did not remit the proceeds from the sale of books to the order during his lifetime, evidencing that it was private property. The order's right to the property rested, the Court believed, on the strength of these earlier Harmony Society cases:

> We are not concerned in the present case with any question of ecclesiastical requirement or monastic discipline. The question is solely one of civil rights. The claim in this suit rests upon the constitution of the complainant corporation, and the obligations inherent in membership. . . . [T]he question here is not one of canon law or ecclesiastical polity. The requirement of complainant's constitution [respecting community property] must be read according to its terms, and its validity must thus be determined.

Happy to avoid delving into canon law, the Court turned to the state law of contract and association. The decedent had been a lifelong member of the order, had committed to its common-fund requirement by accepting membership under the order's constitution and had not withdrawn from the order, and had retained and used proceeds during his life only with permission of his superior. The Court thus held that the order had a claim to decedent's property, which was not against public policy since the order was specifically incorporated under a state statute.[21]

Collectively, this line of cases points to an ideal that religious bodies are free to manage their own internal affairs regarding property, provided that there is actual consent by the members. Further, a certain deference should be given to religious groups to structure their property affairs as they see fit; courts should not second-guess associational arrangements after the fact based on charges by former members or their heirs. Basic principles of contractual consent and the right of individuals to associate as they see fit seem adaptable to such religious organization cases.

Deference (1872–1976)

While the first line of cases called for religious organizations to be treated like any other association, a contemporaneous line of cases asserted that religion is special, and courts must develop distinct methods of dispute resolution that keep them from delving into religious doctrine. The first such case was *Watson v. Jones* (1872), which dealt with an intrachurch property dispute rather than an intact community.

Watson grew out of a complicated set of property facts, but the main issue was that the Walnut Street Presbyterian Church in Louisville, Kentucky, became deeply divided over the issue of slavery during and after the Civil War. A majority of the church's membership opposed slavery and wanted to adhere to the views of the General Assembly of the Presbyterian Church: that southerners who had aided the South in the Civil War or had joined the competing general assembly formed by the southern states (which had stated that slavery was a divine institution) should be required to repent for these sins. But a majority of the church leadership (the elders, trustees, and pastor) of the Walnut Street Church opposed the national general assembly and instead aligned with a competing intermediary synod. This divided the church, with each group claiming to be the "true" church and each claiming the exclusive right to use and control church property. The pro-slavery faction sued in federal court in a federal diversity action.

The Supreme Court held that because the Presbyterian Church was essentially hierarchical in nature, the decision of the highest ruling body within that church was conclusive and binding on the civil courts:

> [W]e think the rule of action which should govern the civil courts, founded in a broad and sound view of the relations of church and state . . . is, that, whenever the questions of discipline, or of faith or ecclesiastical rule, custom, or law have been decided by the highest of these church judicatories to which the matter has been carried, the legal tribunals must accept such decisions as final and binding on them, in their application of the case before them.

The rationale for this case was not difficult, thought the Court, and turned on the fact that appellants had previously consented to the decisional authority of the general assembly before the controversy commenced, even though "they now deny its authority, denounce its action, and refuse to abide by its judgments." The pro-slavery faction could not complain at this late date about the authority of the general assembly to determine which faction was the true church with a right to the church property; and the civil courts could not second-guess the general assembly, for the judges of the civil courts were not "as competent in the ecclesiastical law and religious faith of all these bodies as the ablest men" within the religious group itself.[22]

The year after *Watson*, the Court had occasion to intervene in another internal church dispute in *Bouldin v. Alexander* (1872). The Court was asked to identify the legal trustees for an unincorporated religious society. In its discussion it was critical to the Court that the case involved "temporalities alone" and not "who were [the] church officers." This was important, for, as Justice Strong stated, "we have no power to revise or question ordinary acts of church discipline, or of excision of church membership. . . . [W]e cannot decide who ought to be members of the church, nor whether the excommunicated have been regularly or irregularly cut off."[23]

When asked to rule on an internal church controversy in *Gonzales v. Roman Catholic Archbishop* (1929), the Court followed *Bouldin*'s principle that such matters were beyond its competence. Raul Gonzalez sought appointment to a Roman Catholic chaplaincy in the Philippines (and the salary that came with it). The archbishop refused the appointment because Gonzalez was not a priest (and was in fact only ten years old when presented for appointment). This led to a lawsuit to determine whether Gonzalez was "legally entitled to be appointed the chaplain."[24] Gonzalez claimed that the chaplaincy was governed by canon law in place in 1820, when the will establishing the chaplaincy was probated; it would have permitted a layperson to be appointed to the position. The archbishop countered that the code of canon law of 1917 governed, and that it disallowed someone so young and someone who was not a cleric from such an appointment. The Supreme Court held that it was compelled to accept the decision of the archbishop:

> Because the appointment is a canonical act, it is the function of the church authorities to determine what the essential qualifications of a chaplain are and whether the candidate possesses them. In the absence of fraud, collusion, or arbitrariness, the decisions of the proper church tribunals on matters purely ecclesiastical, although affecting civil rights, are accepted in litigation before the secular courts as conclusive, because the parties in interest made them so by contract or otherwise.[25]

While this key language of "fraud, collusion, or arbitrariness" left the door open for some judicial second-guessing in later cases, in *Gonzales* the Court held that the archbishop's decision must be upheld.

After the religion clauses were incorporated against the states in the 1940s, the Supreme Court converted its earlier holdings on internal church disputes from federal common law to constitutional law. In *Kedroff v. Saint Nicholas Cathedral* (1952),

the Court held that the highest locus of authority as designated by the church structure itself should be followed, even if that authority was foreign. *Kedroff* was striking
in this regard for it involved disputed claims to the archbishop's seat of New York's
St. Nicholas Cathedral, which was affiliated with the Russian Orthodox Church,
governed by the Patriarch in Moscow. Despite New York's stated worries that the
Russian Orthodox Church leadership might well be corrupted by Cold War politics,
the Court nonetheless upheld the internal decision-making of the church (and consequently the right to possess the cathedral itself) by siding with the foreign leadership of the hierarchical Russian Orthodox Church. In so doing, the Court struck
down a New York religious corporation law that would have rejected the authority
of the Moscow patriarch. Justice Reed declared for the Court that a key issue was
that the "controversy concerning the right to use St. Nicholas Cathedral is strictly a
matter of ecclesiastical government." Such a finding rendered the civil courts pow-
erless to interfere in internal church decision making. Justice Reed continued:

> Here [New York's legislature has attempted to] transfer by statute control over
> churches. This violates our rule of separation between church and state. . . . [It also
> violates] a spirit of freedom for religious organizations, an independence from secular
> control or manipulation, in short, power to decide for themselves, free from state in-
> terference, matters of church government as well as those of faith and doctrine. Free-
> dom to select the clergy, where no improper methods of choice are proven, we think,
> must now be said to have federal constitutional protection as a part of the free exercise
> of religion against state interference.[26]

Kedroff thus converted *Watson* into a constitutional principle that religious organizations, by virtue of the free exercise clause, possess a freestanding "independence from secular control or manipulation" and retain the "power to decide for
themselves, free from state interference, matters of church government as well as
those of faith and doctrine." *Kedroff* held to this principle even when it resulted in
the selection of an archbishop and therefore effectuated the transfer and control of
property (the cathedral, or literally the seat of power for the Russian Orthodox
Church in the United States).

Despite the Supreme Court's insistence on the constitutional impermissibility
of judicial interpretation of religious doctrines, some state courts retained vestiges
of the old common law departure-from-doctrine test in property disputes. This doctrine, with a centuries-old pedigree, required a civil court to investigate a dispute
by looking to see which of the competing factions was adhering to older doctrine.
The group that had departed from the older doctrine would then lose. In 1969 the
Court overruled the Georgia Supreme Court in *Presbyterian Church v. Hull Church*
and held directly that the "departure-from-doctrine" standard was unconstitutional.

Hull involved a faction in a local church that was upset about the ordination of
women and some liberal social positions (including membership in the National
Council of Churches). A majority of the local church voted to renounce their affiliation
with the general church and form their own autonomous Presbyterian organization.

Because the Presbyterian Church is hierarchical, though, it was problematic that the "local churchmen made no effort to appeal the Commission's action [of taking over the property for the general church] to higher church tribunals" but instead filed lawsuits. Justice Brennan, for a unanimous Court, categorically rejected further use of the departure-from-doctrine standard in state court proceedings. Justice Brennan held that *Watson v. Jones* had a "clear constitutional ring" and logically led to the conclusion that "civil courts [have] *no* role in determining ecclesiastical questions in the process of resolving property disputes." He continued:

> [T]he First Amendment severely circumscribes the role that civil courts may play in resolving church property disputes. . . . First Amendment values are plainly jeopardized when church property litigation is made to turn on the resolution by civil courts of controversies over religious doctrine and practice. If civil courts undertake to resolve such controversies in order to adjudicate the property dispute, the hazards are ever present of inhibiting the free development of religious doctrine and of implicating secular interests in matters of purely ecclesiastical concern.[27]

Accordingly, the Court seemingly buried the departure-from-doctrine test by holding that it could play "*no* role in any future judicial proceedings." Marginal judicial review per *Gonzalez* was permitted for fraud, arbitrariness, or collusion; deeper judicial investigation was not.

But hidden within *Hull*'s strong discursus on deference to religious tribunals was a carve-out. The Court allowed that not every case involving church property implicated the First Amendment and claimed that "neutral principles of law" could at times be applied in such disputes without constitutional problems. But it did not spell out the contours of that approach. This left an opening for the Georgia Supreme Court, on remand, effectively to ignore the denomination's authority to supervise the local church. The Georgia court instead determined, ostensibly without deciding any questions of religious doctrine, that the property should go to the local church because the deeds were in the name of the local church. The Supreme Court denied certiorari, leading to the anomalous result that the national denomination won a convincing rhetorical victory in the Supreme Court but ultimately lost the case.[28] A similar result occurred in *Maryland and Virginia Eldership of Churches of God v. Church of God at Sharpsburg* (1969), in which the Supreme Court remanded a church property case to a Maryland state court for reconsideration in light of the *Hull* decision. There too the state court awarded the property to the (dissident) local churches rather than the larger denomination. The Supreme Court refused to revisit that Maryland state court determination, since it "involved no inquiry into religious doctrine."[29]

The strength of the *Gonzalez* exception (permitting marginal judicial review of religious decisions) was tested seven years after *Hull* in *Serbian Orthodox Diocese v. Milivojevich* (1976). In that case, the Court overturned the Illinois Supreme Court, which had held that the Serbian Orthodox Church in Belgrade, Yugoslavia, had wrongly suspended and defrocked Bishop Milivojevich. The Serbian Orthodox

Church had become involved in a dispute with Milivojevich, and the church eventually redrew and reorganized his diocese. Milivojevich was upset and purportedly withdrew his diocese from the church; the church countered by defrocking him, dividing his diocese into three parts, and appointing new bishops in his stead. In the ensuing litigation to determine the identity of the true bishop (or bishops), Milivojevich claimed that the church had failed to follow its own internal rules in defrocking him and had followed an "arbitrary" procedure in contravention of *Gonzales*.

Justice Brennan again spoke for the Court and wrote off the "fraud, collusion, or arbitrariness" exception of *Gonzales* as "dictum only" to the rule of *Watson*. There is no room for an "'arbitrariness' exception—in the sense of an inquiry whether the decisions of the highest ecclesiastical tribunal of a hierarchical church complied with church laws and regulations" in a constitutional inquiry, for "this is exactly the inquiry that the First Amendment prohibits." He continued:

> [W]here the resolution of [such] disputes cannot be made without extensive inquiry by civil courts into religious law and polity, the First and Fourteenth Amendments mandate that civil courts shall not disturb the highest ecclesiastical tribunal within a church of hierarchical polity, but must accept such decisions as binding on them, in their application to the religious issues of doctrine or polity before them. . . . [T]his case essentially involves not a church property dispute, but a religious dispute the resolution of which under our cases is for ecclesiastical and not civil tribunals.[30]

As this last excerpt indicates, however, the Court's strong statement on deference to internal church affairs in *Milivojevich* was accompanied by an acknowledgment that there might be cases (of church property disputes or the like) that could still be reviewed by civil courts. Indeed, Justice Rehnquist, dissenting in *Milivojevich*, noted that "blind deference" was neither "counseled by logic nor by the First Amendment." Instead, looking to *Hull* and *Sharpsburg*, he insisted that if lower courts decided matters on "neutral principles of law consistent with the decisions of this Court" then the Constitution was not violated.[31]

Neutral Principles (1979–)

Three years later, in *Jones v. Wolf* (1979), another Georgia case came to the Supreme Court. The local church in Vineville, Georgia, was a member of the Presbyterian Church of the United States (PCUS), which had a hierarchical form of church governance (although it could more rightly be said to be presbyterian rather than strictly hierarchical). A majority of local church members voted to disaffiliate from the PCUS and instead affiliate with the Presbyterian Church of America (PCA). The minority group in the local church ceased to attend and conducted its religious activities elsewhere. Meanwhile, a commission from the PCUS investigated the dispute and determined that the minority faction was "the true congregation of the Vineville Presbyterian Church." The majority faction did not participate in the commission's investigation and did not appeal its decision to a higher tribunal within the PCUS.

On the strength of this internal denominational determination, the minority faction of the local church sued in state court to establish their exclusive right to possess and use the property. The Georgia courts held for the majority of the local church (and thus against the ruling of the national denomination) by applying a "neutral principles of law" approach. Eschewing an "implied trust" theory, which Georgia courts believed to be outlawed by *Hull*, the Georgia courts looked first to see if the governing documents provided for an express trust of church property and, if not, looked to the ownership of legal title. The lower court examined "the deeds to the properties, the state statutes dealing with implied trusts, and the Book of Church Order to determine if there was any basis for a trust in favor of the general [nonlocal] church." Finding nothing, the court awarded the property to the breakaway majority group on the basis of the legal property deeds.

The Supreme Court was deeply divided. Writing for the 5–4 majority, Justice Blackmun found that Georgia's method of resolving the dispute was constitutionally permitted. While acknowledging that "the First Amendment severely circumscribes the role of civil courts in resolving church property disputes," the Constitution "does not dictate that a State follow a particular method of resolving church disputes." Indeed, a state could adopt any one of various approaches for settling church property disputes so long as it did not require civil court resolution of religious doctrine or practice and so long as it deferred to the resolution of issues of religious doctrine or polity by the highest court of a hierarchical church organization. Georgia's "neutral principles" approach "is consistent with the foregoing constitutional principles," the Court held:

> The primary advantages of the neutral principles approach are that it is completely secular in operation, and yet flexible enough to accommodate all forms of religious organization and polity. The method relies exclusively on objective, well-established concepts of trust and property law familiar to lawyers and judges.[32]

In dissent, Justice Powell was confused why the majority engaged in such hairsplitting. In particular, it seemed odd to juxtapose language about the requirement to defer to the highest church authority in matters of church polity and doctrine and then immediately affirm a state court holding counter to the determination of a church tribunal. Justice Powell and three colleagues thought instead that this case was just like *Watson*: the church had authority under its governing documents to resolve the dispute and had done so. The problem, in the dissent's eyes, was that the Court misunderstood the question presented. The question was not ownership of property, for the deeds were in fact clear that the "Vineville Presbyterian Church, or its trustees" were the legal owner. The question was *which faction* constituted the Vineville Presbyterian Church. Answering that question required understanding church polity and then deferring to an internal decision.

The law after *Jones v. Wolf* is both clear and unclear at the same time. Civil courts may *not* decide matters of disputed doctrine or practice. And civil courts are supposed to defer to the highest body in hierarchical religious bodies regarding the resolution of religious doctrine or polity. But civil courts *are* permitted to use either a neutral principles approach or a stricter deference approach, or any other approach consistent with Supreme Court precedent. The weakness is that rather than focusing on the free exercise right of the religious organization, the Court's sole rule about not deciding matters of religious doctrine seems geared toward protecting the civil courts from becoming entangled in religious affairs.

The Court has thus defined the boundaries in which civil courts may operate rather than first carefully defining the scope of the right possessed by the religious groups themselves. This is unfortunate and lacks some of the robustness envisioned by a full articulation of the early principles of religious liberty. As in other matters of free exercise (pp. 162–163), when religious rights are left to the whims and majorities of the political process they become uncertain at best. When matters of federalism are added, such that different approaches are permissible in different states, there is increasing uncertainty for religious organizations that operate or have members in more than one state. And when the constitutional floor for religious liberty is set too low, unpopular religions may receive less protection than they deserve—and courts may out-think themselves in a neutral principles approach by failing to accord proper respect to the prior consent of adherents in the vein of the nineteenth-century cases. *Jones v. Wolf,* for example, seemed to elide the fact that the Court's determination necessarily passed judgment on internal religious matters under the guise of secular terms.[33] While *Jones* counsels that religious bodies should take care to align their secular legal documents in express terms so that civil courts can properly determine them later, this admirable assumption seems naive. Many religious groups are small, have little access to legal advice in advance (or eschew the same), and do not anticipate having disputes with their coreligionists—people with whom they share their deepest beliefs.

Perhaps we will get more direction from the Supreme Court, since each decade averages over one hundred reported decisions on church property disputes. Churches in Georgia, California, Virginia, and elsewhere continue to make headlines by diverging from their national denominations, with current issues focusing on the ordination of homosexuals in leadership positions.[34] In one such case, the majority of parishioners at the oldest Episcopal church in Georgia (Christ Church in Savannah) voted to withdraw from the national church, but the historic church building and the attendant endowment are now the subject of litigation.[35] Because of the relative lack of constitutional uniformity and the lack of First Amendment robustness for religious organizations, the resolution of this and other cases will continue to turn on state law principles as well as constitutional ones—and outcomes may vary significantly depending on where an action is brought.

Employment, Taxation, and More

The lack of definition of the rights of religious organizations qua religious organizations leads to difficulties in a number of other areas besides church property. The most pressing of these cases involve disputes within the employment context, questions about how and when religious organizations can partner with the government in providing social services, and whether a government may or must grant tax benefits. Beyond these are a host of frontier issues involving the interaction of government and religious organizations.

Employment

The church autonomy cases discussed above provide the starting point for decisions concerning employment within and by religious organizations. As we saw earlier, the Supreme Court stated in *Gonzalez v. Roman Catholic Archbishop* (1929) that it would not intervene in a dispute about an internal church position. Doing so would run counter to the principle that civil courts must defer to matters of religious doctrine, polity, and practice. A similar notion was at work in *Kedroff v. Saint Nicholas Cathedral* (1952), where the Court was asked to decide use of the cathedral—but doing so would force the Court to decide who was the rightful bishop of that cathedral. So too in *Serbian Orthodox Diocese v. Milivojevich* (1976), when the Court refused to second-guess a decision of the hierarchical church leadership to appoint (or defrock) bishops of its own choosing. The constitutional principle that religious organizations are entitled to manage their own internal affairs (including employment) without governmental interference won the day, even against claims that the church failed to follow its own internal policy for decision making. The civil court simply could not and should not second-guess such employment decisions.

A more difficult question, at times, is whether antidiscrimination provisions apply directly to religious employers. Typically courts have read a "ministerial exception" into civil rights statutes, especially when they apply to claims brought against houses of worship by ordained ministers.[36] But when the employer is not directly a house of worship but is rather an affiliated religious organization (a teacher at a religious school, a secretary at a religious publishing house, or ministers on the staff of a religious university), lower courts have not been as uniformly solicitous of religious claims to autonomy. This does not mean such employers do not have a First Amendment right to be free from judicial interference, but the Supreme Court has not given clear guidance on this matter. The closest case is *National Labor Relations Board v. Catholic Bishop of Chicago* (1979), where the Court was asked to decide whether the National Labor Relations Act (NLRA) was properly applied to teachers in religious schools. For the purpose of collective bargaining and filing labor complaints, the National Labor Relations Board certified unions for lay teachers in religious schools, claiming authority to do so under the NLRA. The religious schools resisted, claiming a right to be free from such interference in their affairs. On appeal, the Court agreed with the schools, holding that serious constitutional questions would arise if it read the NLRA as granting jurisdiction to the board:

> [I]n the absence of a clear expression of Congress' intent to bring teachers in church-operated schools within the jurisdiction of the Board, we decline to construe the Act in a manner that could in turn call upon the Court to resolve difficult and sensitive questions arising out of the guarantees of the First Amendment Religion Clauses.[37]

While not ruling on whether Congress could have regulated religious schools in this way, the result reiterates the Court's inclination to protect the autonomy of religious organizations generally.

In addition to the constitutional guarantees in employment cases, legislatures often exempt religious employers from civil rights laws in hiring. The best-known of these is the federal exemption (section 702) of Title VII of the Civil Rights Act of 1964. This "ministerial exemption" provision, added by amendment in 1972, states that the federal provisions prohibiting discrimination on the basis of religion do not apply to "any religious corporation, association, educational institution, or society" who hire employees of a particular religion to perform work connected with the activities of the group. The ministerial exemption potentially has wide reach, especially when expanded to noncore functions of a religion.

The statutory exemption was challenged and upheld in the 1987 case of *Presiding Bishop v. Amos,* which held that the establishment clause does not forbid the legislature from allowing religious entities the right to hire exclusively members of their own faith for both secular and religious jobs. In *Amos,* a worker was dismissed from his position as a "building engineer" for a subunit of the local Latter-Day Saints Church because he was not deemed qualified to be a member of that church. After first assuming without deciding that the original, unamended exemption which exempted only religious employees and not secular employees was constitutionally valid, Justice White wrote for the Court that Congress was permitted to exempt "secular nonprofit activities of religious organizations" from Title VII as well. It was not a violation of the "no establishment" principle, per the tripartite *Lemon* test, for Congress to give more protection to religious employers than might otherwise be required by the constitution. Such "benevolent neutrality" did not devolve into an "unlawful fostering of religion" and was therefore permissible.[38]

In short, religious organizations have a right to make significant employment decisions without government interference. This right is at its strongest when the organization is a house of worship and the decisions directly involve theological or ecclesiastical matters concerning leadership of the organization. The claims become weaker as the organization becomes removed from the core mission of the religion and as the employees are less obviously carrying out religious tasks for the organization. Even so, the very questions of how attenuated the organization is or what role the employee is performing often raise doctrinal or theological questions and tend to be quite thorny for courts and religious employers alike. The overlay of statutory protections helps somewhat but can raise its own questions of interpretation.

Social Services

In recent years the question of the extent to which government may partner with religious organizations in providing social services has become increasingly important. Governments have long partnered with religiously affiliated hospitals and, with more hesitation, with religious organizations involved in adoption services. But the Supreme Court's decisions opposing funding to religious schools loomed so large that houses of worship and schools with strong religious connections were excluded from sharing in government funds. In recent years, however, the tide has turned strongly, prompting Professors Lupu and Tuttle to proclaim that some current initiatives "would have been constitutionally unthinkable thirty years ago."[39]

A significant foundation for such cooperation was laid in *Bowen v. Kendrick* (1988). *Bowen* involved a challenge to the Adolescent Family Life Act (AFLA), which authorized federal funding to public or nonprofit organizations, including religious organizations, for services and research about adolescent premarital sexual relations and teen pregnancy. A group of taxpayers sued, claiming that AFLA violated the establishment clause. The Supreme Court held that AFLA was not facially infirm. Walking through the familiar *Lemon* test, the Court held that AFLA was motivated by a legitimate secular legislative purpose (preventing teen pregnancy), did not have the primary purpose of advancing religion (since the act was neutral and any effects were incidental), and did not create an unconstitutional entanglement (since any monitoring would not unduly involve government in the day-to-day affairs). The Court added:

> [T]his Court has never held that religious institutions are disabled by the First Amendment from participating in publicly sponsored social welfare programs. To the contrary, in *Bradfield v. Roberts* (1899) the Court upheld an agreement between the Commissioners of the District of Columbia and a religiously affiliated hospital whereby the Federal Government would pay for the construction of a new building on the grounds of the hospital. In effect, the Court refused to hold that the mere fact that the hospital was "conducted under the auspices of the Roman Catholic Church" was sufficient to alter the purely secular legal character of the corporation. . . .[40]

Congress could therefore constitutionally set up a structure in which funding could flow to religious institutions as well as other civic organizations.

This principle is bounded, though, by *Larkin v. Grendel's Den* (1982), which holds firmly that a government may not cede its governmental function to a religious organization by delegating decisional power. *Larkin* involved a statute that effectively granted veto power to local churches over the issuance of a liquor license to a business within five hundred feet of their property. When a local church objected to such a license, the affected restaurant brought suit and claimed that the statute violated the establishment clause. The Supreme Court agreed, citing *Watson v. Jones* for the notion that government and religious organizations cannot be coextensive: "As [*Watson*] and other cases make clear, the core rationale underlying the Establishment Clause is preventing a 'fusion of governmental and religious functions.'" This kind of entanglement is unconstitutional.[41]

Working within these precedents, the legislative and executive branches have recently been expanding the collaboration between religious-based organizations and government. In 1996 Congress built an expanded role for religious organizations into its welfare reform bill in what is commonly thought of as "Charitable Choice"

provisions. President Bush expanded these partnerships in important ways and established a White House Office of Faith-Based and Community Initiatives. The
purpose of this office was to remove barriers to religious organizations' ability to
participate in federally funded social welfare programs.[42] President Bush's program
faced a legal challenge under the establishment clause, but that was dismissed on
standing grounds by the Supreme Court in *Hein v. Freedom from Religion Foundation* (2007). Thus in light of the current political popularity of the idea of government partnership with faith-based organizations, and via the indirect precedents of
Zelman v. Simmons-Harris (2002) and *Locke v. Davey* (2004) which permit some
governmental funding of religious institutions on an indirect and neutral basis, President Obama has set up a similar White House office. Likely we will continue to
see an evolution and perhaps expansion of governmental partnership with religious
organizations in social services, although some important issues—not least whether
groups may discriminate in hiring if they are receiving government funding—
remain contested.

Taxation

While it is plausible to contend that religious organizations have a constitutional
right to be exempt from taxation, the standard treatment is that exemptions are permissible but not required. Exemptions are neither constitutionally mandated by the
free exercise clause nor constitutionally forbidden by the establishment clause.

Generally speaking, religious organizations are exempt from taxation. Such exemptions are delineated by state and federal statutes, and have gathered support from
history and case law. [43] In *Walz v. Tax Commission* (1970), the leading case, the Court
held that a state statute exempting religious property from taxes did not violate the
establishment clause. Although granting an exemption could be said to amount to
state support (since other taxpayers would have to pay more), the Court was unimpressed with such an argument. A host of historical examples of state and federal tax
exemptions supported upholding a tax exemption for religious organizations, the
Court reasoned. But in *Texas Monthly v. Bullock* (1989), a plurality of the justices
reasoned that a statute conferring tax exemption on the distribution of religious literature without conferring a similar benefit on the distribution of nonreligious literature did violate the establishment clause. And in *Jimmy Swaggart Ministries v. State
Board of Equalization of California* (1990), the Court held that a state is not compelled to confer exemption from a minimal sales and use tax on the distribution of
religious literature; a tax on the sale of religious articles was not a "prior restraint."

This line of cases, with strong support for religious tax exemptions but on a
nonexclusive and even nonmandatory basis in some circumstances, suggests that legislatures have ample room to make decisions regarding taxation. The Court has not
completely dismissed the notion that some free exercise rights attach to tax exemption, but neither has it plainly spelled out these rights. In general, the Court has
left leeway to the legislative and executive branches to sift through the contours of

exemption. The most prominent case in this regard is *Bob Jones University v. United States* (1983), in which a conservative Christian university challenged the revocation of its tax-exempt status. In 1970 the Internal Revenue Service concluded that it could no longer legally justify granting tax-exempt status under section 501(c)(3) to private religious schools that practiced racial discrimination. The IRS notified Bob Jones University of its change in policy in late 1970, announcing its intention to remove the university's tax-exempt status because of racial discrimination in admissions. Until 1971, Bob Jones University completely excluded African Americans; from 1971 to 1975 the university accepted African American applicants only if they were married to another African American. This stemmed from the university's religious belief that interracial dating and marriage were wrong. The university sued the IRS.

Chief Justice Burger, writing for the Court, held that the IRS had the authority and ability (if not the mandate) to revoke the university's tax-exempt status:

> [A] declaration that a given institution is not "charitable" [and therefore not able to have tax-exempt status] should be made only where there can be no doubt that the activity involved is contrary to a fundamental public policy. But there can no longer be any doubt that racial discrimination in education violates deeply and widely accepted views of elementary justice. . . . Racially discriminatory educational institutions cannot be viewed as conferring a public benefit within the "charitable concept" . . . or with the Congressional intent underlying § 170 and § 501(c)(3).

The *Bob Jones* Court also gave short shrift to the university's free exercise claim. Specifically, the Court cited *United States v. Lee* (1982), an earlier tax case, for the proposition that some burdens on free exercise rights were permitted by the Constitution, so long as the state could justify the burden "by showing that it is essential to accomplish an overriding governmental interest" (p. 156). The Court did not contend that the university had no free exercise rights, but rather applied strict scrutiny to the facts and found that the government interest of eradicating racial discrimination in education was compelling and that no "less restrictive means" were available to achieve that governmental interest. The university could choose to forgo state benefits and still practice its religious beliefs, but the Court found that society's commitment to a racial nondiscrimination norm trumped the organization's religious beliefs and practice.[44] Whether other norms could be enforced in similar ways by the state is an open question. But it seems possible that issues of same-sex marriage may blossom into controversies akin to *Bob Jones* since most of the tax exemption cases rest on legislative grace rather than deep-seated constitutional principles.[45]

Frontier Issues

Just as issues of same-sex marriage may implicate the line of tax cases, issues of marriage and divorce raise fundamental questions about the scope of authority of religious organizations and the civil state. The propriety of allowing religious tribunals some amount of jurisdiction over family law has received public discussion and debate in

Canada and the United Kingdom (including commentary by the archbishop of Canterbury). While this notion has not yet garnered widespread support in the United States, there are already interesting examples of cooperation between religion and the state on family law matters via "covenant marriage statutes" and a statute that specifically affects Jewish divorces in New York. Some have called for religious organizations to exercise greater autonomy over marriage and divorce, since it is historically and currently a quintessential area where religion and the civil state each claim jurisdiction and authority. Such issues, including the appropriate role of religious organizations in the formation and dissolution of marriages, are likely to increase.[46]

In the past decade or so, issues of civil and criminal liability for religious organizations have come to the fore, most prominently in cases involving sexual abuse and the Catholic Church. There is no uniform treatment of these cases in the law, as they often touch on sensitive issues of state law, including respondeat superior liability, clergy/penitent privilege, breach of fiduciary duty, child protection laws, and others. They also frequently involve principles of religious organization, theology (e.g., notions of forgiveness), and prudential and constitutional concerns about the role of state intervention in matters that occur within a religious organization.[47] Clearly, the extent to which a court views a religious organization as hierarchical and grants the national organization control over local property affects the likelihood that a court would hold it liable for bad acts committed by employees in specific locales under doctrines of respondeat superior. While some consider this a desirable public policy outcome,[48] it seems odd for that outcome to be dictated by a line of church property cases rather than by independent analysis.

Other issues require attention as well. The interaction of the state and religious schools is treated at some length in Chapter 9 (pp. 207–222). Debates about immigration and the role of religious organizations in that debate—by taking outspoken policy positions or tangible actions—highlight the importance of giving serious consideration to the corporate activity and collective voice of believers. The propriety of discrimination by or within religious organizations arises regularly; several lower federal courts have sustained provisions in the federal Fair Housing Act that allow religious organizations to favor their coreligionists and state laws that allow religious schools and charities to favor their own coreligionist pupils and patrons. And the involvement of religious organizations in government affairs (via direct or indirect lobbying, educating its members, or supporting particular candidates or positions) raises a host of questions, including whether the organization may keep its tax-exempt status and also whether the Constitution permits or contemplates such activity.

Summary and Conclusions

The free exercise of religion principle is not restricted to individuals. Properly understood, it also extends to religious organizations and entities. America's own experience, ideals, and history underscore this—and, as we shall see in the following chapter, international norms strongly recognize that religious groups have rights *as groups*. Too often the concept of separation of church and state has been invoked to support the notion that religious entities, individuals, and norms have no place in the public sphere. A more accurate historical understanding of the phrase illuminates another aspect: that religious entities have the right to be free from undue government influence, control, and interference in their internal activities. When religious organizations choose to participate in governmental benefits, they should be allowed to do so equally. When they choose to assist in providing social services, they should be allowed to do so fairly but on their own terms (provided they accord with basic norms of civil society). When they resort to civil courts for resolution of internal disputes, their internal decisions about internal matters should be respected. This is a challenging arena, but courts and commentators alike must refocus their attention on religious organizations in modern society and continue to craft coherent theories that respect state and church alike.

Notes

1. 397 U.S. 664, 669 (1970).

2. See Robert K. Vischer, *Conscience and the Common Good* (2010).

3. Kathleen A. Brady, "Religious Organizations and Free Exercise: The Surprising Lessons of *Smith*," *Brigham Young University Law Review* 2004: 1633, 1676–1677.

4. Douglas Laycock, "Towards a General Theory of the Religion Clauses: The Case of Church Labor Relations and the Right to Church Autonomy," *Columbia Law Review* 81 (1981): 1373, 1389.

5. 530 U.S. 640 (2000).

6. *Pierce v. Society of Sisters*, 268 U.S. 510 (1925); *National Labor Relations Board v. Catholic Bishop of Chicago*, 440 U.S. 490 (1979).

7. Richard W. Garnett, *Two There Are: Understanding the Separation of Church and State* (2010). While this book is in production, the Court is hearing the case of *Christian Legal Society v. Martinez*, which presents a conflict between the associational rights of a religious student group in setting their own terms of membership and leadership and a state law school's interest in promoting nondiscrimination norms concerning sexual orientation. (*Cert. granted*, 130 S.Ct. 795 (December 7, 2009))

8. For thorough overviews, see William Bassett, *Religious Organizations and the Law* (1998 with updates); James A. Serritella et al., eds., *Religious Organizations in the United States: A Study of Identity, Liberty, and Law* (2006).

9. See Martin E. Marty and James A. Serritella, "Religious Polity," in Serritella, ed., *Religious Organizations*, 85.

10. *Kedroff v. St. Nicholas Cathedral*, 344 U.S. 94, 110 (1952); see also *Watson v. Jones*, 80 U.S. (13 Wall.) 679, 722–727 (1871).

11. See DePaul University Center 1994 Survey of Religious Organizations at the National Level, with results in Rhys H. Williams and John P.N. Massad, "Religious Diversity, Civil Law, and Institutional Isomorphism," in Serritella, ed., *Religious Organizations*, 111, 118.

12. See Virginia Constitution Art. IV, Sec. 14 and West Virginia Constitution Art VI, Sec. 47.

13. See McKinney's *Consolidated Laws of New York*, bk. 50.

14. See Patty Gerstenblith, "Associational Structures of Religious Organizations" in Serritella, ed., *Religious Organizations*, 223; Patricia Carlson, "Unincorporated Associations and Charitable Trusts," in Serritella, ed., *Religious Organizations*, 253; Paul G. Kauper and Stephen C. Ellis, "Religious Corporations and the Law," *Michigan Law Review* 71 (1973): 1499.

15. 13 U.S. (9 Cranch) 43 (1815).

16. See Alice Felt Tyler, *Freedom's Ferment: Phases of American Social History from the Colonial History to the Outbreak of the Civil War* (1962); Yaacov Oved, *Two Hundred Years of American Communes* (1988).

17. 55 U.S. (14 How.) 589 (1852).

18. 60 U.S. (19 How.) 126 (1856).

19. 120 U.S. 377 (1877).

20. 187 U.S. 8 (1902).

21. 234 U.S. 640 (1914).

22. 80 U.S. (13 Wall.) 679, 727–729 (1872).

23. 82 U.S. (15 Wall.) 131, 139–140 (1872); see further Justice Strong's *Two Lectures upon the Relations of Civil Law to Church Polity, Discipline, and Property* (1875).

24. 280 U.S. 1, 11 (1929).

25. 280 U.S. at 16–17.

26. 344 U.S. 94, 110, 116 (1952).

27. 393 U.S. 440, 449 (1969).

28. *Presbyterian Church in United States v. Eastern Heights Presbyterian Church*, 167 S.E.2d 658 (Ga. 1969), cert. denied, 396 U.S. 1041 (1970). See further Patrick J. Schiltz and Douglas Laycock, "Employment in Religious Organizations," in Serritella, ed., *Religious Organizations*, 527, 532–533.

29. 393 U.S. 528 (1969). On remand at 254 A.2d 162 (Md. 1970), appeal dismissed, 396 U.S. 367 (1970).

30. 426 U.S. 696, 713–715, 724–725 (1976). See also Kent Greenawalt, "Hands Off! Civil Court Involvement in Conflicts over Religious Property," *Columbia Law Review* 98 (1998): 1843–1907.

31. *Milivojevich*, 426 U.S. at 733–735 (Rehnquist, J., dissenting).

32. *Jones v. Wolf*, 443 U.S. 595, 603 (1979). See criticism in Douglas Laycock, "Towards a General Theory of the Religion Clauses: The Case of Church Labor Relations and the Right to Church Autonomy," *Columbia Law Review* 81 (1981): 1373–1417.

33. "This reluctance to identify the highest church authority [in *Jones v. Wolf*] undermined the Court's commitment to defer when interpretation of church documents raised religious controversies; touting the avoidance of religious controversies as the advantage of neutral principals encouraged courts to interpret church documents in ways that raised no religious controversies and made secular language and secular rules dispositive. The result was a powerful incentive to define church disputes in secular terms, to ignore any underlying disputes, and by ignoring them, to pretend not to have resolved them." Schiltz and Laycock, "Employment in Religious Organizations," 537.

34. See Jeffrey B. Hassler, "A Multitude of Sins? Constitutional Standards on Legal Resolution of Church Property Disputes in a Time of Escalating Intradenominational Strife," *Pepperdine Law Review* 35 (2008): 399–457.

35. See Brenda Goodman, "A Church Is Divided, and Headed for Court," *New York Times,* December 5, 2007. In October 2009 the trial court ruled in favor of the larger church, and local members have appealed to the Georgia Supreme Court. www.ccesavannah.org/main/about-christ-church/legal-proceedings. For history of Christ Church, see Joel A. Nichols, "Religious Liberty in the Thirteenth Colony: Church-State Relations in Colonial and Early National Georgia," *NYU Law Review* 80 (2005): 1693.

36. See, e.g., *McClure v. Salvation Army,* 460 F.2d 552 (5th Cir. 1973).

37. 440 U.S. 490, 507 (1979).

38. 483 U.S. 327 (1987).

39. Ira C. Lupu and Robert W. Tuttle, "The Faith-Based Initiative and the Constitution," *DePaul Law Review* 55 (2005): 1–118, 4.

40. 487 U.S. 589, 609 (1988).

41. 459 U.S. 116, 126–127 (1982), quoting *Abingdon v. Schempp,* 374 U.S. 203, 222 (1963).

42. See discussion in Lupu and Tuttle, "The Faith-Based Initiative." See also David J. Wright, *Taking Stock: The Bush Faith-Based Initiative and What Lies Ahead,* The Roundtable on Religion and Social Welfare Policy (2009), www.religionandsocialpolicy.org/final_report/full_report_060809.pdf.

43. John Witte, Jr., "Tax Exemption of Religious Property: Religious Anomaly or Valid Constitutional Practice?" *Southern California Law Review* 92 (1991): 363. See also the discussion and analysis in Chapter 9 of the first edition of this volume.

44. 461 U.S. 574, 592, 595–596, 604 (1983).

45. See Douglas Laycock et al., eds., *Same Sex Marriage and Religious Liberty: Emerging Conflicts* (2008).

46. See generally Joel A. Nichols, ed., *Marriage and Divorce in a Multi-Cultural Context: Multi-Tiered Marriage and the Boundaries of Civil Law and Religion* (2010).

47. For an analysis of some of these issues, see *Roman Catholic Diocese of Jackson v. Morrison,* 905 So.2d 1213 (Miss. 2005) (en banc).

48. See Marci A. Hamilton, *Justice Denied: What America Must Do to Protect Its Children* (2008).

12

Toward an Integration of Religious Liberty

The American Experiment in International Context

As we have seen in the last five chapters, the Supreme Court's jurisprudence has seemed meandering at times. It has vacillated between granting free exercise exemptions from generally applicable laws and refraining from crafting such exceptions. It has upheld some public religious monuments and struck down others. It has disallowed some funding for religious schools and allowed other funding. It has refused to intervene in some internal church disputes and rendered decisions in other cases that seem to run counter to internal church authority.

The ample vacillations and variations in the Supreme Court's First Amendment cases can be explained, in part, on factual grounds. The application of a sixteen-word guarantee to dozens of diverse and complex issues over the course of a century and more has inevitably led to conflicting decisions. "The life of the law has not been logic: it has been experience," Oliver Wendell Holmes reminds us. The American law of religious rights and liberties is no exception. And to a lesser extent, personnel changes on the Court over the years have shaped the interpretation and application of the First Amendment.

These vacillations, however, also betray the Court's failure to develop a coherent framework for interpreting and applying the First Amendment. The Court has tended to rely too heavily on mechanical tests of free exercise and establishment and to use these tests as substitutes for legal analysis rather than as guides to it. The Court has tended to pit the establishment and free exercise clauses against each other rather than treating them as twin guarantees of religious rights and liberties. The Court has been too eager to reduce the religion clauses to one or two principles rather than exploring the range of interlocking first principles of the American experiment. The accumulation of these interpretive shortcomings, particularly in the past three decades, has brought the American experiment to a state of acute crisis—both of law and of faith in the law.

The Court needs to develop a more integrated approach to First Amendment questions that incorporates the first principles of religious rights and liberties on which the American experiment was founded and integrates them into the resolution of specific cases. Such a framework is easy enough to draw up on the blackboard or in the pages of a treatise—and a number of important integrative methodologies and frameworks have been offered of late. In the context of the ongoing constitutional experiment in religious liberty—with the thickly entangled work of federal and state courts and legislatures—deliberate and provisional steps are essential to reaching any type of coherent new framework or methodology. There is ample wisdom in Justice O'Connor's caveat in *Kiryas Joel Village School District v. Grumet* (1994):

> It is always appealing to look for a single test, a Grand Unified Theory that would resolve all the cases that may arise under a particular [First Amendment] clause. . . . But the same constitutional principle may operate very differently in different contexts. . . . And setting forth a unitary test for a broad set of cases may sometimes do more harm than good. Any test that must deal with widely disparate situations risks being so vague as to be useless. . . . I think a less unitary approach provides a better structure for analysis. If each test covers a narrower and more homogeneous area, the tests may be more precise and therefore easier to apply. . . . Perhaps eventually under this structure we may indeed distill a unified, or at least a more unified [approach].[1]

Whatever interim steps are taken, the Supreme Court—with the help of Congress, the states, and the academy—must strive for this "more unified approach." Such an approach might come in a variety of forms—in another grand synthetic case in the series of *Watson, Cantwell, Everson, Sherbert,* and *Lemon,* or through comprehensive restatements, congressional statutes, or even another constitutional amendment on religious rights and liberties.

Any integrative approach to the First Amendment must begin with the text and then embrace "the long standing traditions of our people," as Justice Scalia urged in response to Justice O'Connor in *Kiryas Joel.*[2] We believe these traditions are best captured in the role of "essential rights and liberties" first incorporated into the First Amendment. Indeed, the task of this volume has been, in part, to lay out some of the rich resources of this American tradition, both in its genesis and its exodus, which can be profitably drawn into a more integrated understanding of religious liberty today.

An integrative approach to the First Amendment should also consider the emerging traditions of other people. The way of integration is not only the way of the past, the original intent of the eighteenth-century founders of the American experiment. It is also the way of the future, the intent of the emerging world system of law and human rights, in which American law has played and must continue to play a vital part.

Resort to international legal and human rights norms of religious liberty might seem a rather unpromising path to developing a more integrated American constitutional law of religious liberty. Americans are better at exporting their constitutional ideas and institutions than importing those of other peoples, and the canon of applicable international human rights norms that has developed slowly and sporadically since World War II does not often have binding legal effect on the United States. Moreover, there remains political resistance to departing from American exceptionalism.

To keep this parochial veil drawn shut, however, is to deprive the American experiment of a rich source of instruction and inspiration. Comparative legal analysis is always edifying—if for no other reason than to have confirmation, from a fresh perspective, of the validity and utility of one's own legal norms and practices and to gain an idea or two about reforming them.[3] But especially at this time of transition, if not turmoil, in First Amendment law, comparative legal analysis is particularly necessary and salutary.

Several principles and teachings of international human rights help to confirm, refine, and integrate prevailing First Amendment principles and cases. For example, the prioritizing of the principles of liberty of conscience, free exercise, and religious equality in international human rights instruments suggests a prototype for the integration of American free exercise and disestablishment values. The insistence of international human rights instruments that state abridgments of religious rights and liberties be both "necessary" and "proportionate" confirms the strict scrutiny test of American free exercise jurisprudence—demanding both a "compelling state interest" (necessity) and the "least restrictive alternative" of achieving that interest (proportionality). The heavy emphasis on group religious rights in recent international instruments both confirms the American protection of corporate free exercise rights and one core understanding of the doctrine of separation of church and state. The international doctrine of granting "a margin of appreciation" for local religious and political practices could be put to particularly effective use in our federalist system of government.[4] The international debate over the "universalism versus relativism" of human rights has profound implications for the American debate concerning federal and state jurisdiction over religious rights.[5]

In this chapter, then, we return to the early counsel of Francis Bacon, who commended that we should "compare our experiments" and experiences with those of others who so experiment (pp. xxi–xxii). Just as the founders both imported and exported notions of religious liberty, we believe that the way to a more principled, integrative approach to religious liberty lies in returning to importation as well as exportation. An integrative approach must be not only inward-looking but also outward-looking.

International Norms and the Constitution

The mere suggestion that we Americans should look beyond our own borders, our own experiences, and our own texts for discussions of basic rights like religious liberty elicits jeers in some quarters and cheers in others.[6] The further suggestion that the Supreme Court should participate in such an endeavor invites even more skeptics. As we saw at the recent Senate confirmation hearings for Supreme Court justices, it is politically incorrect—at least in that setting—for prospective justices to admit that they might acknowledge the influence of any sources outside the very text of the Constitution and the law of the United States.

Part of the resurgent interest in "foreign law" or "international law," as it is often called, stems from recent Supreme Court decisions that have explicitly invoked external sources. Critics decry such moves as novel and beyond the pale of acceptable constitutional judicial reasoning. Proponents hail such moves, pointing out historical analogs to such modern judicial reasoning and contending that the give-and-take of legal decision making has room for acknowledging that sources other than the text itself can and often do shape judging. While such debates merit far more pages than remain in this volume, we nonetheless turn to them briefly, and then look more specifically at why international norms are relevant for American religious liberty.

Constitutional Interpretation

The Supreme Court has explicitly looked abroad at foreign authority in a trio of recent cases. In *Atkins v. Virginia* (2002), the Supreme Court held that execution of mentally retarded criminals amounted to "cruel and unusual punishment" and therefore violated the Eighth Amendment. To reach this result, Justice Stevens, writing for the majority, looked to "evolving standards of decency" in interpreting the Constitution and held that the death penalty was "excessive" punishment for mentally retarded defendants. In supporting his claim of community "consensus" about the propriety of a death sentence, he looked primarily to state legislatures that prohibit such punishment for mentally retarded defendants. He particularly raised the ire of the dissenters when he quoted, in a footnote, a brief for the European Union as further support for overturning a jury's imposition of the death penalty for a mentally retarded defendant: "[W]ithin the world community," Justice Stevens wrote, "the imposition of the death penalty for crimes committed by mentally retarded offenders is overwhelmingly disapproved."[7] Justice Scalia, in dissent, was unimpressed: "The Prize for the Court's most Feeble Effort to fabricate 'national consensus' must go to its appeal to . . . members of the so-called 'world community,'" among others. The practices of the "world community" are "irrelevant," Scalia said, for their "notions of justice are (thankfully) not always those of our people." The views of "other nations" simply "cannot be imposed upon Americans," "however enlightened" the Court may think those opinions to be.[8]

In the following term the Court directly referenced foreign law when striking down a state sodomy statute in *Lawrence v. Texas* (2003). In *Lawrence*, Justice Kennedy wrote for the Court and reversed its holding in *Bowers v. Hardwick* (1986), which had upheld the constitutionality of a sodomy law. "The reasoning and holding in *Bowers* have been rejected elsewhere," he wrote. He cited cases from the European Court of Human Rights and noted that these cases were binding in forty-five nations. The values that undergirded the prior case, he reasoned, were not "share[d] with a wider civilization," and this provided additional support to an "emerging awareness" that prohibitions on private sexual conduct of this sort could no longer be upheld.[9] Justice Scalia again dissented, this time decrying all elements of the majority's rationale: he disbelieved that an "emerging awareness" could form the basis for establishing a fundamental right at all, and even more disbelieved that "[c]onstitutional entitlements . . . spring into existence . . . because *foreign nations* decriminalize conduct." He thought reference to and reliance upon what non-Americans did was dicta; it was not only "meaningless" but also "dangerous," for it meant that the Court was imposing "foreign moods" or "fads" on Americans.[10]

The Court again looked externally in *Roper v. Simmons* (2005). Justice Kennedy, for the majority, struck down the application of the death penalty to juveniles. He found that the national consensus and the Court's own judgment deemed that application of the death penalty to minors is disproportionate and therefore impermissible. Justice Kennedy looked expressly to international covenants and other human rights treaties, and to the fact that the United States was outside the norm—indeed "the only country in the world"—in giving official sanction to the death penalty for juveniles, to support his finding of disproportionality. Such an international consensus, "while not controlling our outcome, does provide respected and significant confirmation for our own conclusions," he wrote.[11] Justice O'Connor agreed with this methodology even if not its specific application in the case: "[T]he existence of an international consensus," she noted, "can serve to confirm the reasonableness of a consonant and genuine American consensus."[12] For Justice Scalia, once again in dissent, this was beyond the pale. "[T]he basic premise of the Court's argument—that American law should conform to the laws of the rest of the world—ought to be rejected out of hand," he said. It is "sophistry," not "reasoned decision-making," to apply international norms in some cases, when the norms support one's own predilections, but not in others. (In this regard, he pointed out that the Court had not yet looked to the "views of other countries" to temper its more rigid reading of the establishment clause.) It is for the executive and legislative branches to decide what treaties to ratify and what international instruments to expressly adopt, he claimed; the Court oversteps its bounds when it looks to external norms, even if the result that obtains is salutary.[13]

Unsurprisingly, these cases have generated a wealth of academic and public commentary. The Supreme Court justices have taken their views outside the Court's walls and pressed their positions for and against the use of "foreign law" in public lectures and interviews. Legislators have chimed in, usually by voicing their strong displeasure at the idea of these unelected justices considering anything "un-American" in their decision-making. Politicians exercise the few options remaining to them by giving public political speeches about the impropriety of any judicial interpretation that references "foreign law" (as it is typically called), and by directly questioning all prospective justices about the proper role of foreign law during confirmation hearings.

Not to be outdone, academic authors have penned a burgeoning literature on the use of international and foreign authority, as well as the propriety of the same. Some posit that the Supreme Court and proponents of "constitutional comparativism" are

still "in search of a theory," since the Court's recent uses of foreign authority do not
fit neatly into preexisting constitutional theories. Other writers work hard to provide just such theories.[14] And still others have endeavored to comb the case law for
the historical usage of "foreign law" by the Supreme Court. Perhaps surprisingly to
some modern critics, the practice of referring to foreign law is not new, although it
has increased in recent years. But Justice Scalia's reticence at its use may be somewhat
merited, for historically the Court has cited "foreign law" in some of "the most problematic [cases] in the Court's history," such as the pro-slavery case of *Dred Scott v.
Sandford* (1857) and the anti-polygamy case of *Reynolds v. United States* (1879).[15]

Part of the confusion in this arena comes from failing to distinguish between
"foreign law" and "international law" or neglecting to clarify the reason and rationale for adducing any "foreign authority." It is one thing for the Supreme Court to
analyze an international treaty signed by the president and ratified by the Senate. It
is quite another to cite case law from a foreign jurisdiction that relies on specific foreign law. It is one thing for the Court to look at how foreign courts have interpreted
language in particular international agreements that also bind the United States. It
is quite another for the Court to adopt conclusively language from aspirational international documents that lack enabling legislation. Most modern debates fall between these extremes, but distinctions and clarifications are made too infrequently.
All too quickly matters devolve into an "overly simplistic, all-or-nothing debate in
which policymakers argue the relative merits of so-called 'foreign authority,' but
demonstrate little understanding of what that term means."[16]

"Foreign law" properly refers to positive law enacted by the sovereign of another
nation. "Comparative law" refers to investigating and comparing the laws of two or
more different nations. "International law" may refer to public international law or
private international law, to binding treaties or hortatory pronouncements. It may
have its own accountability regime or leave enforcement to local laws and courts. It
may be of the highest order deriving from natural law or may lack moral suasion at
present. These and other vagaries plague this topic and evade easy discussion, and
even the cases we have seen do not always clarify the issue or explain to what use they
are putting foreign authority. *Atkins*, for example, merely referenced a brief submitted
by the European Union regarding sentiments abroad. *Lawrence* specifically cited case
law from the European Court of Human Rights. And *Roper* looked to the International Covenant on Civil and Political Rights and the Convention on the Rights of
the Child, among others, to bolster its decision. None of these cases pointed to foreign law as dispositive, and they actually used differing foreign authorities in differing
ways. All too often, though, commentators and even justices fail to distinguish
whether they object to the invocation of comparative foreign law, to international
law (including human rights law), or to some combination of the same.

The invocation of any foreign authority, seemingly external to the Constitution,
does present problems—not least of which is an "international countermajoritarian
difficulty," whereby courts, by relying on external norms, may overrule the will of
the people as expressed through their local legislatures.[17] And as Justice Scalia has

famously objected to the use of foreign authority, "We must never forget that it is a Constitution . . . we are expounding."[18] But just as blithe acceptance of the virtues of comparative analysis is naive and unmerited, so too is cavalier dismissal of the possibility of deeper engagement and learning. Merely stating that we are expounding and interpreting a Constitution begs rather than answers the question. How are we to expound and interpret it? What sources are appropriate for that endeavor, and why? If text and history are the starting points, must they be the ending points also? What if text and history do not provide solid answers? And might there be other norms that govern us?

International Religious Liberty

Within this larger debate, the topic of whether and how to use international norms holds particular nuance in the area of religious liberty. To date, the Supreme Court has not issued a First Amendment religious liberty case that explicitly invokes or involves international law or foreign sources. But there is more to commend the Court to look to international norms with regard to religious liberty than with other topics, particularly if the Court focuses on international human rights law and not on comparative foreign law.

First, as the founders believed, every person has the "right" to form his or her own opinions about religion, and the attendant right to act on those beliefs according to the dictates of conscience, as Madison taught. In modern international law, there is little talk of "natural rights" these days—but certainly talk of rights and liberties, both positive and negative, including a notion of *jus cogens*. Rights delineated by international instruments may lack inherent enforcement mechanisms but are pressed on governments by moral suasion with hopes that they will be reified in local law. *Jus cogens*, though, need not be specifically delineated even in local law, for it has peremptory norms of general international law, accepted as binding by the international community of nations. No derogation is permitted from *jus cogens*, and no modification of it is permitted without subsequent consensus from the international community. Prohibitions on genocide, slavery, torture, and piracy traditionally fall within the category of *jus cogens*. The long and deep history of religious liberty, both in the United States and abroad, places it within a category of "rights" that should be reified in American law. And quite arguably, an international norm already exists concerning the right to be free from religious persecution and the right to be free from government interference with one's religious convictions and actions, peaceably held. This would push religious liberty, or at least some of its key components, into the realm of *jus cogens*—in the sense of a liberty that must already be recognized at law without any enabling legislation or other accountability regime needed.

Second, the international norms on religious liberty are—in many ways—the very norms of the American experiment itself. Most of what appears in modern international human rights instruments captures the best of American and other Western constitutional learning on religious liberty and other matters as well. For example, both the Universal Declaration of Human Rights (1948) and the great International Covenants of 1966 encapsulate and elaborate President Franklin Roosevelt's famous "four freedoms" from his 1941 speech: (1) freedom of speech and expression; (2) freedom of "every person to worship God in his own way"; (3) freedom from want; and (4) freedom from fear.[19] As Mary Ann Glendon has shown, Eleanor Roosevelt was indispensable in crafting the modern human rights regime, and other Americans were also involved.[20] More recent international provisions on religious rights were also forged, in no small measure, by the efforts of American politicians, diplomats, jurists, theologians, and activists. To compare First Amendment law with international norms is, in a real sense, to judge American law by an international standard that it helped shape.[21]

We will see that all six principles of religious liberty are prominent in the international instruments—and several principles and teachings of international human rights could help confirm, refine, and integrate prevailing First Amendment religious liberty jurisprudence.

Third, comparing American laws on religious liberty to international norms will help integrate not only American law and international law but also American domestic and foreign policy. Using international norms on religious liberty as a benchmark is not new; our government does this on a regular basis with respect to other countries. Using those same norms to measure U.S. law will merely judge America by the standards that we use to judge other countries. And using those same norms will merely ask the judiciary to work in harmony with the executive and legislative branches, which are already looking to international norms on religious liberty to inform decision making.

Each year, both the U.S. State Department and the Office of International Religious Freedom (an executive branch agency) and the related United States Commission on International Religious Freedom (with appointments made by both executive and congressional branches) issue reports on religious liberty. These reports judge the laws, policies, and activities regarding religion in nations around the world in light of prevailing international norms on religious liberty. This reporting is specifically intended to shape U.S. foreign policy and opinion, and these bodies are charged with making recommendations to Congress and the executive branch on responses, including the imposition of economic sanctions, to countries that fall short of international standards.

The commission and the State Department office, as well as an ambassador at large for religious freedom and an adviser on religious freedom to the National Security Council, were created by the mandate of the International Religious Freedom Act (IRFA) of 1998.[22] Congress passed IRFA largely in response to lobbying from evangelical Christians and their political allies, some of whom seemed odd companions except for their agreement on this key issue. IRFA affirms the importance of religious freedom, as reflected in American history and law and in various international human rights instruments, and it decries the resurgence of religious repression and persecution around the world. IRFA thus has as its professed aim "to condemn violations of religious freedom, and to promote, and to assist other governments in the promotion of, the fundamental right to freedom of religion."

As Jeremy Gunn has said, "With the adoption and implementation of IRFA, the United States has become the [nation] that most visibly promotes the rhetoric of freedom of religion in the international arena."[23] This is admirable and fitting, given the prominent place of religious liberty in America's past and present, in its law and lore. IRFA has produced some tangible and laudable results—and it further commends us to look at home to those same international norms we use when looking abroad.

The International Framework of Religious Liberty

International religious rights and liberties have deep roots in classical Roman law, medieval canon law, and early modern Protestant and Catholic legal traditions.[24] Their definitive modern formulation, however, came after World War II, with the promulgation of the Universal Declaration of Human Rights (1948). Four international instruments, elaborating the Declaration, contain critical protections of religious rights and liberties: (1) the International Covenant on Civil and Political Rights (1966) ("the 1966 Covenant"), (2) the United Nations Declaration on the Elimination of All Forms of Intolerance and of Discrimination Based on Religion or Belief (1981) ("the 1981 Declaration"), (3) the Concluding Document of the Vienna Follow-up Meeting of Representatives of the Participating States of the Conference on Security and Cooperation in Europe (1989) ("the 1989 Vienna Concluding Document"), and (4) the 1992 United Nations Declaration on the Rights of the Persons Belonging to National or Ethnic, Religious, and Linguistic Minorities ("the 1992 Minorities Declaration").[25]

The 1966 Covenant largely repeats the capacious guarantee of religious rights and liberties first announced in the 1948 Universal Declaration of Human Rights. Article 18 reads:

> 1. Everyone shall have the right to freedom of thought, conscience and religion. This right shall include freedom to have or to adopt a religion or belief of his choice, and freedom, either individually or in community with others and in public or private, to manifest his religion or belief in worship, observance, practice and teaching.

> 2. No one shall be subject to coercion which would impair his freedom to have or to adopt a religion or belief of his choice.

> 3. Freedom to manifest one's religion or beliefs may be subject only to such limitations as are prescribed by law and are necessary to protect public safety, order, health, or morals or the fundamental rights and freedoms of others.

> 4. The States Parties to the present Covenant undertake to have respect for the liberty of parents and, when applicable, legal guardians to ensure the religious and moral education of their children in conformity with their own convictions.[26]

Article 18 distinguishes between the right to freedom of religion and the freedom to manifest one's religion—the rough equivalent of what American law labels as liberty of conscience and free exercise of religion, respectively. The right to freedom of religion—the freedom to have, to alter, or to adopt a religion of one's choice—is an absolute right from which no derogation may be made and which may not be restricted or impaired in any manner. Freedom to manifest or exercise one's religion—individually or collectively, publicly or privately—may be subject only to such limitations as are prescribed by law and are necessary to protect public safety, order, health, or morals or the fundamental rights and freedoms of others. The latter provision is an exhaustive list of the grounds allowed to limit the manifestation of religion. The requirement of necessity implies that any such limitation on the manifestation of religion must be proportionate to its aim to protect any of the listed state interests. Such limitations must not be applied in a manner that would vitiate the rights guaranteed in Article 18—an ideal that is often honored in the breach, even in many advanced Western countries.[27]

Article 20.2 of the 1966 Covenant calls for states parties to prohibit "any advocacy of national, racial, or religious hatred that constitutes incitement to discrimination, hostility, or violence." Articles 2 and 26 require equal treatment of all persons before the law and prohibit discrimination based, among other grounds, on religion. Article 27 further guarantees to religious and cultural minorities "the right to enjoy their own culture" and "to profess and practise their own religion."

The 1981 Declaration elaborates the religious liberty provisions that the 1966 Covenant adumbrated. Like the 1966 Covenant, the 1981 Declaration on its face applies to "everyone," whether "individually or in community," "in public or in private." Articles 1 and 6 of the 1981 Declaration set forth a lengthy illustrative catalog of rights to "freedom of thought, conscience, and religion," repeating but also illustrating more concretely the 1966 Covenant's guarantees of liberty of conscience and free exercise of religion. Article 6 enumerates these rights as follows:

(a) To worship or assemble in connection with a religion or belief and to establish and maintain places for these purposes;

(b) To establish and maintain appropriate charitable or humanitarian institutions;

(c) To make, to acquire and use to an adequate extent the necessary articles and materials related to the rites or customs of a religion or belief;

(d) To write, issue, and disseminate relevant publications in these areas;

(e) To teach a religion or belief in places suitable for these purposes;

(f) To solicit and receive voluntary financial and other contributions from individuals and institutions;

(g) To train, to appoint, to elect, or to designate by succession appropriate leaders called for by the requirements and standards of any religion or belief;

(h) To observe days of rest and to celebrate holy days and ceremonies in accordance with the precepts of one's religion or belief; and

(i) To establish and maintain communications with individuals and communities in matters of religion and belief at the national and international levels.[28]

The 1981 Declaration also focuses on the religious rights of children and their parents. It guarantees the rights of parents (or guardians) to organize life within their household and educate their children "in accordance with their religion or beliefs." Such parental responsibility within and beyond the household, however, must be discharged in accordance with the "best interests of the child." At minimum, the parents' religious upbringing or education of their child "must not be injurious to his physical or mental health or to his full development." Moreover, the declaration provides more generically, "the child shall be protected from any form of discrimination on the ground of religion or belief. He shall be brought up in a spirit of understanding, tolerance, friendship among peoples, peace and universal brotherhood, respect for freedom of religion or belief of others, and in full conscience that his energy and talents should be devoted to the service of his fellow men."[29] The declaration leaves juxtaposed the parents' right to rear and educate their children in accordance with their own religion and beliefs and the state's power to protect the best interests of the child, including the lofty aspirations for the child's upbringing. Despite ample debate on this point, the drafters offered no specific principles to resolve the disputes that would inevitably arise between the rights of parents and the powers of the state operating *in loco parentis*. Some further guidance on this subject is provided by the 1989 UN Convention on the Rights of the Child—though the issue of parental rights over their child's religious upbringing and welfare remains highly contested in international and domestic law.[30]

As these children's rights provisions illustrate, the 1981 Declaration, like the 1966 Covenant, allows the "manifestation of religion" to be subjected to "appropriate" state regulation and adjudication. The 1981 Declaration permits states to enforce against religious individuals and institutions general regulations designed to protect public safety, order, health, or morals, or the fundamental rights and freedoms of others. It is assumed, however, that in all such instances, the grounds for such regulations are enumerated and explicit and that such regulations abide by the international legal principles of necessity and proportionality.

The 1981 Declaration includes more elaborate prohibitions than the 1966 Covenant on religious discrimination and intolerance. It bars religious "discrimination by any State, institution, group of persons, or person." And it defines such discrimination as "any distinction, exclusion, restriction or preference based on religion or belief, and having as its purpose or as its effect nullification or impairment of the recognition, enjoyment or exercise of human rights or fundamental freedoms on an equal basis." All discrimination based on religion or belief, the declaration insists, is "an affront to human dignity" and a "disavowal" of the "fundamental freedoms" that form the cornerstone of national and international peace and cooperation. Accordingly, the declaration calls on all States Parties "to take effective measures to prevent and eliminate" such discrimination "in all fields of civil, economic, political, social, and cultural life," including rescinding laws that foster discrimination and enacting laws that forbid it.[31]

The 1989 Vienna Concluding Document extends the religious liberty norms of the 1981 Declaration, particularly for religious groups. Principle 16 rounds out the list of enumerated rights guarantees quoted above from the 1981 Declaration:

16. In order to ensure the freedom of the individual to profess and practice religion or belief the participating States will, *inter alia,*

A. take effective measures to prevent and eliminate discrimination against individuals or communities, on the grounds of religion or belief in the recognition, exercise and enjoyment of human rights and fundamental freedoms in all fields of civil, political, economic, social and cultural life, and ensure the effective equality between believers and non-believers;

B. foster a climate of mutual tolerance and respect between believers of different communities as well as between believers and non-believers;

C. grant upon their request to communities of believers, practicing or prepared to practice their faith within the constitutional framework of their states, recognition of the status provided for them in their respective countries;

D. respect the right of religious communities to establish and maintain freely accessible places of worship or assembly; organize themselves according to their own hierarchical and institutional structure; select, appoint and replace their personnel in accordance with their respective requirements and standards as well as with any freely accepted arrangement between them and their State; solicit and receive voluntary financial and other contributions;

E. engage in consultations with religious faiths, institutions and organizations in order to achieve a better understanding of the requirements of religious freedom;

F. respect the right of everyone to give and receive religious education in the language of his choice, individually or in association with others;

G. in this context respect, *inter alia,* the liberty of parents to ensure the religious and moral education of their children in conformity with their own convictions;

H. allow the training of religious personnel in appropriate institutions;

I. respect the right of individual believers and communities of believers to acquire, possess, and use sacred books, religious publications in the language of their choice and other articles and materials related to the practice of religion or belief;

J. allow religious faiths, institutions and organizations to produce and import and disseminate religious publications and materials;

K. favorably consider the interest of religious communities in participating in public dialogue, inter alia, through mass media.[32]

A number of these religious group rights provisions in the Vienna Concluding Document reflect the international right to self-determination of peoples. This right has long been recognized as a basic norm of international law and is included, among other places, in Article 1.1 of the 1966 Covenant. The right to self-determination has its fullest expression in the 1992 Minorities Declaration. This right belongs to "peoples" within pluralistic societies. It guarantees a religious community the right to practice its religion, an ethnic community the right to promote its culture, and a linguistic community the right to speak its language without undue state interference or unnecessary legal restrictions. The 1992 Minorities Declaration recognizes that "the promotion and protection of the rights" of religious, cultural, and linguistic minorities is "an integral part of the development of a society as a whole and within a democratic framework based on the rule of law." Accordingly, it calls on states to respect and to pass implementing legislation that protects and promotes the rights of cultural, religious, and linguistic minorities "to enjoy their own culture, to profess and practice their own religion, and to use their own language, in private and in public, freely and without interference or any form of discrimination." It further provides that "States shall take measures to create favorable conditions to enable persons belonging to minorities to express their characteristics and to develop their culture, language, religion, traditions and customs, except where specific practices are in violation of national law and contrary to international standards."[33] So conceived, the right to religious self-determination provides religious groups some of the same strong protections that are afforded to religious individuals under the freedom of conscience guarantee.

These are the basic international religious rights provisions on the books. Various regional instruments, notably the European Charter on Human Rights (1950), the American Convention on Human Rights (1969), and the African Charter on Human and People's Rights (1981), elaborate some of these guarantees. Various religious declarations and treaties involving religious bodies, notably the recent concordats between the Vatican and Italy, Spain, and Israel, as well as the Universal Islamic Declaration of Human Rights (1981) and the Cairo Declaration on Human Rights in Islam (1990), reflect the religious concerns of their cosigners.[34] But the foregoing four instruments capture the common lore of current international human rights norms on religious rights and liberties.

These instruments highlight many legal issues that have confronted national and international tribunals over the past half century: how to protect religious minorities within a majoritarian religious culture—particularly controversial groups like Muslims, Mormons, Baha'is, Jehovah's Witnesses, Scientologists, members of the Unification Church, and indigenous or first peoples who often bring charges of religious and cultural discrimination. How to place limits on religious and antireligious exercises and expressions that cause offense or harm to others. How to adjudicate challenges that a state's proscriptions or prescriptions run directly counter to a party's core claims of conscience or cardinal commandments of the faith. How to balance private and public exercises of religion, including the liberty of conscience of one party to be left alone and the free exercise right of another to proselytize. How to negotiate the complex needs and norms of religious groups without according them too much sovereignty over their members or too little relief from secular courts in the event of fundamental rights violations by religious tribunals. How to adjudicate intra- or interreligious disputes that come before secular courts for resolution. And how to determine the proper levels of state cooperation with and support for religious officials and institutions in the delivery of vital social services—child care, education, charity, medical services, and disaster relief, among others.

International Norms and American Laws Compared

The United States has ratified the 1966 Covenant. None of the fourteen reservations, understandings, or declarations that the United States declared to the instrument seeks to avoid or evade the religious liberty standards set out in the document. The 1966 Covenant, however, is not self-executing. It "does not, by itself, create private rights enforceable in U.S. courts."[35] It requires implementing legislation to become effective, and no such law to date has been issued.[36] Yet the 1966 Covenant holds out a high standard of religious liberty that the United States has pledged to support.

The 1981 Declaration, 1989 Vienna Concluding Document, and 1992 Minorities Declaration are not binding legal instruments on the United States. Nonetheless, as collective expressions of common international opinion (if not common international law) on the meaning and measure of religious liberty, these instruments carry ample moral, intellectual, and diplomatic suasion. Moreover, these instruments have increasingly begun to be mined and analyzed in academic literature and parsed and applied in cases before a number of national and international courts, commissions, and committees (especially in Europe).[37]

These international human rights instruments both confirm and prioritize several of the founding principles of religious liberty in America—liberty of conscience, freedom of exercise, religious equality, religious pluralism, separation of church and state, and no establishment of religion. The principles of liberty of conscience, individual and corporate free exercise of religion, and equality of a plurality of religions before the law form the backbone of the international norms on religious liberty. Liberty of conscience rights, with their inherent protections of religious voluntarism and prohibitions against religious coercion, are absolute rights from which no derogation can be made. The exercise of religion may be regulated only to protect either the fundamental rights of others or public health, safety, welfare, and morals, and the burden caused by the regulation must be "proportionate" to achieving that stated interest. Equality of religions before the law must be protected and affirmatively fostered by the state, particularly to ensure the equal protection and treatment of religious and cultural minorities. A vast pluralism of forms and forums of religion and belief deserve protection—whether ancient or new, individual or communal, internal or external, private or public, permanent or transient.

International human rights instruments further confirm the American principles of corporate free exercise rights and the basic separation of the state from churches and other religious groups. Religious groups organized for purposes of religious worship, education, charity, and other causes have the fundamental right to function in expression of their founding religious beliefs and values and must enjoy a level of autonomy in their own affairs. The state may regulate these religious groups only on stated grounds that are necessary and proportionate. Conspicuously absent from international human rights instruments, however, are the more radical demands for separationism rooted in the popular American metaphor of a "wall of separation between church and state." *Everson v. Board of Education* (1948), *McCollum v. Board of Education* (1948), and other early establishment clause cases maintained that religious liberty requires the absolute separation of church and state and the cessation of state support for religion, particularly religious schools. Only the secular state can guarantee religious liberty, it was argued, and only separation can guarantee the state's neutrality on religious matters. Such views, which still pervade popular opinion in America, are not reflected in international human rights instruments nor, indeed, widely shared by other nation-states around the world.[38]

If they were hypothetically applied in the United States, the international instruments would commend several lines of Supreme Court cases protecting liberty of conscience rights. These include a series of cases from *Arver v. United States* (1918) to *Welsh v. United States* (1970), where the Court upheld federal statutes that granted conscientious objection status to religious pacifists. These also include several early free exercise cases from *West Virginia Board of Education v. Barnette* (1943) to *Torcaso v. Watkins* (1961) that protected parties from coerced participation in swearing pledges and oaths as well as the later establishment cases of *Lee v. Weisman* (1992) and *Santa Fe Independent School District v. Doe* (2000) that protected parties from coerced participation in public prayers and ceremonies. These liberty of conscience cases also include a series of Sabbatarian cases, from *Sherbert v. Verner* (1963) onward, that relieved parties from having to choose between adherence to a core commandment of conscience and a set of government benefits to which they were otherwise entitled. The international instruments norms make it unequivocally clear that private parties have the right to choose, change, or reject religion without compulsion, control, or conditions imposed by the state.

Particularly younger children, as the 1981 Declaration and 1989 UN Convention on the Rights of the Child underscore, cannot be compelled to participate in religious or secular activities to which their parents object. Several American cases have confirmed this, based on the landmark case of *Wisconsin v. Yoder* (1972). To be sure, parental rights to control their child's religious upbringing must be balanced against the state's duty to protect the best interest of that child. The international instruments would likely confirm the Supreme Court case *Prince v. Massachusetts* (1944), which insisted that a minor child could not proselytize on the street corner at night in violation of child labor laws, even if the child's guardian regarded that activity as essential to the child's religious upbringing. These instruments would also uphold *Jehovah's Witnesses v. King County Hospital* (1968), which insisted that a minor child be given a necessary blood transfusion and other medical care, even though the parents wanted to treat the child by prayer alone as a test and testimony of faith. Endangering a child's life and limb is an automatic trigger for state intervention—notwithstanding parental religious interests to the contrary.

The international instruments would strongly commend the "strict scrutiny" test for free exercise claims. This was the test developed by the Supreme Court in *Sherbert v. Verner* (1963) and *Wisconsin v. Yoder* (1972) and recaptured by Congress in the Religious Freedom Restoration Act (RFRA) (1993) and the Religious Land Use and Institutionalized Persons Act (RLUIPA) (2000). The test provides that when the state imposes a substantial burden on the free exercise of a claimant's religion, the state must show that it is pursuing a compelling or overriding purpose, has used the least restrictive alternative for achieving that purpose, and has engaged in no religious discrimination in drafting or applying the law in question. Absent such a showing, the state must either rescind the law or provide the burdened party with an exemption from full compliance. This American strict scrutiny test is the rough equivalent of the "necessity" and "proportionality" standard of the international human rights instruments, particularly as set forth in the 1966 Covenant.

Just as in international law, so in First Amendment law, this strict scrutiny regime of free exercise is not "strict in theory, but fatal in fact."[39] Even in the *Sherbert* and *Yoder* heyday of 1963–1989, when the Supreme Court had strict scrutiny as its stated free exercise standard, government won nearly half the time, especially in cases where parties claimed free exercise exemption from taxation and social security laws. These holdings are consistent with prevailing international and comparative law standards that all parties, including religious parties, must comply with a fairly administered tax scheme.[40]

While they would applaud a strict scrutiny regime, the international instruments would find little to commend in the narrower reading of the free exercise clause introduced by the Supreme Court in *Bowen v. Roy* (1986), *Lyng v. Northwestern Indian Cemetery Protective Association* (1988), and *Employment Division v. Smith* (1990). These latter cases, which now control application of the First Amendment free exercise clause by the federal courts, effectively reduce the free exercise guarantee to a type of heightened rational basis review, except when blatant discrimination is involved. In particular, the *Smith* Court held that laws judged to be "neutral and generally applicable" will pass constitutional muster regardless of the burden cast on religion or the nature of the power exercised by government. Even a discretionary law or policy that crushes a central belief or practice of a free exercise claimant will survive constitutional challenge if it is neutrally drafted and generally applicable to all. Only if the law is not neutrally drafted or generally applicable will government be required to demonstrate a compelling government interest that overrides the burdened free exercise right. Such a harsh, religion-blind neutrality leaves religious minorities vulnerable to the machinations of state legislators and judges who tend to keep their eyes on majoritarian sentiment and the next election. This runs directly counter to the strong solicitude for religious minorities mandated especially by the 1966 Covenant and the 1992 Minorities Declaration.

It is especially troublesome that the *Bowen, Lyng,* and *Smith* cases involved claims by Native Americans to special protection for their religious sites and rites. The right to self-determination of indigenous peoples, particularly their religious self-determination, is an important international human rights principle, and it requires unusual solicitude by nation-states. Congress, in fact, had recognized this responsibility in passing the American Indian Religious Freedom Act (1978), which called officials "to protect and preserve for American Indians their inherent right of freedom to believe, express, and exercise the[ir] traditional religions . . . including but not limited to access to sites, use and possession of sacred objects, and the freedom to worship through ceremonials and traditional rites."[41] The Supreme Court's cavalier treatment of Native American religious liberty claims is a substantial blight on its First Amendment record. The Court's special accommodations of Adventist Sabbatarianism in *Sherbert* and Amish communitarianism in *Yoder* come much closer to the solicitude mandated by international human rights instruments.

Moreover, international norms would have little patience with the patently discriminatory treatment of other religious minorities in America. The Court's failure to consider accommodating the distinctive theology of polygamous marriage among Mormons, the special Sabbatarian needs of Jews, and the religious worship patterns of Muslims, as well as the nontraditional sites and rites of Native Americans, all run directly counter to the cardinal principles of equality and nondiscrimination mandated by a number of international human rights instruments. International norms demand not only general toleration of religious minorities but special solicitude for their religious needs that often are not accommodated in majoritarian laws and policies.

The international norms on equality and nondiscrimination would, however, applaud the free speech equal access and equal treatment cases from *Widmar v. Vincent* (1981) to *Good News Club v. Milford Central School* (2001) that give religious parties equal access to forums, facilities, and even funds made available to like-positioned nonreligious parties. They would likewise commend recent establishment clause cases like *Agostini v. Felton* (1997), *Mitchell v. Helms* (2000), and *Zelman v. Simmons-Harris* (2002) that treated religious and nonreligious schools alike in the distribution of general government-funded educational services and materials. Nothing in international law or First Amendment law requires the state to make public forums or state funds available to private parties. But when the state does offer these forums or funds, it may not discriminate against otherwise eligible religious claimants in granting access or distributing them.

The international instruments would also commend cases like *McDaniel v. Paty* (1978) that removed special state prohibitions on religious ministers participating in political office. It would also uphold the recent case of *Watchtower Bible and Tract Society v. Village of Stratton* (2002) and several earlier free exercise and free speech cases that prohibited discriminatory licensing requirements against religious solicitors in public places. Nondiscriminatory and neutrally applied "time, place, and manner" regulations on all public speech, including religious and political speech and activities, is as permissible under the international instruments as it is under First Amendment law. But again, singling out religious solicitors for special restrictions or requirements violates the essential religious liberty principle of equality and nondiscrimination.

The principles of structural pluralism (or group rights) set out in the international instruments would endorse the many lines of cases and statutes protecting the forms and functions of religious associations, whether worship centers, religious schools and charities, or other such groups. Various Supreme Court cases upholding general regulation of these bodies in furtherance of health, safety, and welfare, and in exercise of regulatory, taxation, and police power would likewise pass muster. The principle of structural pluralism, especially as elaborated in the Vienna Concluding Document, would look askance, however, at a case like *Jones v. Wolf* (1979), which permitted government resolution of intrachurch disputes involving "neutral principles" of law. The "deference test" maintained by the Supreme Court from *Watson v. Jones* (1872) to *Serbian Orthodox Diocese v. Milivojevich* (1976) would find greater favor under international human rights instruments as a proper form of intrareligious dispute resolution. Also favorably received at international law would be the cases of *NLRB v. Catholic Bishop of Chicago* (1979) and *Presiding Bishop v. Amos* (1987), which protected the employment decisions of religious employers, including their right to engage in religious discrimination in their core employment decisions.

This same principle of structural pluralism might also look askance at a case like *Bob Jones University v. United States* (1983), which withheld tax-exempt status from a religious university that engaged in racial discrimination on the basis of its religious convictions. The holding of the *Bob Jones* case is intuitively attractive, given the tragic history of slavery and discrimination against African Americans—just as holdings in modern Germany outlawing any private discrimination against Jews are intuitively attractive, given that county's tragic history of anti-Semitism. But international norms of religious rights protect even unpopular and prejudicial policies of a religious body that are firmly grounded and sincerely held—so long as such policies do not threaten or violate the life or limb of its members or impair any party's liberty of exit from the religious body.[42] As new battles begin to rage over religious groups' solicitude (or not) over same-sex marriage, these issues seem poised to return to the fore.

The absence of a no establishment of religion principle in international human rights instruments would not call into question the entire line of establishment clause cases that have emerged since 1947, principally on issues of religion and education. Many of these cases serve to protect the principles of liberty of conscience, free exercise, religious equality, and religious pluralism in a manner consistent with prevailing international instruments. But when there is a clash between such principles and the principle of no religious establishment, international norms would give preference to the former—as do American cases upholding the principle of accommodation.

The international instruments do not have an equivalent to the *Lemon* test, which requires that a law or policy will pass constitutional muster under the establishment clause only if it (1) has a secular purpose, (2) has a primary effect that neither inhibits or prohibits religion, and (3) fosters no excessive entanglement between religious and political officials. This test, while ignored or reformulated by several later Supreme Court cases, still finds favor among lower federal courts in the absence of a consistently applied alternative. The *Lemon* test is consistent with international instruments insofar as it protects nonreligious or religious minorities from coerced support for or participation in majoritarian religions, and protects various religious communities from undue intrusion or regulation by the state. The *Lemon* test goes further than international instruments, however, in requiring a secular purpose for a state law or policy. The key to international religious liberty is not the secular nature of the law but the freedom of each individual to accept or reject available religions.

Moreover, the realm of education—where parental religious rights and preferences receive especially strong protection—is not the ideal place for undue zealotry in application of disestablishment values. To be sure, the international instruments would not countenance, anymore than the First Amendment coerced, religious exercises in school classrooms—such as mandatory participation in prayers, pledges, confessions of faith, Bible reading, and the like—however strong the countervailing parental preferences. But using the Constitution to purge tax-supported public schools of virtually all religious symbols, texts, and traditions in favor of purportedly neutral and secular tropes stands in considerable tension with international principles of religious equality and parental religious rights. It also fails to recognize what the international instruments have long recognized—that peaceable religious, nonreligious, and antireligious "thought, conscience, and belief" are all "religious" and are all deserving of religious liberty protection.

Finally, the absence of a universal definition, or common method of defining, religion in American law would meet criticism under international norms. The current system of leaving such definitions to individual states and statutes, courts, and agencies has introduced a bewildering array of legal definitions of "religion." Some courts and legislatures make a simple common-sense inquiry into the existence of religion. Others defer to the good faith self-declarations of religion by the claimant. Some seek to find analogies between existing religions and new religious claimants. Others insist on evidence of a god or something transcendent that stands in the same position as a god. And still others analyze the motives for founding a religious organization or adopting a religious belief, the presence and sophistication of doctrines explicating the beliefs, practice, and celebration of religious rites and liturgies, the degree of formal training required for the religious leaders, the strictures on the ability of members to practice other religions, the presence and internal enforcement of a set of ethical rules of conduct, and other factors.[43] All this results in considerable inequality and potentially discriminatory treatment of religious claims and claimants.

It may not be apt to adopt the capacious definition of religion set out in international human rights instruments—particularly given that under the First Amendment one definition of religion must be usefully applied to both the free exercise clause and the establishment clause. But the term "religion" must be assigned some consistent boundaries to be useful, at least for a constitutional rights regime. No universal definition can easily embrace every religious dimension of modern culture. No bright line test can readily resolve all penumbral cases. Fairness commands as broad a legal definition of religion as possible, so that no legitimate religious claim is excluded. Prudence commends a narrower definition, so that not every claim becomes religious (and thus no claim becomes deserving of special religious rights protection). To define "religion" too closely is to place too much trust in the capacity of the lexicon or the legislature. But to leave the term undefined is to place too much faith in the self-declarations of the claimant or the discernment of local judges and administrators.

Summary and Conclusions

The American experiment in religious liberty is unique, and some degree of American exceptionalism should certainly be preserved. The First Amendment's establishment clause, firmly embodying a notion largely absent in international law, could be the first exhibit in support of this proposition and one could deduce others discussed in this volume. But at the same time, America's experiment with religious liberty is connected to a deep history abroad and is inseparable from the current plight of religious (and nonreligious) individuals and groups around the world who seek religious freedom. It is intertwined with the text and ideas of international instruments.

Looking to international norms allows for recalibration and repristination of our own first principles of religious liberty. If we are careful, we will find the core of America's own ideas of religious liberty in those norms. Those conceptions of religious liberty have been reinterpreted, reused, and sometimes reformulated by others abroad who have experimented with them. As we seek to reinvigorate America's experiment in religious liberty, we would be well served to consider what the international norms have to teach us.

Notes

1. *Kiryas Joel Village School District v. Grumet,* 512 U.S. 687, 718–721 (1994) (O'Connor, J., concurring). See also *Rosenberger v. University of Virginia,* 515 U.S. 819, 846–849 (1995) (O'Connor, J., concurring).

2. *Kiryas Joel,* 512 U.S. at 751 (Scalia, J., dissenting).

3. See, e.g., International Law and Religion Symposium, *Brigham Young Law Review* (2001): 413 (2002): 205; Johan D. van der Vyver and John Witte, Jr., eds., *Religious Human Rights in Global Perspective: Religious Perspectives* (1996).

4. Clovis C. Morrisson Jr., "Margin of Appreciation in European Human Rights Law," *Revue des droits de l'homme* 6 (1973): 263–286.

5. John D. Kelsay and Sumner B. Twiss, eds., *Religion and Human Rights* (1998 [1994]).

6. See, e.g., several thoughtful essays in Michael Ignatieff, ed., *American Exceptionalism and Human Rights* (2005).

7. 536 U.S. 304, 316 n. 21, 321 (2002).

8. 536 U.S. at 347–348 (Scalia, J., dissenting).

9. 539 U.S. 558, 572 573, 576–577 (2003).

10. 539 U.S. at 598 (Scalia, J., dissenting).

11. 543 U.S. 551, 575–578 (2005).

12. 543 U.S. at 604–605 (O'Connor, J., dissenting).

13. 543 U.S. at 622–628 (Scalia, J., dissenting).

14. Roger Paul Alford, "In Search of a Theory for Constitutional Comparativism," *UCLA Law Review* 52 (2005): 639–714; Sarah H. Cleveland, "Our International Constitution," *Yale Journal of International Law* 31 (2006): 1–125.

15. Steven G. Calabresi and Stephanie Dotson Zimdahl, "The Supreme Court and Foreign Sources of Law: Two Hundred Years of Practice and the Juvenile Death Penalty Decision," *William and Mary Law Review* 47 (2005): 743–909, at 907. See *Reynolds v. United States,* 98 U.S. 145, 164 (1878) ("Polygamy has always been odious among the northern and western nations of Europe, and, until the establishment of the Mormon Church, was almost exclusively a feature of the life of Asiatic and of African people").

16. Melissa A. Waters, "Creeping Monism: The Judicial Trend Toward Interpretive Incorporation of Human Rights Treaties," *Columbia Law Review* 107 (2007): 628–705, at 632.

17. Roger Paul Alford, "Misusing International Sources to Interpret the Constitution," *American Journal International Law* 41 (2004): 57, 58–62. But compare T. Alexander Aleinikoff, "Thinking Outside the Sovereignty Box: Transnational Law and the U.S. Constitution," *Texas Law Review* 82 (2004): 1989–2016.

18. *Thompson v. Oklahoma,* 487 U.S. 815, 869 n. 4 (1988) (Scalia, J., dissenting).

19. See "Roosevelt's Eighth Annual Message to Congress (January 6, 1941)," in *State of the Union Messages of the Presidents, 1790–1966,* ed. F. Israel (1966), 3:1; Louis B. Sohn, *The Human Rights Movement: From Roosevelt's Four Freedoms to the Interdependence of Peace, Development, and Human Rights* (1982).

20. See Mary Ann Glendon, *A World Made New: Eleanor Roosevelt and the Universal Declaration of Human Rights* (2001).

21. Louis Henkin, "Rights, American and Human," *Columbia Law Review* 79 (1979): 405; Paul Gordon Lauren, *The Evolution of International Human Rights: Visions Seen* (2003).

22. International Religious Freedom Act of 1998, 22 U.S.C.A. 6401, 112 Stat. 2787, and amended by 116 Stat. 1408. See Allen D. Hertzke, *Freeing God's Children: The Unlikely Alliance for Global Human Rights* (2004). See also Joel A. Nichols, "Evangelicals and Human Rights: The Continuing Ambivalence of Evangelical Christians' Support for Human Rights," *Journal of Law and Religion* 24 (2009): 629–662.

23. T. Jeremy Gunn, "The United States and the Promotion of Freedom of Religion and Belief," in *Facilitating Freedom of Religion or Belief: A Deskbook*, ed. Tore Lindholm et al. (2004): 721–746, 722.

24. John Witte, Jr., *The Reformation of Rights: Law, Religion, and Human Rights in Early Modern Calvinism* (2008).

25. "1966 Covenant": UN Doc. A/6316 (1968), available in Ian Brownlie and Guy S. Goodwin-Gill, *Basic Documents on Human Rights*, 5th ed. (2006), 358–374; "1981 Declaration": U.N. Doc. A/RES/36/55 (1982), available in Brownlie and Goodwin-Gill, *Basic Documents*, 74–77; "1989 Vienna Concluding Document": 28 I.L.M. 527, available in Brownlie and Goodwin-Gill, *Basic Documents*, 845–848; "1992 Minorities Declaration": G.A. Res. 47/135 (18 Dec. 1992), available in Brownlie and Goodwin-Gill, *Basic Documents*, 134–137. For overviews and critical analyses of these and related documents regarding religious liberty, see Natan Lerner, *Religion, Secular Beliefs, and Human Rights: 25 Years After the 1981 Declaration* (2006); Lindhom et al., eds., *Facilitating Freedom of Religion or Belief*.

26. 1966 Covenant, Art. 18.1–18.4.

27. Symposium, "The Permissible Scope of Legal Limitations on the Freedom of Religion and Belief," *Emory International Law Review* 19 (2005): 465–1320.

28. 1981 Declaration, Art. 6.

29. Ibid., Arts. 5.1, 5.2, 5.4, 5.5, and 5.3, respectively.

30. U.N. Doc. A/44/25; see further Symposium, "What's Wrong with Rights for Children?" *Emory International Law Review* (2006): 1–239.

31. 1981 Declaration, Arts. 2.1, 2.2, 3, and 4.1–2, respectively.

32. Vienna Concluding Document, Principle 16.

33. 1992 Minorities Declaration, preamble and Arts. 1–2, 4.2, respectively.

34. See the collection of documents in Brownlie and Goodwin-Gill, *Basic Documents*.

35. David P. Stewart, "United States Ratification of the Covenant on Civil and Political Rights: The Significance of the Reservations, Understandings, and Declarations," *DePaul Law Review* 42 (1993): 1183, 1202ff.

36. Louis Henkin, "U.S. Ratification of Human Rights Conventions: The Ghost of Senator Bricker," *American Journal of International Law* 89 (1995): 341; Gerald Neumann, "The Global Dimension of RFRA," *Constitutional Commentary* 14 (1997): 33.

37. For Europe and UN, especially, see Paul M. Taylor, *Freedom of Religion: UN and European Human Rights Law and Practice* (2005); Carolyn Evans, *Freedom of Religion Under the European Convention on Human Rights* (2001); Malcolm D. Evans, *Religious Liberty and International Law in Europe* (1997). See also Liam Gearon, ed., *Human Rights and Religion: A Reader* (2002). For a comparative constitutional analysis of foreign law on free speech, see

Ronald J. Krotoszynski Jr., *The First Amendment in Cross-Cultural Perspective: A Comparative Legal Analysis of the Freedom of Speech* (2006).

38. See John Witte, Jr., "Facts and Fictions About the History of Separation of Church and State," *Journal of Church and State* 48 (2006): 15–45; Steve Monsma and Chris Soper, *The Challenge of Pluralism: Church and State in Five Democracies* (1997).

39. Kent Greenawalt, *Religion and the Constitution: Free Exercise and Fairness* (2006), 215 (quoting Gerald Gunther).

40. See esp. *United States v. Lee*, 455 U.S. 252 (1982); *Jimmy Swaggart Ministries v. Board of Equalization of California*, 493 U.S. 378 (1990).

41. 42 U.S.C. sec. 1996 (1978).

42. See Natan Lerner, *Group Rights and Discrimination in International Law*, 2d ed. (2002).

43. See, e.g., T. Jeremy Gunn, "The Complexity of Religion and the Definition of 'Religion' in International Law," *Harvard Human Rights Journal* 16 (2003): 189.

Concluding Reflections

Writing in the context of the United States Constitutional Convention of 1787, John Adams, the great Massachusetts jurist and future American president, offered a robust appraisal of the new American experiment:

The people in America have now the best opportunity and the greatest trust in their hands, that Providence ever committed to so small a number, since the transgression of the first pair [Adam and Eve]; if they betray their trust, their guilt will merit even greater punishment than other nations have suffered, and in the indignation of Heaven. . . . The United States have exhibited, perhaps, the first example of governments erected on the simple principles of nature; and if men are now sufficiently enlightened to disabuse themselves of artifice, imposture, hypocrisy, and superstition, they will consider this event as a [new] era in history. Although the detail of the formation of the American governments is at present little known or regarded either in Europe or in America, it may hereafter become an object of curiosity [for it is] destined to spread over the northern part of . . . the globe. The institutions now made in America will not wholly die out for thousands of years. It is of the last importance, then, that they should begin right. If they set out wrong, they will never be able to return, unless it be by accident to the right path.[1]

More than two centuries later, Adams's sentiments prove remarkably prescient. The eighteenth-century American founders did indeed begin on the right path of liberty, and today we enjoy ample freedom of religion as a consequence. American models of religious liberty have had a profound influence around the globe, and they now figure prominently in a number of national constitutions and international human rights instruments.

To be sure, as Adams predicted, there has always been "a glorious uncertainty in the law" of religious liberty and a noble diversity of understandings of its details.[2] This was as true in Adams's day as in our own. In Adams's day, there were competing models of religious liberty more overtly theological than his—whether Puritan, Evangelical, or Anglican in inspiration. There were also competing models more overtly philosophical than his—whether Classical, Republican, or Enlightenment in inclination. Today, these and other founding models of religious liberty have born ample progeny, and the great rivalries among them are fought out in the courts, legislatures, and academies throughout the land.

Prone as he was to a dialectical model of religious liberty, Adams would likely approve of our rigorous rivalries of principle—so long as all rivals remain committed to constitutional ideals of democracy, liberty, and rule of law. But Adams would also likely insist that we reconsider his most cardinal insights about the necessary dialectical nature of religious freedom and religious establishment. Too little religious freedom, Adams had insisted, is a recipe for hypocrisy and impiety. But too much religious freedom is an invitation to depravity and license. Too firm a religious establishment breeds coercion and corruption. But too little religious establishment allows secular prejudices to become constitutional prerogatives. Somewhere between these extremes, Adams believed, a society must find its balance.

The balance that Adams and other founders often struck between the freedom of all private religions and the establishment of one public Christian religion can no longer serve in our day. But the balance that the Supreme Court has often struck between the freedom of all private religions and the establishment of one public secular religion also can no longer serve. Somewhere between these extremes, our society must now find a new constitutional balance.

One key to restriking this constitutional balance today lies in the eighteenth-century founders' most elementary and most essential insight—that religion is special and is accorded special protection in the Constitution. "[W]e cannot repudiate that decision," Douglas Laycock writes, "without rejecting an essential feature of constitutionalism, rendering all constitutional rights vulnerable to repudiation if they go out of favor."[3] The founders' vision was that religion is more than simply a peculiar form of speech and assembly, privacy and autonomy. Religion is a unique source of individual and personal identity, involving "duties that we owe to our Creator, and the manner of discharging them," as Madison put it. Religion is also a unique form of public and social identity, involving a vast plurality of sanctuaries, schools, charities, missions, and other forms and forums of faith. Individual and corporate, private and public entities and exercises of religion—in all their self-defined varieties—properly deserve the protection of the First Amendment.

A second key to restriking this constitutional balance today lies in the founders' insight that to be enduring and effective, the constitutional process must seek to involve all voices and values in the community—religious, areligious, and antireligious alike. Constitutionalism ultimately demands ecumenism to be effective and enduring. Thus in creating the state and federal constitutions, the founders stretched the role of delegates and ratifiers to the furthest edges of conscience and credulity. Believers and skeptics, churchmen and statesmen, Protestants and Catholics, Republicans and *Philosophes,* Quakers and Jews—many of whom in decades and centuries past had slandered and slaughtered each other with a vengeance—now came together in a rare moment of solidarity. The founders understood that creating a proper law of religious liberty required that all religions have liberty to participate in both its creation and its unfolding.

A third key to restriking this constitutional balance today lies in repristinating the six basic principles of religious liberty that the founders set forth. The founders designed the First Amendment free exercise and establishment clauses as twin guarantees of religious liberty for all. The free exercise clause outlawed government *proscriptions* of religion—actions that unduly burdened the conscience, restricted religious expression and activity, discriminated against religion, or invaded the autonomy of churches and other religious bodies. The establishment clause outlawed government *prescriptions* of religion—actions that unduly coerced the conscience, mandated forms of religious expression and activity, discriminated in favor of religion, or improperly allied the state with churches or other religious bodies. Both the free exercise and the establishment clauses thereby provided complementary protections to the other constitutive principles of the American experiment—liberty of conscience, freedom of religious expression, equality of plural faiths before the law, and separation of church and state.

These three key insights of the American experiment were not only part of the original vision of the eighteenth-century founders, but they were also part of the original vision of the Supreme Court as it founded a modern national law of religious liberty. All three of these insights recur in *Cantwell v. Connecticut* (1940) and *Everson v. Board of Education* (1947), the two cases that first applied the First Amendment religion clauses to the states and inaugurated the modern era of religious liberty in America.

Cantwell and *Everson* declared anew that religion had a special place in the Constitution and deserved special protection in the nation. In a remarkable countertextual reading, the Court took it upon itself to enforce the First Amendment religion clauses against all levels and branches of government in the nation—whether federal, state, or local; whether executive, legislative, or regulatory. "*Congress* shall make no law. . . . " now became, in effect, "*Government* shall make no law respecting an establishment of religion, or prohibiting the free exercise thereof."

Cantwell and *Everson* also declared anew that all religious voices were welcome in the modern constitutional process concerning religious liberty. These two cases welcomed hitherto marginal voices: *Cantwell* welcomed a devout Jehovah's Witness who sought protections for his unpopular missionary work. *Everson* welcomed a skeptical citizen who sought protection from paying taxes in support of religious schools. Subsequent cases have drawn into the constitutional dialogue a whole host of rival religious and antireligious groups—Catholics, Protestants, and Orthodox, Jews, Muslims, and Native Americans, Mormons, Quakers, and Krishnas, alongside a variety of skeptics, cynics, and secular iconoclasts.

And *Cantwell* and *Everson* declared anew the efficacy of the six founding principles of the American experiment. The free exercise clause, the *Cantwell* Court declared, protects "freedom of conscience and freedom to adhere to such religious organization or form of worship as the individual may choose." It "safeguards the free exercise of the chosen form of religion," the "freedom to act" on one's beliefs. It protects a "plurality of forms and expressions" of faith, each of which deserves equal protection under the law. "The essential characteristic of these liberties is, that under their shield many types of life, character, opinion and belief can develop unmolested and unobstructed."[4] The establishment clause, the *Everson* Court echoed, means that no government "can set up a church"; "can force or influence a person to go or to remain away from church against his will or force him to profess a belief or disbelief in any religion"; can "punish [a person] for entertaining or professing religious beliefs or disbeliefs, for church attendance or non-attendance"; "can, openly or secretly, participate in the affairs of any religious organizations or groups, or vice versa." Government may not exclude "individual Catholics, Lutherans, Mohammedans, Baptists, Jews, Methodists, Nonbelievers, Presbyterians, or the members of any faith, because of their faith, or lack of it, from receiving the benefits of public welfare legislation" or participating in the American public arena.[5] Such was the original vision of the eighteenth-century founders—and also the original vision of the United States Supreme Court at the start of the modern era of religious liberty.

A good deal of this volume has been devoted to documenting the Supreme Court's repeated departures from these original insights in both its free exercise and establishment cases. Far from being special and specially protected, religion has often become a suspect category in modern constitutional law. The free exercise clause no longer accords religious individuals or groups special exemptions from general laws that burden core claims of conscience or central commandments of the faith. Such religious exemptions now come only from the legislature, and even then the Court has sometimes ignored them or struck them down. The establishment clause does not include religious individuals or religious groups among those naturally eligible for government benefits, forums, and programs. Such religious entitlements come only if they are sufficiently buffered by nonreligious entitlements and so long as they are not directed to "sectarian" ends.

Far from openly engaging and valuing all religious voices and values in modern constitutional dialogue, the Supreme Court has often been notorious in its harsh treatment of some religious groups. No Jew, no Muslim, and no Native American has ever won a free exercise case before the Supreme Court, despite numerous efforts. And when Christians have sought to inject their concerns for equal treatment into neutral legislation, the Supreme Court has often struck down these laws as "ingenious and self-serving schemes" that violate the establishment clause.

Far from judiciously balancing the multiple principles on which the American religious experiment was founded, the modern Supreme Court has often taken more reductionist approaches. In its early free exercise cases, the Court applied the principles of liberty of conscience, freedom of religious expression, religious pluralism and equality, and separation of church and state. Since the mid-1980s, however, the Court has reduced the free exercise clause to the single principle of neutrality. In its early establishment cases, the single principle of separation of church and state dominated the Court's reasoning. Since the mid-1980s, individual justices have slowly imported into their analyses new principles of religious equality and liberty of conscience, but now the recent trend has likewise been toward a simple neutrality standard.

Such criticisms, and the ample volumes of others that can be found in the literature, have not been lost on the Supreme Court. In the past two decades, the Court seems to be charting something of a new constitutional course to offset some of these criticisms and to return to some of the original vision of the First Amendment. The Court has, in effect, taken up John Adams's challenge cited at the beginning of this chapter: how to balance the freedom of all religions with the maintenance of a public religion that is neither a newly established secularism nor a traditionally established Christianity. The Court has not yet crafted a coherent new First Amendment logic, let alone a consistent new test, to address this question. But some of these recent cases hold signposts of a new way to protect religious freedom: both private and public forms of religion deserve constitutional freedom and support, though neither may be established or preferred.

Tradition has become one strong vector in the Court's recent First Amendment cases. The Court had used arguments from tradition a few times before, as part of broader rationales for upholding religious tax exemptions and Sabbath day laws. In *Marsh v. Chambers* (1983), however, this argument from tradition became the exclusive basis for upholding a state legislature's practice of funding a chaplain and opening its sessions with his prayers. Writing for the Court, Chief Justice Burger defended such practices as a noble survival of the traditional public role of religion in American life and law:

> In light of the unambiguous and unbroken history of more than 200 years, there can be no doubt that the practice of opening legislative sessions with prayer has become part of the fabric of our society. To invoke Divine guidance on a public body entrusted with making the laws is not, in these circumstances, an "establishment" of religion [but] simply a tolerable acknowledgement of beliefs widely held among the people of this country. . . . "[W]e are a religious people whose institutions presuppose a Supreme Being."[6]

Arguments from tradition, though by themselves rarely convincing, can sometimes bolster a broader rationale for upholding traditional features of a public religion and a religious public. Tradition can sometimes serve effectively as something of a "null hypothesis"—to be overcome by strong constitutional arguments rather than discarded by simple invocations of principle. As Holmes once put it: "If a thing has been practiced for two hundred years by common consent, it will need a strong case for the Fourteenth Amendment to affect it."[7] Innocuous long-standing practices, therefore, such as religious tax exemptions, military and prison chaplains, public displays of the Decalogue, religious artwork and literature in state museums and libraries, and official coinage, oaths, proclamations, and pledges that invoke the name of God and other religious language might well be justified—particularly when private parties are not coerced into participating in or endorsing this language.

Arguments from tradition, though, are also inherently limited in their ability to define and defend the public place of religion today. Such arguments perforce assume a traditional definition of what a public religion is—a common system of beliefs, values, and practices drawn eclectically from the multiple denominations within a community. In the religiously homogeneous environment of John Adams's day, a public religion of the common denominator and common denomination still had the doctrinal rigor, liturgical specificity, and moral suasion to be effective. In the religiously heterogeneous environment of our day—with more than one thousand incorporated denominations on the books—no such effective common religion can be readily devised or defended.

More recent cases suggest a budding new way of defining and defending the legal place of religion in public and private life. The Court has repeatedly upheld government policies that support the public access and activities of religious individuals and groups—so long as these religious parties act voluntarily, and so long as nonreligious parties also benefit from the same government support. Under this logic, Christian clergy are just as entitled to run for state political office as nonreligious candidates. Church-affiliated pregnancy counseling centers may be funded as part of a broader federal family counseling program. Religious student groups may have equal access to state university and public school classrooms that are open to nonreligious student groups. Religious school students are just as entitled to avail themselves of general scholarships, remedial, and disability services as public school students. Religious groups are given equal access to public facilities or civic education programs that are already open to other civic groups. Religious parties are just as entitled as nonreligious parties to display their symbols in public forums. Religious student newspapers are just as entitled to public university funding as those of nonreligious student groups. Religious schools are just as entitled as other private schools to participate in a state-sponsored educational improvement or school voucher or educational program.

Such holdings have been defended on wide-ranging constitutional grounds—as proper accommodations of religion under the establishment clause, as necessary protections of religion under the free speech or free exercise clauses, and as simple applications of the equal protection clause, among other arguments.

One theme common to many of these cases, however, is that public religion must be as free as private religion. Not because the religious groups in these cases are really nonreligious. Not because their public activities are really nonsectarian. And not because their public expressions are really part of the cultural mainstream. To the contrary, these public groups and activities deserve to be free just because they are religious, just because they engage in sectarian practices, just because they sometimes take their stand above, beyond, and against the mainstream. They provide leaven and leverage for the polity to improve.

A second theme common to these cases is that the freedom of public religion sometimes requires the support of the state. Today's state is not the distant, quiet sovereign of Jefferson's day from whom separation was both natural and easy. Today's modern welfare state, whether for good or ill, is an intensely active sovereign from whom complete separation is impossible. Few religious bodies can now avoid contact with the state's pervasive network of education, charity, welfare, child care, health care, family, construction, zoning, workplace, taxation, security, and other regulations. Both confrontation and cooperation with the modern welfare state are almost inevitable for any religion. When a state's regulation imposes too heavy a burden on a particular religion, the free exercise clause should provide a pathway to relief. When a state's appropriation imparts too generous a benefit to religion alone, the establishment clause should provide a pathway to dissent. But when a general government scheme provides public religious groups and activities with the same benefits afforded to all other eligible recipients, establishment clause objections are viewed as counter to the public good.

A third theme common to these cases is that a public religion cannot be a common religion. Today our public religion must be a collection of particular religions, not the combination of religious particulars. It must be a process of open religious discourse, not a product of ecumenical distillation. All religious voices, visions, and values must be heard and deliberated in the public square. All public religious services and activities, unless criminal or tortious, must be given a chance to come forth and compete, in all their denominational particularity.

Some conservative Evangelical and Catholic groups today have seen and seized on this insight better than most. Their rise to prominence in the public square in recent years should not be met with glib talk of censorship or habitual incantation of Jefferson's mythical wall of separation. The rise of the so-called Christian right should be met with the equally strong rise of the Christian left and the Christian middle, as well as Jewish, Muslim, and other religious groups who test and contest its premises, prescriptions, and policies. That is how a healthy democracy works. The real challenge of the new Christian right is not to the integrity of American politics but to the apathy of American religion. It is a challenge for people of all faiths and of no faith to take their place in the marketplace.

A fourth teaching of these cases is that freedom *of* public religion also requires freedom *from* public religion. Government must strike a balance between coercion and freedom. The state cannot coerce citizens to participate in religious ceremonies and subsidies that they find odious. But the state cannot prevent citizens from participating in public ceremonies, programs, and forums just because they are religious. It is one thing to prevent government officials from delegating their core police powers to religious bodies, quite another thing to prevent them from facilitating the charitable services of voluntary religious and nonreligious associations alike. It is one thing to outlaw government prescriptions of prayers, ceremonies, and symbols in public forums, quite another thing to outlaw governmental accommodations of private prayers, ceremonies, and symbols in these same public forums.

Individuals should exercise a comparable prudence in seeking protection from public religion. In the public religion schemes of nineteenth-century America, it was not so much the courts as the frontier that provided this freedom—a place away from it all, where one could escape with one's conscience and coreligionists. Today, the frontier still provides this freedom—if not physically in small towns and wild mountains, then virtually in our ability to sift out and shut out the public voices of religion that we do not wish to hear.

Modern technology and modern privacy make escape to the frontier considerably easier than it was in the days of covered wagons and mule trains. Just turn off the tel-evangelists. Block the religious advocate's emails. Dump their pleas for funds. Turn away the missionary at your door. Close your eyes to the city crucifix that offends. Cover your ears to the public prayer that you can't abide. Forgo the military chap-lain's pastoral counseling. Skip the legislative chaplain's prayers. Walk by the town hall's menorah and star. Don't read the Decalogue posted in the courthouse. Don't join the religious student group. Don't vote for the collared candidate. Don't visit the military chaplain. Don't browse the Evangelicals' newspapers. Avoid the services of the Catholic counselors. Shun the readings of the Scientologists. Turn down the trinkets of the colporteurs. Turn back the ministries of the hate mongers. Such es-capes to the virtual frontier, the law does and will protect—with force if necessary. Such voluntary self-protection from religion will ultimately provide far greater reli-gious freedom for all than pressing yet another tired constitutional case.

Notes

1. C. F. Adams, ed. *The Works of John Adams* (Bostson, 1850–1856), vols. 4–6, 4:290, 292–293, 298. See also James Madison in *Federalist* 37, writing of the formation of the Con-stitution: "It is impossible for the man of pious reflection not to perceive in it a finger of the Almighty hand."

2. Adams, *Works,* 9:629–632, at 630.

3. Douglas Laycock, "Religious Liberty as Liberty," *Journal of Contemporary Legal Issues* 7 (1996): 313–356, at 314.

4. 310 U.S. 296, 303–304, 310 (1940).

5. 330 U.S. 1, 16 (1947).

6. 463 U.S. 783 (1983), quoting *Zorach v. Clauson,* 343 U.S. 306, 313 (1952).

7. *Jackman v. Rosenbaum,* 260 U.S. 22, 31 (1922).

Drafts of Federal Religion Clauses (1787–1789)

Drafts Proposed by the State Ratification Conventions

1. "The rights of conscience shall be held inviolable; and neither the legislative, executive, nor judicial powers of the United States, shall have authority to alter, abrogate, or infringe any part of the constitutions of the several States, which provide the preservation of liberty in matter of religion."—Pennsylvania Minority Proposal, December 15, 1787.

2. "[T]hat the said Constitution be never construed to authorize Congress to infringe the just liberty of the press, or the rights of conscience."—Massachusetts Minority Proposal, February 6, 1788.

3. "That no persons conscientiously scrupulous of bearing arms, in any case, shall be compelled personally to serve as a soldier."—Maryland Minority Proposal, April 21, 1788.

4. "That there be no national religion established by law; but that all persons be equally entitled to protection in their religious liberty."—Maryland Minority Proposal, April 21, 1788.

5. "That all warrants, without oath, or affirmation of a person conscientiously scrupulous of taking an oath, to search suspected places, or to seize any person, or his property, are grievous and oppressive. . . . "—Maryland Majority Proposal, April 21, 1788.

6. "Congress shall make no laws touching religion, or to infringe the rights of conscience."—New Hampshire Proposal, June 21, 1788.

7. "All warrants . . . to search suspected places, or seize any freeman, his papers or property, without information upon Oath (or affirmation of a person religiously

scrupulous of taking an oath) of legal and sufficient cause, are grievous and oppressive . . . and ought not to be granted."—Virginia Proposal, June 26, 1788.

8. "That religion, or the duty which we owe to our creator, and the manner of discharging it, can be directed only by reason and conviction, not by force or violence, and therefore all men have an equal, natural and unalienable right to the free exercise of religion according to the dictates of conscience, and that no particular religious sect or society ought to be favored or established by law in preference to others."—Virginia Proposal, June 26, 1788.

9. "That the people have an equal, natural, and unalienable right freely and peaceably to exercise their religion, according to the dictates of conscience; and that no religious sect or society ought to be favored or established by law in preference to others."—New York Proposal, July 26, 1788.

10. "That any person religiously scrupulous of bearing arms ought to be exempted, upon payment of an equivalent to employ another to bear arms in his stead. That religion, or the duty which we owe to our Creator, and the manner of discharging it, can be directed only by reason and conviction, not by force or violence; and therefore all men have an equal, natural, and unalienable right to the free exercise of religion according to the dictates of conscience, and that no particular religious sect or society ought to be favored or established by law in preference to others."—North Carolina Proposal, August 1, 1788; Repeated by Rhode Island, June 16, 1790.

Drafts Debated in the First Congress (1789)

11. "The civil rights of none shall be abridged on account of religious belief or worship, nor shall any national religion be established, nor shall the full and equal rights of conscience be in any manner, or any pretext infringed."—Draft Proposed to the House by James Madison, June 8, 1789.

12. "No state shall violate the equal rights of conscience, or the freedom of the press, or the trial by jury in criminal cases."—Draft Proposed to House by James Madison, June 8, 1789.

13. "[N]o religion shall be established by law, nor shall the equal rights of conscience be infringed."—Draft Proposed to House by Committee of Eleven, July 28, 1789.

14. "[N]o person religiously scrupulous shall be compelled to bear arms."—Draft Proposed to House by Committee of Eleven, July 28, 1789.

15. "[N]o State shall infringe the equal rights of conscience, nor the freedom of speech or of the press, nor of the right of trial by jury in criminal cases."—Draft Proposed to House by Committee of Eleven, July 28, 1789.

16. "Congress shall make no laws touching religion, or infringing the rights of conscience."—Draft Proposed by Charles Livermore on August 15, 1789; Passed by the House.

17. "[T]he equal rights of conscience, the freedom of speech or of the press, and the right of trial by jury in criminal cases, shall not be infringed by any State."—Draft Proposed by Charles Livermore on August 17, 1789; Passed by the House.

18. "Congress shall make no law establishing religion, or to prevent the free exercise thereof, or to infringe the rights of conscience."—Revised Draft Proposed by Fisher Ames on August 20, 1789; Passed by the House.

19. "No person religiously scrupulous shall be compelled to bear arms in person." —Revised Draft Passed by the House, August 20, 1789.

20. "Congress shall make no law establishing religion, or prohibiting the free exercise thereof, nor shall the rights of conscience be infringed."—Final Draft Proposed by the Style Committee, Passed by the House, and Sent to the Senate, August 25, 1789.

21. "Congress shall make no law establishing One Religious Sect or Society in preference to others, nor shall the rights of conscience be infringed."—Draft Proposed and Defeated in the Senate, September 3, 1789.

22. "Congress shall not make any law, infringing the rights of conscience, or establishing any Religious Sect or Society."—Draft Proposed and Defeated in the Senate, September 3, 1789.

23. "Congress shall make no law establishing any particular denomination of religion in preference to another, or prohibiting the free exercise thereof, nor shall the rights of conscience be infringed."—Draft Proposed and Defeated in the Senate, September 3, 1789.

24. "Congress shall make no law establishing religion, or prohibiting the free exercise thereof."—Draft Proposed and Passed by the Senate, September 3, 1789.

25. "Congress shall make no law establishing articles of faith or a mode of worship, or prohibiting the free exercise of religion. . . . "—Draft Proposed and Passed by the Senate, and Sent to the House, September 9, 1789.

26. "Congress shall make no Law respecting an establishment of Religion, or prohibiting the free exercise thereof."—Draft Proposed by Joint House-Senate Committee on September 24, 1789 and Passed by House and Senate on September 25, 1789.

State Constitutional Provisions on Religion (as of 1947)

(continues)

APPENDIX TWO
State Constitutional Provisions on Religion (as of 1947)

State and Year of Constitution	does preamble use "God" or other religious language?	a liberty or right of conscience clause?	a free exercise clause?	a clause against coercion or compulsion to religion or religious support?	a conscientious objection to arms or pacifism clause?	an equality of religion clause?	a clause indicating no state preference for or among religions?	a disestablishment clause?	a clause prohibiting the mandatory payment of money or tithes?	a prohibition on religious test oaths for holding public office?	a prohibition on religious tests or oaths for serving on a jury or as a witness?	a prohibition on religious tests or oaths for voting?	is a tax exemption given to religious property or bodies?	a prohibition against state funding for religious education?	a prohibition against state funding of religion more generally?
Alabama (1901)[1]	yes	yes		yes			yes	yes	yes	yes	—	—	yes	yes	yes
Arizona (1912)	yes	yes								yes	yes	—	yes	yes	yes
Arkansas (1874)	yes	yes	yes	yes			yes	yes	yes	no	no	yes	yes		
California (1879)	yes	yes	yes		yes		yes			—	yes	—	yes	yes	yes
Colorado (1876)	yes	yes	yes	yes			yes			—	—	—		yes	yes
Connecticut (1818)	yes	yes	yes	yes		yes	yes		yes				yes	yes	
Delaware (1897)	yes	yes	yes	yes			yes		yes	yes			yes	yes	

NOTE: These provisions are drawn, in large measure, from Chester James Antieau, Phillip Mark Carroll, and Thomas Carroll Burke, *Religion Under the State Constitutions* (Brooklyn, 1965), 173–239, with some corrections and refinements drawn from the state constitutions in F. Thorpe, ed., *The Federal and State Constitutions*, 7 vols. (Washington, 1909), and *Constitutions of the United States: National and State* (New York, 1962). Because this list depicts only the status of the state constitutions in 1947, Alaska and Hawaii are omitted, as they were not yet states.

[1]The year listed for each state constitution is the year of adoption. Some state constitutions were amended between the year of adoption and 1947. This table incorporates such changes and thus provides a statement of the status of religious liberty in the states in the year 1947.

(continues)

APPENDIX TWO (continued)

State and Year of Constitution	does preamble use "God" or other religious language?	a liberty or right of conscience clause?	a free exercise clause?	a clause against coercion or compulsion to religion or religious support?	a conscientious objection to arms or pacifism clause?	an equality of religion clause?	a clause indicating no state preference for or among religions?	a disestablishment clause?	a clause prohibiting the mandatory payment of money or tithes?	a prohibition on religious test oaths for holding public office?	a prohibition on religious tests or oaths for serving on a jury or as a witness?	a prohibition on religious tests or oaths for voting?	is a tax exemption given to religious property or bodies?	a prohibition against state funding for religious education?	a prohibition against state funding of religion more generally?
Florida (1887)	yes	yes	yes		yes		yes			—	yes	—	yes	yes	yes
Georgia (1945)	yes	yes			yes				yes	yes	—	—	yes	yes	yes
Idaho (1890)	yes	yes	yes	yes	yes		yes			—	—	—	yes	yes	yes
Illinois (1870)	yes	yes	yes	yes	yes		yes			—	—	—	yes	yes	yes
Indiana (1851)	yes	yes	yes	yes	yes		yes			yes	yes	—		yes	
Iowa (1857)	yes	yes		yes	yes	yes		yes		yes	yes	—			
Kansas (1861)	yes	yes		yes	yes	yes	yes		yes	yes	yes	yes	yes	yes	
Kentucky (1891)	yes	yes		yes	yes	yes	yes		yes	—	—	—	yes	yes	
Louisiana (1921)	yes	yes		yes	yes		yes	yes	yes	—	—	—	yes	yes	
Maine (1820)	yes	yes	yes					yes		yes	—	—			
Maryland (1867)	yes	yes		yes					yes	no	no	—			
Massachusetts (1780)	yes	yes	yes		yes		yes			—	—	—	yes	yes	yes
Michigan (1890)	yes	yes	yes	yes	yes				yes	—	yes	yes		yes	yes
Minnesota (1857)	yes	yes		yes					yes	yes	yes	yes		yes	yes

(continues)

APPENDIX TWO (continued)

State and Year of Constitution	does preamble use "God" or other religious language?	a liberty or right of conscience clause?	a free exercise clause?	a clause against coercion or compulsion to religion or religious support?	a conscientious objection to arms or pacifism clause?	an equality of religion clause?	a clause indicating no state preference for or among religions?	a disestablishment clause?	a clause prohibiting the mandatory payment of money or tithes?	a prohibition on religious test oaths for holding public office?	a prohibition on religious tests or oaths for serving on a jury or as a witness?	a prohibition on religious tests or oaths for voting?	is a tax exemption given to religious property or bodies?	a prohibition against state funding for religious education?	a prohibition against state funding of religion more generally?
Mississippi (1890)	yes	yes								no	—	—			yes
Missouri (1945)	yes	yes					yes			yes	yes	—	yes	yes	yes
Montana (1889)	yes	yes	yes	yes			yes			—	—	—	yes	yes	yes
Nebraska (1875)	yes	yes	yes	yes			yes			yes	yes	—	yes	yes	
Nevada (1864)	yes	yes		yes			yes			—	yes	—	yes	yes	yes
New Hampshire (1784)		yes	yes		yes	yes			yes	—	—	—			
New Jersey (1947)	yes	yes		yes			yes		yes	yes	yes	—	yes	yes	yes
New Mexico (1913)	yes	yes		yes			yes	yes		yes	yes	yes	yes	yes	yes
New York (1894)	yes	yes	yes		yes	yes				—	—	—	yes		
North Carolina (1868)	yes		yes		yes		yes			no	yes	—	yes	yes	yes
North Dakota (1889)	yes		yes		yes		yes			yes	yes	—	yes	yes	
Ohio (1851)	yes		yes	yes						yes	—	—	yes		
Oklahoma (1906)	yes									yes	yes	yes	yes	yes	yes
Oregon (1859)		yes								yes	yes	—	yes	yes	yes

APPENDIX TWO *(continued)*

State and Year of Constitution	does preamble use "God" or other religious language?	a liberty or right of conscience clause?	a free exercise clause?	a clause against coercion or compulsion to religion or religious support?	a conscientious objection to arms or pacifism clause?	an equality of religion clause?	a clause indicating no state preference for or among religions?	a disestablishment clause?	a clause prohibiting the mandatory payment of money or tithes?	a prohibition on religious test oaths for holding public office?	a prohibition on religious tests or oaths for serving on a jury or as a witness?	a prohibition on religious tests or oaths for voting?	is a tax exemption given to religious property or bodies?	a prohibition against state funding for religious education?	a prohibition against state funding of religion more generally?
Pennsylvania (1874)	yes	yes		yes	yes		yes		yes	no	—	—	yes	yes	yes
Rhode Island (1843)	yes	yes	yes	yes	yes					yes	—	—		yes	yes
South Carolina (1895)	yes	yes	yes		yes		yes	yes		no	—	—	yes	yes	yes
South Dakota (1889)	yes	yes	yes	yes	yes		yes		yes	—	yes	—	yes	yes	yes
Tennessee (1870)		yes	yes	yes	yes		yes		yes	yes	yes	—	yes	yes	yes
Texas (1876)	yes	yes	yes	yes	yes				yes	no	yes	—	yes	yes	yes
Utah (1895)	yes	yes	yes	yes	yes				yes	yes	yes	yes		yes	yes
Vermont (1793)		yes	yes			yes		yes		—	—	yes	yes		
Virginia (1902)				yes			yes		yes	yes	yes	yes	yes	yes	yes
Washington (1889)	yes			yes	yes		yes			yes	yes	—		yes	yes
West Virginia (1872)	yes	yes	yes	yes	yes		yes		yes	yes	yes	—	yes	yes	
Wisconsin (1848)	yes	yes					yes		yes	yes	yes	—	yes	yes	yes
Wyoming (1890)	yes	yes			yes		yes			yes	yes	—	yes	yes	yes

United States
Supreme Court Decisions
Relating to Religious Liberty

APPENDIX THREE
United States Supreme Court Decisions Relating to Religious Liberty

#	Issue	Case	Citation	Year	Ratio	Author	Holding
1	Church Property	Terrett v. Taylor	13 U.S. (9 Cranch) 43	1815	7-0	Story, J.	State may not rescind the properly obtained charter of the Episcopal Church and expropriate the church's lands.
2	Church Property	Town of Pawlet v. Clark	13 U.S. (9 Cranch) 292	1815	6-0	Story, J.	Royal grant of land to Church of England was not completed, and therefore Episcopal Church had no claim of right or title after the Revolution when the new sovereign claimed the land for other purposes.
3	Charitable Bequest	Vidal v. Girard's Executors	43 U.S. (2 How.) 127	1844	7-0	Story, J.	Testamentary bequest for establishment of school for orphans is valid notwithstanding provisions derogatory of Christianity.
4	Federalism	Permoli v. First Municipality of New Orleans	44 U.S. (3 How.) 589	1844	8-0	Catron, J.	United States Constitution does not protect citizens' religious liberties in regard to the respective states.
5	Church Property	Goesele v. Bimeler	55 U.S. (14 How.) 589	1852	8-0	McLean, J.	Heirs of member of communitarian religious group cannot recover share of property from the religious society.

NOTE: This chart is modeled, in part, after Carl Esbeck's chart, "Table of United States Supreme Court Decisions Relating to Religious Liberty, 1789–1994," *Journal of Law and Religion* 10 (1994): 573–588, as updated at http://law.hamline.edu/files/pdfs/jlr/pdfs/U.S.SupremeCt.05-07.pdf.

¹The "ratio" typically includes two numbers: the majority and the dissenters. If justices concur in the judgment but not in the opinion, they are listed following the number of the majority, designated by "/". We have not differentiated among dissenting opinions but rather listed them all together. Similarly, concurring opinions are not listed separately unless they concur in the judgment only. As a shorthand way of denoting the ratio in more complicated cases, we have simply designated the ratio as "Pluralities." In such cases, if the author is listed as "opinion of the Court," then the opinion garnered a majority of votes, and there was disagreement only beyond the majority. If the author is listed as "for the plurality," then there was no clear majority, though there was sufficient consensus for a judgment, and the named author rendered the judgment of the Court.

(continues)

APPENDIX THREE *(continued)*

#	Issue	Case	Citation	Year	Ratio	Author	Holding
6	Church Property: Civil Court Relief	Smith v. Swormstedt	57 U.S. (16 How.) 288	1853	9-0	Nelson, J.	A Court may sit in equity and divide jointly held property to carry out a voluntarily reached agreement of the church.
7	Church Property	Baker v. Nachtrieb	60 U.S. (19 How.) 126	1856	9-0	Campbell, J.	Defecting member of communitarian religious group may not recover share of property from the religious society.
8	Mandatory Oath	Cummings v. Missouri	71 U.S. (4 Wall.) 277; dissent attached to Ex parte Garland, 71 U.S. (4 Wall.) 397	1866	5-4	Field, J.	State may not deprive priest of the right to preach for failure to take a mandatory oath disavowing support/sympathy for the cause of the Confederate states.
9	Church Property	Watson v. Jones	80 U.S. (13 Wall.) 679	1871	6-2	Miller, J.	Civil courts should defer to the judgment of the highest religious authority in determining which of two internal religious factions is entitled to disputed property.
10	Church Property: Internal Church Governance	Bouldin v. Alexander	82 U.S. (15 Wall.) 131	1872	9-0	Strong, J.	Courts have no power to question acts of internal church discipline or excommunication; the rule of the church's highest internal tribunal must govern property disputes dependent on doctrine.
11	Polygamy; First Application of Free Exercise Clause	Reynolds v. United States	98 U.S. 145	1879	9-0	Waite, C.J.	Upheld federal criminal law prohibiting polygamy and denied a Mormon's free exercise claim to the practice, stating that beliefs could not be regulated but actions could.
12	Polygamy	Miles v. United States	103 U.S. 304	1881	9-0	Woods, J.	Prosecutor may ask prospective jurors at voire dire about polygamy, including whether it is religiously required; calling second wife to testify against husband violates spousal testimonial privilege.

(continues)

APPENDIX THREE *(continued)*

#	Issue	Case	Citation	Year	Ratio	Author	Holding
13	Sunday Law	*Soon Hing v. Crowley*	113 U.S. 703	1885	9-0	Field, J.	Upheld local Sunday law as a day of rest from labor, not as promotion of religion.
14	Polygamy	*Murphy v. Ramsey*	114 U.S. 15	1885	9-0	Matthews, J.	Upheld laws disenfranchising known and suspected bigamists.
15	Polygamy	*Clawson v. United States*	114 U.S. 477	1885	9-0	Blatchford, J.	Polygamy conviction upheld over challenge that Mormons were wrongly excluded from serving on grand jury.
16	Tax Exemptions	*Gibbons v. District of Columbia*	116 U.S. 404	1886	9-0	Gray, J.	Allowed property tax scheme that exempted "church buildings, and grounds actually occupied by such buildings" but not land owned by but not used for the church.
17	Polygamy	*In re Snow*	120 U.S. 274	1887	9-0	Blatchford, J.	Multiple convictions for polygamy against a man are improper because they cover the same time period, and are thus only one offense.
18	Church Property	*Speidel v. Henrici*	120 U.S. 377	1887	9-0	Gray, J.	Defecting member of communitarian religious group may not recover share of property from the religious group.
19	Polygamy	*Ex parte Hans Nielsen*	131 U.S. 176	1889	9-0	Bradley, J.	Mormon man was improperly convicted of adultery after pleading guilty to improper co-habitation; same facts for plea could not be used for the adultery offense.
20	Polygamy	*Davis v. Beason*	133 U.S. 333	1890	9-0	Field, J.	Upheld a conviction for falsely taking a (mandatory) oath renouncing polygamy.
21	Polygamy	*The Late Corporation of the Church of Jesus Christ of Latter Day Saints v. United States*	136 U.S. 1, with decree entered (as modified) at 140 U.S. 665 (1891)	1890	6-3	Bradley, J.	Upheld government's dissolution of the Mormon Church's corporate charter and the confiscation of its property for continued advocacy of polygamy.

(continues)

APPENDIX THREE *(continued)*

#	Issue	Case	Citation	Year	Ratio	Author	Holding
22	Polygamy	*Bassett v. United States*	137 U.S. 496	1890	9-0	Brewer, J.	Conviction for polygamy reversed where testimony of wife was taken, in contravention of marital testimonial privilege.
23	Church Staff Hiring	*Church of the Holy Trinity v. United States*	143 U.S. 457	1892	9-0	Brewer, J.	Refused to apply a new federal law forbidding contracts with foreign aliens to a church seeking to hire a foreign cleric.
24	Church Property	*Catholic Bishop of Nesqually v. Gibbon*	158 U.S. 155	1895	9-0	Brewer, J.	Grant of tract of land by a federal agency to a church still in occupancy could not be later retracted by act of Congress, despite the fact that land was made by donation and not a sale.
25	Sunday Law	*Hennington v. Georgia*	163 U.S. 299	1896	7-2	Harlan, J.	State may enact Sunday closing laws pursuant to its police power, such that laws prohibiting operation of trains does not violate the dormant commerce clause.
26	Building Grants; First Application of Establishment Clause	*Bradfield v. Roberts*	175 U.S. 291	1899	9-0	Peckham, J.	Upheld, against establishment clause challenge, the allocation and distribution of federal funds to build religious hospital.
27	Sunday Law	*Petit v. Minnesota*	177 U.S. 164	1900	9-0	Fuller, C.J.	Barber shops do not have to be included in "works of necessity or charity" that may remain open on Sundays.
28	Church Property	*Schwartz v. Duss*	187 U.S. 8	1902	5-2	McKenna, J.	Dismissing suit seeking distribution of property where claimants were never members of religious group and the group had not dissolved.

(continues)

APPENDIX THREE (continued)

#	Issue	Case	Citation	Year	Ratio	Author	Holding
29	Property Rights	Lowrey v. Hawaii (I)	206 U.S. 206	1907	8-0	McKenna, J.	Condition, prescribing the teaching of Christian training at a school, in land grant from foreign mission board to government requires that either the Christian teaching continue or that a payment option to grantors be exercised; Hawaii statute forbidding governmental aid to denominational school does not alter result.
30	Religious School Funding; Indian Trust Disbursement	Quick Bear v. Leupp	210 U.S. 50	1908	9-0	Fuller, C.J.	Upheld federal distribution of funds (under an Indian treaty) to Catholic schools that offered education to Native Americans.
31	Treaty; Church Property	Ponce v. Roman Catholic Apostolic Church	210 U.S. 296	1908	9-0	Fuller, C.J.	Confirmed church's title to property acquired from Spanish government before the U.S. annexation of Puerto Rico.
32	Incorporation Rights; Religious College	Berea College v. Kentucky	211 U.S. 45	1908	5/2-2	Brewer, J.	Conviction of religious college for violation of state segregation laws is not unconstitutional since state holds power to incorporate educational institutions.
33	Property Rights	Lowrey v. Hawaii (II)	215 U.S. 554	1910	8-0	McKenna, J.	Condition in land grant from foreign mission board to government must be strictly interpreted; teaching general Christianity was insufficient when teaching a definite Congregational and Presbyterian doctrine was contemplated.
34	Church Property	Order of St. Benedict v. Steinhauser	234 U.S. 640	1914	9-0	Hughes, J.	Upheld communal ownership of property within monastic order and granted the Order title to the estate of deceased life-long member.

(continues)

APPENDIX THREE *(continued)*

#	Issue	Case	Citation	Year	Ratio	Author	Holding
35	Religious Exemptions	Crane v. Johnson	242 U.S. 339	1917	9-0	McKenna, J.	State statute did not violate equal protection clause when it criminalized non-religious "drugless practitioner" of medicine but exempted Christian Scientists.
36	Conscientious Objection	Selective Draft Law Cases (Arver v. United States)	245 U.S. 366	1918	9-0	White, C.J.	Upheld as constitutional Congress's power to define conscientious objector status and Congress's restriction of the status to ordained ministers, theology students, and members of well-recognized pacifist sects.
37	Religious School Curriculum	Meyer v. Nebraska	262 U.S. 390; dissent attached to Bartels v. Iowa, 262 U.S. 412	1923	7-2	McReynolds, J.	State statute mandating English-only instruction in all grade schools held unconstitutional, as applied to private religious school.
38	Religious School Attendance	Pierce v. Society of Sisters	268 U.S. 510	1925	9-0	McReynolds, J.	Invalidated state law mandating attendance at public schools as violation of rights of private schools and of parents.
39	Religious School Regulation	Farrington v. Tokushige	273 U.S. 284	1927	9-0	McReynolds, J.	States may not impose unduly intrusive and stringent accreditation and regulatory requirements on religious and other private schools.
40	Naturalization Qualifications; Conscientious Objection	United States v. Schwimmer	279 U.S. 644	1929	6-3	Butler, J.	Permitted the denial of citizenship to pacifist who refused to swear an oath to take up arms in defense of the country.
41	Internal Church Dispute	Gonzalez v. Roman Catholic Archbishop	280 U.S. 1	1929	9-0	Brandeis, J.	Refused to overturn the internal decision-making of religious body regarding proper appointee to ecclesiastical office.

(continues)

APPENDIX THREE *(continued)*

#	Issue	Case	Citation	Year	Ratio	Author	Holding
42	Religious School Subsidization: Textbooks	*Cochran v. Louisiana State Board of Education*	281 U.S. 370	1930	9-0	Hughes, C.J.	Upheld state policy of furnishing textbooks to public and religious school students over objection of taxpayer that this constituted a taking of his private property in violation of the Fourteenth Amendment due process clause.
43	Naturalization Qualifications	*United States v. Macintosh*	283 U.S. 605	1931	5-4	Sutherland, J.	Refusal to take oath to bear arms in defense of the United States, except with qualifications, is a valid reason to bar a person's naturalization as a U.S. citizen.
44	Naturalization Qualifications	*United States v. Bland*	283 U.S. 636	1931	5-4	Sutherland, J.	Refusal to bear arms in defense of the United States is a valid reason to bar a person's naturalization as a U.S. citizen.
45	Conscientious Objection	*Hamilton v. Regents of the University of California*	293 U.S. 245	1934	9-0	Butler, J.	Due process clause of Fourteenth Amendment, though to be construed broadly, confers no right to exemption for pacifists from mandatory ROTC training at state university.
46	Federal Jurisdiction; Distribution of Religious Literature	*Coleman v. City of Griffin*	302 U.S. 636, letting stand 189 S.E. 427 (Ga. Ct. App. 1936)	1937	9-0	Per curiam	No federal question presented in appeal of city ordinance prohibiting distribution of religious literature on religion grounds; same ordinance addressed substantively in Lovell v. City of Griffin, 303 U.S. 444 (1938).
47	Distribution of Religious Literature	*Lovell v. City of Griffin*	303 U.S. 444	1938	8-0	Hughes, C.J.	Invalidated city ordinance prohibiting distribution of religious literature for violating freedom of the press.
48	Distribution of Religious Literature	*Schneider v. State of New Jersey (Town of Irvington)*	308 U.S. 147	1939	7-1	Roberts, J.	Invalidated local ordinance prohibiting distribution of religious literature for violating freedom of speech and freedom of the press.

(continues)

APPENDIX THREE *(continued)*

#	Issue	Case	Citation	Year	Ratio	Author	Holding
49	Licensing; Free Exercise Clause Incorporated	Cantwell v. Connecticut	310 U.S. 296	1940	9-0	Roberts, J.	Free exercise clause expressly applied to the states through the Fourteenth Amendment; city licensing law, requiring religious groups to procure a license in advance but giving discretion to local administrators to deny such licenses, held unconstitutional.
50	Flag Salute	Minersville School Board v. Gobitis	310 U.S. 586	1940	7/1-1	Frankfurter, J.	Provided no free exercise exemption from public school requirement of saluting and pledging allegiance to the American flag.
51	Licensing	Cox v. New Hampshire	312 U.S. 569	1941	9-0	Hughes, C.J.	City may require all groups to obtain a license/permit and pay a reasonable fee, consonant with the expense incurred by the city to administer the license and maintain public order during and after the parade/procession.
52	Fighting Words	Chaplinsky v. New Hampshire	315 U.S. 568	1942	9-0	Murphy, J.	Cursing a police officer is not the exercise of "religion" or speech protected by the First Amendment.
53	Distribution of Religious Literature	Jones v. Opelika (I)	316 U.S. 584	1942	5-4	Reed, J.	Local ordinance requiring license fee on distribution of all literature, and reserving discretion of revocation, may constitutionally be applied to distributors of religious literature.
54	Distribution of Religious Literature	Jamison v. Texas	318 U.S. 413	1943	8-0	Black, J.	Local ordinance prohibiting distribution of religious pamphlets in the public square and door to door is unconstitutional.

(continues)

APPENDIX THREE (continued)

#	Issue	Case	Citation	Year	Ratio	Author	Holding
55	Licensing	*Largent v. Texas*	318 U.S. 418	1943	8-0	Reed, J.	City ordinance that requires permit to solicit orders for books but reserves to city official discretion to deny permits is unconstitutional as applied to religious publications.
56	Distribution of Religious Literature	*Jones v. Opelika (II)*	319 U.S. 103; dissents attached to Murdock v. Pennsylvania (City of Jeannette), 319 U.S. 117, and Douglas v. City of Jeannette, 319 U.S. 166	1943	5-4	Per curiam (relying on Justice Douglas's opinion in Murdock v. Pennsylvania, and Chief Justice Stone's dissent in Jones v. Opelika (I))	Explicitly overruled Jones v. Opelika (I), 316 U.S. 584 (1942); state may not prohibit distribution of religious literature; even if ordinance is "nondiscriminatory" on its face, the liberties guaranteed by the First Amendment are in a preferred position.
57	Distribution of Religious Literature; Flat License Tax	*Murdock v. Pennsylvania (City of Jeannette)*	319 U.S. 105; additional dissent attached to Douglas v. City of Jeannette, 319 U.S. 166 (1943)	1943	5-4	Douglas, J.	A flat tax on all persons soliciting or selling goods is a "prior restraint" on those exercising their constitutional right to exercise their religion through distributing tracts and is thus unconstitutional.
58	Distribution of Religious Literature	*Martin v. Struthers*	319 U.S. 141; additional dissent attached to Douglas v. City of Jeannette, 319 U.S. 166 (1943)	1943	5-4	Black, J.	Ordinance forbidding door to door distribution of religious pamphlets and circulars is unconstitutional because it violates free speech and press.
59	Federal Jurisdiction; Flat License Tax	*Douglas v. City of Jeannette*	319 U.S. 157	1943	7/2-0	Stone, C.J.	Case not properly in federal court; same ordinance addressed substantively in Murdock v. Pennsylvania (City of Jeannette), 319 U.S. 105 (1943).

(continues)

APPENDIX THREE (continued)

#	Issue	Case	Citation	Year	Ratio	Author	Holding
60	Religious Speech; Flag Salute	Taylor v. Mississippi	319 U.S. 583	1943	9-0	Roberts, J.	Overturning convictions of Jehovah's Witnesses for advocating, through words and pamphlets, a refusal to salute the flag/state.
61	Flag Salute	West Virginia State Board of Education v. Barnette	319 U.S. 624	1943	6-3	Jackson, J.	Overruled Minersville School Board v. Gobitis, 310 U.S. 586 (1940); First Amendment provides exemption from mandatory participation in rituals that parties conscientiously oppose, including saluting the flag in a public school classroom.
62	Parent/Guardian Rights	Prince v. Massachusetts	321 U.S. 158	1944	5-4	Rutledge, J.	State criminal law regulating child labor, applied to guardian of nine-year-old girl distributing religious tracts on the public streets in the evening, is not a denial or abridgment of free exercise rights.
63	Flat License Tax; Distribution of Religious Literature	Follett v. Town of McCormick	321 U.S. 573	1944	5/1-3	Douglas, J.	City may not impose flat license tax on minister distributing religious literature.
64	Religious Fraud	United States v. Ballard	322 U.S. 78	1944	5-4	Douglas, J.	Truth of religious belief is not subject to the scrutiny of a jury, but jury may be called on to decide the sincerity of defendant's belief.
65	Conscientious Objection	In re Summers	325 U.S. 561	1945	5-4	Reed, J.	Refusal of bar admission to conscientious objector who refused to swear oath that he would serve in military not a free exercise violation.
66	Polygamy	Chatwin v. United States	326 U.S. 455	1946	7/1-0	Murphy, J.	Defendant who persuaded minor female to join him in "celestial" marriage not guilty of violating Federal Kidnapping Act.

(continues)

APPENDIX THREE *(continued)*

#	Issue	Case	Citation	Year	Ratio	Author	Holding
67	Distribution of Religious Literature	*Marsh v. Alabama*	326 U.S. 501	1946	5-3	Black, J.	Statute imposing criminal penalties for distribution of religious literature in company owned town is unconstitutional, per free exercise and speech clauses.
68	Distribution of Religious Literature	*Tucker v. Texas*	326 U.S. 517	1946	5-3	Black, J.	Statute imposing criminal penalties for distribution of religious literature in company owned town is unconstitutional, per free exercise and speech clauses.
69	Naturalization Qualifications; First Application of Article VI Test Oath Clause	*Girouard v. United States*	328 U.S. 61	1946	5-3	Douglas, J.	Government may not require a party who is conscientiously opposed to swear a military test oath before receiving naturalized citizenship status, per free exercise clause and Article VI ban on religious test oaths.
70	Polygamy	*Cleveland v. United States*	329 U.S. 14	1946	5/1-3	Douglas, J.	Upheld convictions of members of polygamous sect for transporting plural wives across state lines in violation of the Mann "White Slave" Act.
71	Conscientious Objection	*Eagles v. Samuels*	329 U.S. 304	1946	9-0	Douglas, J.	Civilian panel could properly determine that defendant failed to establish right to preministerial deferment under Selective Service Act.
72	School Transportation; Incorporation of Establishment Clause	*Everson v. Board of Education*	330 U.S. 1	1947	5-4	Black, J.	Expressly applied establishment clause to the states through the Fourteenth Amendment; but it is not establishment of religion for states to provide school bus transportation to religious and public school children alike.
73	Polygamy	*Musser v. Utah*	333 U.S. 95	1948	5/1-3	Jackson, J.	Conviction for polygamy vacated and remanded for consideration of state law questions.

(continues)

APPENDIX THREE *(continued)*

#	Issue	Case	Citation	Year	Ratio	Author	Holding
74	Public School On-Campus Release Time	McCollum v. Board of Education	333 U.S. 203	1948	6/1/1-1	Black, J.	Disallowed public school "release time" program, wherein students were released from regular classes once a week to be able to participate in religious classes, which were held on campus.
75	Religious Speech	Saia v. New York	334 U.S. 558	1948	5-4	Douglas, J.	City ordinance prohibiting sound amplification, reserving discretion to police chief but giving no criteria for exercising that discretion, violates free speech because it operates as a prior restraint.
76	Conscientious Objection	Gara v. United States	340 U.S. 857, affirming, by an equally divided Court, 178 F2d 38 (6th Cir. 1949)	1950	4-4	Per curiam	Upheld conviction for counseling another person conscientiously to object to draft registration and for actively opposing Selective Service Act.
77	Licensing	Niemotko v. State of Maryland	340 U.S. 268	1951	7/1/1-0	Vinson, C.J.	City may not deny a permit to use a public park for religious purposes when the applicable statute lacks clear criteria for such denials.
78	Licensing	Kunz v. New York	340 U.S. 290; concurrence attached to Niemotko v. Maryland, 340 U.S. 273 (1991)	1951	6/1/1-1	Vinson, C.J.	City may not deny a license to a Baptist minister to preach in a public park because the licensing regulation improperly gave local officials discretion to deny licenses.
79	Standing	Doremus v. Board of Education	342 U.S. 429	1952	6-3	Jackson, J.	Party lacks standing to challenge Bible reading in public school when the student has already graduated.
80	Release Time from Public Schools	Zorach v. Clauson	343 U.S. 306	1952	6-3	Douglas, J.	Upheld the constitutionality of granting students release time from public schools to attend religious education or services.

(continues)

APPENDIX THREE (continued)

#	Issue	Case	Citation	Year	Ratio	Author	Holding
81	Censorship	Joseph Burstyn, Inc. v. Wilson	343 U.S. 495	1952	6/2/1-0	Clark, J.	State law requiring permit for commercial showing of films but allowing censorship of films that are "sacrilegious" is a prior restraint and thus an unconstitutional violation of freedoms of speech and press.
82	Church Property; Internal Church Governance	Kedroff v. Saint Nicholas Cathedral	344 U.S. 94	1952	8-1	Reed, J.	State religious incorporation law may not prohibit foreign religious authority from selecting church leaders and shift control to local church authorities; internal church law must be allowed to decide who makes such a decision.
83	Public Forum	Fowler v. Rhode Island	345 U.S. 67	1953	7/1/1-0	Douglas, J.	Struck down ordinance that prohibited religious speech but allowed for religious services in a public park because it was religiously discriminatory.
84	Licensing	Poulos v. New Hampshire	345 U.S. 395	1953	6/1-2	Reed, J.	Ordinance that leaves officials no discretion in granting permits but nevertheless requires payment of a sliding-scale fee to pay for city expenses incurred because of the permitted activity is constitutional.
85	Conscientious Objection	United States v. Nugent	346 U.S. 1	1953	5-3	Vinson, C.J.	Conscientious objector refusing to submit to induction into armed services has not shown the statute to be unconstitutional; Selective Service not required to disclose full FBI file on claimants.
86	Conscientious Objection	Sicurella v. United States	348 U.S. 385	1955	7-2	Clark, J.	Willingness to fight in "theocratic" wars does not disqualify a Jehovah's Witness who would otherwise qualify for exemption as a conscientious objector.

(continues)

APPENDIX THREE   *(continued)*

#	Issue	Case	Citation	Year	Ratio	Author	Holding
87	Conscientious Objection	*Simmons v. United States*	348 U.S. 397	1955	5/2-2	Clark, J.	Reversed conviction of defendant who was denied fair conscientious objection hearing because of government's failure to supply him "fair resume" of materials from his FBI files.
88	Conscientious Objection	*Gonzales v. United States*	348 U.S. 407	1955	6-3	Clark, J.	Reversed conviction of defendant who was denied fair conscientious objection hearing because of government's failure to supply him "fair resume" of materials from his FBI files.
89	Loyalty Oath	*First Unitarian Church v. County of Los Angeles*	357 U.S. 545; concurrence and dissent attached to *Speiser v. Randall*, 357 U.S. 513, 538 (1958)	1958	7/1-1	Brennan, J.	Government may not require a party who is conscientiously opposed to swear a loyalty oath as a prerequisite to receiving a tax exemption.
90	Church Property: Internal Church Governance	*Kreshik v. St. Nicholas Cathedral*	363 U.S. 190	1960	9-0	Per curiam	In follow-up to *Kedroff v. St. Nicholas Cathedral*, state court cannot make same decisions forbidden to legislature; internal church authorities are entitled to make own decisions.
91	Sunday Laws	*McGowan v. Maryland*	366 U.S. 420	1961	6/2-1	Warren, C.J.	Upheld state law proscribing certain business and commercial activity on Sunday against establishment clause challenge.
92	Sunday Laws	*Two Guys from Harrison Allentown, Inc. v. McGinley*	366 U.S. 582; concurrence and dissent attached to *McGowan v. Maryland*, 366 U.S. 459, 561 (1961)	1961	6/2-1	Warren, C.J.	Sunday closing law does not violate establishment clause.
93	Sunday Laws	*Braunfeld v. Brown*	366 U.S. 599; other opinions attached to *McGowan v. Maryland*, 366 U.S. 459, 561 (1961)	1961	Pluralities	Warren, C.J. (for the plurality)	Statute disallowing sales on Sunday does not violate free exercise rights of Jewish appellant, who is a strict Saturday Sabbatarian.

(continues)

APPENDIX THREE   (continued)

#	Issue	Case	Citation	Year	Ratio	Author	Holding
94	Sunday Laws	Gallagher v. Crown Kosher Super Market of Massachusetts	366 U.S. 617; other opinions attached to McGowan v. Maryland, 366 U.S. 459, 561, and to Braunfeld v. Brown, 366 U.S. 610, 616	1961	Pluralities	Warren, C.J. (for the plurality)	Sunday closing law does not violate free exercise rights of owner of kosher supermarket, Orthodox Jewish customers, or rabbis with a duty to inspect kosher markets per Jewish dietary laws.
95	Mandatory Public Office Oath	Torcaso v. Watkins	367 U.S. 488	1961	7/2-0	Black, J.	Requirement of mandatory oath affirming belief in God as a prerequisite for holding public office is unconstitutional.
96	Prayer in Public School	Engel v. Vitale	370 U.S. 421	1962	6-1	Black, J.	Disallowed state program of daily (nondenominational) prayer in public school classrooms.
97	Federal Jurisdiction; Sunday Laws	Arlan's Department Store v. Kentucky	371 U.S. 218; letting stand 357 S.W.2d 708 (Ky. 1962)	1962	8-1	Per curiam	Dismissed for lack of federal question; state court decision allowed to stand, upholding regulation that provided exemption from Sunday closing law only for those whose religion required rest on another day.
98	Bible Reading in Public School	Abington School District v. Schempp	374 U.S. 203	1963	8-1	Clark, J.	Mandatory Bible reading in public school classrooms violates establishment clause.
99	Unemployment Compensation Benefits	Sherbert v. Verner	374 U.S. 398	1963	6/1-2	Brennan, J.	Free exercise clause forbids state to deny unemployment compensation to claimant discharged from a job that would require her to work on her Sabbath.
100	Bible Reading in Public School	Chamberlain v. Public Instruction Board	377 U.S. 402	1964	6-3	Per curiam	Reading the Bible and reciting the Lord's Prayer in public school is unconstitutional.
101	Prisoner's Rights	Cooper v. Pate	378 U.S. 546	1964	9-0	Per curiam	Muslim prisoner entitled to hear on the merits that he was denied access to religious publications.

(continues)

APPENDIX THREE *(continued)*

#	Issue	Case	Citation	Year	Ratio	Author	Holding
102	Conscientious Objection	*United States v. Seeger*	380 U.S. 163	1965	9-0	Clark, J.	Section 6(j) of Selective Service Act should be construed broadly, such that claimants may qualify for conscientious objector status if their belief is "sincere and meaningful" and occupies in their life "a place parallel to that filled by the God of those admittedly qualifying for the exemption."
103	Medical Care; Parent/ Guardian Rights	*Jehovah's Witnesses v. King County Hospital*	390 U.S. 598; affirming 278 F.Supp. 488 (W.D. Wash)	1968	7-2	Per curiam	Blood transfusions may be administered to children, even if the parents are religiously opposed.
104	Standing	*Flast v. Cohen*	392 U.S. 83	1968	8-1	Warren, C.J.	Federal taxpayer has standing to challenge appropriation of federal funds for religious schools under the establishment clause.
105	Religious School Subsidization: Textbooks	*Board of Education v. Allen*	392 U.S. 236	1968	6-3	White, J.	Upheld state law requiring textbooks of "secular subjects" be provided to all students in the state, whether attending public or private (religious or other) schools.
106	Teaching Evolution in Public Schools	*Epperson v. Arkansas*	393 U.S. 97	1968	8/1-0	Fortas, J.	State criminal law which prohibited the teaching of evolution in a public school or state university violates the establishment clause.
107	Conscientious Objection	*Oestereich v. Selective Service System*	393 U.S. 233	1968	5/1-3	Douglas, J.	Individual who qualified for exemption based on religion could not be denied that exemption for conduct unrelated to the merits of that exemption in absence of legislative authorization.

(continues)

APPENDIX THREE *(continued)*

#	Issue	Case	Citation	Year	Ratio	Author	Holding
108	Internal Church Governance: Church Property	*Presbyterian Church in the United States v. Mary Elizabeth Blue Hull Memorial Presbyterian Church*	393 U.S. 440	1969	9-0	Brennan, J.	Internal church disputes, including property disputes, should be governed by internal church law; civil courts may not use "departure from doctrine" standard, and should defer to the highest internal church authority.
109	Church Property	*Maryland and Virginia Churches v. Sharpsburg Church*	396 U.S. 367	1970	9-0	Per curiam	Civil courts may resolve church property disputes as long as they do not involve inquiry into church doctrine.
110	Tax Exemptions	*Walz v. Tax Commission*	397 U.S. 664	1970	8-1	Burger, C.J.	Upheld state property tax exemption for church property against establishment clause challenge.
111	Conscientious Objection	*Welsh v. United States*	398 U.S. 333	1970	4/1-3	Black, J. (for the plurality)	Section 6(j) must be construed broadly; persons whose consciences, "spurred by deeply held moral, ethical, or religious beliefs," do not allow them to be an "instrument of war" are entitled to conscientious objector status.
112	Conscientious Objection	*Mulloy v. United States*	398 U.S. 410	1970	8-0	Stewart, J.	Review board must consider new evidence submitted for reclassification by petitioner who had returned to faith of his youth.
113	Conscientious Objection	*Gillette v. United States*	401 U.S. 437	1971	7/1-1	Marshall, J.	Congress may exempt persons opposed to participating in all wars, but not those objecting to participation in a particular war, from military service without violating the First Amendment.
114	Employment	*Dewey v. Reynolds Metals Co.*	402 U.S. 689; affirming, by an equally divided Court, 429 F.2d 324 (6th Cir. 1970)	1971	4-4	Per curiam	Rejected free exercise claim of a Sabbatarian who claimed he was wrongfully discharged on the basis of his religious beliefs.

(continues)

APPENDIX THREE *(continued)*

#	Issue	Case	Citation	Year	Ratio	Author	Holding
115	Religious School Subsidization: Textbooks	*Lemon v. Kurtzman (I)*	403 U.S. 602	1971	6/1/1-0	Burger, C.J.	Establishment clause requires laws to have (1) a secular purpose; (2) primary effect that neither advances nor inhibits religion; and (3) no excessive entanglement of church and state; statute that reimbursed religious schools for costs of teaching secular subjects violates (3).
116	Construction Grants	*Tilton v. Richardson*	403 U.S. 672; additional opinions attached to Lemon v. Kurtzman (I), 403 U.S. 642, 661 (1971)	1971	Pluralities	Burger, C.J.	Upheld federal grants that supported construction of library, science, and arts buildings at religious colleges as well as secular colleges.
117	Conscientious Objection	*Clay v. United States*	403 U.S. 698	1971	7/1-0	Per curiam	Reversed conviction of black Muslim for refusing induction notice when the government conceded pacifism based on religious belief and sincerity.
118	Prisoner's Rights	*Cruz v. Beto*	405 U.S. 319	1972	6/1/1-1	Per curiam	Buddhist prisoner must be given "reasonable opportunity" to free exercise of religion.
119	Compulsory Education	*Wisconsin v. Yoder*	406 U.S. 205	1972	6-1 (but dissenting opinion concurred in part)	Burger, C.J.	Granted free exercise exemption to Amish, which exempted them from full compliance with compulsory school attendance law.
120	Religious School Subsidization	*Lemon v. Kurtzman (II)*	411 U.S. 192	1973	4/1-3	Burger, C.J. (for the plurality)	Lemon v. Kurtzman (I), 403 U.S. 602 (1971), should not be applied retroactively.
121	Religious School Subsidization: Textbooks	*Norwood v. Harrison*	413 U.S. 455	1973	7/2-0	Burger, C.J.	State may loan textbooks on secular subjects to religious schools, but not if those schools discriminate on racial grounds.

(continues)

APPENDIX THREE *(continued)*

#	Issue	Case	Citation	Year	Ratio	Author	Holding
122	Religious School Subsidization	*Levitt v. Committee for Public Education and Religious Liberty*	413 U.S. 472	1973	5/3-1	Burger, C.J.	States may not reimburse religious schools for most costs incurred to administer standardized tests and to prepare mandated state records.
123	Revenue Bonds	*Hunt v. McNair*	413 U.S. 734	1973	6-3	Powell, J.	Upheld issuance of revenue bonds for religious colleges.
124	Religious School Subsidization	*Committee for Public Education and Religious Liberty v. Nyquist*	413 U.S. 756	1973	Pluralities	Powell, J. (opinion of the Court)	Disallowed state reimbursement for low-income parents for part of religious school tuition; disallowed tax deduction for low-income parents whose children attended religious schools; disallowed direct grants to private schools; disallowed direct grants to private schools serving low-income students for maintenance and repair costs.
125	Religious School Subsidization	*Sloan v. Lemon*	413 U.S. 825; additional opinions attached to Committee for Public Education and Religious Liberty v. Nyquist, 413 U.S. 798, 813 (1973)	1973	6-3	Powell, J.	Disallowed state reimbursement to parents for portion of religious school tuition.
126	Education Benefits; Conscientious Objection	*Johnson v. Robison*	415 U.S. 361	1974	8-1	Brennan, J.	Statute that grants education benefits to military draftees but not to draftees who perform civilian alternative service is not unconstitutional.
127	Education Benefits; Conscientious Objection	*Hernandez v. Veterans' Administration*	415 U.S. 391	1974	8/1-0	Brennan, J.	Vacated a Ninth Circuit dismissal, for lack of jurisdiction, of a former conscientious objector's challenge to the statute at issue in Johnson v. Robinson, 415 U.S. 361 (1974) and remanded for reconsideration in light of that case.

(continues)

APPENDIX THREE (continued)

#	Issue	Case	Citation	Year	Ratio	Author	Holding
128	Title I; Religious School Subsidization	Wheeler v. Barrera	417 U.S. 402	1974	6/1/1-1	Blackman, J.	State receiving Title I funds must provide "comparable" but "not identical" services to disadvantaged students in both public and private schools, or forfeit Title I funds.
129	Conscientious Objection; Taxes	United States v. American Friends Service Committee	419 U.S. 7	1974	8-1	Per curiam	Upheld collection of taxes from those conscientiously opposed to having their taxes support the military.
130	Religious School Subsidization: Textbooks	Meek v. Pittenger	421 U.S. 349, overruled by Mitchell v. Helms, 530 U.S. 793 (2000)	1975	Pluralities	Stewart, J. (for the plurality)	State may loan textbooks, but not other various supplies and film, nor various counseling and other personnel, even if those were mandated by state policy.
131	Internal Church Governance	Serbian Orthodox Diocese v. Milivojevich	426 U.S. 696	1976	6/1-2	Brennan, J.	Internal church law must govern internal church matters, including removal from ecclesiastical posts; civil courts may not give marginal review to ecclesiastical decisions, even if they appear arbitrary, collusive, or fraudulent.
132	Construction Grants	Roemer v. Maryland Public Works Board	426 U.S. 736	1976	3/2-4	Blackmun, J. (for the plurality)	Upheld a state construction grant program that aided religious colleges alongside secular colleges.
133	Title VII; Employment	Parker Seal Company v. Cummins	429 U.S. 65, affirming, by an equally divided Court, 516 F.2d 544 (6th Cir. 1975)	1976	4-4	Per curiam	Employer did not make sufficient effort to accommodate Sabbatarian.
134	State Motto	Wooley v. Maynard	430 U.S. 705	1977	Pluralities	Burger C.J. (opinion of the Court)	State cannot require, upon pain of criminal sanctions, display of state motto on vehicle license plates that violates religious owner's religious convictions.

(continues)

APPENDIX THREE *(continued)*

#	Issue	Case	Citation	Year	Ratio	Author	Holding
135	Title VII; Employment Accommodation	*Trans World Airlines, Inc. v. Hardison*	432 U.S. 63	1977	7-2	White, J.	Employer's attempted accommodation of employee's religious beliefs was reasonable; no obligation to violate union contracts or incur additional costs without express congressional intent.
136	Religious School Subsidization	*Wolman v. Walter*	433 U.S. 229, overruled by *Mitchell v. Helms*, 530 U.S. 793 (2000)	1977	Pluralities	Blackmun, J. (for the plurality)	State may provide various personnel, diagnostic services, and standardized testing but may not loan instructional materials to private schools or to parents or provide transportation for field trips by private schools.
137	Title VII; Employment Accommodation	*Parker Seal Company v. Cummins*	433 U.S. 903, vacating 429 U.S. 65 (1976)	1977	8-0	Vacated and remanded	Vacated and remanded for consideration in light of Trans World Airlines, Inc. v. Hardison, 432 U.S. 63 (1977).
138	Religious School Subsidization	*New York v. Cathedral Academy*	434 U.S. 125	1977	6-3	Stewart, J.	Disallowed reimbursement of religious schools for state-mandated record keeping.
139	Clergy Disqualified from Public Office	*McDaniel v. Paty*	435 U.S. 618	1978	4/2/1/1-0	Burger J. (for the plurality)	State constitutional prohibition against clergy holding political office is unconstitutional.
140	Labor Law	*National Labor Relations Board v. Catholic Bishop of Chicago*	440 U.S. 490	1979	5-4	Burger, C.J.	Denied jurisdiction to the NLRB over a Catholic school's teachers, based on the rights of a religious group to function separately from the state.
141	Church Property: Internal Church Governance	*Jones v. Wolf*	443 U.S. 595	1979	5-4	Blackmun, J.	Courts may decide intrachurch property disputes using "neutral principles of law," and thus avoid deferring all decision making to internal church authorities.
142	Religious School Subsidization	*Committee for Public Education and Religious Liberty v. Regan*	444 U.S. 646	1980	5-4	White, J.	Upheld reimbursement of religious schools for "actual costs" of state-mandated tests and reporting.

(continues)

APPENDIX THREE (continued)

#	Issue	Case	Citation	Year	Ratio	Author	Holding
143	Abortion and Religion	Harris v. McRae	448 U.S. 297	1980	5-4	Stewart, J.	Upheld congressional restrictions on Medicaid-funded abortions.
144	Ten Commandments in Public School	Stone v. Graham	449 U.S. 39	1980	5-4	Per curiam	Struck down state statute that required the posting of a plaque bearing the Ten Commandments on the wall of each public school classroom.
145	Unemployment Compensation Benefits	Thomas v. Review Board, Indiana Employment Security Division	450 U.S. 707	1981	7/1-1	Burger, C.J.	Government may not deny unemployment benefits to claimant who refused to accept employment, based on individual religious beliefs, at a job that produced parts that would be used in military armaments.
146	Religious Schools and Unemployment Compensation Taxes	St. Martin Evangelical Lutheran Church v. South Dakota	451 U.S. 772	1981	8/1-0	Blackmun, J.	The word "church" in the Federal Unemployment Tax Act exempting service performed in the employ of a church applies to schools that have no separate legal existence from a church.
147	Distribution of Religious Literature; Charitable Solicitation Law	Heffron v. International Society for Krishna Consciousness	452 U.S. 640	1981	Pluralities	White, J. (opinion of the Court)	Regulation requiring all persons and groups wishing to sell, exhibit, or distribute materials at a fair to do so from a rented booth does not violate First Amendment rights of itinerant religious group.
148	Equal Access	Widmar v. Vincent	454 U.S. 263	1981	7/1-1	Powell, J.	When a state university creates a limited public forum open to voluntary student groups, religious groups must be given "equal access" to that forum.
149	Standing	Valley Forge Christian College v. Americans United for Separation of Church and State	454 U.S. 464	1982	5-4	Rehnquist, J.	Religious liberty litigant, as federal taxpayer, lacked standing to challenge federal donation of property to religious organizations.

(continues)

APPENDIX THREE (continued)

#	Issue	Case	Citation	Year	Ratio	Author	Holding
150	Tax Exemption	United States v. Lee	455 U.S. 252	1982	8/1-0	Burger, C.J.	Denied free exercise exemption from social security taxes for Amish employer.
151	Prayer in Public School	Treen v. Karen B.	455 U.S. 913; affirming 653 F.2d 897 (5th Cir. 1981)	1982	9-0	Affirmed on appeal	Affirmed, without comment, a Fifth Circuit opinion that struck down a statute authorizing student volunteers to lead prayer in public school classrooms.
152	Charitable Solicitation Law	Larson v. Valente	456 U.S. 228	1982	5-4	Brennan, J.	Disallowed state law requiring only certain religious organizations to make revenue reports.
153	Charitable Solicitation Law	Rusk v. Espinoza	456 U.S. 951; affirming 634 F.2d 477 (10th Cir. 1980)	1982	7-2	Affirmed on appeal	Affirmed, without comment, a Tenth Circuit opinion that struck down ordinance requiring officials to distinguish between "religious" and "secular" activities of religious bodies for licensing and regulation purposes.
154	Federal Jurisdiction; Unemployment Tax	California v. Grace Brethren Church	457 U.S. 393	1982	7-2	O'Connor, J.	Federal district court did not have jurisdiction to hear case involving state tax.
155	Zoning; Delegation of Civil Power	Larken v. Grendel's Den	459 U.S. 116	1982	8-1	Burger, C.J.	States may not grant veto power to churches over whether a liquor license will be granted to a facility within 500 feet of the church property.
156	Tax Exempt Status	Bob Jones University v. United States	461 U.S. 574	1983	7/1-1	Burger, C.J.	Upheld IRS decision to remove federal tax-exempt status from religious university that engaged in racial discrimination, on the basis of its religious convictions, in matriculation and employment decisions.

(continues)

APPENDIX THREE *(continued)*

#	Issue	Case	Citation	Year	Ratio	Author	Holding
157	State Income Tax Deduction	*Mueller v. Allen*	463 U.S. 388	1983	5-4	Rehnquist, J.	Upheld state law that allowed parents of private school children to claim state income tax deductions for the costs of "tuition, transportation, and textbooks."
158	Legislative Prayer	*Marsh v. Chambers*	463 U.S. 783	1983	6-3	Burger, C.J.	Upheld, against establishment clause challenge, the state practice of appointing legislative chaplains to offer prayers at the General Assembly.
159	Religious Display	*Lynch v. Donnelly*	465 U.S. 668	1984	5-4	Burger, C.J.	Upheld government practice of displaying nativity scene as part of holiday display in city park.
160	Conscientious Objection	*Wayte v. United States*	470 U.S. 598	1985	7-2	Powell, J.	"Passive enforcement policy" and "beg policy" of Selective Service System do not violate First (or Fifth) Amendment.
161	Religious Display	*Village of Scarsdale v. McCreary*	471 U.S. 83; affirming, by an equally divided Court, 739 F.2d 716 (2d Cir. 1984)	1985	4-4	Per curiam	Accommodation of displaying a nativity scene, at no expense to city, is not a violation of establishment clause.
162	Fair Labor Standards Act	*Tony and Susan Alamo Foundation v. Secretary of Labor*	471 U.S. 290	1985	9-0	White, J.	Application of Fair Labor Standards Act does not obstruct core religious functions of a foundation.
163	Moment of Silence in Public School	*Wallace v. Jaffree*	472 U.S. 38	1985	5/1-3	Stevens, J.	Struck down state law providing for moments of silence (for prayer or meditation) in public schools.
164	Driver's License Photograph	*Jensen v. Quaring*	472 U.S. 478, affirming, by an equally divided Court, 728 F.2d 1121 (8th Cir. 1984)	1985	4-4	Per curiam	Struck down requirement that applicant submit to having color photograph taken to affix on driver's license as an unconstitutional burden on applicant's free exercise of her sincerely held religious beliefs.

(continues)

APPENDIX THREE *(continued)*

#	Issue	Case	Citation	Year	Ratio	Author	Holding
165	Sabbath Laws	Estate of Thornton v. Caldor	472 U.S. 703	1985	8-1	Burger, C.J.	Struck down state law that allowed private sector employees to pick their Sabbath, which employers had to accommodate.
166	Religious School Subsidization: Shared Time Programs	Grand Rapids School District v. Ball	473 U.S. 373	1985	Pluralities	Brennan, J. (opinion of the Court)	States may not lend public school personnel to teach remedial and enrichment courses in religious schools.
167	Title I; Remedial Services	Aguilar v. Felton	473 U.S. 402, overruled by Agostini v. Felton, 521 U.S. 203 (1997)	1985	5-4	Brennan, J.	States may not use public school teachers to hold remedial educational programs to indigent children in classrooms leased from religious schools.
168	State Aid for Vocational Education at Religious College	Witters v. Washington Department of Services for the Blind	474 U.S. 481	1986	8/1-0	Marshall, J.	Upheld state program furnishing aid to a visually impaired student attending a Christian college for vocational education.
169	Military Regulations	Goldman v. Weinberger	475 U.S. 503	1986	5-4	Rehnquist, J.	Military officer does not have free exercise right to wear his yarmulke on duty.
170	Standing	Bender v. Williamsport Area School District	475 U.S. 534	1986	5-4	Stevens, J.	School board member has no standing, in his capacity as a parent, to appeal a board decision affecting the religious rights of his child in the school.
171	Social Security Number Requirement	Bowen v. Roy	476 U.S. 693	1986	Pluralities	Burger C.J. (for the plurality)	Agency's use of social security number does not violate free exercise rights of Native American who believes such use would impair his child's spirit.
172	Federal Jurisdiction	Ohio Civil Rights Commission v. Dayton Christian Schools	477 U.S. 619	1986	5/4-0	Rehnquist, J.	Federal district courts should abstain from adjudicating pending state proceedings as long as federal plaintiff has opportunity to litigate his constitutional claim.

(continues)

APPENDIX THREE (continued)

#	Issue	Case	Citation	Year	Ratio	Author	Holding
173	Title VII: Employment Accommodation	Ansonia Board of Education v. Philbrook	479 U.S. 60	1986	Pluralities	Rehnquist, C.J. (opinion of the Court)	Employer not required to accept employee's preferred religious accommodation.
174	Unemployment Compensation Benefits	Hobbie v. Unemployment Appeals Commission of Florida	480 U.S. 136	1987	6/1/1-1	Brennan, J.	Government may not deny unemployment benefits to claimant, a new religious convert, who was discharged for refusing to work on her Sabbath.
175	Religious Discrimination	Shaare Tefila Congregation v. Cobb	481 U.S. 615	1987	9-0	White, J.	Jews may rely on racial clause of civil rights statute for cause of action against desecrators of synagogue.
176	Prisoner's Rights	O'Lone v. Estate of Shabazz	482 U.S. 342	1987	5-4	Rehnquist, C.J.	Denied free exercise accommodation for Muslim prisoner to engage in collective Friday worship.
177	Overbreadth Doctrine	Airport Commissioners of Los Angeles v. Jews for Jesus	482 U.S. 569	1987	9-0	O'Connor, J.	Airport regulation banning all "first amendment activities" within a public (or nonpublic) forum is a violation of the free speech clause.
178	Creationism in Public School	Edwards v. Aguillard	482 U.S. 578	1987	6/1-2	Brennan, J.	Struck down state statute that required, in public schools, teaching of both creation and evolution, if a theory of origins was taught at all.
179	Employment Discrimination	Corporation of the Presiding Bishop of the Church of Jesus Christ of Latter-Day Saints v. Amos	483 U.S. 327	1987	5/2/1/1-0	White, J.	Upheld exemption of religious school from civil rights prohibition against religious discrimination; religious employer not required to retain employee who has lapsed from its faith.

(continues)

APPENDIX THREE (continued)

#	Issue	Case	Citation	Year	Ratio	Author	Holding
180	Standing	Karcher v. May	484 U.S. 72	1987	8/1-0	O'Connor, J.	State legislators cannot appeal an establishment case involving a moment of silence law for which they voted, but which the legislature has chosen not to appeal.
181	Native American Rights	Lyng v. Northwest Indian Cemetery Protective Association	485 U.S. 439	1988	5-3	O'Connor, J.	Construction of road through section of national forest regarded as sacred ground by three tribes does not violate free exercise clause; American Indian Religious Freedom Act provides no cause of action.
182	Unemployment Compensation Benefits	Employment Division, Oregon v. Smith (I)	485 U.S. 660	1988	5-3	Stevens, J.	State must determine whether religious use of peyote is legal under state law.
183	Standing	United States Catholic Conference v. Abortion Rights Mobilization	487 U.S. 72	1988	8-1	Kennedy, J.	A nonparty witness held in contempt had standing to challenge federal court's jurisdiction over case.
184	Religious Social Agency Subsidization	Bowen v. Kendrick	487 U.S. 589	1988	5-4	Rehnquist, C.J.	Upheld federal funding of Catholic counseling centers for pregnant teenagers, in implementation of the Adolescent Family Life Act.
185	Tax Exemption	Texas Monthly v. Bullock	489 U.S. 1	1989	3/2/1-3	Brennan, J. (for the plurality)	State sales tax exemption exclusively for religious periodicals violates establishment clause.
186	Unemployment Compensation Benefits	Frazee v. Illinois Department of Employment Security	489 U.S. 829	1989	9-0	White, J.	State may not deny unemployment benefits to claimant who refused to take a job that might require him to work on Sunday.
187	Tax Deductions	Hernandez v. Commissioner of Internal Revenue	490 U.S. 680	1989	5-2	Marshall, J.	Upheld denial of charitable deduction for contributions to the Church of Scientology, given in return for religious services.

(continues)

APPENDIX THREE *(continued)*

#	Issue	Case	Citation	Year	Ratio	Author	Holding
188	Religious Display	*County of Allegheny v. ACLU*	492 U.S. 573	1989	Pluralities	Blackmun, J. (for the plurality)	Disallowed county's practice of allowing a privately funded nativity scene in front of its courthouse but upheld the display of a menorah on courthouse grounds.
189	Tax Exemption	*Jimmy Swaggart Ministries v. Board of Equalization of California*	493 U.S. 378	1990	9-0	O'Connor	Levy of state sales and use taxes on religious articles is not a prior restraint.
190	Unemployment Compensation Benefits	*Employment Division, Oregon v. Smith (II)*	494 U.S. 872	1990	5/1-3	Scalia, J.	Denial of unemployment compensation benefits to Native American who was discharged for sacramental use of peyote, a proscribed narcotic, does not violate free exercise clause.
191	Tax Deductions	*Davis v. United States*	495 U.S. 472	1990	9-0	O'Connor, J.	Upheld denial of charitable deduction for contribution in return for religious services.
192	Equal Access	*Board of Education of the Westside Community Schools v. Mergens*	496 U.S. 226	1990	4/2/2-1	O'Connor, J. (for the plurality)	Equal Access Act, which applies *Widmar v. Vincent*, 454 U.S. 263 (1981) rule to public high schools, does not violate establishment clause.
193	Title VII; Employment Discrimination	*EEOC v. Arabian American Oil Co.*	499 U.S. 244	1991	5/1-3	Rehnquist, C.J.	Nondiscrimination in employment rules of Title VII do not apply outside U.S. to U.S. employers who employ U.S. citizens abroad.
194	Graduation Prayers in Public School	*Lee v. Weisman*	505 U.S. 577	1991	5-4	Kennedy, J.	Ecumenical prayer by Jewish rabbi at a public middle school graduation ceremony violates establishment clause.

(continues)

APPENDIX THREE (continued)

#	Issue	Case	Citation	Year	Ratio	Author	Holding
195	Forum Analysis; Religious Solicitation	*International Society for Krishna Consciousness v. Lee*	505 U.S. 672	1992	Pluralities	Rehnquist, C.J. (opinion of the Court)	An airport terminal operated by a public authority is a nonpublic forum, and therefore a ban on distribution of religious literature and solicitation need only satisfy a reasonableness standard; the ban on solicitation here is reasonable.
196	Distribution of Religious Literature	*Lee v. International Society for Krishna Consciousness*	505 U.S. 830	1992	5-4	Per curiam	Ban on distribution of religious materials in airport terminals is invalid under First Amendment, as it does not satisfy a reasonableness standard.
197	Mootness, IRS Summons	*Church of Scientology of California v. United States*	506 U.S. 9	1992	9-0	Stevens, J.	Compliance with an enforcement order to surrender taped conversations does not render moot an appeal concerning the lawfulness of the search claim.
198	Equal Access	*Lamb's Chapel v. Center Moriches Union Free School District*	508 U.S. 384	1993	6/2/1-0	White, J.	Public school that opens its school facilities, during nonschool time, to various voluntary community groups may not exclude only those with religious viewpoint; equal access must be given.
199	Ritual Sacrifice of Animals	*Church of the Lukumi Babalu Aye, Inc. v. City of Hialeah*	508 U.S. 520	1993	9-0, but concurring opinions	Kennedy, J. (opinion of the Court, except as to Part II.A.2)	Local ordinance discriminating against ritual sacrifice of animals violates the free exercise clause.
200	Religious School Subsidy: Interpreter	*Zobrest v. Catalina Foothills School District*	509 U.S. 1	1993	5-4	Rehnquist, C.J.	State's provision of an interpreter to disabled student at religious high school does not violate establishment clause.
201	Delegation of Civil Power	*Board of Education of Kiryas Joel Village School District v. Grumet*	512 U.S. 687	1994	4/1/1-3	Souter, J. (for the plurality)	State's creation of a single public school district within an exclusively Satmar Hasidic community violates establishment clause.

(continues)

APPENDIX THREE *(continued)*

#	Issue	Case	Citation	Year	Ratio	Author	Holding
202	Religious Display	*Capitol Square Review and Advisory Board v. Pinette*	515 U.S. 753	1995	4/3-2	Scalia, J. (for the plurality)	City may not ban private display of KKK cross in an otherwise open public forum.
203	Equal Access	*Rosenberger v. Rector and Visitors of the University of Virginia*	515 U.S. 819	1995	5-4	Kennedy, J.	State university must grant equal access to funding for voluntary religious student groups as for voluntary nonreligious student group.
204	Title I; Remedial Services	*Agostini v. Felton*	521 U.S. 203	1997	5-4	O'Connor, J.	Overturned Aguilar v. Felton (1985); the mere presence of a state employee in a religious institution is not per se unconstitutional, and thus the state may provide Title I remedial services to students at religious schools.
205	Free Exercise Standard of Review	*City of Boerne v. Flores*	521 U.S. 507	1997	5/1-3	Kennedy, J.	Religious Freedom Restoration Act (1993), which required use of the compelling state interest test for free exercise cases, declared unconstitutional, as applied to the state.
206	Religious School Subsidy	*Mitchell v. Helms*	530 U.S. 793	2000	4/2-3	Thomas, J. (for the plurality)	Federally funded state policy to lend educational materials directly to public and private schools does not violate the establishment clause simply because many of the private schools receiving aid are religiously affiliated; Meek v. Pittinger (1975) and Wolman v. Walter (1977) overruled.
207	Student Prayer at Public School Football Games	*Santa Fe Independent School District v. Doe*	530 U.S. 290	2000	6-3	Stevens, J.	School policy instituting student-led, student-initiated "invocations" prior to public high school football games violates the establishment clause.

(continues)

APPENDIX THREE *(continued)*

#	Issue	Case	Citation	Year	Ratio	Author	Holding
208	Equal Access	*Good News Club v. Milford Central School*	533 U.S. 98	2001	5/1-3	Thomas, J.	Public school's exclusion of Christian children's club from meeting on school property after hours was unconstitutional viewpoint discrimination, and was not required to avoid establishment of religion.
209	Licensing	*Watchtower Bible and Tract Society v. Village of Stratton*	536 U.S. 150	2002	6-2/1	Stevens, J.	Ordinance requiring door to door solicitors and canvassers to obtain a permit containing one's name violates constitutional free speech and free exercise rights because of its breadth and unprecedented nature, and is not narrowly tailored to the stated interest of preventing fraud, crime, and privacy intrusion.
210	Religious School Subsidy: Voucher	*Zelman v. Simmons-Harris*	536 U.S. 639	2002	5-4	Rehnquist, C.J.	School voucher program, enacted for valid secular purpose of providing educational assistance to poor children in demonstrably failing public school system, does not violate the establishment clause because program was neutral toward religion and government aid to religious schools was the result of parents' "true private choices."
211	State Scholarship Program	*Locke v. Davey*	540 U.S. 712	2004	7-2	Rehnquist, C.J.	State scholarship program established to assist payment of academically gifted students' postsecondary education expenses for all students, except those pursuing a theology degree, does not violate the free exercise clause.
212	Pledge of Allegiance; Standing	*Elk Grove Unified School District v. Newdow*	542 U.S. 1	2004	5/1/1/1-0	Stevens, J.	Noncustodial father lacked standing to bring establishment case on behalf of his minor daughter challenging school district's policy that required teacher-led recitation of the Pledge of Allegiance, with phrase "one nation under God."

(continues)

APPENDIX THREE   (continued)

#	Issue	Case	Citation	Year	Ratio	Author	Holding
213	Prisoner's Rights	Cutter v. Wilkinson	544 U.S. 709	2005	9-0	Ginsburg, J.	RLUIPA is upheld against establishment clause challenge.
214	Religious Display	Van Orden v. Perry	545 U.S. 677	2005	4/1-1	Rehnquist, C.J. (for the plurality)	A display of the Ten Commandments outside the Texas State Capitol in the context of other memorials does not violate the establishment clause.
215	Religious Display	McCreary County v. ACLU	545 U.S. 844	2005	5-4	Souter, J.	County display of the Ten Commandments in the courthouse violates the establishment clause because circumstances that indicate the reasons for the display are religious.
216	Preliminary Injunction; Controlled Substances	Gonzales v. O Centro Espirita Beneficiente Uniao Do Vegetal	546 U.S. 418	2006	8-0	Roberts, C.J.	Federal government failed to prove a compelling interest, as required by RFRA, in regulating hoasca as a Schedule I narcotic against religious group's need to use it for sacramental purposes.
217	Standing	Hein v. Freedom from Religion Foundation	551 U.S. 587	2007	5-4	Alito, J.	Establishment clause challenge to federal agency's use of federal funds in support of "faith-based initiatives" dismissed because plaintiffs lacked standing per Flast v. Cohen.
218	Religious Display	Pleasant Grove City v. Summmum	555 U.S. ___ (129 S.Ct. 1125)	2009	8/1-0	Alito, J.	City lawfully denied request by minority religious group to post its monument among other religious monuments on city property; establishment clause could not be used to force city to speak in certain ways.

(continues)

APPENDIX THREE *(continued)*

#	Issue	Case	Citation	Year	Ratio	Author	Holding
219	Religious Display; Standing	*Salazar v. Buono*	__ U.S. __ (slip opinion)	2010	3/2-4	Kennedy, J. (for the plurality)	Remand is necessary in case where plaintiff sought to enforce an injunction to remove a Latin cross from a national park despite subsequent Congressional statute mandating the sale of that land to a private party.
220	Religious Group Membership; Discrimination	*Christian Legal Society v. Martinez*		2010			(Pending at time of printing)

Index